The Governors of Indiana

The Governors of Indiana

EDITED BY

LINDA C. GUGIN AND JAMES E. ST. CLAIR

PUBLISHED BY THE INDIANA HISTORICAL SOCIETY PRESS
IN COOPERATION WITH THE
INDIANA HISTORICAL BUREAU, STATE OF INDIANA
INDIANAPOLIS 2006

© 2006 Indiana Historical Society Press. All rights reserved.
Illustrations © 2006 Governors' Portraits Collection,
Indiana Historical Bureau, State of Indiana
www.IN.gov/history

Printed in China

This book is a publication of the
Indiana Historical Society Press
450 West Ohio Street
Indianapolis, Indiana 46202-3269 USA
www.indianahistory.org

Telephone orders 1–800–447–1830
Fax orders 317–234–0562
Online orders @ shop.indianahistory.org

The paper in this publication meets the minimum requirements of American
National Standard for Information Sciences—Permanence of Paper for Printed
Library Materials, ANSI Z39.48-1984.

Library of Congress Cataloging-in-Publication Data

The governors of Indiana / edited by Linda C. Gugin and James E. St. Clair
    p. cm.
  Includes bibliographical references and index.
  ISBN 0-87195-196-7 (cloth : alk. paper)
  1. Governors—Indiana—Biography. 2. Indiana—Politics and government. 3.
Indiana—History. I. Gugin, Linda C. II. St. Clair, James E.
Title.

  F525.G69 2006
  997.2009'9—dc22

                                            2005056796

*To all public servants who have worked
on behalf of the citizens of Indiana
in all three branches of state government.*

Table of Contents

Acknowledgments. xi

Contributors xiii

Indiana Governors: Powers and Personal Attributes 1
Linda C. Gugin, James E. St. Clair, Thomas P. Wolf

William Henry Harrison, January 10, 1801–July 1812 18
Douglas E. Clanin

John Gibson, July 4, 1800–January 10, 1801 and
June 1812–May 1813. 28
John R. Bierly

Thomas Posey, March 3, 1813–November 7, 1816 32
John Thornton Posey

Jonathan Jennings, November 7, 1816–September 12, 1822. 40
Carl E. Kramer

Ratliff Boon, September 12–December 5, 1822 48
Carl E. Kramer

William Hendricks, December 5, 1822–February 12, 1825 52
C. Martin Rosen

James B. Ray, February 12, 1825–December 7, 1831 60
David G. Vanderstel

Noah Noble, December 7, 1831–December 6, 1837 70
David G. Vanderstel

David Wallace, December 6, 1837–December 9, 1840 80
Jeffery A. Duvall

Samuel Bigger, December 9, 1840–December 6, 1843 88
Gregory A. Bartlett

James Whitcomb, December 6, 1843–December 26, 1848 94
David L. Baker

Paris C. Dunning, December 26, 1848–December 5, 1849 106
Thomas D. Kotulak

Joseph A. Wright, December 5, 1849–January 12, 1857 112
Bradford W. Sample

Ashbel P. Willard, January 12, 1857–October 4, 1860 124
James E. St. Clair

Abram A. Hammond, October 4, 1860–January 14, 1861 132
James E. St. Clair

Henry S. Lane, January 14–16, 1861 136
James E. St. Clair

Oliver P. Morton, January 16, 1861–January 23, 1867 140
Ed Runden

Conrad Baker, January 23, 1867–January 13, 1873 152
Randall T. Shepard

Thomas A. Hendricks, January 13, 1873–January 8, 1877 160
Ralph D. Gray

James D. Williams, January 8, 1877–November 20, 1880 166
Rebecca S. Shoemaker

Isaac P. Gray, November 20, 1880–January 10, 1881 and
January 12, 1885–January 14, 1889 174
J. Michael Walsh, Dennis Walsh, James E. St. Clair

Albert G. Porter, January 10, 1881–January 12, 1885 184
Jeffery A. Duvall

Alvin P. Hovey, January 14, 1889–November 23, 1891 190
Kathy L. Nichols

Ira J. Chase, November 23, 1891–January 9, 1893 198
Alan K. Wild

Claude Matthews, January 9, 1893–January 11, 1897. 204
  Deborah A. Howard

James A. Mount, January 11, 1897–January 14, 1901. 210
  Charles S. Ewry

Winfield T. Durbin, January 14, 1901–January 9, 1905 216
  Raymond H. Scheele

J. Frank Hanly, January 9, 1905–January 11, 1909 224
  Raymond H. Scheele

Thomas R. Marshall, January 11, 1909–January 13, 1913 232
  Peter T. Harstad

Samuel M. Ralston, January 13, 1913–January 8, 1917 244
  Ray E. Boomhower

James P. Goodrich, January 8, 1917–January 10, 1921. 250
  Dane Starbuck

Warren T. McCray, January 10, 1921–April 30, 1924 260
  Tony L. Trimble

Emmett F. Branch, April 30, 1924–January 12, 1925 268
  Tony L. Trimble

Edward L. Jackson, January 12, 1925–January 14, 1929. 274
  Jason S. Lantzer

Harry G. Leslie, January 14, 1929–January 9, 1933 280
  Alfred L. Knable, Jr.

Paul V. McNutt, January 9, 1933–January 11, 1937 288
  Linda C. Gugin

M. Clifford Townsend, January 11, 1937–January 13, 1941. 300
  James L. McDowell

Henry F. Schricker, January 13, 1941–January 8, 1945 and
January 10, 1949–January 12, 1953 308
  James L. McDowell

Ralph F. Gates, January 8, 1945–January 10, 1949 316
  Jason S. Lantzer

George N. Craig, January 12, 1953–January 14, 1957 32
  Hugo C. Songer

Harold W. Handley, January 14, 1957–January 9, 1961 330
Joseph L. Wert

Matthew E. Welsh, January 9, 1961–January 11, 1965 336
James Philip Fadely

Roger D. Branigin, January 11, 1965–January 13, 1969 346
Ray E. Boomhower

Edgar D. Whitcomb, January 13, 1969–January 9, 1973 352
Ronald J. Allman II

Otis R. Bowen, January 9, 1973–January 13, 1981 360
Raymond H. Scheele

Robert D. Orr, January 13, 1981–January 9, 1989 368
Ralph D. Gray

Birch Evans Bayh III, January 9, 1989–January 13, 1997 376
Clifford L. Staten

Frank L. O'Bannon, January 13, 1997–September 13, 2003 384
Cary G. Stemle

Joseph E. Kernan, September 13, 2003–January 10, 2005 394
John E. Findling

Mitchell E. Daniels Jr., January 10, 2005–Current 402
Jim Shella

Index 409

Acknowledgments

First, we want to thank the staff of the Indiana Historical Society Press who readily embraced this project and provided valuable advice and assistance at every stage in its development. In particular, we are grateful to Thomas A. Mason, Paula Corpuz, Kathleen M. Breen, Ray E. Boomhower, and Rachel M. Popma for their encouragement and expert guidance. Working on this project renewed our appreciation for the vast resources of the Indiana Historical Society. Anyone interested in exploring Indiana history will find invaluable what the Society collects, preserves, and makes widely available.

Without the hard work and scholarship of the contributing authors this book would not have been possible, and we thank them for their writing and research skills that chronicle the contributions of the fifty men who have served Indiana as governor. Collectively the authors' essays provide a rich and revealing tapestry of Indiana's political history.

We also want to thank our own institution, Indiana University Southeast, for generously providing financial support in the form of a sabbatical leave and a summer faculty fellowship. The staff and resources of the IU Southeast library were, as always, helpful and supportive. In addition, we received valuable assistance from the Indiana State Library, whose staff unfailingly tracked down information that we were unable to locate elsewhere. No request went without a prompt reply. We also appreciate the fact that Pam Bennett, director of the Indiana Historical Bureau has graciously given the Society permission to use the official portraits from its governors' collection in this book. The librarians in the Indiana Room of the New Albany–Floyd County Public Library also provided expert assistance.

Contributors

RONALD J. ALLMAN II
Associate professor of journalism, Indiana University Southeast. Faculty
adviser to the campus weekly newspaper. Contributing author to *Creative
Strategy in Advertising* by A. Jerome Jewler and Bonnie L. Drewniany.

DAVID L. BAKER, JD
Retired university counsel. Author of entry for Kentucky in *Colliers
Encyclopedia* and "The Joyce Family Murders: Justice and Politics in
Know-Nothing Louisville," *Register of the Kentucky Historical Society*
(Summer 2004).

GREGORY A. BARTLETT
Former reporter for several publications, including the *Louisville Eccentric Observer* and the *Elizabethtown (KY) News-Enterprise*. Also held position of editor with ProQuest Information and Learning, Louisville.

JOHN R. BIERLY
Freelance writer. American correspondent for British popular culture
magazine, *Impact.*

RAY E. BOOMHOWER
Managing editor, *Traces of Indiana and Midwestern History*. Author of
*Jacob Piatt Dunn, Jr.: A Life in History and Politics, 1855–1924; The Country
Contributor: The Life and Times of Juliet V. Strauss*; and *Gus Grissom: The Lost*

Astronaut. Contributor to the *Encyclopedia of Indianapolis* and the *American National Biography.*

DOUGLAS E. CLANIN
Retired editor, researcher, Indiana Historical Society. Editor, the William Henry Harrison Papers and the Lew and Susan Wallace Papers Project.

JEFFERY A. DUVALL
Doctoral candidate in U.S. history at Purdue University; dissertation topic: Twentieth-century Tobacco Culture in the Ohio River Valley. Teaching assistant, Purdue University; reference assistant, Indiana University–Purdue University Indianapolis; and former research assistant for The Polis Center.

CHARLES S. EWRY
Staff writer, *Corydon Democrat.*

JAMES PHILIP FADELY, PhD
Director of College Counseling and AP history instructor, University High School, Carmel, Indiana. Author of *Thomas Taggart: Public Servant, Political Boss, 1856–1929* and "Editors, Whistle Stops, and Elephants: The Presidential Campaign of 1936 in Indiana," *Indiana Magazine of History* (June 1989). Has taught at Indiana University Bloomington, Indiana University–Purdue University Indianapolis, Butler University, and University of Indianapolis.

JOHN E. FINDLING, PhD
Professor emeritus of history, Indiana University Southeast. Author of various works in the area of world's fairs and expositions and the Olympic Games, including *Chicago's Great World's Fairs.* Coauthor of *Fair America* and coeditor of *Encyclopedia of the Modern Olympic Movement.*

RALPH D. GRAY, PhD
Professor emeritus of history, Indianapolis University–Purdue University Indianapolis. Author and editor of a number of books, including *Alloys*

and Automobiles: The Life of Elwood Haynes; *The National Waterway: A History of the Chesapeake and Delaware Canal*; *Gentlemen from Indiana: National Party Candidates, 1836–1940*; *IUPUI: The Making of an Urban University*; and *Meredith Nicholson: A Writing Life* (forthcoming 2007). Also a frequent contributor to *Traces of Indiana and Midwestern History.*

LINDA C. GUGIN, PhD

Professor of political science, Indiana University Southeast. Coeditor of *The Governors of Indiana*; coauthor of *Sherman Minton: New Deal Senator, Cold War Justice* and *Chief Justice Fred M. Vinson of Kentucky: A Political Biography.*

PETER T. HARSTAD, PhD

Retired executive director of the Indiana Historical Society. Author of *Gilbert N. Haugen: Norwegian-American Farm Politician* and frequent contributor to *Traces of Indiana and Midwestern History.*

DEBORAH A. HOWARD, JD

Chair, Department of Law, Politics and Society, University of Evansville. Has published and made several conference presentations in the areas of discrimination law, employment law, and women's studies, including "The Role of Women in a Modern Global Culture" in *American Culture in an Era of Globalization* and also "Sex Discrimination in Employment: Rules Without Remedies," presented at an international conference in Lodz, Poland. Publication in proceedings pending.

ALFRED L. KNABLE JR., MD

Practicing physician in New Albany, Indiana, and Louisville, Kentucky; associate clinical professor of dermatology, University of Louisville Medical School. Frequent contributor to medical textbooks and journals.

THOMAS D. KOTULAK, PhD

Associate professor of political science, Indiana University Southeast. Author of biographical profiles of former Indiana senator

William Jenner and former congressman Ray Madden in *The Scribner Encyclopedia of American Lives* and also "Litigating Civil Liberties Under the Indiana State Constitution: The Problematic Promise of *Price v. State*," *Journal of the Indiana Academy of Social Sciences* (2001).

CARL E. KRAMER, PhD
Vice president of Kramer Associates Inc., a consulting firm specializing in public history, community development, and public relations. Adjunct faculty, history, Indiana University Southeast. Author of numerous books and articles, mainly focusing on the history of southern Indiana and the Louisville metropolitan area. Author of *This Place We Call Home: A History of Clark County, Indiana* (forthcoming 2007).

JASON S. LANTZER, PhD
Visiting lecturer with the Indiana University School of Continuing Studies. Dissertation topic: Prohibition in America. Has taught at Indiana University Bloomington, Indiana University–Purdue University Indianapolis, and Franklin College.

JAMES L. MCDOWELL, PhD
Professor of political science, Indiana State University. Author of "Indiana's Venerable Constitution: 150 Years Old and Counting" in *Traces of Indiana and Midwestern History* (Fall 2001); "Single Subject Provisions in State Government" in *Spectrum: The Journal of State Government* (Spring 2003); and "The Bayhing of Indiana Politics: The Changing Face of Campaign Finance in the Hoosier State" in *Money, Politics and Campaign Finance Reform Law in the States.*

KATHY L. NICHOLS
Associate director of Farmington Historical Home, Louisville. Wrote "Lord Michael Killanin" entry in *Dictionary of Olympics* and "Voices Seldom Heard," article published by the Indiana Historical Society for an exhibit at the Carnegie Center for Art & History.

JOHN THORNTON POSEY, JD

Retired attorney, author of *General Thomas Posey: Son of the American Revolution.* His articles on Governor Thomas Posey have appeared in *Virginia Cavalcade, Indiana Magazine of History,* and *Illinois Historical Journal.*

C. MARTIN ROSEN

Director of library services at Indiana University Southeast. Frequent contributor of feature stories and performance reviews to the *Louisville Courier-Journal* and *Louisville Eccentric Observer.*

ED RUNDEN

Retired history teacher at Corydon Central High School. Regular columnist for the *Corydon Democrat,* a weekly newspaper. Worked as a reporter/wire editor for the *Elgin Daily Courier,* United Press International, and the Associated Press. Freelance writer for variety of publications, including *Encyclopedia Britannica.*

BRADFORD W. SAMPLE

Director, general studies, College of Adult & Professional Studies, Indiana Wesleyan University, Marion, Indiana. Doctoral candidate in American history at Purdue University. Former special assistant and editorial assistant at the Indiana Historical Society. Author, "A Truly Midwestern City: Indianapolis on the Eve of the Great Depression," *Indiana Magazine of History* (June 2001).

RAYMOND H. SCHEELE, PhD

Professor of political science, Ball State University. Author of *Larry Conrad of Indiana: A Biography* and several journal articles in public administration and state government.

RANDALL T. SHEPARD, JD

Chief Justice, Indiana Supreme Court. Former president, Conrad Baker Foundation, Evansville. Coauthor with David Bodenhamer, executive director of The Polis Center at Indiana University–Purdue

University Indianapolis, of *The History of Indiana Law* (forthcoming 2006).

JIM SHELLA
Political reporter, WISH-TV, Indianapolis, and host and producer of *Indiana Week in Review* for public television station WFYI. Twice awarded Sagamore of the Wabash; recipient of the Larry Conrad Award from the Indianapolis Press Club.

REBECCA S. SHOEMAKER, PhD
Professor of history, Indiana State University. Author of "James D. Williams: Indiana's Farmer Governor" in *Their Infinite Variety: Essays on Indiana Politicians.* Author, *The White Court: Justices, Rulings, and Legacy.* Also editor of *The Biographical Directory of the Indiana General Assembly.*

HUGO C. SONGER, JD
Senior judge, state of Indiana and former Dubois County Circuit Court Judge. Retired member, Indiana Board of Law Examiners. Author of *Dufftown: Rural Life in Southern Indiana during the Great Depression and World War II.*

JAMES E. ST. CLAIR
Professor of journalism, Indiana University Southeast. Coeditor, *The Governors of Indiana;* coauthor of *Sherman Minton: New Deal Senator, Cold War Justice* and *Chief Justice Fred M. Vinson of Kentucky: A Political Biography.*

DANE STARBUCK, JD
Attorney, Carmel, Indiana, and author of *The Goodriches: An American Family.*

CLIFFORD L. STATEN, PhD
Professor of political science and dean of the School of Social Sciences, Indiana University Southeast. Author of *The History of Cuba* and several articles, including "U.S. Foreign Policy since World War II: An

Essay on the Corrective Qualities of Reality," in *American Diplomacy* (July 2005).

CARY G. STEMLE
Editor, *Louisville Eccentric Observer.* Former staff writer for *Business First of Louisville* and the *Corydon Democrat,* where he covered Governor Frank O'Bannon.

TONY L. TRIMBLE
Psychologist for the Federal Drug Aftercare Program in Indianapolis. Author of the manuscript "The Squire of Orchard Lake: Governor Warren T. McCray," available at the Indiana State Library. Has written extensively on the Civil War, including as a contributor to the *Encyclopedia of Indianapolis.*

DAVID G. VANDERSTEL, PhD
Executive director, National Council on Public History, Indianapolis and adjunct professor of history, Indiana University–Purdue University Indianapolis. Assistant editor of the *Encyclopedia of Indianapolis.*

DENNIS L. WALSH, JD
Claims attorney for Fidelity & Deposit Insurance, Bloomington. Served as co-state manager of Indiana for Voter News Service, a joint operation of the Associated Press, FOX, ABC, CNN, NBC, and CBS.

J. MICHAEL WALSH, EdS
Interim director, consultant, Indiana University High School, School of Continuing Studies, Indiana University. Faculty facilitator for Project Aspire, Indiana Academy, Ball State University; vice president of operations and former general manager, Bloomington Pops Orchestra. Retired middle-school principal, Tri-North, Bloomington.

JOSEPH L. WERT, PhD
Associate professor of political science, Indiana University Southeast. Author of *Study of Bill Clinton's Presidential Approval Ratings* and

several entries in *Encyclopedia of the Presidency*. Coauthor of "Campaigns and Elections in Indiana," in *Indiana, Politics and Public Policy*, second edition.

ALAN K. WILD
Copy editor, *Louisville Courier-Journal*; adjunct faculty, journalism, Indiana University Southeast; former chief copy editor, *Chillicothe (Ohio) Gazette*. Eight articles published in *Boys' Life* magazine.

THOMAS P. WOLF, PhD
Professor emeritus of political science, Indiana University Southeast. Editor and contributor, *Franklin D. Roosevelt and Congress*. Published various works on political leadership including Franklin D. Roosevelt, Winston Churchill, Harold Macmillan, Willy Brandt, Robert Lovett, Christian Herter, and various Indiana political figures. Contributed several entries to reference works on the U.S. presidency and on American political parties.

Indiana Governors: Powers and Personal Attributes

LINDA C. GUGIN
JAMES E. ST. CLAIR
THOMAS P. WOLF

Historically, the office of governor in Indiana has been a weak institution compared to the strength of the state legislature and in contrast to the office of governor in some other states. Over time, in response to crises, state and national reform efforts, partisan politics, and the force of personality of its occupants, the office has been transformed into one with considerably more power than what is prescribed in the constitutions of 1816 and 1851.

Under the formal powers of the office—those provided for in state constitutions and state practices—governors have the authority to appoint and remove public employees, submit a state budget for legislative consideration, veto legislation, reorganize the administrative structure, and determine staff size in the governor's office.

The power relationship between the governor and the legislature changed significantly in 1972 when voters approved a constitutional amendment allowing the governor to serve two consecutive terms. Otis R. Bowen (1973–81), the first governor to benefit from this change, acknowledged how important the prospect of his holding office for eight years was. "We were able to pursue tax-reform legislation with a lot more conviction and success," he said.

Under the Constitution of 1816, the governor served a three-year term and was prohibited from serving more than six years in a nine-year period. Of the governors serving under this constitution, five served more than three years—Jonathan Jennings (1816–22), James B. Ray (1825–31), Noah Noble (1831–37), James Whitcomb (1843–48), and

Joseph A. Wright (1849–57), in office for seven years because he was governor when the 1851 Constitution lengthened the term to four years. Still, a governor could not serve more than four years in an eight-year period, making the official a lame duck from the moment he took office. Between 1851 and 1972, two governors served longer than four-year terms. Isaac P. Gray served one year, 1880–81, after succeeding Governor James D. Williams (1877–80), who died in office, and was then elected in his own right in 1884 for a four-year term. Henry F. Schricker served two separate terms, 1941–45 and 1949–53.

Term limits aside, the length of gubernatorial tenure has varied widely. Of the first forty-nine territorial and state governors, ten, or more than one-fifth, did not complete their terms. Four died in office: Ashbel P. Willard (1857–60), Williams, Alvin P. Hovey (1889–91), and Frank L. O'Bannon (1997–2003). In a four-month period in late 1860 and early 1861, Indiana had four governors, starting with the death of Willard, who was succeeded by Abram A. Hammond. He was followed by Henry S. Lane, who served only three days before resigning to assume his position in the U.S. Senate. Lane was promptly succeeded by Oliver P. Morton (1861–67). All governors since 1972 have served eight years, with the exception of O'Bannon and Joseph E. Kernan (2003–05).

Although the constitution vests the governor with the power to appoint and remove state employees, occasionally the general assembly has tried to assert its control over this function. The first battle over appointive powers occurred in 1889 between the Democratic legislature and Hovey, a Republican, over an appointment for trustee of the School for the Blind. The issue was settled when the state supreme court ruled in favor of the legislature. Two years later the legislature further restricted the governor's appointive powers over members of executive agencies. In 1895 the state's high court again affirmed the power of the general assembly to make administrative appointments under both the 1816 and 1851 constitutions.

When Paul V. McNutt assumed office in 1933, however, there was no question of who held the upper hand. McNutt, considered one of Indiana's most powerful chief executives, engineered major changes in the appointive powers of the office, largely by expanding the system of patronage and placing it under his control. His success in this effort resulted from his "own desire for political power, the depth of the Depression which created thousands of political job seekers, and the return of the Democrats to the statehouse after long years out of power." McNutt added to his powers by imposing state control over who received licenses to import, manufacture, and sell alcoholic beverages and through his creation of the infamous Two Percent Club. Under this arrangement, those who got their jobs through patronage were expected to "voluntarily" kick back 2 percent of their pay to the party. The power of the McNutt machine led to calls for a merit system, and the governor responded by allowing a limited one to be established in the Department of Public Welfare and the Division of Unemployment.

Despite this modest reform, Indiana's patronage system "was nearly unparalleled in the mid and late twentieth century," which made the appointive powers of Indiana governors among the strongest in the country. They remain strong, though by the mid-1980s, patronage in Indiana was "but a pale shadow of its former condition." Nonetheless, patronage continues to be more prevalent in Indiana than in most states.

One of the most significant reforms of the patronage system came during the administration of Robert D. Orr (1981–89), who persuaded the general assembly to remove license branch offices from party control and place them under the state merit system. Before, the party of the governor controlled the operations of these branches, assuring the winning party thousands of patronage appointments and a guaranteed source of income. After a modification of the system in 1977, profits were split between both parties.

While changes in hiring practices for state employees have lessened the power of governors, their authority over the budgetary process has increased. In 1941 the financial reins of the state were placed in the hands of a four-person bipartisan group of state legislators consisting of one Democrat and one Republican from each house, appointed by the governor to two-year terms. This body prepared the budget submitted to the legislature every two years and was the legislature's oversight committee for the expenditure of state funds. Even though the governor appointed the members of the committee, "he frequently found his freedom of choice quite limited if he expected to have successful working relations with the General Assembly, since a powerful legislator would exact his appointment to the committee as a price for this cooperation during the session."

In 1960 this arrangement was declared unconstitutional by the Indiana Supreme Court as a violation of the doctrine of separation of powers. A bill drafted by Governor Matthew E. Welsh (1961–65) in consultation with leaders of both parties in both houses was approved in 1961 and gave the governor direct responsibility for preparing the state budget to be submitted to the legislature. A four-member Budget Advisory Committee replaced the old Budget Committee to serve as a liaison with the general assembly, and the governor's budget director was given the full authority of the old Budget Committee.

Welsh said that "this transfer of authority from one branch of the government to another was, without question, the most significant action taken by any legislature since 1941." Although the State Budget Committee remains in existence, the real power over the budget lies with the State Budget Agency, which is directly accountable to the governor. Bowen, noting the distinction between the two organizations, said, "The governor appoints the Budget Agency Chairman, and he actually prepares the budget with the governor's supervision. Only then does he present it to the Budget Committee." Of course, the legislature retains the power to approve the budget, and while governors seldom get all that they want, they still have enormous influence in the budget process.

The executive and legislative branches have also battled over attempts to reorganize the administrative structure of government. Governors want the ability to create or eliminate agencies and to realign responsibilities within the administrative area for the sake of efficiency and to make the bureaucracy more amenable to their policy goals. Any reorganization proposal requires approval of the general assembly. Such proposals have often been the source of conflict between the governor and the legislature.

The evolution of the state's administrative structure grew willy-nilly until the 1930s. More than one hundred agencies and responsibilities had been created piecemeal "with little attention given to integration or co-ordination of the total system. . . . By 1933 Indiana government had achieved twentieth-century proportions in bureaucratic size, but it remained at nineteenth-century levels in its degree of centralization and integration." McNutt's famous Executive Reorganization Act of 1933, which combined all state agencies and commissions into eight departments each controlled by a board appointed by him, brought order to this unwieldy and arcane structure. The act further provided that all employees in these departments would be appointed by the governor and serve at his pleasure. Although this scheme did not lack for critics, it was applauded by groups as diverse as the Indiana Chamber of Commerce, the Indiana Federation of Labor, and the Indiana Farm Bureau.

McNutt's reorganization plan was credited with bringing some measure of administrative rationality to the operations of state government, but it did not meet the test of time. When Republicans regained control of the state legislature after 1940, they passed legislation aimed at weakening the power of Schricker, a Democrat. Among the four proposals approved by the legislature were measures repealing the 1933 Executive Reorganization Act and stripping away some of the governor's powers of appointment. Schricker vetoed all of the bills, claiming they violated the governor's constitutional power as chief executive. Although the general assembly again passed the four bills, they were all subsequently declared unconstitutional in the case of *Tucker et al. v. State* decision.

Other governors since McNutt have attempted major administrative restructuring, most notably Ralph F. Gates (1945–49) and George N. Craig (1953–57), but neither was able to gather sufficient support from the legislature to implement their plans. Today Indiana still lacks the traditional cabinet style of government that is found in many other states. New departments have been added to create more efficiency and coordination in certain policy areas. Recent examples of changes in the administrative structure are Governor Evan Bayh's (1989–97) creation of the Family Social Services Administration and Governor Mitch Daniels's (2005–present) Department of Agriculture.

While the veto is one of a chief executive's most potent weapons, Indiana governors have one of the weakest veto powers in the nation. The governor has only what is known as a package veto, in which he must reject a bill in its entirety. There is no line-item veto, which would permit him to veto specific items in a piece of legislation, particularly certain measures in a budget bill. Only six other states prohibit the line-item veto. Nor does the governor enjoy the power of the pocket veto, whereby all bills remaining on the governor's desk are automatically vetoed if the legislature has adjourned during the allotted time for action by the governor. Fifteen states permit the exercise of the pocket veto, but this power was ruled unconstitutional by the state supreme court in 1969 when Edgar D. Whitcomb (1969–73) was governor. In Indiana the governor has only seven days to act, and the veto can be overridden by a simple majority. In many states the governor's veto requires a two-thirds majority. Bowen was unsuccessful in his attempt to persuade the legislature to pass a constitutional amendment requiring a two-thirds majority in each house to override the governor's veto. His proposal was never called up for consideration by House Speaker and fellow Republican Kermit Burrous, who was not interested in approving a measure that would weaken the power of the legislature.

Despite formal limits on the governor's veto power, in practice it still has considerable force. As one observer said, "Look it up, and I think you will see that few legislators—even those of the opposite party—will vote to override a veto." Research bears this out. Of the 3,240 bills passed from 1971 to 1981, for example, only 117 were vetoed by the governor, and only eleven of these vetoes were overridden.

The use of the veto has varied widely from governor to governor. During the pioneer period (1815–50) Democrat James Whitcomb held the record for the most vetoes during a single session—fifteen. Democrat Roger D. Branigin (1965–69) has the distinction of exercising the most vetoes in a single session in modern times. In 1965, even though his own party held solid majorities in both houses, he vetoed fifty-four bills. When Republicans gained control of the legislature in 1967, he vetoed forty-six more bills.

One final measure of a governor's formal power is the extent to which he has the ability to appoint an array of staff personnel for his office, people who provide political and policy advice to the governor or handle important functions such as media relations, speech writing, legislative liaison, and constituency service. As executive powers of the governor have expanded, so has the need for staff. As a rule, governors in the nineteenth century had only one or two assistants. By 1961 the governor's staff under Welsh had grown to a dozen staff members. Ten years later, Bowen's staff consisted of more than twenty members. Daniels had forty-five staff members in his first year in office.

While formal gubernatorial powers are a key factor in a governor's ability to be effective, other variables such as electoral mandate, partisan control of the legislature, and critical circumstances such as war and depression are pertinent. Also, not to be overlooked are personal attributes such as age, political experience, and ambition. The governors who enjoyed the greatest success have been skillful in drawing upon these more informal sources of power as "tools of persuasion" to supplement the formal powers available to them.

A governor's success in office is determined largely by the extent to which he is able to persuade members of the legislature to approve his policy initiatives. As a general rule, governors who have been blessed with a legislature controlled by the same party have enjoyed greater success than those who confronted a legislature controlled by the opposition or a divided legislature with each house controlled by a different party. Democrat McNutt, one of the state's most successful governors, was blessed with overwhelming Democratic majorities in both houses. They offered no serious opposition to his reorganization of state government that centralized power in the hands of the governor, his tax reforms, or his various social welfare programs aimed at ameliorating the effects of the Great Depression. In 1973 Republican Bowen achieved his key legislative proposal—property tax reform—because of solid Republican majorities in both houses.

Partisan control of the legislature by the governor's party has not always guaranteed success, however. Republicans Craig and Edgar

Whitcomb met with opposition from the GOP-controlled legislature during their administrations. In both of these cases divisions within the party prevented these governors from achieving much of their legislative agenda. As previously noted, Democrat Branigin had problems with a Democratic legislature, and he vetoed a record number of bills passed by his partisans.

Governors who have had to deal with divided legislative control have often been frustrated in their objectives. Since 1831, when legislative control was clearly assigned to one party or the other, governors dealt with divided legislatures thirty-one times. Bowen served four years out of eight with a divided legislature, which forced him to make many policy compromises. Likewise, proposals by Democrats Bayh and O'Bannon were curtailed by strong Republican majorities in the state senate. On the other hand, Democrat Welsh enjoyed a modicum of success in his first two years, even though the senate was held by Republicans and his own party had only a two-vote margin in the house.

Governors who have been in the weakest position were those faced with opposition-controlled legislatures. Under such administrations gubernatorial-legislative conflicts have been the most strident. There have been five instances when governors were confronted by a legislature with both houses controlled by the opposite party. In 1941 Democrat Schricker's confrontation with a hostile Republican legislature that tried to reduce the office of governor to that of a caretaker resulted in a supreme court ruling that the governor *is* the chief executive. In 1963 Welsh won approval from an opposition-controlled legislature for a tax compromise that established a sales tax and replaced the gross income tax with an income tax on individuals and a corporate income tax. However, he won the compromise only after calling a special session of the legislature.

Historical circumstances have also had an impact on gubernatorial power. The two most outstanding examples in Indiana history are Morton's term during the Civil War and McNutt's term during the Great Depression. Both of these men achieved extraordinary amounts of power, although under different circumstances and by different means. Morton became governor the same year that the Civil War broke out. While he used his power as governor to provide President Abraham Lincoln with a reliable source of manpower throughout the war and equipped Indiana soldiers with arms, munitions, and uniforms, he also used the war as a means to attack his Democratic opponents for disloyalty to the nation in order to help his own political career. His most audacious power grab occurred in 1863 when the Republicans bolted the Democrat-controlled legislature, ending the legislative session without the passage of a state budget. The legislature did not convene again for two years, during which time Morton seized power through extralegal and extraconstitutional means and ran the state without legislative appropriations. Despite his dictatorial exercise of power, his popularity increased. He was easily reelected in 1864 and Republicans gained majorities in both houses.

Morton has been called "the most powerful governor of Indiana during the nineteenth century." His twentieth-century counterpart is McNutt, whose path to power was facilitated by the economic crisis of the Great Depression. Unlike Morton, whose exercise of power rested on questionable legal grounds, McNutt's accumulation of power was sanctioned by the Democrat-controlled legislature. His governmental reorganization plan, concentrating power in the governor's office, was reinforced by a greatly expanded system of patronage that gave the governor extraordinary powers of appointment, and by the establishment of the Two Percent Club. In addition, McNutt's agenda for social legislation, addressing the economic dislocations of the Depression, steamrolled through the compliant legislature. His record of legislative victories has never been matched by any subsequent governor.

Personal attributes, previous legislative experience, and ambition also play a role in the power potential of any given governor. Conventional wisdom holds that prior legislative experience can be an important asset for a governor. In Indiana that premise has not always proved to be valid. There are cases in point and exceptions all around. Twenty-nine governors served in the legislature before becoming governor; four of these served in both houses. Prior legislative experience was more common under the first constitution (1816–50). Eight of the ten governors who served in that period were members of the

legislature. Of the thirty-seven men who have served under the 1851 constitution, twenty-one have had legislative experience. Three of these have
been Speakers of the House—Emmett F. Branch (1924–25), Harry G.
Leslie (1929–33), and Bowen.

Some governors with prior legislative experience did enjoy fairly
good relations with the legislature. Wright, who was governor under
both constitutions, had previously served in both the house and senate. Legislative-executive conflicts were at a minimum during his term,
and his vetoes were generally upheld, owing in part to Democratic
control of the legislature during most of his two terms. From 1890
to 1930 the three governors "who came closest to exercising powerful leadership independent of the legislature" were J. Frank Hanly
(1905–09), Thomas R. Marshall (1909–13), and Samuel M. Ralston
(1913–17). Both Ralston and Hanly had legislative experience. As governors they also had the advantage of large majorities in both houses.
Of the eight governors who served between 1930 and 1970 four had
been members of the legislature. Harold W. Handley (1957–61) experienced less conflict with the legislature than any of the governors of
the period. Also during this time Welsh was fairly successful in getting
policies accepted by the general assembly, even though he confronted
a divided legislature for two years and one completely controlled by
the opposite party for two years.

Of the three governors who had been House Speakers, Branch,
Leslie, and Bowen, the latter had the best relationship with the legislature. Branch served for only one year after Warren T. McCray (1921–
24) was imprisoned for mail fraud. Leslie was a more of a caretaker
governor, and his relationship with the legislature was relatively calm.
Bowen had an especially good relationship with the legislature during his first two years in office when his party controlled the legislature, achieving his primary policy initiative of property tax reform.
However, Democrats controlled at least one house half of the time he
served, and in those years his success rate was not as strong, though
relations with the legislature were generally cordial.

Lack of legislative experience may have affected the terms of at
least three governors. Neither Gates nor Craig had legislative expe-

rience, and despite the advantage of a legislature controlled by the same party, both had a difficult time gaining legislative approval of their proposals. Bayh's relationship with the legislature may also have suffered because of his lack of legislative experience. His first two years with the legislature were rocky, and he acknowledged before leaving office that in retrospect he should have done more to develop a more conciliatory relationship with the general assembly.

It is notable that the two most powerful governors in the state's history, Morton and McNutt, did not serve in the state legislature before ascending to office, proving that such experience is not a prerequisite to success.

Success in politics is closely linked to personal ambition. All of those who succeeded in becoming governor obviously possessed strong aspirations for power and prestige. For some, however, their ambitions reached beyond the office of governor. They aspired to be members of Congress, vice president, and even president. A few succeeded.

Only Indiana's first territorial governor, William Henry Harrison (1800–12), became president of the United States. Harrison died in office after serving for one month, the shortest term of any president. Two former governors became vice president. Thomas A. Hendricks (1873–74), the nephew of Indiana's third governor William Hendricks (1822–25), was elected vice president with Grover Cleveland in 1884, but died after eight months in office. Marshall served as vice president under Woodrow Wilson from 1913 to 1921.

The state's first governor, Jennings, left the governor's office upon election to the U.S. House of Representatives. Six governors became U.S. senators. Four of these were elected to the U.S. Senate while they were governor—William Hendricks; James Whitcomb; Lane, who served only three days before giving up the governor's office to become senator; and Morton. These men were all elected to the Senate by the general assembly. This route to the Senate ended in 1913 with the ratification of the Seventeenth Amendment to the U.S. Constitution that provided for popular election of U.S. senators. After leaving office, Wright was appointed to the Senate by Morton to replace Senator

Jesse D. Bright, who had been expelled from office. Wright served from 1862 to 1863. Bayh is the only governor who became senator through popular election.

The ambition of some governors to attain higher office often influenced their conduct as the state's chief executive. The most outstanding example was McNutt, whose lifelong ambition was to be elected president. In 1932, the same year that he was elected governor, he was already attempting to play a role in national politics, but it was not a good debut. By withholding the support of the Indiana delegates to the Democratic National Convention, he prolonged Franklin D. Roosevelt's nomination for the presidency, an act of obstinacy that Roosevelt never forgot or forgave.

As governor, McNutt calculated how his actions might affect his chance to become president. He took every opportunity to demonstrate his control over party nominations and to thwart anyone who might harm his political reputation. His active cooperation with the federal government in implementing New Deal programs was also viewed as way to gain support from Roosevelt. Most impressive was McNutt's mastery of the political process, as evidenced by his success in centralizing power in the governor's office and developing patronage to a fine art.

McNutt created a finely tuned machine for managing the legislature by working with a small inner circle of advisers who developed the governor's policy proposals in secret and then worked the legislature to assure their passage. His record of number of policy accomplishments, coupled with his handsome looks and effective oratorical style, would almost have guaranteed McNutt the presidency save for Roosevelt's hold on the office. Almost as soon as McNutt left the governor's office in 1937, he launched his bid for the Democratic nomination in 1940, but his hopes were dashed when Roosevelt announced on the eve of the convention that he would seek a third term. McNutt withdrew from the race and hoped he might get the vice presidential nomination, but it was not to be.

According to many observers, Bayh was another governor whose conduct in office was often influenced by his ambition for higher office. His cautious approach to policy making helped to establish him as a solid centrist who could attract support from a broad spectrum of voters, as evidenced by his 80 percent approval rating at the end of his second term. When he left the governor's office he touted his record of a balanced budget without tax increases, a large budget surplus, and nationally acclaimed welfare reform that required more responsibility on the part of recipients. His record helped him handily win the race for U.S. Senate in 1998 and reelection in 2004. By 2006 he was among the top contenders for the Democratic Party nomination for president in 2008, a prize that many say he was eyeing even before he became governor.

Gray was one of the earlier governors whose career was marked by ambitions for higher office. He served briefly as governor for three months following the death of Williams in 1880. Oddly at the time he had lost in his bid to become the party nominee for governor for the next term. However, four years later he was elected governor and soon after set his sights on winning the U.S. Senate seat held by Benjamin Harrison, whose term expired in 1888, one year before Gray's term as governor was to expire. However, Gray's carefully crafted plans to be elected by the state legislature went awry when his lieutenant governor resigned, making it impossible for Gray to leave the office without a successor. The chain of events that followed culminated in fistfights on the floor of the state senate and the threat of even worse violence. This "black day in the history of the General Assembly" helped fuel the movement for a constitutional amendment for the popular election of senators.

As the discussion of how governors used their formal and informal powers demonstrates, there are many differences in how the first fifty men who served as Indiana's chief executive carried out their responsibilities, but there are also some common threads woven into their lives and backgrounds.

The practice of law is one such commonality. By far, the path into politics for most Hoosier governors has been the legal profession. Thirty-one, or nearly two-thirds, were attorneys, if for some it was only for a part of their working years. Others were businessmen, farmers, newspaper publishers, teachers, or physicians. One was a minister. The three territorial governors were essentially public servants, spending their careers either in the military or in government office, elective or appointive.

Military service was a common experience for about half of the state's governors. Among those with especially distinguished military records were Harrison, the first territorial governor, who gained widespread fame for his victories at the Battle of Tippecanoe in 1811 and at the Battle of the Thames in 1813; Thomas Posey, the second territorial governor, who displayed great courage and leadership in many battles during the American Revolution; Hovey, who displayed great valor during the Civil War; Craig, who was part of the Normandy invasion during World War II and saw action throughout Europe; Edgar Whitcomb, who was a fighter pilot in the Pacific during World War II and a prisoner of war; and Kernan, also a fighter pilot, who was shot down over North Vietnam in the early 1970s and held as a prisoner of war for nearly a year.

Several governors used their activities with veterans organizations as springboards into political life. For example, the leadership positions that Ira J. Chase (1891–93) held in the Grand Army of the Republic, an influential group of Union veterans, were instrumental in giving him the recognition and prominence necessary to launch his venture into politics. McNutt skillfully used his experience as state commander and later as national commander of the American Legion, the nation's largest veterans organization, to build a political following. Similarly, top positions in the state and national Legion organizations proved helpful for the entry of Gates and Craig into politics.

No native-born Hoosier served as governor until Morton assumed the office in 1861. In all, twenty governors were born in Indiana. During the period from the election of James P. Goodrich (1917–21) to that of Handley, every governor was an Indiana native. Seven governors were born in Pennsylvania. Kentucky and Ohio were the birthplaces of four governors each; other native states of governors included Virginia, Illinois, and Michigan. Within Indiana, the community of Brookville became home to four governors: Ray, Noble, David Wallace (1837–40), and Hammond.

Of the fifty governors, thirty attended an institution of higher education, though some for only a brief period. Eleven attended the Bloomington campus of Indiana University, or its predecessor, for either undergraduate or graduate studies or both. Wright was the first to attend what became Indiana University; at the time he was a student it was called Indiana Seminary. Other Indiana colleges and universities that have at least one governor among their alumni include Hanover College, DePauw University, Wabash College, Franklin College, the University of Notre Dame, and Purdue University. Marshall, one of the most intellectually gifted governors, graduated from Wabash at the age of nineteen, achieving high marks and campus leadership roles in the process.

The personal lives of Indiana's chief executives tended to reflect the times in which they lived. All married. John Gibson, who twice served as acting territorial governor, married a member of the Mingo tribe of Native Americans. Through much of the nineteenth century, many governors were married more than once. This was not due to divorce but to the deaths of spouses, often at childbirth or soon thereafter, a common occurrence during those times. A few, including Williams and Winfield T. Durbin (1901–05), were married for decades to their only wife. James Whitcomb married while serving as governor, but his wife died a little over a year later after the birth of their daughter.

The average age of Indiana governors upon entering office was about fifty years old. Harrison was just twenty-seven when he was appointed territorial governor. Ray, at thirty-one, was the youngest to be elected governor. In the twentieth century, the youngest was thirty-four-year-old Bayh. Williams was the oldest, elected to office when he was sixty-nine.

Although Indiana is generally considered to be a Republican stronghold, at least in presidential elections, the party ties of its governors present a different pattern. Since the time candidates became affiliated with the two major parties in the mid-nineteenth century, twenty-one Democrats have served as governor and an identical number of Republicans have held the office. Three of Indiana's governors were Whigs, and earlier governors either were independent of party affiliation or were loosely identified with a national party.

The continuous length of time that one of the major parties has held the governor's office has been modest. The longest stretch for any party was twenty years, from January 1969 to January 1989, when the Republican Party prevailed. This period of party dominance was facilitated by the change in the law that permitted a governor to serve two consecutive four-year terms. Five Democrats held the post from December 1843 until January 1861, or seventeen years. The next longest tenure of one party was the Republican era of January 1916 to January 1933, or sixteen years, a total matched by the Democrats from January 1989 to January 2005. At different times one party has occupied the office for twelve consecutive years: the Republicans from January 1861 to January 1873 and the Democrats from January 1933 to January 1945. Perhaps the most notable fact about party control of the Indiana governorship is that at the beginning of 2005, Democrats had held the office for eighty-one years and ten months; Republicans for eighty years and two months.

Indiana has never had a female governor, but as the twenty-first century got under way, there was a hint that the male monopoly might soon end, as two women served as lieutenant governor. The first was Katherine (Kathy) Davis, chosen by Kernan to succeed him when he became governor upon the death of O'Bannon. Daniels selected Rebecca (Becky) Skillman as his running mate in the 2004 election, and she became Indiana's first elected female lieutenant governor.

FOR FURTHER READING

Madison, James H. *Indiana through Tradition and Change: A History of the Hoosier State and Its People, 1920–1945.* Vol. 5, *The History of Indiana.* Indianapolis: Indiana Historical Society, 1982.

————. *The Indiana Way: A State History.* Bloomington: Indiana University Press; Indianapolis: Indiana Historical Society, 1986.

Owen, James. "Formal Power of the Governor of Indiana: A Comparative Assessment." *Proceedings of the Indiana Academy of the Social Sciences.* Vol. 22. The Academy, 1987.

Walsh, Justin E. *The Centennial History of the Indiana General Assembly, 1816–1978.* Indianapolis: The Select Committee on the Centennial History of the Indiana General Assembly, 1987.

Welsh, Matthew. *View from the State House: Recollections and Reflections, 1961–1965.* Indianapolis: Indiana Historical Bureau, 1981.

William Henry Harrison

January 10, 1801–July 1812

DOUGLAS E. CLANIN

WHEN WILLIAM HENRY HARRISON BECAME THE FIRST GOVER-
nor of the Indiana Territory in 1801, most of the territorial land was
held by Native Americans. Through his successful negotiation of a
series of eleven treaties from 1803 through 1809, Harrison was able to
secure the southern third of what is now modern Indiana and most
of what is now present-day Illinois for white settlement. These treaties
probably had a greater impact on the development of the Midwest
than anything else Harrison accomplished during his time in office.
Whether they are viewed today positively or negatively, the treaties do
represent Harrison's most enduring legacy as governor.

The youngest son of Benjamin Harrison, a signer of the Declaration of Independence, and Elizabeth Bassett Harrison, William Henry
was born on February 9, 1773, at the family plantation, Berkeley, in
Charles City County, Virginia. Young Harrison received tutoring at
home and attended Hampden-Sidney College from 1787 to 1790. He
also studied medicine briefly in Richmond, Virginia, and under the
tutelage of Doctor Benjamin Rush in Philadelphia. He married Anna
Tuthill Symmes on November 25, 1795, over the objections of her
father, Judge John Cleves Symmes, a noted land speculator in New
Jersey and in what later became Ohio. During the forty-five years they
were married, the Harrisons had ten children, including John Scott,
the father of a future president, Benjamin Harrison.

Although just twenty-seven years old when he was appointed governor of the Indiana Territory by President John Adams on May 13,

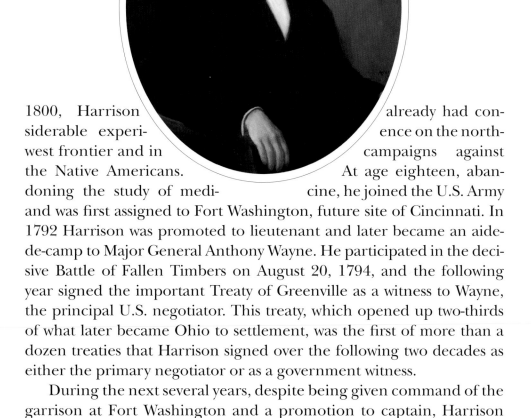

1800, Harrison already had considerable experience on the northwest frontier and in campaigns against the Native Americans. At age eighteen, abandoning the study of medicine, he joined the U.S. Army and was first assigned to Fort Washington, future site of Cincinnati. In 1792 Harrison was promoted to lieutenant and later became an aide-de-camp to Major General Anthony Wayne. He participated in the decisive Battle of Fallen Timbers on August 20, 1794, and the following year signed the important Treaty of Greenville as a witness to Wayne, the principal U.S. negotiator. This treaty, which opened up two-thirds of what later became Ohio to settlement, was the first of more than a dozen treaties that Harrison signed over the following two decades as either the primary negotiator or as a government witness.

During the next several years, despite being given command of the garrison at Fort Washington and a promotion to captain, Harrison began to tire of military life, and he resigned effective June 1, 1798. A month later Adams appointed Harrison secretary of the Northwest Territory, making him responsible for keeping the territorial records, which included laws made by the governor, land claim decisions, and land survey reports.

Harrison served as secretary of the territory a little more than a year. Then, by using census figures, territorial leaders determined that enough freeholders lived in the Northwest Territory for officials to hold an election to choose a delegate to the U.S. Congress. Harrison won this election, held in October 1799, by one vote over Arthur St. Clair Jr., son of the territorial governor.

Shortly after Harrison took his seat in Congress two months later, that body named him chairman of the Committee on Public Lands. During the session, the committee capped its work with the passage of the Land Act of 1800. This legislation liberalized methods of purchasing lands by cutting minimum land purchases in half to 320 acres in some areas, setting the price of land at two dollars per acre, reducing credit terms, and establishing four additional land districts in the area that became Ohio in 1803.

In early May 1800 Harrison was instrumental in obtaining the division of the Northwest Territory into the eastern territory, still referred to as the Northwest Territory, comprising what later became Ohio and eastern Michigan, and the western territory, designated the Indiana Territory, consisting of lands that later became western Michigan, part of eastern Minnesota, and all of Indiana, Illinois, and Wisconsin.

Initially, Harrison was reluctant to accept his appointment as governor of the new Indiana Territory because it would take him away from family, friends, and landholdings in the Cincinnati area. However, he soon accepted. Harrison was one of the few Federalist Party appointees who retained his post after the elections of two presidents from the Democratic-Republican Party: Thomas Jefferson and James Madison. They reappointed Harrison governor of the Indiana Territory in 1803, 1806, and 1809. When Harrison was reappointed territorial governor by Jefferson on February 8, 1803, the president also granted him "full power to conclude and sign any treaty or treaties, which may be found necessary." Armed with this broad authorization, Harrison set out to acquire the maximum amount of Indian land for settlers.

When the government of the Indiana Territory began on July 4, 1800, only John Gibson, the territorial secretary, had arrived in Vincennes. For six months, Gibson served as acting governor and made a number of initial appointments to territorial offices.

On January 10, 1801, Harrison and the three territorial judges assembled in Vincennes to assume the reins of government. Until the

Indiana Territory House of Representatives met in preliminary session on February 1, 1805, Harrison and the judges were in charge. Harrison made numerous appointments to the various territorial and county offices. Using a Pennsylvania law as their model, the governor and the judges created and then oversaw the territory's legal system.

Harrison and his allies also attempted to introduce slavery into the territory, although it violated Article 6 of the Ordinance of 1787. On November 22, 1802, Harrison called for a general convention of delegates from the four counties in the Indiana Territory to ask Congress to repeal this ban on slavery. Twelve delegates, meeting in Vincennes for eight days in December, called for the suspension of Article 6 for ten years. Although a committee of the U.S. House of Representatives approved the convention's resolution in 1804, the full House rejected it.

Meanwhile, in 1803, Harrison and the territorial judges enacted a law that allowed for contracts between masters and servants who were former slaves and required that servants fulfill these contracts. Further, an 1805 territorial law gave masters the right to establish the length of a term of servitude. In 1810 the Indiana General Assembly repealed both laws.

Harrison was assigned additional duties in 1804 when Congress divided the Territory of Louisiana into two regions for administrative purposes and gave Harrison the northern portion, which it named the District of Louisiana. He took office in Saint Louis on October 1, 1804, and made several appointments throughout the district. In less than a year, Congress changed the district to the Louisiana Territory and directed that it be presided over by a governor and three judges. On July 4, 1805, Brigadier General James Wilkinson took over as governor of the new territory.

Changes were also in store for the Indiana Territory, which advanced into the second stage of government following approval by freeholders in a September 1804 referendum. As a result, nine men were elected to sit in the first territorial House of Representatives. During their preliminary session on February 1, 1805, they sent Jefferson a list of ten nominees for the first territorial legislative council, the "upper house" under the second stage of government. In turn, Jefferson asked Harrison to select five men from the list of nominees to serve in the first council.

After Indiana passed into the second stage of government, Harrison gradually began to lose his political hold on the territory. There were two main reasons for this development. First, under the new form of government, Harrison no longer had legislative powers except for an absolute veto over legislation he found offensive or unconstitutional, such as bills he vetoed in 1808 because they infringed on his power to appoint officeholders. Second, the Indiana Territory became smaller when Michigan and Illinois became independent territories on June 30, 1805, and March 1, 1809, respectively. After the latter division, Indiana assumed approximately its modern boundaries.

The last of the major modifications in the shape and size of the Indiana Territory placed Vincennes, where Harrison and his family lived, on its western border. As population increased along the Ohio River and the eastern portion of the territory, freeholders increasingly demanded that the capital be moved from Vincennes to a more eastern site. The principal candidate for the new capital was Corydon, located some eighty-five miles southeast of Vincennes. Harrison vigorously resisted all attempts to move the capital from Vincennes, but on May 1, 1813, Corydon became the new territorial capital.

Another factor that contributed to Harrison's waning political power was the ascendancy of strong democratic leaders such as Jonathan Jennings, who led the drive to make Corydon the capital. During Harrison's last half dozen years of service as territorial governor, Jennings was his principal political foe. In April 1807 Jennings arrived in Vincennes to practice law, but in the following year he moved to Clark County and began to rally the antislavery, anti-Harrison forces. On May 22, 1809, Jennings won election as Indiana delegate to Congress, where he served until his election in 1816 as the first Indiana state governor.

As Harrison's tenure as territorial governor wound down after 1809, he remained unwilling or unable to adapt to the changing political realities that were represented by Jennings and the majority of the new settlers who were moving into the territory. These settlers sided with Jennings's democratic policies and joined with him in signing petitions that supported Indiana statehood. In addition, Harrison's string of treaty signings was ended during this time by the increasing protests of some Native Americans who wanted no contact with the whites and no more land sales to them. These tribal groups, led by the Shawnee Prophet and his brother Tecumseh, gravitated almost inexorably into a conflict with Jeffersonian Indian policies. From the viewpoint of these Native American leaders and their followers, the surprise was not that the Shawnee Prophet and his followers fought with Harrison and his troops at the Battle of Tippecanoe near present-day Lafayette, Indiana, on November 7, 1811, but that this clash of arms did not occur sooner.

Fearing further hostilities, Harrison, in early May 1812, sent his wife and their children to Cincinnati, where they lived near Judge Symmes and other family members and friends. On June 18, 1812, the United States declared war on Great Britain, and Harrison made his final departure from Vincennes shortly thereafter, apparently without making his future intentions known. For a six-month period, Gibson carried out the duties of both the secretary and the governor.

Harrison made several trips to Kentucky during the summer of 1812, probably in an effort to obtain a military appointment from that state, which he received in late August when the outgoing Kentucky governor made him a major general and head of the state militia. He relinquished this position about a month later when the U.S. government commissioned him to command the Northwest Army. Harrison continued to draw his governor's salary, as well as his federal military pay, from early September 1812 until he was forced to resign as Indiana territorial governor on December 28, 1812.

The high point in Harrison's military service in the War of 1812 was the decisive victory he and his troops achieved on October 5, 1813, at a pivotal battle near Moravian Town on the Thames River in Upper Canada (now Ontario). In the Battle of the Thames, Major General Henry Procter commanded British troops, and Tecumseh led the Native American forces. Tecumseh was killed during the battle, and with his death, Indian opponents of the United States lost their principal leader. Harrison commanded the Northwest Army until a dispute with Secretary of War John Armstrong led to his resignation from the army in late May 1814.

Harrison then returned to politics, serving Ohio during an eight-year period as a member of the state senate as well as in the U.S. House of Representatives and the U.S. Senate. After service in these elective offices, he was the U.S. Minister to Colombia from May 1828 until the end of September 1829, when President Andrew Jackson recalled him. For several years after his recall, Harrison was not only in a political wilderness but also struggled to overcome a series of family tragedies and economic reversals. In 1835 Harrison made numerous high-profile and popular tours of the Midwest that helped to lift him out of his political isolation. The following year, he attended several rallies that commemorated the twenty-fifth anniversary of the Battle of Tippecanoe. During these events, several Whig Party leaders began to see Harrison's potential as a presidential candidate.

In the 1836 presidential race, the Whigs split their votes between Harrison, Daniel Webster, and Hugh L. White. Despite this divided vote, Harrison managed to carry seven of the twenty-six states, receiving seventy-three votes in the Electoral College. Nevertheless, Martin Van Buren, the Democratic candidate, had 170 electoral votes and won the election.

The Whigs worked diligently against Van Buren during his presidential term, and the panic of 1837, caused in part by western land speculation, greatly aided the Whigs in this endeavor. During the depression, Harrison's political support continued to grow, centering around his core supporters—veterans of the War of 1812 and members of the Anti-Masonic Party.

When the Whigs met for their national convention in Harrisburg, Pennsylvania, in December 1839, only Harrison and Kentucky's Henry Clay were candidates for the party's presidential nomination. Since Whig leaders wanted to control the presidency if they won the election, they chose Harrison to be their candidate. They perceived that he was a weaker, more compliant man than the ambitious Clay. Vice presidential candidate John Tyler of Virginia joined Harrison on the ticket. Whig leaders chose Tyler in a move designed to placate southern members of their party, who were upset by the leadership's rejection of their champion, Clay.

The Whigs did not draft a platform at the convention, and instead party leaders instructed Harrison and Tyler to avoid taking a stand on any controversial issue, such as slavery, the tariff, or the economy. Harrison's war record became the focus of the campaign, along with the symbols of a log cabin and a jug of hard cider to create the illusion that Harrison came from a humble background. This strategy was full of irony because Harrison had governed the Indiana Territory (and for a brief time the District of Louisiana) as a "Virginia-born aristocrat."

Regardless of the unorthodox nature of their campaign, the Whigs won the 1840 presidential election. The ticket of "Tippecanoe and Tyler, Too," carried nineteen of the twenty-six states and won 234 electoral votes, though their majority in the popular vote totaled fewer than 150,000 votes. The Democrats, led by the incumbent Van Buren, collected only sixty electoral votes.

Harrison was able to savor his triumph for only a few months. Worn down by the rigors of the campaign and by the duties of his office, Harrison contracted pneumonia shortly after his inauguration on March 4, 1841. He died on April 4, 1841, at the age of sixty-eight. Harrison, the oldest man elected president until Ronald Reagan, was the first chief executive to die in office. His remains were placed in the family vault, in which were later interred the remains of Anna Harrison and those of at least ten other family members. The Harrison family burial vault, topped by a monument, is located just west of North Bend, Ohio, near the site of Harrison's farm.

Portrait by Theodore Clement Steele (1916), Governors' Portraits Collection, Indiana Historical Bureau, State of Indiana.

FOR FURTHER READING

Clanin, Douglas E., ed. *A Guide to the Papers of William Henry Harrison, 1800–1815.* 2nd ed. Indianapolis: Indiana Historical Society, 1999.

Esarey, Logan, ed. *Messages and Letters of William Henry Harrison.* Vol. 1, *1800–1811.* Indianapolis: Indiana Historical Commission, 1922.

Goebel, Dorothy Burne. *William Henry Harrison: A Political Biography.* Indianapolis: Historical Bureau of the Indiana Library and Historical Department, 1926.

Gunderson, Robert G. "William Henry Harrison: Apprentice in Arms." *Northwest Ohio Quarterly* 65 (Winter 1993): 3–29.

Hickey, Donald R. *The War of 1812: A Forgotten Conflict.* Urbana and Chicago: University of Illinois Press, 1989.

Stevens, Kenneth R., comp. *William Henry Harrison: A Bibliography.* Westport, CT: Greenwood Press, 1998.

Webster, Homer J. *William Henry Harrison's Administration of Indiana Territory.* Indiana Historical Society Publications, vol. 4, no. 3. Indianapolis: Sentinel Printing Company, 1907.

Woollen, William Wesley, Daniel Wait Howe, and Jacob Piatt Dunn, eds. *Executive Journal of Indiana Territory, 1800–1816.* 1900. Reprint with revisions, Indianapolis: Indiana Historical Society, 1985.

Collections of Harrison's papers can be found in the William Henry Smith Memorial Library, Indiana Historical Society, Indianapolis; the Indiana State Archives, Indianapolis; the Library of Congress, Washington, D.C.; and the National Archives, Washington, D.C.

John Gibson

July 4, 1800–January 10, 1801 and June 1812–May 1813

JOHN R. BIERLY

JOHN GIBSON, SOMETIMES REFERRED TO AS INDIANA'S SEC-
ond territorial governor, was actually secretary of the territory for its
entire sixteen-year existence, from 1800 to 1816. He did, however,
serve as acting governor during two critical periods, from July 1800
to January 1801, and from the summer of 1812 to the spring of 1813.
The task of organizing the government and militia of the far-flung,
newly created territory, which encompassed 80 percent of the former
Northwest Territory, fell to the sixty-year-old Gibson, who arrived in
Vincennes, the territorial capital, on July 22, 1800. The governor, William Henry Harrison, only twenty-seven years old at the time of his
appointment by President John Adams, did not arrive at the capital
until January 10, 1801.

Meanwhile, Gibson, who had spent his life up to that point along
the Allegheny frontier as a soldier, trader, judge, and politician,
appointed judges for the various courts, clerks, a sheriff, a treasurer,
and a recorder. He also began naming officers to the militia. Shortly
after Harrison's arrival in Vincennes, Gibson assumed other duties
besides his secretarial ones, including being named a justice of the
peace, county recorder of Knox County, and a judge of the quarter
sessions court, which tried petty crimes and misdemeanors.

John Gibson was born in Lancaster, Pennsylvania, on May 23, 1740,
to George and Elizabeth de Vinez Gibson. He never attended college,
but by all accounts was well educated. At age seventeen, he joined General John Forbes's successful campaign to take Fort Duquesne (now

Pittsburgh) from the French. When the Revolutionary War started, Gibson raised a regiment of troops, was appointed a colonel, and fought in New York and on the western frontier. After the war, he returned to Pittsburgh to resume his trading business. In 1788 Gibson was elected a member of the convention that wrote the first constitution of Pennsylvania. He served for several years as a common pleas judge of Allegheny County and as general of the state militia.

In one of his first acts as secretary, Gibson completed a census of the Indiana Territory. The yearlong investigation determined the population of the vast region, consisting of the present-day states of Indiana, Illinois, Michigan, Wisconsin, and a part of Minnesota, numbered 4,875 free whites and 135 slaves. Vincennes, with its population of 714, including eight slaves, was the largest settlement. The land also was home to numerous French settlers and, of course, Native Americans, who lived in the forests and along the streams of the mostly wilderness territory.

As Harrison sought to fulfill his mandate from Washington to increase the American population in the territory and get the tribes to cede additional lands for settlement, he had a valuable resource in Gibson, someone with long and varied experience with Indians. Gibson had acquired the nickname "Horsehead" from the Native Americans, which they bestowed as a compliment to his horse sense. Gibson had been a trader, had fought them, and had lived with them for several years in southwest Virginia—learning their language and customs—after his capture and near-execution. He was about to be burned at the stake, along with several other white men, when an old squaw intervened on his behalf and promptly adopted him. Gibson was also married for a time to a sister of Logan, the renowned Mingo chief, but eventually left his life with the tribe and his wife to resume his business as a trader.

Gibson and Logan again crossed paths after a group of Virginia settlers murdered a dozen Mingos, including Logan's mother and sister, Gibson's former wife. In retaliation, Logan, who before had always been peaceful toward settlers, conducted raids that killed thirteen whites, sparking Lord Dunmore's War in 1774. Gibson, who became part of the expedition assembled to fight the Mingo and Shawnee, was asked by Dunmore to negotiate with Logan. According to Gibson's account of their meeting, they went for a walk in the woods and Logan, "after shedding [an] abundance of tears," gave Gibson a copy of his famous speech in which he lamented his sense of betrayal by whites and pledged to continue waging war against settlers, which he did. Gibson later interpreted the speech for Dunmore.

In his roles as territorial secretary and acting governor, Gibson continued to be intimately involved in Native American affairs. He was present when Shawnee leader Tecumseh, accompanied by four hundred armed warriors, came to Vincennes in the summer of 1810 to talk with Harrison about the massive cession of land in the territory by other tribes to the United States. As Tecumseh's words became more heated and threatening, Gibson, who understood Shawnee, summoned a twelve-man guard, whose quick appearance on the scene kept the situation from escalating out of hand.

It was just a matter of time, though, before widespread warfare with the Native Americans came. When it did, Harrison, responsible for the defense of settlers, left Vincennes to assume military commands, first at the Battle of Tippecanoe and then during the War of 1812, leaving Gibson in the capital to act as governor and to cope with the outbreak of hostilities in the territory. One of Gibson's first acts was to seek help for stemming the siege at Fort Harrison, under the command of Captain Zachary Taylor, the future president. As a result of Gibson's pleas, thousands of reinforcements of Kentucky militia and regular army troops marched into Indiana to join the fighting. Gibson was also concerned that those Native Americans seeking peace with the United States not be drawn into the opposition by some inadvertent military action. For instance, when dispatching militia to Clark and Harrison counties in southern Indiana, Gibson, in a message to the troops' commander, forbid him "from proceeding against the Delawares without permission." At the time, the tribe was in peace negotiations with a presidential commission.

Gibson, who officially became acting governor after Harrison resigned in late 1812 to accept a commission as major general of the Army of the Northwest, held this position until Thomas Posey, appointed governor by President James Madison, assumed the office in May 1813. Before returning to his job as secretary, Gibson oversaw the relocation of records and offices from Vincennes to the new Indiana capital of Corydon, then situated just about in the center of the settled territory. At about the same time, Gibson County in southwestern Indiana was formed and named for the acting governor.

With the advent of statehood in 1816, Gibson's duties as secretary ended, and he returned to Pennsylvania, living at Braddock's Field near Pittsburgh. He died there on April 10, 1822.

No documented portrait of John Gibson has been located as of the date of this publication.

FOR FURTHER READING

Cayton, Andrew R. L. *Frontier Indiana.* Bloomington: Indiana University Press, 1996.

National Cyclopaedia of American Biography. New York: James T. White and Company, 1906.

Woollen, William Wesley. *Biographical and Historical Sketches of Early Indiana.* Indianapolis: Hammond and Company, 1883.

Thomas Posey

March 3, 1813–November 7, 1816

JOHN THORNTON POSEY

ALTHOUGH INDIANA ATTAINED STATEHOOD DURING THE governorship of Thomas Posey, historians have tended to marginalize his role in that process. A veteran Revolutionary War officer, he had previously held high public office in three states, bringing a wealth of military and governing experience to a territory under attack from without and bitterly split into political factions within. Under his moderating, nonpartisan leadership, the most immediate needs of the rapidly growing population were met, the political environment stabilized, and a diverse and scattered territory coalesced into a worthy candidate for admission to the Union.

President James Madison named Posey to replace William Henry Harrison, and he was confirmed by the Senate on March 2, 1813. But Posey was not universally welcomed in Indiana. The territory was then locked in bitter factionalism between proslavery followers of Harrison, scorned as "the Virginia aristocrats," and an antislavery coalition that had gained control of the legislature under the leadership of Jonathan Jennings, territorial delegate to Congress. Many in Indiana viewed Posey as just another Harrison, and Jennings had lobbied in the Senate to defeat his confirmation.

Even before his arrival in the territory, Posey met the issue head-on, writing the acting governor, John Gibson, that "I am as much opposed to slavery as any person whatever; I have disposed of what few I had some time since. . . . I shall never sanction a law for slavery or any modification of it," and promised to "neither meddle or inter-

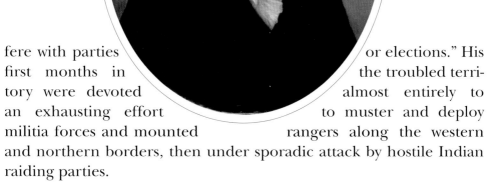

fere with parties or elections." His first months in the troubled territory were devoted almost entirely to an exhausting effort to muster and deploy militia forces and mounted rangers along the western and northern borders, then under sporadic attack by hostile Indian raiding parties.

Posey was, by his own account, "born of respectable parentage" near the Potomac in Virginia on July 9, 1750. His actual ancestry, though, has been a matter of considerable speculation, beginning with an assertion in a Cincinnati newspaper in 1871, more than fifty years after Posey's death, that he was the illegitimate son of George Washington. Although that possibility was subsequently discussed in many news articles, serious historical works, and biographical encyclopedias, the claim has never been proved or disproved, and the true story most likely will never be known.

What is more certain is that Posey grew up in the household of Captain John Posey at Rover's Delight, a property bordering Washington's Mount Vernon. The captain was Washington's longtime friend, frequent hunting companion, and fellow vestryman, a well-regarded member of the Fairfax County gentry community. Young Thomas received a "tolerable english education" from the neighborhood free school and private tutelage, but did not advance beyond the secondary level. Captain Posey, meanwhile, became increasingly dependent upon and indebted to Washington and in 1768 forfeited his entire estate to the frugal squire of Mount Vernon. At age eighteen, Thomas set out to make his own way in life in the frontier town of Staunton, Virginia.

Posey established himself in the saddlery trade and married Martha Mathews, niece of the town's prominent innkeeper. His first military service was in Lord Dunmore's War as commissary general in a force of volunteer militia under Colonel Andrew Lewis, sent by the colonial governor against hostile tribes in the trans-Appalachian region. At the Battle of Point Pleasant on October 10, 1774, the eight hundred frontiersmen defeated a Native American coalition led by the able Shawnee war chief Cornstalk, opening the region to white settlement.

Posey eagerly embraced the cause of colonial independence, serving first on the revolutionary Botetourt County Committee of Correspondence. On March 20, 1776, he was commissioned a captain in the Continental army, raising at his own expense a company of fellow veterans of Point Pleasant. His subsequent seven-year military record in the American Revolution is notable for its wide-ranging scope, participation in the nation's greatest victories, and many acts of personal bravery and leadership under fire.

Posey's unit played a leading role in driving the governor, John, Earl of Dunmore, from Gwynn's Island in Chesapeake Bay, his last foothold on Virginia soil. After joining Washington's main army in 1777, Posey commanded a company in Colonel Daniel Morgan's famed Rifle Regiment, composed entirely of frontier marksmen. As a component of General Horatio Gates's forces in upstate New York, Morgan's five-hundred-man corps played a key role in the battles leading to the British surrender at Saratoga, a turning point in the Revolutionary War.

During the bitterly cold winter at Valley Forge, the riflemen guarded the perimeter of the main army, skirmishing almost daily with enemy scouting and foraging parties. Promoted to major on April 30, 1778, Posey led his troops in the Battle of Monmouth and then marched his battalion to New York's northern border, guarding outlying American settlements from raids by Canadian rangers and British-allied tribes of the Iroquois League. He was one of eight battle-tested battalion commanders selected for Brigadier General Anthony Wayne's Light Infantry Corps. In the July 15, 1779, assault on Stony Point, a heavily fortified promontory dominating the Hudson River between the two contending main armies, he was one of the first to fight his way over the highest parapet. Posey shouted the watchword, "The fort's our own," and led a relentless charge across the parade grounds, forcing more than six hundred British defenders to throw down their arms in surrender.

After the corps disbanded, Posey returned to Virginia, where he recruited and led a new battalion at the American-French siege at Yorktown. Now a lieutenant colonel, Posey witnessed the surrender of General Charles Cornwallis's army on October 19, 1781. His unit then marched to join Wayne's small force besieging enemy-occupied Savannah. On the dark, moonless night of June 24, 1782, their camp was overrun by a horde of British-allied Creek warriors under war chief Guristersigo. They were repulsed only after Wayne and Posey, swords drawn, personally led a counterattack. Soon thereafter, the enemy peacefully evacuated both Savannah and Charleston, and Posey had the high honor of leading the advance guard into the latter city. When the war officially ended, he returned to Virginia and resigned his commission on March 10, 1783.

Posey's first wife, Martha, had died in childbirth during the war, leaving three sons, only one of whom lived to maturity. On January 22, 1784, the former saddler, his stature as a war hero and gentleman now firmly established, married Mary Alexander Thornton, a widow of means with three children and impressive connections in Virginia gentry society. For eighteen years, with one notable exception, Posey lived the life of a planter and country squire at Greenwood, a secluded estate near Fredericksburg, adding nine more children to the family circle. He held several appointive state and local positions, but other than a losing race for Congress in 1797, was not politically active. Only another call to military service in his country's interests could lure the retired soldier from his comfortable life.

A coalition of Miami Indian tribes had decisively defeated two American military expeditions sent in 1790 and 1791 to open the Ohio

Territory to white settlement. On March 11, 1793, Posey accepted a brigadier general's commission from President Washington and marched again under Wayne in a five-thousand-man legion ordered to establish American hegemony in the region. When the army went into winter quarters, he took home leave, stopping at the nation's capital in Philadelphia to lobby Congress for increases in the pay and benefits of the soldiers. He was dismayed to learn that Wayne's second in command, General James Wilkinson, had systematically undermined the commander's character and authority in a series of anonymous reports to government officials. Feeling compromised by divided loyalty between his two superiors, both Revolutionary comrades in arms, Posey resigned his commission on February 20, 1794, missing the Battle of Fallen Timbers on August 20, 1794. Wilkinson, long after his death, was found to have been a longtime paid secret agent of Spain.

In the spring of 1802 Posey exercised his seven-thousand-acre military land warrant and moved his entire household to the frontier settlement of Henderson in western Kentucky. Within two years, he was elected to the state senate and on November 10, 1804, was chosen as its speaker, and in 1805, as de facto lieutenant governor. After presiding over the senate until December 29, 1807, he withdrew from the 1808 governor's race in favor of another prominent Revolutionary officer and fellow Virginian, General Charles Scott. He later served briefly as major general of the state militia. The outbreak of war in 1812 found him temporarily residing in Baton Rouge, Louisiana, where the sixty-two-year-old patriot promptly raised a volunteer company and on September 14, 1812, accepted a commission as its captain from General James Wilkinson, then commander of American forces in the southwest. But within weeks, Governor William C. C. Claiborne gave Posey an interim appointment as one of Louisiana's first U.S. senators. Arriving in Washington on December 6, he served in the Senate until his successor arrived on February 5, 1813, while also assisting acting Secretary of War James Monroe with staff work at the War Office.

From Washington it was on to Indiana and new challenges as the state's last territorial governor. His relationship with an unfriendly general assembly began inauspiciously in the new capital at Corydon in December 1813 when, after delivering a conciliatory welcoming address, he was forced by poor health to withdraw to his home in Jeffersonville. The legislators viewed his midsession absence as a display of aristocratic arrogance, issuing a sharp rebuke to the ailing governor. Nevertheless, they enacted many of his proposals, and for the balance of his three-year term of office, legislators and the governor worked in close harmony to address the many concerns of the growing population. The militia was reformed along traditional military lines, the judicial system was expanded and reorganized, new counties and towns were created, critical road work and other infrastructure was approved, banks were chartered, and the first steps were taken toward free public education. Posey apparently was even-handed and nonpartisan in his appointments to territorial and local offices.

As statehood replaced slavery as the major issue in the territory, the dominant Jennings coalition pressed hard for home-rule status after a special census in 1815 met the required population threshold of sixty thousand. In December of that year the assembly petitioned Congress to call a constitutional convention. Posey, who had hailed the prospect of statehood at the assembly's opening session, signed the memorial despite grave private doubts that the territory's struggling residents could sustain the heavy financial burden it would impose upon them. He also expressed concern that the territory lacked qualified people to assume the various offices of government. Delegate Jennings, however, deftly guided the measure through Congress, and by the summer of 1816 a state constitution was crafted and an election for state offices was set for August 5. After a short but spirited campaign, Jennings defeated Posey for governor by a vote of 5,211 to 3,934 and was sworn into office on November 7, 1816.

Within weeks of leaving office, Posey was appointed Indian agent for the lower Wabash and spent the last two years of his life befriending and counseling the Wea, Kickapoo, and Potatwatomi, whose brother tribes he had fought as enemies on many past battlefields. His last political foray was an ill-advised and losing campaign in 1817 for the congressional seat of Jennings ally William Hendricks. Posey died on March 19, 1818, and lies in an elaborately inscribed sarcophagus at Shawneetown, Illinois.

Posey was a better soldier and statesman than a politician. Most of his public service was in appointed, rather than elected, positions. He was not the father of Indiana statehood, a title more properly belonging to his political opponent and successor in office, Jennings. As his term of office neared its end, once-hostile legislators of his time, in declaring their "perfect approbation of your official conduct as Governor," defined Posey's true contribution to Indiana history: "During your administration, Sir, many then existing evils have been remedied; and we particularly admire the calm, dispassionate, impartial conduct of your administration, which has produced the salutary effect of quieting the violence of party spirit . . . under your auspices, we have become as one people."

Portrait by John Bayless Hill (1869), Governors' Portraits Collection, Indiana Historical Bureau, State of Indiana.

FOR FURTHER READING

Barnhart, John D. and Dorothy L. Riker. *Indiana to 1816: The Colonial Period.* Vol. 1, *The History of Indiana.* Indianapolis: Indiana Historical Bureau and Indiana Historical Society, 1971.

Dunn, Jacob P. *Indiana and Indianans: A History of Aboriginal and Territorial Indiana and the Century of Statehood.* 5 vols. Chicago: American Historical Society, 1919.

Esarey, Logan, ed. *Messages and Letters of William Henry Harrison.* 2 vols. Indianapolis: Indiana Historical Commission, 1922.

Johnston, Henry P. *The Storming of Stony Point on the Hudson, Midnight, July 15, 1779.* 1900. Reprint, New York: Da Capo Press, 1971.

Madison, James H. *The Indiana Way: A State History.* Bloomington: Indiana University Press; Indianapolis: Indiana Historical Society, 1990.

Nelson, Paul David. *Anthony Wayne: Soldier of the Early Republic.* Bloomington: Indiana University Press, 1985.

Posey, John Thornton. *General Thomas Posey: Son of the American Revolution.* East Lansing: Michigan State University Press, 1992.
———. "Rascality Revisited: In Defense of General James Wilkinson." *The Filson Club History Quarterly* 74, no. 4 (Fall 2000).
Woollen, William Wesley. *Biographical and Historical Sketches of Early Indiana.* Indianapolis: Hammond and Company, 1883.

Posey's papers are in the William H. English Collection, William Henry Smith Memorial Library, Indiana Historical Society, Indianapolis.

Jonathan Jennings

November 7, 1816–September 12, 1822

CARL E. KRAMER

AS THE FIRST STATE GOVERNOR, JONATHAN JENNINGS FACED the daunting challenges of placing Indiana on a sound financial footing, implementing a court system, and developing rudimentary educational and internal improvements systems, while also attempting to prevent government from becoming so burdensome that it obstructed personal advancement and enterprise.

Throughout his career in territorial, state, and federal politics, Jennings vigorously defended the rights and equality of white men against the forces of aristocracy and corruption, represented in his view by Governor William Henry Harrison and others whom he believed viewed government as a tool to advance their own wealth and position at the expense of the average citizen. Jennings, one historian observed, "believed, in a vague but intense and impetuous fashion, in the rights of white men, the value of popular democracy, and the evils of slavery."

Jennings was born in 1784, probably in Hunterdon County, New Jersey, and was the sixth child of Jacob and Mary Kennedy Jennings. His father was a practicing physician and Dutch Reformed minister. In the early 1790s the Jennings family moved to Fayette County, Pennsylvania, where the elder Jennings accepted a pastorate at Dunlap's Creek. The family was very close, and Jonathan developed particularly close attachments with an older brother, Ebenezer, and a younger sister, Ann. After receiving his elementary education at home, Jennings attended a grammar school at Canonsburg, Pennsylvania, where he stud- ied Greek, Latin, and higher math- ematics. His classmates included Wil- liam Hendricks and William Wick, both of whom would become political associates in Indiana. After grammar school, Jennings apparently read law for a time with John Simonson in Washington, Pennsylvania. By 1806 he had moved to Steubenville, Ohio, where his elder brother, Obadiah, practiced law.

Jennings's stay in Ohio was brief. Later in 1806 he moved to Jeffersonville, the seat of justice for Clark County, Indiana Territory. After a short stay, he moved in early 1807 to Vincennes, then the capital of the Indiana Territory. He was admitted to the bar in April and served as clerk of the land office and assistant clerk of the territorial legislature while struggling to attract clients. He also engaged in several disastrous business ventures, including an ill-fated land speculation scheme that forced him to sell land to pay his debts. In September 1807 Jennings was elected clerk of the board of trustees of Vincennes University, of which Harrison was president. Jennings soon became enmeshed in the board's internal politics, and he and Harrison quickly crossed swords. Although information about the conflict is sketchy, it resulted in Jennings's resignation in May 1808. While very real substantive differences divided Harrison and Jennings during the years that followed, personal animosities stemming from university politics undoubtedly shaped the latter's path to the governor's office over the next eight years.

Realizing his chances for advancement in Vincennes were limited, Jennings returned to Clark County and stayed briefly in Jeffersonville before settling permanently in Charlestown. The timing of the move was propitious. Jennings had predicated his move on the belief that his political fortunes would be greater in the eastern part of the territory and that the capital soon would be transferred to Clark County. But his action proved even more timely when in February 1809 Congress divided Indiana to create the new Illinois Territory and declared that Indiana's territorial delegate to Congress would be elected by the voters rather than the legislature. Meanwhile, residents of Clark County and southeastern Indiana were growing increasingly resentful of efforts by Harrison and his allies to persuade Congress to open the territory to slavery and to maintain its existence through a tortured interpretation of indentured servitude.

Seizing an opportunity to mesh his own resentment against Harrison with those of the electorate, Jennings launched a vigorous campaign for congressional delegate, declaring his opposition to slavery and Harrison's system of patronage politics, both of which he considered aristocratic tendencies. As important as his message was his style. Traversing Clark, Harrison, and Dearborn counties, Jennings courted voters directly, treating them like friends, drinking with them, and often helping with their work or joining in their games before mounting the stump. Whether it was his message, his style, or a combination of the two that attracted the electorate, Jennings won a plurality in a three-way race and in late November took his seat in Washington. He was reelected in 1811, 1812, and 1814.

On August 8, 1811, Jennings married nineteen-year-old Ann Gilmore Hay, a native of Harrodsburg, Kentucky, and daughter of one of Charlestown's leading politicians. Ann Hay Jennings died in March 1826 after a long illness; Jennings married Clarissa Barbee on October 19, 1827. Neither marriage produced children. Although a gregarious politician, Jennings suffered periods of despondency, and his style may well have reflected a fear of loneliness. His personal insecurities, combined with the casual drinking and camaraderie of the campaign trail, probably fostered the alcoholism that ultimately ruined his career. As has been noted, "by the 1820s, Jennings was a well-known sot, a convivial drunk."

During his congressional tenure, Jennings closely tended to the concerns of his constituents. He supported relief measures for those who, because of the shaky credit system, were at risk of losing land purchased under the Land Act of 1800, secured passage of a bill to strengthen defense of frontier settlements from attack by hostile tribes, and promoted the development of roads in Ohio and Indiana. But he also used his position to chip away at Harrison's gubernatorial powers. Soon after his arrival in Washington, he made an unsuccessful effort to block Harrison's reappointment. In 1810, however, Congress prohibited most gubernatorial appointees from serving in the territorial assembly and extended the franchise to all white men over twenty-one who had lived in the territory for a year and paid a county or territorial tax. Jennings failed to win congressional approval of other democratizing measures, such as direct election of sheriffs and allowing appeals from territorial courts to federal courts. But the territorial legislature took matters into its own hands by passing legislation that further weakened the governor's control of the political process. When Harrison resigned in late 1812 to resume military service in the war against the British, Indiana was a very different place from what it had been when he arrived nearly twelve years earlier.

In December 1815, the War of 1812 having been successfully concluded, Jennings took his most important initiative, presenting a petition from the territorial legislature asking Congress to authorize an election for delegates to a constitutional convention to determine if Indiana should become a state. The following month he introduced a statehood Enabling Act, which Congress passed on April 11, 1816. Jennings was elected one of five Clark County delegates to the convention, which convened in June at Corydon, then the territorial capital. As a reward for his success in pushing through the Enabling Act and as a symbol of the strength of the anti-Harrison faction, Jennings was promptly elected the convention's president. Under his leadership, the convention crafted a constitution that embodied the democratizing values that Jennings and the territorial legislature had supported for a decade and created a structure of governance that exalted the legislature at the expense of the governor.

In August Jennings defeated Territorial governor Thomas Posey and took office as Indiana's first state governor in November 1816. During his tenure of nearly six years, Jennings concentrated primarily on six broad objectives: establishing a court system to secure swift and certain justice; organizing an educational system that reached from the common schools to a state university; creating a state banking system; preventing illegal efforts to capture and enslave blacks entitled to their freedom; organizing a state library; and developing a plan of internal improvements. That Jennings experienced limited success in achieving these objectives is as much a reflection of the governor's limited powers and the state's impoverished financial condition as it is upon his political skills and knowledge of the issues.

Jennings's powers were perhaps most limited in the area of justice, where his primary responsibility was to nominate the three judges of the state supreme court, who were confirmed by the state senate. Except for a president judge appointed by the legislature, county circuit courts were elected by the voters, as were justices of the peace. Immediately after the first general assembly convened, Jennings called to its attention the constitution's ambitious vision of a system of free public education extending from the common school to the university level. But the document also conditioned action on the ability and willingness of counties to finance such a system. Thus the assembly paid little more than lip service to the subject. It empowered county commissioners to appoint school superintendents and the voters to elect trustees and authorized them to oversee the leasing of land in section sixteen of each congressional township for school purposes. But few pioneer Hoosiers were concerned enough about education to support the imposition of the taxes necessary to fund public education. Similarly, the state's penury postponed any initiative toward creation of a state library until the administration of Governor James B. Ray in 1826.

In the field of banking, Jennings signed legislation passed in 1817 to create the State Bank of Indiana, which converted the Bank of Vincennes, chartered by the territorial assembly, into the new institution's headquarters branch and established branches at Brookville, Corydon, and Vevay. The new bank soon became a federal depository, but it also became engulfed in the wave of speculation and political wrangling that triggered the panic of 1819 and was forced to suspend specie payment. Soon thereafter the federal treasury suspended deposits, and by 1821 the bank was insolvent. For several years thereafter, Hoosiers depended largely on the Bank of the United States, especially its Louisville branch, and the Farmers and Mechanics Bank of Madison, which held a territorial charter, for banking services. Meanwhile, Jennings received severe criticism for failing to supervise the bank more carefully and for not initiating an investigation that might have uncovered wrongdoing of its officials. But as historian Dorothy Riker noted, "The blame must be placed more on the general ignorance of economic laws and the dishonesty of some of the men in charge of the Bank rather than on the conduct of the governor."

Confronted with a "road system" that was little more than a network of rude Indian and buffalo trails, implementing a program of internal improvements was one of Jennings's highest priorities. The first state legislative session gave county commissioners the authority to open, relocate, and vacate roads; to appoint local citizens as township road supervisors; and to compel men between the ages of eighteen and fifty to provide labor for road construction. In 1821 Jennings persuaded the legislature to appropriate $100,000 from the Three Percent Fund, a pool of money received from federal land sales for construction of roads and canals, to build twenty-two state roads that would link most of the state's larger communities with Indianapolis, the purposed new capital. But the scale of the plan far exceeded the money available, and very few miles of road were constructed during Jennings's tenure.

As a longtime opponent of slavery in Indiana, Jennings urged legislators in November 1816 to make it illegal to seize free blacks and sell them into slavery. But he also believed Indiana was a white man's country, and he equally objected to efforts by people in other states to make the Hoosier State "a refuge from the possession of their lawful owners." In response, the assembly imposed heavy fines on persons who knowingly aided escaped slaves and created personal liberty safeguards to persons of color not available in federal law. Those attempting to seize and return a fugitive were required to obtain an arrest warrant from a local court, present their case before a jury trial, and pay the cost of the trial. Anyone who seized a person in violation of the law was branded "guilty of man stealing."

Jennings's greatest political crisis resulted not from a legislative conflict but from a federal appointment that excited the ambitions of a rival, Lieutenant Governor Christopher Harrison. In 1818 President James Madison appointed the governor to serve with Lewis Cass and Benjamin Parke as commissioners to negotiate the Treaty of St. Marys, or the New Purchase Treaty, by which the Miami relinquished most of their tribal lands in central Indiana. Because the state constitution prohibited anyone holding federal office from serving as governor, Harrison claimed that Jennings had vacated his office, and Harrison began exercising the powers of the chief executive. After Jennings returned to Corydon and reclaimed his office, Harrison and his allies urged the assembly to initiate impeachment proceedings. But the legislators refused the bait, and in 1819 Jennings sealed his victory by defeating Harrison by a large majority in his bid for reelection.

In September 1822, shortly before his term ended, Jennings resigned as governor after being elected to the U.S. House of Representatives, where he represented the Second Congressional District until 1830. In Congress he successfully supported appropriations to build the National Road and the Wabash and Erie Canal and to improve navigation on the Wabash River. He also advocated construction of a canal around the north side of the Falls of the Ohio, but that effort failed. By the late 1820s he had become increasingly addicted to alcohol, and in 1830 he lost a reelection bid to John Carr, another popular Clark County politician and hero of the War of 1812. He lived with his wife Clarissa on their farm outside Charlestown until his death on July 26, 1834. He is buried in the Charlestown cemetery.

Portrait by Theodore Clement Steele (1916), Governors' Portraits Collection, Indiana Historical Bureau, State of Indiana.

FOR FURTHER READING

Carmony, Donald F. *Indiana, 1816–1850: The Pioneer Era.* Vol. 2, *The History of Indiana.* Indianapolis: Indiana Historical Bureau and Indiana Historical Society, 1998.

Cayton, Andrew R. L. *Frontier Indiana.* Bloomington: Indiana University Press, 1996.

Mills, Randy K. *Jonathan Jennings: Indiana's First Governor.* Indianapolis: Indiana Historical Society Press, 2005.

Riker, Dorothy L. "Jonathan Jennings." *Indiana Magazine of History* 28 (December 1932): 223–39.

Jennings's gubernatorial papers are in the Indiana State Archives, Indianapolis. Scattered letters can be found in the William Henry Smith Memorial Library, Indiana Historical Society, Indianapolis, and the Indiana State Library, Indianapolis.

Ratliff Boon

September 12–December 5, 1822

CARL E. KRAMER

RATLIFF BOON, INDIANA'S SECOND GOVERNOR, SERVED FOR only eighty-four days and accomplished virtually nothing while completing the second term of Governor Jonathan Jennings. Nevertheless, Boon was a prominent pioneer politician who served a lengthy tenure in Congress and was instrumental in building the Democratic Party in Indiana.

Boon was born on January 18, 1781, to Jesse and Kessiah Boon, though sources differ on his birthplace, with some listing it in Georgia and others in Franklin County, North Carolina. When Boon was a child, his family moved to Warren County, Kentucky, and later settled in Danville, where he attended the public schools and learned the gunsmith's trade. In 1809 Boon moved to the Indiana Territory, settling in what soon became Warrick County. There he bought land and established a farm about two miles west of the present city of Boonville, which is named for him. He soon plunged into politics and in 1813 was elected Warrick County treasurer, a position he held until 1816, when he was elected to the new Indiana House of Representatives. During his tenure he played a leading role in dividing Warrick into Vanderburgh, Spencer, and Warrick counties. After serving two one-year terms, he was elected to the state senate.

In the wake of a conflict with Jennings over his service on the federal commission that negotiated the New Purchase Treaty, Lieutenant Governor Christopher Harrison resigned his office in December 1818. Boon was one of several politicians who vied to replace him

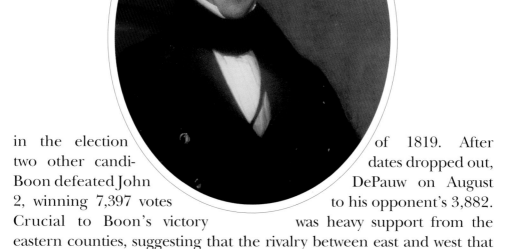

in the election of 1819. After two other candi-dates dropped out, Boon defeated John DePauw on August 2, winning 7,397 votes to his opponent's 3,882. Crucial to Boon's victory was heavy support from the eastern counties, suggesting that the rivalry between east and west that characterized the territorial period was beginning to wane.

Boon was reelected lieutenant governor on August 12, 1822, defeating William Polke and two other candidates by a huge margin. Meanwhile, he ascended to the governorship one month later, when Jennings resigned to assume his seat in the U.S. House of Representatives. During his brief gubernatorial tenure, Boon's primary initiative was to point out the need to reapportion the general assembly to provide legislative representation for residents in several new central Indiana counties that had been created from the territory gained through the New Purchase Treaty. The legislature responded by forming three new house seats and one new senate seat. Boon resumed the office of lieutenant governor on December 5, 1822, serving with Governor William Hendricks, who had relinquished his seat in Congress to run unopposed to succeed Jennings as the state's chief executive.

After serving through the 1823–24 legislative session, Boon resigned as lieutenant governor on January 30, 1824, to run for Congress as a supporter of Andrew Jackson, who was locked in a fierce battle with Secretary of State John Quincy Adams and Speaker of the

House Henry Clay for Hoosier votes in the presidential contest. Boon won the election on August 2, but he lost his seat two years later to Thomas H. Blake of Terre Haute, who charged that the congressman had not been sufficiently vigorous in supporting navigational improvements on the Wabash River and the Wabash and Erie Canal. Boon regained the congressional seat in 1828 and served until 1839. Throughout his tenure he supported Jackson's political fortunes, land preemption rights for settlers, and appropriations for western internal improvements. In 1836 he was defeated in a bid for the U.S. Senate by Oliver H. Smith.

Boon was married on August 13, 1801, to Deliah Anderson, and they were the parents of seven children. After Boon completed his tenure in Congress, he and his wife moved to Pike County, Missouri, where he spearheaded an unsuccessful political revolt against the powerful U.S. Senator Thomas Hart Benton. He died on November 20, 1844, in Louisiana, Missouri, where he is buried in Riverview Cemetery.

Portrait by James Forbes (1870), Governors' Portraits Collection, Indiana Historical Bureau, State of Indiana.

FOR FURTHER READING

Carmony, Donald F. *Indiana, 1816–1850: The Pioneer Era.* Vol. 2, *The History of Indiana.* Indianapolis: Indiana Historical Bureau and Indiana Historical Society, 1998.

Esarey, Logan, ed. *Messages and Papers of Jonathan Jennings, Ratliff Boon, William Hendricks, 1816–1825.* Indianapolis: Indiana Historical Commission, 1924.

Boon's gubernatorial papers are in the Indiana State Archives, Indianapolis. Scattered letters are in the William Henry Smith Memorial Library, Indiana Historical Society, Indianapolis.

William Hendricks

December 5, 1822–February 12, 1825

C. MARTIN ROSEN

IN 1937, A CENTURY AFTER WILLIAM HENDRICKS LEFT PUB-
lic service, Indiana adopted a motto that in large measure reflects
Hendricks's far-reaching vision for the state: The Crossroads of America. Throughout his career, Hendricks, the state's third governor, was
a proponent of internal improvements, especially canals and roads,
that would eventually create the transportation infrastructure necessary for Indiana to become a national crossroad. For more than
two decades, from 1813 to 1837, a period that saw Indiana grow from
a thinly settled territory to a vibrant state, Hendricks was a popular
leader who served in the territorial legislature, represented the state
in the U.S. House of Representatives and the U.S. Senate, and served
a partial term as governor.

As governor, he implemented a series of steps that placed the state
on a sound footing with regard to both its finances and its legal codes.
And despite pressure from his constituents in the southern part of
the state, in 1825 Hendricks signed the legislation to move the capital
from Corydon to Indianapolis.

A popular figure in a period before party politics had come to
Indiana, Hendricks was the founder of what would become a family dynasty. He and his brothers, Thomas and John, who settled in
Greensburg and Shelbyville respectively, and their descendants eventually accounted for two U.S. Senators, two congressmen, two governors, a vice president (Thomas A. Hendricks), and a host of local
political leaders and state legislators.

The son of Abraham and Ann Jamison Hendricks, William Hendricks was born in Westmoreland County, Pennsylvania, on November 12, 1782. His father served in the state legislature. As a youth, Hendricks worked as a farmhand and laborer and then attended Jefferson College at Canonsburg, Pennsylvania, where he befriended Andrew Wylie, the first president of the state seminary that would eventually become Indiana University.

After graduating in 1810, Hendricks moved to Cincinnati, where he taught school, studied law, and was admitted to the bar. Though there is some uncertainty about the date, it is likely he settled in Madison, Indiana, in 1812. In 1816 he married Ann Parker, daughter of Colonel John Paul, founder of Madison; they had two sons, both of whom were killed during the Civil War. Years later, after he had been elected to Congress, Hendricks wrote to his constituents that he arrived in Madison "without acquaintances, friends, wealth or patronage."

But he soon established himself. In February 1813, though lacking an official portfolio, Hendricks traveled to Vincennes to attend the territorial general assembly; he was elected clerk of the house of representatives. That summer, he also founded the *Madison Western Eagle*, the second newspaper in the territory.

Though party politics were nonexistent in the territory, an emergent struggle for political power pitted two factions against one another. The western faction, led by William Henry Harrison and Thomas Posey, was based in Vincennes. The Harrison faction favored maintaining territorial status—and the strong central powers held by the appointed territorial governor—and protecting the rights of slaveholders. In the eastern counties, the Jonathan Jennings faction, based in Corydon, advocated statehood, which implied an elected governor with limited powers, and wanted to end all vestiges of slavery in the state.

Hendricks and his newspaper aligned with the Jennings faction. In 1813 two pivotal events suggested that the Jennings faction was in the ascendancy: the territorial capital was relocated from Vincennes to Corydon, and Hendricks was appointed the territorial printer, taking the position away from Elihu Stout of Vincennes, a Harrison adherent and publisher of the first Indiana newspaper, the *Vincennes Indiana Gazette*, which later became the *Vincennes Western Sun*.

In November 1813 Hendricks became an elected member of the territorial legislature, filling the unexpired term of a Jefferson County representative who had resigned. Later that year he would be reelected and then be elected speaker of the house. By April 1814 he ended his relationship with the *Western Eagle* to focus on his law practice, which included serving as prosecuting attorney for Jefferson and Switzerland counties; in addition, he held the mail contract for delivery to several Indiana towns along the Ohio and Kentucky borders. In November 1814 President James Madison appointed him U.S. Attorney for the territory, a post he would hold until statehood.

When Indiana's constitutional convention convened in June 1816, Hendricks again was not an official delegate, but he attended and was elected to serve as secretary. On the major questions, the Jennings faction prevailed over the Harrison faction: statehood was adopted, and the new constitution prohibited slavery.

In August 1816, barely a month after Indiana adopted its constitution, Hendricks was elected to the U.S. House of Representatives, where he was seated in November, though the state had not yet been officially admitted into the Union. Eventually, he was elected four times, winning his last election, in 1822, by a margin of ten to one.

As a congressman, Hendricks was involved in the key issues related to the westward expansion. He served on the Select Committee on Roads and Canals, was involved in the legislation enabling statehood for Illinois and Missouri, and pressed for the acquisition and survey of tribal lands, which in 1816 accounted for two-thirds of the area of Indiana. Regarding the most contentious national issue of his time, Hendricks was actively opposed both to strengthening the rights of slave owners to recover fugitive slaves and to permitting the expansion of slavery in the western territories and states.

In 1822 Hendricks and the state's first governor, Jennings, switched places. Each resigned his office to run for that of the other. In the governor's race, Hendricks was unopposed and received 18,340 votes, and Jennings was elected to Congress.

Though he would serve as governor of the young state for only three years, Hendricks was a driving force in four major areas: he placed the state's finances on a sound footing, laid the groundwork for improving its roads and waterways, rationalized its chaotic statutes, and signed the legislation that moved the state capital to its current location in Indianapolis.

In 1822 Indiana still suffered under the lingering effects of the economic convulsion known as the panic of 1819. It was an implosion that had a devastating effect on the western states, where credit had spurred a great speculative expansion. In the wake of expansion driven by the War of 1812 and the Napoleonic Wars came tightening credit, doubts about the soundness of banknotes, and an inevitable pullback from a period of exuberant growth. The resulting contraction stifled agriculture, industry, and growth. When Hendricks took office, the state had an operating deficit of $4,000 a year and an accumulated debt of $25,000. In addition, it had an economy with few prospects for quick recovery. In response, Hendricks improved the tax collection system, imposed tougher standards on tax collectors, imposed penalties for late payments, and freed up more public land for sale. But he also signed stay-of-execution bills that protected overextended debtors from their creditors. His tactics worked. In January 1825 he reported to the legislature that the operating budget was in balance and the debt had been reduced by $10,000.

In addition, Hendricks recognized that the state's agricultural and manufacturing prospects were hindered by the difficulty of getting goods to market. If Indiana were to flourish, transportation routes were key, he believed. His focus was on building roads and canals and clearing obstructions from navigable streams. At the national level, he lobbied for an extension of the Cumberland Road through Ohio and Indiana. In the state, he pressed for a canal at the Falls of the Ohio, a canal between the Maumee and Wabash rivers to link the Ohio River and Lake Erie, the clearing of the Vincennes rapids in the Wabash River, and a road system that would connect the southern Indiana settlements and Indianapolis.

While the waterway projects would not be completed during his tenure, and the Ohio River canal would eventually be built as a Kentucky project, Hendricks had laid the groundwork through surveys and studies. On roads, he made more progress. The state legislature had continued a territorial law that mandated compulsory road work for able-bodied men, work that entailed cutting trees to below axle height so that wagons could travel through forested lands. That labor pool permitted many miles of roads to be opened during Hendricks's term.

As governor, Hendricks inherited a system of state and territorial statutes that had never been organized, revised, or rationalized. In 1822 the legislature authorized Hendricks to make the revisions, which entailed substantial rewriting not only to correct editorial problems, but to resolve major inconsistencies and ambiguities in criminal, probate, and other areas. The most controversial aspect of his revisions may have been the inclusion of a gag rule that imposed as much as a $500 fine for malicious criticism of the government and its officers, a rule that some suggested was an attack on freedom of the press. In any event, he completed the task, declined compensation, and was widely praised for bringing order to the state's legal system.

Finally, the constitution adopted by the state in 1816 called for Corydon to remain the capital until at least 1825. In 1820 a commission proposed that the capital be relocated to Indianapolis, a proposal

approved by the legislature in 1824. Though there was much speculation that Hendricks would defer to the south and veto the legislature's
decision, he signed the bill, which required the government to convene in Indianapolis in January 1825, though the only public building
in the town was a courthouse. Hendricks himself was not involved in
the development of the capital, having resigned his office in February
after being elected by the legislature to the U.S. Senate.

During two terms in the Senate, he remained actively involved in
work related to the western expansion, including road and canal work,
the acquisition of tribal lands, and the struggle over slavery, to which
he remained an eloquent opponent. Within the state, he was a proponent of education and served as a trustee of Indiana University from
1829 to 1840; he also had an active interest in Hanover College.

In 1836 Hendricks ran for a third term in the Senate. Though
affiliated with the Democrats in Congress, throughout his career he
had maintained nonpartisan independence. Once again, he ran as a
nonpartisan, but the forces of party politics were growing in Indiana;
Hendricks had lackluster support and even opposition from some
Indiana Democrats, and in an election that required nine ballots, he
was defeated by Oliver H. Smith, a Whig.

He returned home, practiced law, and managed his estate, which
included significant real estate holdings. On May 16, 1850, while overseeing the building of a family vault, he fell ill and died. A few weeks
later, an anonymous letter to the *Madison Daily Courier* summarized
his career: "In all the offices he held in the State, he acquitted himself
with honor, and gave general satisfaction to his constituents. His State
papers while Governor of the State are all marked with prudence and
good sense, and will certainly 'stand the test of scrutiny and time.'"

Portrait by Samuel Burtis Baker (1926), Governors' Portraits Collection, Indiana Historical Bureau, State of Indiana.

FOR FURTHER READING

Esarey, Logan, ed. *Messages and Papers of Jonathan Jennings, Ratliff Boon,
William Hendricks, 1816–1825*. Indianapolis: Indiana Historical
Commission, 1924.

Hill, Frederick Dinsmore. "William Hendricks: Indiana Politician and Western Advocate, 1812–1850." PhD diss., Indiana University, 1972.

Hendricks's gubernatorial papers are in the Indiana State Archives, Indianapolis.

James B. Ray

February 12, 1825–December 7, 1831

DAVID G. VANDERSTEL

JAMES BROWN RAY, THE STATE'S FOURTH GOVERNOR, ROSE rapidly in Indiana politics, and his fall was just as fast. Ray, a young lawyer from Kentucky and resident of Brookville, the first of three consecutive governors from that community, assumed office on February 12, 1825, a week before he turned thirty-one. Some newspaper editors even questioned Ray's eligibility, believing him to be younger than the constitutionally required age of thirty. By the time he left as governor nearly seven years later, still a young man of thirty-seven, his political career was over.

Ray's rise to the position of chief executive resulted from a chain of events triggered first by the resignation of Lieutenant Governor Ratliff Boon in 1824 and then the resignation of Governor William Hendricks the following year. Both men resigned after being elected to Congress—Boon to the House of Representatives and Hendricks to the Senate. With Hendricks's resignation and the office of lieutenant governor vacant, Ray, who had been elected president pro tempore of the state senate in 1824 and reelected to the post the following year, was next in the line of succession and became acting governor. After completing the few months remaining in Hendricks's term, he was elected governor in his own right in August of 1825 and reelected in 1828.

When Ray came into office, Indiana was a young state undergoing significant changes, most notably in its population. In the span of five years, from 1825 to 1830, the number of people in the state grew

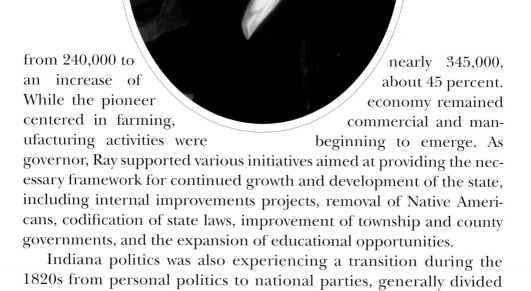

from 240,000 to nearly 345,000, an increase of about 45 percent. While the pioneer economy remained centered in farming, commercial and manufacturing activities were beginning to emerge. As governor, Ray supported various initiatives aimed at providing the necessary framework for continued growth and development of the state, including internal improvements projects, removal of Native Americans, codification of state laws, improvement of township and county governments, and the expansion of educational opportunities.

Indiana politics was also experiencing a transition during the 1820s from personal politics to national parties, generally divided along an axis of Henry Clay–John Quincy Adams followers, known as National or Jeffersonian Republicans, and Jacksonian Democrats. The former advocated protective tariffs, a national bank, and federally financed internal improvements, while the latter supported cheap western land, removal of Native Americans, and state-financed internal improvements. With Hoosiers drawn both to Adams's position on internal improvements, believing it would benefit the West, and to Jackson for his military career and common origins, Ray attempted to steer a nonpartisan course. Parties, he felt, tended to make principle subservient to political calculation and management, and thus "should be viewed as aiming a fatal blow at the public tranquility."

Ray, born in Jefferson County, Kentucky, on February 19, 1794, to William Ray, a Revolutionary War veteran, and Phebe Ann Brown Ray, was one of twelve children. He received his education in common schools before moving to Cincinnati, where he studied law, was admitted to the bar in 1816, and served briefly as deputy clerk of Hamilton County, Ohio. Ray relocated to Brookville in the neighboring new state of Indiana in 1818, where he practiced law and got his start in politics. In four years' time, from 1821 to 1825, he vaulted from the state legislature, first as a representative and then as a senator, to the governor's office.

In announcing that he was running for a full three-year term as governor in the regular summer election of 1825, Ray said, "I have lived in this Western country thirty years—am a native—a republican—the friend of civil and religious liberty—to the freedom of the press, to law—have long been an open advocate for Internal Improvement—for domestic industry—a friend to education—to freedom and to peace—to equal privileges—to my country, her interests, inhabitants and glory." His candidacy drew decidedly different responses, with supporters praising his "industry, integrity, and his record as a legislator," and detractors describing him as "pompous, poorly educated, ill-equipped for the job." Despite such attacks, Ray won on August 1, 1825, defeating Indiana Supreme Court Justice Isaac Blackford 13,040 votes to 10,418. His stance on internal improvements likely gave him the election over a better-educated and politically situated candidate.

Ray began his tenure as governor during a period of relative prosperity and growth for Indiana, and he saw improved transportation as crucial to its continued progress. In his first message to the Indiana General Assembly on December 8, 1825, after noting the economic impact of Ohio's successful internal improvements program, Ray said that Indiana's future depended upon a program of canal construction that would create "a great commercial thoroughfare . . . through the interior of our state." Continuing, he added that canals were a "means of giving a new impulse to the agricultural and manufacturing interests of the country, and improving the finances of the state."

Two years later, however, Ray had a change of heart and, in a demonstration of progressive thinking during the time of "canal mania," began promoting railroad construction over canals. In 1827 he organized an effort to encourage the newly formed Baltimore Rail Road Company to extend its line west through Indiana, a development that eventually occurred in the 1850s, and he discussed his preference for railroads with the general assembly in his December message. Noting that other states were building railroads because they were faster and less expensive than other modes of transportation, Ray asked legislators to seek permission from Congress to allow construction of a railroad on land intended for a canal. A senate committee, however, concluded that all evidence pointed to the "usefulness, practicality, durability, and economy" of canals, which made it "inexpedient to waste time upon the subject of railways." Although his critics accused him of promoting "utopian projects," Ray remained a staunch advocate of railroads throughout his life. His opponents also claimed that his embrace of railroads held up construction of the Wabash and Erie Canal, though it was other factors that caused a lengthy delay in getting the project under way.

Another of Ray's internal improvements initiatives was construction of the Michigan Road, a highway that would extend from the Ohio River through Indianapolis to Lake Michigan. The project was contingent upon concluding a treaty with the Native Americans who occupied the land, and Ray, in a letter to Adams, indicated his desire to help negotiate such a treaty. In 1826 the president named Ray, Governor Lewis Cass of Michigan Territory, and Indian agent John Tipton to a federal commission to negotiate with the Miami and Potawatomi for the purchase of land and subsequent removal of the tribes. Negotiations were concluded in the fall of 1826 with the tribes ceding nearly one million acres, which allowed for the construction of the Michigan Road.

The negotiations energized Ray's opponents. They cited Cass's and Tipton's extensive experience with the Native Americans and faulted Ray for delaying the talks because of his inexperience, although the actual problem rested with federal officials who initially rejected the

commissioners' choice of lands. More important, however, Ray's critics, including several state legislators, charged him with violating Indiana's constitution, which prohibited the governor from holding any
federal office. A state representative presented a resolution declaring
that Ray had "forfeited" his right as governor by serving as a treaty
commissioner. Following the defeat of the resolution by a vote of 31
to 27, the governor asserted that he had done nothing wrong and had
sought only to advance the state's interests by opening tribal lands for
settlement and building a road from the Ohio River to Lake Michigan. Within a year, Ray appointed three commissioners to establish
the route from the lake to Indianapolis.

Ray believed the state's advancement also depended upon expanding educational opportunities, asserting in a message to the legislature that "no subject [was] more worthy" of its attention "than that of
providing means for the education of all classes of society, rich and
poor together, in the same manner and at the same school." He proposed the sale of public lands to organize schools in each township,
employ qualified teachers, and extend education to females. Furthermore, in 1825 the Indiana State Seminary opened in Bloomington
with thirteen young men under the tutelage of Baynard Rush Hall, a
Presbyterian minister. Following positive reports regarding the profi-
ciency of students and teachers, Ray recommended in 1828 that the
seminary be elevated to a college. By an act of the general assembly on
January 24, 1828, the school became Indiana College (later Indiana
University).

Likewise, Ray linked the removal of Native Americans from the
state to progress. He considered the Miami and Potawatomi a blight,
as he made clear in a message to legislators. After indicting them for
their "growing indolence," "alarming intemperate habits," "primitive
simplicity of manners," and "destitution of any moral code," Ray concluded that the tribes "have, by some unaccountable fatality, acquired
all of the vices of the whites, with but few of their virtues." Ray called
for a "change of relation between the parties," which would extend
state law over the tribes. This would either bring the Native Americans
"to an equality with the citizen, and subjected to his burdens," or force

them to move farther west, which would open their land to settlement by whites. The "change of relation" never occurred, and Native American removals continued apace.

Ray also supported efforts to send freed slaves to Liberia. In remarks that sharply contrasted with the harsh words he used about Native Americans, Ray, in support of colonization, called blacks the "long degraded and unhappy members of the human family" who had been "oppressively torn by the hand of tyranny, to gratify the most sacrilegious cupidity." Ray said, "We long to celebrate the jubilee of freedom—of general and unconditional emancipation, of every soul held in bondage, because his skin is dark." The colonization movement, however, was never successful.

In yet another initiative, Ray sought to simplify state statutes by codifying Indiana's civil and criminal laws. He recommended modeling the new code upon the laws of Louisiana, which were based upon the Napoleonic Code, to make state laws understandable to the general public. Ray pledged to assume this responsibility at his own expense, but two years later, with no evident progress, he requested funds for an assistant to move the process forward. In the final legislative session under Ray, the general assembly appointed a joint committee to generate the Revised Code of 1831.

Ray's first term in office was marked by other notable events, including the beginnings of a new statehouse in Indianapolis. Under his leadership, the general assembly authorized the sale of lands to finance construction of the project. The governor also issued a last-minute pardon to spare the life of a seventeen-year-old who was convicted along with four men in the murders of nine Native Americans near Pendleton in Madison County, an incident known as the Fall Creek Massacre. It reportedly was the first time whites were convicted for murdering Indians. On May 12, 1825, Ray had the honor of greeting General Marquis de Lafayette at Jeffersonville, an occasion he said "will ever be a source of the most grateful recollection."

Ray never truly escaped controversy and the political feuding that was present from almost his first days in office to his last. An especially bitter dispute erupted in 1827 between the state treasurer,

Samuel Merrill, and the governor. Merrill, a Dartmouth-educated easterner who had supported Blackford's gubernatorial candidacy in 1825, waged a personal attack through the newspapers, embarrassing Ray by charging him with questionable behavior, fraud, and using his office for personal gain. Many, including Governor Cass of Michigan Territory, vouched for Ray's honorable conduct. Merrill's petty and baseless charges illustrated the vicious personal politics of the era, which, in this case, may have contributed to Ray's inability to win future political contests.

At times, Ray was his own worst enemy. He announced for reelection and vowed to remain independent from national parties. Pro-Jackson men in Indiana approached him to run as the Jacksonian candidate for governor, and Ray indirectly consented on the condition that the offer and his reply remain secret. He said, "I am in your hands. Dispose of *me* and my *name*, as you in your wisdom think proper. I wish to be elected Governor of the State on my *merits*—shall not become a partizan—shall have no objections to receiving the united support of the Jacksonians— shall not undo what they think fit to do, in state elections."

Shortly thereafter, the pro-Clay editor of the *Brookville Repository* published an interview with Ray, who unadvisedly announced his support for the Adams administration and agreed with the statement that the Jacksonian opposition was an "outrageous, violent faction." Upon reading this, the Jacksonians published their "secret" agreement with Ray, thus creating a political controversy weeks prior to the election. Ray, however, reiterating his independence from any party, was reelected on August 4, 1828, defeating Israel T. Canby, the Jackson candidate, and Harbin H. Moore, the Adams candidate, receiving 15,131 votes to Canby's 12,251 and Moore's 10,898.

Not surprisingly, political conflicts continued to plague Ray's second term. The general assembly questioned his failure to prepare the revised code of laws, which led critics to discredit the governor and Ray to respond angrily. Another battle arose over the governor's appointments to the Indiana Supreme Court. The state senate strongly favored the reappointment of incumbent justices Isaac Blackford, Jesse L. Holman, and James Scott, whose terms expired on December 31, 1830.

Ray apparently delayed the appointments to gain support for his own election to the U.S. Senate, a bid that he lost. He eventually appointed to the court Blackford and two members from the senate, individuals who, according to Ray's enemies, "would lend whatever weight they could to Ray's election to the Senate two years later."

During his last years as governor, Ray lost his influence and effectiveness. He was defensive in his work with the legislature, alleged a conspiracy against him, and portrayed himself as a "victim of misrepresentation and malicious envy." Critics complained of his hotheadedness and inability to handle criticism. On December 7, 1831, the day following Ray's farewell address, Noah Noble, one of Ray's opponents, was sworn in as governor of Indiana. Ray's political career was over at the young age of thirty-seven.

Upon leaving public office, Ray attempted to resume his law practice in Indianapolis, but business never met expectations. He continued to seek political office, though unsuccessfully. Ray was one of five candidates for Congress from the Second District in 1831, though he lost by nearly three thousand votes to John Carr, a Jacksonian Democrat. He announced his intention to run for Congress on the Jackson ticket in 1833, but withdrew when assured of his loss. Ray failed in later bids to become a commissioner of the Wabash and Erie Canal in 1835, Marion County Clerk in 1835, and again for Congress in 1837.

Ray embarked upon assorted business ventures, which, like his political comeback attempts, also proved unsuccessful. He joined with W. M. Tannehill in 1833 to publish *The Hoosier* in Greencastle, but the paper was short lived. Ray possessed a license to sell merchandise and opened an office for buying and selling land, but the ventures never succeeded. By 1837 Ray had moved to Centerville, establishing a law practice with brother Martin M. Ray and a dry goods and grocery store with a nephew. He returned to Indianapolis around 1846 to "open a Law, conveyancing, writing, abstract-making, land-agency, general and emigrants' intelligence and counsel office" on Washington Street. Ray remained a staunch advocate for railroads to the end of his life, announcing in the *Indianapolis Sentinel* of December 31, 1846, "I want a printing office to advocate my four National Railways, from Indianapolis, Ia., to the Atlantic and Pacific Oceans, and Lake Michigan and Gulf of Mexico."

During the summer of 1848, Ray fell ill while traveling to Wisconsin. He was returned to a relative's home in Cincinnati, where he died of cholera on August 4, 1848. Ray was buried in Spring Grove Cemetery in Cincinnati. His will, probated in Marion County, showed substantial property holdings, including two lots in Indianapolis and more than seven hundred acres of land in Hendricks, Marion, Marshall, and Wayne counties.

Ray was married to Mary Riddle, daughter of Colonel John Riddle of Hamilton County, Ohio, in December 1818. The couple had two children before Mary died on July 4, 1823. Following his election as governor, Ray married Esther Booker of Centerville in September 1825; they had five children.

Portrait by Jacob Cox (before 1840), Governors' Portraits Collection, Indiana Historical Bureau, State of Indiana.

FOR FURTHER READING

Barnhart, John D., and Donald Carmony. *Indiana: From Frontier to Industrial Commonwealth.* Vol. 1. New York: Lewis Historical Publishing, 1954.

Buley, R. Carlyle. *The Old Northwest: Pioneer Period, 1815–1840.* 2 vols. Indianapolis: Indiana Historical Society, 1950.

Carmony, Donald F. *Indiana, 1816–1850: The Pioneer Era.* Vol. 2, *The History of Indiana.* Indianapolis: Indiana Historical Bureau and Indiana Historical Society, 1998.

Journal of the Senate of the State of Indiana, 1825–1830. Indianapolis: State Printer.

Riker, Dorothy L., and Gayle Thornbrough, eds. *Messages and Papers Relating to the Administration of James Brown Ray, Governor of Indiana, 1825–1831.* Indianapolis: Indiana Historical Bureau, 1954.

Sobel, Robert, and John Raimo. *Biographical Directory of the Governors of the United States, 1789–1978.* Vol. 1. Westport, CT: Meckler Books, 1978.

Noah Noble

December 7, 1831–December 6, 1837

DAVID G. VANDERSTEL

THROUGHOUT HIS TWO TERMS AS GOVERNOR, NOAH NOBLE was best known for promoting internal improvements. As a devoted disciple of Henry Clay, he embraced the principles of the "American System" and advocated in his first message to the Indiana General Assembly "the opening of new and artificial channels of commercial intercommunication between the several states." He said it was the duty of state government "to improve our rivers, and by making lateral roads and canals, to facilitate the conveyance of the various commodities of our State."

Noah Noble was born in Berryville, Frederick (now Clarke) County, Virginia, on January 14, 1794. He was one of fourteen children of Doctor Thomas Noble, a physician, and Elizabeth Claire Sedgwick Noble. In the early 1800s Thomas sold his lands and moved his family first to Campbell County and then Boone County, Kentucky, where in 1807 he acquired a three-hundred-acre plantation with slaves along the Ohio River. Noah followed his eldest brother James to Brookville in the Indiana Territory, where he joined the militia and eventually acquired property. In 1817 Noah was commissioned lieutenant colonel of the Seventh Regiment Indiana Militia and became an early initiate of the Harmony Lodge of Free and Accepted Masons.

He embarked upon numerous enterprises with brother-in-law Enoch D. John, including operating the Brookville Hotel, speculating in land, and running a fulling mill with wool carding machines on the East Fork of the Whitewater River. Noble engaged in trading under

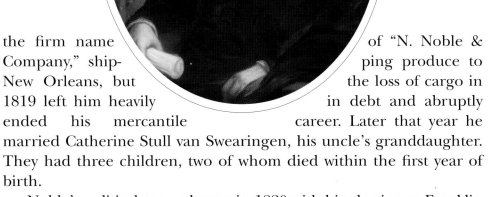

the firm name of "N. Noble & Company," ship-ping produce to New Orleans, but the loss of cargo in 1819 left him heavily in debt and abruptly ended his mercantile career. Later that year he married Catherine Stull van Swearingen, his uncle's granddaughter. They had three children, two of whom died within the first year of birth.

Noble's political career began in 1820 with his election as Franklin County Sheriff, a race in which he received twice as many votes as his nearest competitor; he won all but nine of the 1,186 votes cast in his 1822 reelection bid. Voters chose Noble as their state representative in 1824, electing him to the first assembly to sit at the new capital of Indianapolis. Noble apparently possessed a respectable record and won reelection to the Indiana House in 1825, but gave up his seat. In late 1825 President John Quincy Adams, probably at the recommendation of Noah's brother, U.S. senator James Noble, appointed him to fill the post of Receiver of Public Moneys for the Indianapolis Land Office, a position previously held by Noah's next-oldest brother Lazarus, who had recently died. As receiver, Noble maintained the records and accounts of land sales and transferred funds quarterly to the U.S. Bank at Cincinnati; he lost the post when Andrew Jackson became president in 1829.

Finding himself out of public office for the first time in nearly a decade, Noble became involved once again in several private ventures.

However, his time out of the public arena was brief. Friends had been suggesting that he run for governor, a proposition helped along in the 1829–30 session of the general assembly when the position of contract commissioner for the Michigan Road was created and political allies of Noble's inserted his name for the office into the legislation.

Noble, backed by supporters of Clay, known as National Republicans and later as Whigs, announced his candidacy for governor in May 1831. David Wallace, a fellow resident of Brookville, was a candidate for lieutenant governor on the same ticket. The Jacksonian Democrats selected James G. Read for governor and Amos Lane for lieutenant governor.

As the campaign proceeded, both camps exchanged personal charges. Noble's supporters charged Read, who had served as Receiver of Public Moneys at the Jeffersonville Land Office, with drawing a commission while campaigning. Democrats, in turn, accused Noble of campaigning while holding the position of Michigan Road commissioner. The most serious charge was that Noble had sold a black girl into slavery after she had reportedly obtained her freedom while residing in a free state. Noble explained that the girl, who had accompanied him to Indiana, properly belonged to his father-in-law, who intended to reclaim the girl but had then directed Noble to sell her instead. The incident clearly influenced the antislavery element against him. In the 1831 election, Noble received only twenty-six votes for governor from Hendricks County, home to a sizable Quaker population.

Noble, at age thirty-seven, became the state's fifth governor, winning the election on August 1, 1831, with 23,518 votes to Read's 21,002. Milton Stapp, an independent candidate, had 6,894 votes. Wallace won the race for lieutenant governor. While Clay men won the governorship and dominated the general assembly, Jacksonians won all three seats in Congress. Noble won a second term three years later, again defeating Democratic challenger Read; this time he had 36,773 votes to Read's 27,257. Wallace was reelected as lieutenant governor.

Upon becoming governor, Noble purchased several out lots on the east edge of Indianapolis. He cleared the land, planted an orchard and vineyard, pastured his animals, and constructed a spacious brick home. Noble brought some of his family's emancipated slaves from Kentucky to live, one of whom supposedly served as a model for Harriet Beecher Stowe's "Uncle Tom."

Noble assumed office during a period of economic prosperity, population growth, and national development. Increasing numbers of people were moving to western states and purchasing government lands made available through Jackson's Native American removal policies. It was a period in which the national parties were debating issues of banks, tariffs, states' rights, and distribution of proceeds from public land sales—all issues that would impact Indiana's new governor.

Noble's predecessor, James B. Ray, had initiated the construction of roads and planning for waterways, but it was Noble who oversaw the actual development and expansion of that network. Work began on the Wabash and Erie Canal in 1832, covering a route from Ohio through Lafayette and Terre Haute before ending at Evansville. Work also began to improve navigation on the Wabash River. Unlike Ray, who had been a major proponent of railroads, Noble strongly favored canals. He and the legislature allowed the incorporation of railroads and surveying of routes throughout the state, but Noble remained suspect of railroads, considering them to be monopolies.

During his first term Noble recommended several steps regarding statewide improvements, all rejected by legislators. Since money from the federal government's Three Per Cent Fund, the principal source of funding for roads, was often slow in arriving, Noble suggested that Indiana borrow $100,000 to $150,000 over fifteen years to fund roadwork immediately. The measure was never approved. He also called for the creation of a board of internal improvements whose mission would be to "collect and digest information" on improvements. The general assembly, while expressing enthusiasm for improvements, rejected Noble's idea, which resulted in the incorporation of numerous private companies to build roads, railroads, and bridges without an overall coordinated effort.

When Noble began his second term, however, the political climate had changed and "public sentiment was mounting in favor of an extensive state program of internal improvements." In short order, the general assembly approved the Mammoth Internal Improvements Bill, handing Noble what appeared at the time the capstone of his tenure in office. The legislation created a Board of Internal Improvements, consisting of three canal commissioners and six appointees of the governor who would supervise building a vast network of canals, roads, and railroads and be authorized to borrow up to $10 million (nearly $200 million in today's dollars) at 6 percent interest for twenty-five years. The largest appropriations went to canals, a mode of transportation that Noble believed to be superior to railroads or turnpikes because they "were cheaper, they were more permanent, and better adapted to the convenience and habits of the people and the character and products of the state."

Noble was concerned about how the state would pay the interest on the massive debt it was about to incur. Accordingly, he recommended a tax increase of 50 percent, a proposal legislators rejected. It had been widely believed that income from tolls, rents, and generation of water power would be more than adequate to meet debt obligations. The failure to provide for increasing the state treasury was compounded by a provision in the legislation that permitted bonds to be purchased on credit.

For the moment, though, passage of the Internal Improvements Bill was cause for celebration throughout Indiana and was hailed by Hoosiers as the way of binding the state to the rest of the nation and the world. Some prescient observers, however, including former state legislator Calvin Fletcher, an Indianapolis attorney, were not so sanguine. He wrote in his diary on April 22, 1836, "that there is a great danger of a *crash* engaging speculators & holders of real estate & that will take place in 18 months that all prudent men will prepare for it in the meantime." In his December 1836 address, Noble, less than a year after passage of the internal improvement legislation, was still expressing optimism about the eventual success of the system, but continued to press for a tax increase. The 1836–37 session responded with an increase in the ad valorem tax, with a third of the additional revenue going to pay interest on the internal improvements loan.

This mild measure was hardly adequate when the panic of 1837 hit the nation and the state, causing serious economic depression, rising interest rates, and a suspension of specie payments by banks. Noble recommended a plan to prioritize the improvement projects and extend the timetables to survive the economic crisis. But in August 1839, after Noble had left office, the state suspended work on these projects, abandoning many totally and allowing private companies to salvage others.

In his first address as governor, Noble identified several themes that would shape his six years in office. His first priority was creating a "general system of education" that would meet the needs of a developing state. In order to perpetuate "our free institutions," Noble said, "it is not enough that we provide a few who are qualified to sit in the councils, or guide the helm of state—we must commence at the fountain of power, with the great mass of the people, to cultivate and enlighten the public mind, by a diffusion of the benefits of education."

Noble returned to the subject of education in the following year's address to the general assembly. Noting the enormous need, he said that "there are not less than one hundred thousand children" in the state who lacked a public school education. "If they receive it," Noble said, "they can succeed us in the professions, arts, sciences, commerce, and agriculture, and safely take upon themselves the charge of self government, continuing our institutions, with such improvements as the lights of experience may point out." He made two recommendations, neither apparently enacted. One would have apportioned any state budget surplus to schools, and the other would have excused from militia duties those individuals who "contributed in money or labor, one dollar and upwards" to schools.

In 1833 Noble turned his attention to the need for "competent persons to instruct in our township schools," and he called for the creation of a state seminary to prepare young men as teachers for the state's common schools and a "preparatory department" with Indiana College, later Indiana University. Legislators in the 1833–34 session responded by chartering the Indiana Teachers' Seminary in Madison and the Wabash Manual Labor College and Teachers' Seminary in

Crawfordsville, which became Wabash College. Noble also sought legislation to overhaul schools by creating township school districts and electing school commissioners and township and district trustees who would handle proceeds from land sales, build and maintain school buildings, and examine and employ teachers.

Continuing as an advocate for improved education, Noble served as president of the State Education Convention in Indianapolis in January 1837, which "launched a vigorous and comprehensive appeal for improving and extending public common schools." The two-day non-partisan meeting, which drew about 250 people, included "prominent Whigs and Democrats, natives of both southern and northern states, and leaders from the Presbyterians, Methodists, and Baptists." The convention adopted a resolution that said "a good common education has the highest claims upon our attention, inasmuch as it lays the surest foundation for civil liberty, social order and private happiness." A memorial was also sent to the legislature that contained a number of recommendations on such items as an expanded school calendar, funding, teacher training, and the creation of a state board of public instruction. The movement to strengthen education in the state was derailed, however, when the state's financial condition collapsed from the effects of the depression in the late 1830s and early 1840s and the failed Internal Improvements System.

When Noble became governor, the nation was embroiled in a great debate over the future of the Second Bank of the United States. Jackson's veto of the bank's charter and subsequent removal of funds to his "pet banks" stimulated action to establish another state bank in Indiana. Noble did not actively campaign for a bank and left the decision to the general assembly, which created the Second State Bank on January 28, 1834. The legislation authorized ten branches, with the head office in Indianapolis, and capital of $1.6 million that was to be divided equally among the ten branches. By late 1835 Noble acknowledged that the bank had had a "most healthful and beneficial influence on the enterprise and various pursuits of our citizens."

Tax reform and legislative apportionment were among other issues Noble addressed during his time in office. Noble claimed that state revenue came primarily from poll taxes and a tax on land, the assessment of which was "defective, unequal, and unnecessarily expensive in administration," Noble said. He advocated the adoption of the ad valorem system by which capital, real estate, and personal property would be taxed according to its value. The change, he argued, was essential to ensure equal distribution of the tax burden among landholders. The general assembly adopted the governor's recommendations on February 7, 1835. A year after the change, state revenue from taxes increased about 25 percent, to $64,437 from the previous year's total of $51,278.

In December 1833 Noble, noting the "great increase" in population in the northern part of the state, recommended to the general assembly that it add three representatives and one senator for several northern counties to correct the inequity in representation. In this instance, the legislature agreed with the governor and approved his recommendation, but in the general apportionment of 1836 it ignored his advice to not materially increase the number of lawmakers. Instead, the legislature, taking into account that twenty-one new counties had been formed since the 1831 apportionment and that the state's population had grown to "an estimated 100,000 white males twenty-one years and older," increased the number of senate districts from thirty-one to forty-seven and house districts from seventy-seven to one hundred. The change was significant because "for the first time members of the House from Central Indiana had more voting power than members from Southern Indiana."

The erection of a new statehouse in Indianapolis was also one of Noble's principal accomplishments. The structure was to be financed by the sale of four sections of land reserved in the original congressional donation of 1816 and from additional land sales authorized in 1831. The general assembly selected plans submitted by architects Ithiel Town and A. J. Davis of New York City that showed a Greek-style building, constructed of stone and modeled on the Parthenon, with a large Roman dome at the center. Completed at a cost of $60,000, the statehouse opened for the 1835–36 legislative session. It was, as Noble commented, "an edifice worthy of the state, and being dedicated to the public interests, within these walls the representatives of the people will annually assemble to perform some of the most important duties ever delegated to man."

When Noble first campaigned in 1831, he claimed that the office of governor should not be a stepping-stone to higher office and promised not to accept any other offices. During his 1834 campaign, however, he did not repeat that pledge and later sought to replace William Hendricks as U.S. Senator in 1836 and John Tipton in 1838; both efforts were unsuccessful. After leaving office in December 1837, Noble served two years as a member of the Board of Internal Improvements and then as Fund Commissioner until January 1842. He received an offer to become commissioner of the General Land Office in Washington, D.C., but declined because of Indiana's poor economic situation.

As governor, Noble was not an innovative leader, though he saw himself as the elected servant of the people. Regarding his work with the general assembly, Noble wrote, "the confidence between the two branches of the government has been uniform and reciprocal." Opponents, however, continued to blame him for placing the state deeply in debt, which ultimately led to the drafting of Indiana's second constitution in 1850–51 and a provision that prohibited the state from incurring debt. Nevertheless, Noble laid the groundwork for numerous reforms and improvements that would enhance the Hoosier economy and society. Noble died in Indianapolis on February 8, 1844, at the age of fifty.

Portrait by Jacob Cox (before 1840), Governors' Portraits Collection, Indiana Historical Bureau, State of Indiana.

FOR FURTHER READING

Buley, R. Carlyle. *The Old Northwest: Pioneer Period, 1815–1840.* 2 vols. Indianapolis: Indiana Historical Society, 1950.

Carmony, Donald F. *Indiana, 1816–1850: The Pioneer Era.* Vol. 2, *The History of Indiana.* Indianapolis: Indiana Historical Bureau and Indiana Historical Society, 1998.

Fatout, Paul. *Indiana Canals.* West Lafayette, IN: Purdue University Press, 1972.

Glass, James A. "The Architects Town and Davis and the Second Indiana Statehouse." *Indiana Magazine of History* 80 (December 1984): 329–47.

Reifel, August J. *History of Franklin County, Indiana, Her People, Industries, and Institutions.* Indianapolis: B. F. Bowen, 1915.

Riker, Dorothy L., and Gayle Thornbrough, eds. *Messages and Papers Relating to the Administration of Noah Noble, Governor of Indiana, 1831–1837.* Indianapolis: Indiana Historical Bureau, 1958.

Thornbrough, Gayle, ed. *The Diary of Calvin Fletcher.* Vol.1, *1817–1838.* Indianapolis: Indiana Historical Society, 1972.

Noble's papers are in the Indiana State Library, Indianapolis.

David Wallace

December 6, 1837–December 9, 1840

JEFFERY A. DUVALL

VIEWED AS THE POLITICAL HEIR OF POPULAR OUTGOING
Governor Noah Noble, David Wallace swept into office on the combined strength of the Whigs' domination of state politics and his own
cautiously optimistic support of the simultaneous completion of projects outlined in the Internal Improvements System of 1836. Although
Wallace quickly modified his stance on the best means of implementing the program—calling for the completion of the "most profitable
and commercial points" so that "the State may be realizing something
from them" while "finishing the remainder"—he remained the "pro"
internal improvements governor in the eyes of the electorate and
quickly found his sole term in office overwhelmed by the resulting
financial disaster.

The oldest of seven children, David Wallace was born on April 4,
1799, in Mifflin County, Pennsylvania, to Andrew Wallace and Eleanor
Jones, whom the family claimed was the niece of Revolutionary War
hero John Paul Jones. Andrew, a surveyor, newspaper publisher, and
tavern owner, moved his family to Miami County, Ohio, in 1807, where
he was elected the county's first treasurer. During the War of 1812 he
forged a friendship with General William Henry Harrison while serving as his quartermaster. After the war Andrew settled in Cincinnati,
where he published the *Cincinnati Liberty Hall Gazette and Cincinnati
Mercury* newspaper for two years. In 1817, however, he sold his interest
in the paper and relocated his family to Brookville, Indiana, where he
operated a tavern.

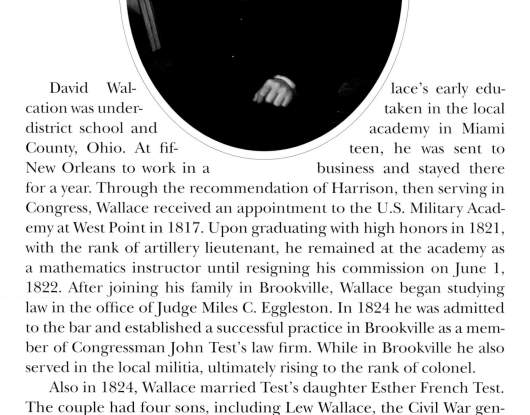

David Wallace's early education was undertaken in the local district school and academy in Miami County, Ohio. At fifteen, he was sent to New Orleans to work in a business and stayed there for a year. Through the recommendation of Harrison, then serving in Congress, Wallace received an appointment to the U.S. Military Academy at West Point in 1817. Upon graduating with high honors in 1821, with the rank of artillery lieutenant, he remained at the academy as a mathematics instructor until resigning his commission on June 1, 1822. After joining his family in Brookville, Wallace began studying law in the office of Judge Miles C. Eggleston. In 1824 he was admitted to the bar and established a successful practice in Brookville as a member of Congressman John Test's law firm. While in Brookville he also served in the local militia, ultimately rising to the rank of colonel.

Also in 1824, Wallace married Test's daughter Esther French Test. The couple had four sons, including Lew Wallace, the Civil War general, diplomat, and author of the bestseller *Ben-Hur*. Following the death of his first wife in 1834, Wallace married Zerelda Sanders in 1836. The daughter of a prominent Indianapolis physician and sister-in-law of Doctor Richard Gatling, inventor of the Gatling gun, Zerelda organized the Indiana Women's Christian Temperance Union in 1874 and served as its first president. In 1878 she helped found the Equal Suffrage Society of Indianapolis and also served as its first president.

In 1881 she lobbied the state legislature for women's rights, suffrage, and prohibition, and from 1883 to 1888 she headed the national WCTU franchise department. David and Zerelda had six children, three of whom (two daughters and a son) survived to adulthood.

Wallace began his career in politics as a National Republican, winning three consecutive elections to the lower house of the Indiana General Assembly (representing Franklin County) between 1828 and 1831. In 1831 he was elected the state's lieutenant governor, serving under Noah Noble. Both men were reelected to the same positions as members of the Whig Party in 1834. While serving as lieutenant governor, Wallace moved his family to Covington, Indiana, near the Illinois border. Following his election as governor in 1837 he settled in Indianapolis permanently.

As lieutenant governor, Wallace was an advocate for the adoption of the charter of the State Bank of Indiana and widely recognized as a skilled orator. It was his support of the Internal Improvements Act of 1836, however, that proved to be the most significant factor in his election as governor in 1837. Winning close to 55.5 percent of the vote and carrying fifty-two of the state's eighty-one counties, Wallace's election was viewed as a ratification of the internal improvements plan. Indeed, his claim during the campaign that an "extra hen and chickens" would be sufficient to cover the cost of any additional taxes that might need to be levied against the state's farmers in order to pay for the project bound the success of Wallace's administration to the success or failure of the improvements program from its inception.

That the Internal Improvements System was doomed to failure before Wallace took office, however, now seems clear. While the call for such a program dated back to at least 1825, at the time the bill was passed in 1836 there had still been no topographical survey of the state and no consultation with engineers in order to determine which projects should take priority or what was even feasible to attempt. Calling for the completion of three major canal projects, a railroad linking Madison to Lafayette via Indianapolis, and a macadamized road from New Albany to Vincennes, the Internal Improvements Act was a daring piece of forward-thinking legislation. But "at a time when the state's normal revenues averaged less than $75,000 a year," the authorized appropriation of $10 million was "beyond the comprehension of either the legislators or the ordinary citizens" of the state. Maintaining that the system would be self-sustaining, the state's lawmakers failed to provide for a means of paying interest on the loans necessary to implement the program. In the first year alone, the state borrowed a staggering $3.8 million, at 5 percent interest, from eastern banks and foreign investors. The following year the commissioners in charge of the improvement fund borrowed another $1.6 million just as the panic of 1837 drove the nation's economy into the most serious depression in its history, up to that point. In 1838 an additional $1.7 million was borrowed, leading to a combined interest payment of $193,000 due on the state's loans in a year in which Indiana's total tax revenue only came to $45,000. By 1840 all work on the Internal Improvements System ceased, and the state was bankrupt.

Although the problems associated with the execution of the internal improvements program beleaguered his tenure in office, it was his decision to enforce the removal of the Potawatomi from the state in 1838 that remains Wallace's single most controversial act as governor. Following the passage of the federal Indian Removal Act in 1830, the Indiana General Assembly petitioned Congress to enact the program in Indiana. Claiming disingenuously that it was in the best interests of the tribes to be removed from the state, Hoosier lawmakers were primed to begin the enforced removal of the Miami and the Potawatomi just as Wallace entered his first year in office. When the Potawatomi, under the leadership of Menominee, proved unwilling to comply with the removal, Wallace ordered Senator John Tipton to recruit an armed militia and forcibly round up Menominee's band and escort them, under heavy guard, out of the state. On September 4, 1838, some eight hundred Potawatomi began the first leg of a poorly organized march that ended in Kansas after months of sickness, hardship, and death. Remembered as the Trail of Death, forty-two Indians, mostly children, died during the removal.

As governor, Wallace is credited with working to develop the state's resources and to improve its common schools. Twice he supported renewing David Dale Owen's appointment as geologist for the state in order to allow Owen time to complete his geological survey of Indiana. Unfortunately, Owen's reports led Wallace to hold a distorted view of the state's mineral wealth, and his prediction in 1838 that "Mishawaka, South Bend, and their vicinity," would soon become the "Pittsburgh of Indiana" proved to be all too false. Also with the state plunging into financial ruin as the Internal Improvements System faltered, the legislature failed to act on any of Wallace's recommendations regarding education reform. Wallace was the first governor to occupy the new state mansion, and he was the first governor of Indiana to officially proclaim November 28 as Thanksgiving Day. He is also credited with only vetoing two pieces of legislation. Still, it is the failure of the Internal Improvements System of 1836 that remains the most important event of Wallace's term as governor.

Recognizing the need for strict economy in light of the growing debt and the rising expense of the various improvements projects, Wallace urged the adoption of a modified plan of simultaneous construction in 1838–39. Believing that the proceeds generated by a completed Wabash and Erie Canal combined with surplus revenue from the federal government would be enough to pay both the interest on the state's loans and complete the entire package of improvements, Wallace urged the legislature to reorganize both the Board of Internal Improvements and the engineering corps in order to make both bodies more efficient. He also lobbied for the Wabash and Erie Canal to be extended to Terre Haute. Although Wallace succeeded in getting almost everything he asked for from the general assembly, his victory quickly turned to failure when it became clear in 1839 that neither Indiana nor Ohio was going to complete its portion of the Wabash and Erie Canal in time to salvage the state's finances. In August 1839 work on all the improvement projects came to a halt and charges of misappropriation of funds began to flood the state. By December 1839 Wallace was forced to inform the legislature that "every foot" of the completed canal system was "almost valueless" and would remain so until it was connected to Lake Erie. In 1840, with only about 140 of the projected 1,160 miles of canal completed, the Whigs determined that Wallace was too closely identified with the now-unpopular Internal Improvements System to win reelection and selected Samuel Bigger to be their candidate for governor that year.

After a brief return to private practice as an attorney in Indianapolis, Wallace was elected to Congress as a Whig in 1841. Serving a single term, his most notable achievement was casting the deciding vote on the House Ways and Means Committee in favor of a $30,000 appropriation to Samuel F. B. Morse to support his work on the telegraph. In 1843, following his defeat for reelection—due largely to his opponent's characterization of his support of Morse as a foolish waste of public funds—Wallace returned to Indianapolis and his private law practice. In 1850–51 he represented Marion County at the Indiana Constitutional Convention, and in 1856 he was elected judge of the court of common pleas in Marion County, a position he held with distinction until his death. Wallace achieved some public vindication for his support of the telegraph in 1858 when he was selected to give the main address at Indianapolis's celebration of the successful laying of the trans-Atlantic cable. Wallace died in Indianapolis on September 4, 1859, and was buried in Crown Hill Cemetery.

Portrait by Jacob Cox (ca. 1840), Governors' Portraits Collection, Indiana Historical Bureau, State of Indiana.

FOR FURTHER READING

Carmony, Donald F. *Indiana, 1816–1850: The Pioneer Era.* Vol. 2, *The History of Indiana.* Indianapolis: Indiana Historical Society and Indiana Historical Bureau, 1998.

Dunn, Jacob Piatt. *Indiana and Indianans: A History of Aboriginal and Territorial Indiana and the Century of Statehood.* 5 vols. Chicago: American Historical Society, 1919.

Madison, James H. *The Indiana Way: A State History.* Bloomington: Indiana University Press; Indianapolis: Indiana Historical Society, 1986.

Martin, John Bartlow. *Indiana: An Interpretation.* Bloomington: Indiana University Press, 1992.

Nowland, John H. B. *Early Reminiscences of Indianapolis, with Short Biographical Sketches of Its Early Citizens, and a Few of the Prominent*

Business Men of the Present Day. Indianapolis: Sentinel Book and Job Printing House, 1870.

Riker, Dorothy L., ed. *Messages and Papers Relating to the Administration of David Wallace: Governor of Indiana, 1837–1840*. Indianapolis: Indiana Historical Bureau, 1963.

Walsh, Justin E. *The Centennial History of the Indiana General Assembly, 1816–1978*. Indianapolis: The Select Committee on the Centennial History of the Indiana General Assembly, 1987.

Woollen, William Wesley. *Biographical and Historical Sketches of Early Indiana*. Indianapolis: Hammond and Company, 1883.

A scattering of Wallace letters can be found in the collections of the Indiana State Library and the William Henry Smith Memorial Library, Indiana Historical Society, Indianapolis.

Samuel Bigger

December 9, 1840–December 6, 1843

GREGORY A. BARTLETT

STRIKING AN OPTIMISTIC TONE IN HIS INAUGURAL ADDRESS on December 9, 1840, Samuel Bigger, Indiana's seventh governor and the last Whig to hold the office, claimed that "much may be done towards rescuing the State from her present condition." He, in fact, failed in his three years of service to make any headway in lifting Indiana from the economic abyss that had been caused in large measure by the sale of state bonds to finance the overly ambitious, ill-conceived, and mismanaged public works projects of canals, railroads, and roads launched four years earlier. The state's debt, a staggering $15 million when Bigger came into office, was hardly unchanged by the time he left. His generally unproductive and undistinguished tenure led noted Indiana historian and editor Gayle Thornbrough to conclude, "Seldom, if ever, has the chief executive seemed to have had so little impact on the affairs of state as . . . Governor Bigger." Still, she conceded, given the enormity of the state's troubles, "it is doubtful that any man, no matter how strong or wise, could have led Indiana out of the morass in which she was floundering."

Bigger's position of political prominence, albeit brief, came during a time of disarray and decline for Indiana Whigs. The party took the unusual step of bypassing the incumbent, David Wallace, as its gubernatorial candidate in 1840 and instead unanimously selected the thirty-eight-year-old Bigger, who as a sitting judge for four years had been out of active politics and thus not tainted by the contretemps surrounding the Mammoth Internal Improvements Bill of 1836, commonly referred

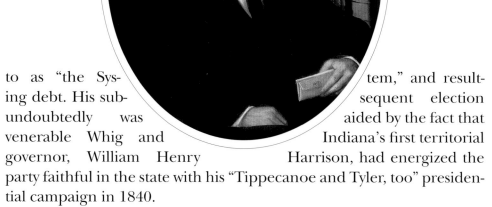

to as "the Sys-tem," and result-ing debt. His sub-sequent election undoubtedly was aided by the fact that venerable Whig and Indiana's first territorial governor, William Henry Harrison, had energized the party faithful in the state with his "Tippecanoe and Tyler, too" presidential campaign in 1840.

Born on a farm in Warren County, Ohio, on March 20, 1802, Samuel Bigger was the son of Colonel John Bigger, both a western pioneer who fought in the American Revolution and a distinguished Whig who served twenty years in the Ohio legislature. After graduating with honors from Ohio University in Athens, Bigger studied law in Lebanon, Ohio. In 1829 he moved to Liberty, Indiana, in Union County, and was married a year later to Ellen Williamson. He moved to Rushville in Rush County, where he joined the law practice of Oliver H. Smith, a prominent Whig politician who served in the Indiana House of Representatives, Congress, and the U.S. Senate. From 1833 to 1835 Bigger was a member of the Indiana House and in 1835 was narrowly defeated for Speaker by Colonel James Gregory. The next year Bigger became a circuit court judge, a position he held until resigning in early 1840 to run for governor.

In the campaign, which matched Bigger against Democrat Tilghman A. Howard, who had resigned his seat in Congress for the race, the collapse of the internal improvement system, naturally, was a central issue. For his part, Bigger said that while he had personally opposed the projects, he now supported the so-called classification approach, which meant resuming work on only those projects that would be the least costly to complete and would have the greatest potential for generating revenue. Howard was branded by the Whig press as a supporter of the discredited public works program from the beginning. In the end, though, what mattered was Harrison's popularity and position as the Whig standard-bearer. Bigger defeated Howard by a comfortable margin, 62,932 to 54,274, and Whigs took control of both houses of the legislature.

However, the financial challenges facing the state, brought on by the System, proved too daunting for the Bigger administration and the Indiana General Assembly to overcome. Interest on the debt was accumulating at a rate of more than $500,000 a year at a time when the state was only taking in about half that amount in tax revenue. The state, which defaulted on its debt in July 1841, continued piling up indebtedness until a final settlement of the internal improvement debt was reached in 1847.

Still, Bigger and the general assembly did attempt some measures aimed at alleviating the crisis. Acting upon the governor's recommendation, the legislature approved a classification system in 1841 that assigned priorities for completing the different state transportation projects, all of which had been idle since the summer of 1839. However, as Thornbrough noted, the legislation was "doomed to start with" because it was to be funded by revenue from the "suspended debt" of the state, or securities the state held as collateral from bond sales that turned out to be virtually worthless. Finally, under a measure that was passed the following year, three projects were turned over to private companies for completion: the Whitewater Canal, from Brookville at the western branch of the Whitewater River to Lawrenceburg on the Ohio River; the Cross-Cut Canal, connecting the Wabash and White rivers as part of the Wabash and Erie Canal; and the Madison and Indianapolis Railroad.

In an effort to shore up Indiana's sagging financial condition, Bigger and the general assembly sought to ensure that the state was realizing the full potential of property taxes as a source of revenue. Their attention to this issue followed a report by the state auditor estimating that more than two million acres of taxable land in the state had escaped assessment in 1840 and also noting the wide variations in how similar pieces of property were valued for tax purposes. In response, the legislature passed a law in 1841 creating equalization boards in each county and a state board to judge whether assessments throughout the state were fair and equal. The public reacted quickly and strongly against the provision for the State Board of Equalization, mistakenly believing "that the state board could raise or lower taxes at will, and also that raising valuation meant raising taxes." Because of the outcry, the state board was repealed by the general assembly the next year.

While the transfer of some internal improvement projects to private companies meant a portion of the moribund System would be salvaged, there still remained demands for an accounting of what went wrong and who was responsible. Bigger, after receiving a report that investigated the state's debt, said flatly that the state had been in many instances the victim of "imposition and fraud." He added that "some of those upon whom we relied for the means of progressing with our public works, have not kept their faith with us." Investigating committees, while finding faulty legislation was partly to blame, saved their most scathing conclusions for several of the fund commissioners. These officials, who were responsible for the finances of the public works, were charged with a host of wrongdoing, including "convoluted negotiations, improper loans of state property, backdating of letters and receipts, negligence and confusion, and improper connections with swindlers."

The financial calamity created by the internal improvements program also ensnarled the State Bank of Indiana, generally considered a sound and conservatively managed institution. Unwittingly, the bank was stuck with a debt of $700,000 after its branches loaned that amount to contractors working on some of the projects. Bigger made repayment of the debt a priority, and the general assembly eventually approved the issuing of treasury notes that erased the debt.

Although Bigger's term as governor was mostly consumed by the state's financial woes, there were a few positive developments. For instance, the Wabash and Erie Canal, which was separate from the internal projects, was moving ahead, though Indiana was still having some difficulty in financing its portion. Begun at Fort Wayne in 1832 after the state received a federal land grant to spur its construction, the canal reached Lafayette in 1841, and Bigger, in his last message to the general assembly in 1843, was able to report that construction of the fifty-mile link between Lafayette and Terre Haute "was progressing more rapidly than anticipated." Ultimately, the 468-mile canal, the longest in the United States, extended from Evansville to Toledo.

Perhaps Bigger's main achievement as governor was his work with the state treasurer, George H. Dunn, on the revision of Indiana codes, a job that had languished for years after unsuccessful attempts by a joint committee of the general assembly and the state supreme court. One legislator called it "the best consolidation of . . . statutes and common law decisions ever presented to the people of this State."

Despite the black financial cloud that hung over Bigger's administration, he still managed to come close to being reelected for another three-year term, losing to James Whitcomb, the first Democrat to be elected governor, by a little more than two thousand votes. While the state's dire financial condition obviously was an issue in the campaign, what tipped the election may have been a disparaging comment that Bigger, a Presbyterian, made about Methodists when he was a state representative. When Methodists in the state sought the legislature's help in 1834 in gaining some representation on the Presbyterian-dominated board of trustees and faculty at what is now Indiana University, Bigger, during legislative debate on the matter, said that there was "not a Methodist in America with sufficient learning to fill a professor's chair." Whether the insult, to which Democratic newspapers devoted considerable attention, determined the outcome is impossible to say. However, at the time Methodists in Indiana outnumbered Presbyterians by a four-to-one ratio.

After leaving office in December 1843, Bigger settled in Fort Wayne, where he formed what became a highly respected law practice with Joseph K. Edgerton. In late 1845 Bigger rejected, without giving a clear explanation, a movement to nominate him for governor again. He died in Fort Wayne on September 9, 1846, after a brief illness.

Portrait by Jacob Cox (1841), Governors' Portraits Collection, Indiana Historical Bureau, State of Indiana.

FOR FURTHER READING

Clark, Robert D. "Matthew Simpson, the Methodists, and the Defeat of Governor Samuel Bigger, 1843." *Indiana Magazine of History* 50 (March 1954): 23–33.

Samuel Bigger: Fort Wayne's Forgotten Man. Fort Wayne: Staff of the Public Library of Fort Wayne and Allen County, 1953.

Thornbrough, Gayle, ed. *Messages and Papers Relating to the Administration of Samuel Bigger: Governor of Indiana, 1840–1843.* Indianapolis: Indiana Historical Bureau, 1964.

Woollen, William Wesley. *Biographical and Historical Sketches of Early Indiana.* Indianapolis: Hammond and Company, 1883.

James Whitcomb

December 6, 1843–December 26, 1848

DAVID L.BAKER

JAMES WHITCOMB WAS ONCE DESCRIBED AS "ONE OF THE most cautious and timid men in the world." Yet Indiana's eighth governor left a bold record of accomplishment. He is credited with saving the state from insolvency, establishing benevolent institutions for the physically and mentally disabled, advocating the first system of free public education, mobilizing the state's participation in the Mexican War, and setting the stage for the second Indiana Constitution. Indiana's first Democratic chief executive was not universally loved, but was widely respected as an intellectual and as a political strategist.

James Whitcomb was born on December 1, 1795, in Rochester, Windsor County, Vermont, the fourth of ten children of John W. and Lydia Parmenter Whitcomb. When James was eleven years old the family moved to a farm near Cincinnati, Ohio, where the future governor was raised on "hard work and coarse fare." John was often displeased with his son's bookishness, but James gained a reputation as the brightest boy in the community. Young Whitcomb found work as a schoolteacher and continued to teach during vacations to pay his fees at Transylvania University in Lexington, Kentucky. After graduation in 1819 he remained in Lexington for five years as he prepared for the bar and then practiced law there for two years.

Influenced perhaps by his exposure in early manhood to the life of academe and cavalier tastes of Kentucky's bluegrass culture, Whitcomb developed a demeanor that belied his rustic roots. He was an accomplished violinist and composed several works for that instru-

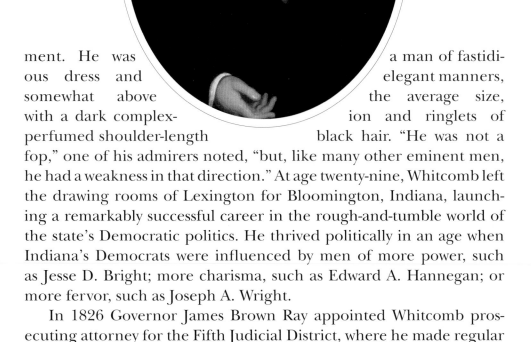

ment. He was a man of fastidious dress and elegant manners, somewhat above the average size, with a dark complexion and ringlets of perfumed shoulder-length black hair. "He was not a fop," one of his admirers noted, "but, like many other eminent men, he had a weakness in that direction." At age twenty-nine, Whitcomb left the drawing rooms of Lexington for Bloomington, Indiana, launching a remarkably successful career in the rough-and-tumble world of the state's Democratic politics. He thrived politically in an age when Indiana's Democrats were influenced by men of more power, such as Jesse D. Bright; more charisma, such as Edward A. Hannegan; or more fervor, such as Joseph A. Wright.

In 1826 Governor James Brown Ray appointed Whitcomb prosecuting attorney for the Fifth Judicial District, where he made regular circuits of fifteen of the state's then fifty-one counties and began accumulating political capital. He was elected in 1830 to the first of two three-year terms in the state senate, where he was noted for his addiction to tobacco and his frugal habits. He was known to insert a pin in his cigar stump when it became too short to hold, and he once chided a fellow smoker for wasting a match when coals from a nearby grate were available to ignite his cheroot. In his first year at Indianapolis, Whitcomb also became one of the drafters of the charter of the Indiana Historical Society.

In Whitcomb's last legislative session, the general assembly approved the gargantuan Internal Improvements System of 1836. The System consisted of nine separate projects, ranging from canals to turnpikes to railroads, to be built throughout the state and financed by bonds to be paid off from revenues generated by the projects. Whitcomb spoke out against the scheme but in the end voted in favor of it, he later said, because his constituents had directed him "to go for the bill." In the next session, the Monroe County senatorial seat would be occupied by Paris C. Dunning, a fellow Democrat and a young lawyer in Whitcomb's law offices.

Whitcomb's political career, meanwhile, moved to the national stage, assisted through the influence of Tilghman A. Howard, his Bloomington law partner and a former Tennessee lawmaker who had been one of that state's electors for his friend Andrew Jackson in 1828. Though Whitcomb was rumored to be favored for a judicial appointment, Jackson ultimately selected him to serve as commissioner of the newly reorganized U.S. General Land Office—reporting directly to the president. The Land Office was a vast, politically sensitive bureaucracy with responsibility for all public lands. The office had been reorganized to absorb the office of Surveyor General of the United States, and a solicitor had been added to handle a heavy backlog of disputed claims under treaties with various Native American tribes, Britain, France, and Spain. Whitcomb taught himself French and Spanish in order to deal with the documentation of these cases.

In 1839 Whitcomb recruited Indiana state geologist David Dale Owen to make a survey of about eleven thousand square miles in Wisconsin and Iowa. Owen received his commission on August 17, hired and instructed 138 assistants, and finished his work in November—a remarkable feat of scientific management. Whitcomb was replaced in 1841 by Whig president John Tyler, who named another Hoosier, Terre Haute attorney Elisha Mills Huntington, as commissioner.

It was in Terre Haute that Whitcomb reestablished his Indiana law practice, which became highly successful. He invested in real estate in nearby Vermillion County, where he built a country home, Hazel Bluff, on twelve hundred acres. His Terre Haute home became a regular meeting place for Democratic strategists with whom Whitcomb had maintained contact and in 1840 he stumped the state for Howard in his unsuccessful bid for the governorship that year. It was not surprising that the Democrats named Whitcomb as the party's standard-bearer in the 1843 gubernatorial race against incumbent Samuel Bigger.

Whitcomb's name recognition grew with the publication of his tract called *Facts for the People in Relation to a Protective Tariff*, in which he opposed the protective tariff. He dealt with the complex issue in language geared to typical Indiana farmers and artisans. "The most difficult national question can be understood by any man who is able to attend to his own business without the aid of a guardian and if he will think for himself," Whitcomb wrote. Democrats paid to circulate the pamphlet, with its thrifty author subscribing $20 to the effort. Lieutenant gubernatorial candidate Jesse Bright, a state senator from Madison, put up $200 and would make substantial financial contributions to the 1843 campaign.

In addition, Whitcomb's oratorical skills served him well throughout the campaign. Nearly forty years later, Governor (and later, Vice President) Thomas A. Hendricks recalled one of Whitcomb's early speeches as "the greatest political speech I ever heard." Hendricks said, "There was not in it a vulgarism or an appeal to low sentiment. He addressed reason, emotion, sympathy. The multitude stood enraptured." As the audience dispersed, they "fell into grave and serious conversation about what they had heard," according to Hendricks, "and the impression remained." But campaign rhetoric was not key to the 1843 election. Democrats counted on the state's internal improvements debacle to hand them a victory.

The Mammoth Internal Improvements System was in shambles with the national economic depression following the financial panic of 1837. The System also suffered from unsound financial practices, engineering setbacks, and alleged corruption. Virtually all the projects, except the separately authorized Wabash and Erie Canal, had been abandoned. Bondholders had not been paid since July 1, 1841. It was estimated that the total debt for internal improvements was nearly

$12 million, with interest accumulating at about $650,000 annually at a time when ordinary expenditures for state government were less than $115,000 a year. The internal improvement fiasco had been a bipartisan blunder, but the Whig Party had the misfortune to hold control of both houses of the general assembly, the governorship, and all statewide offices during much of the time the disaster unfolded.

Whitcomb's margin of victory—barely two thousand votes—is not itself overwhelming, but it represented an electoral swing for the "New Democracy" of more than 10,500 votes from Bigger's landslide win over Howard three years earlier. The final tally was Whitcomb, 60,784; Bigger, 58,721; and 1,683 for Doctor Elizur Deming, the first antislavery candidate of the Liberty Party. Though the antislavery vote was not a decisive factor, about three-fourths of the support for the Liberty Party came from the forty counties favoring Bigger. Many explanations have been suggested for the Whig collapse, including low turnout and an increase in foreign voters. One theory cited political intervention by the Methodist Church on behalf of its Wesleyan brother, Whitcomb, against his Presbyterian opponent. But no explanation of the Whig failure is more persuasive than the crippling effect of the internal improvement debacle.

When Whitcomb was inaugurated in December 1843, he acknowledged he could not submit "specific recommendations" to address the financial disaster. But he began to take steps to restore confidence in state government and end the official paralysis brought on by legislative obsession with internal improvements. He declared a rollback of salaries and perquisites of state officials as part of a cost containment program that would lead him to veto more legislation than any of his predecessors.

Whitcomb's ascension to the governor's office in 1843 coincided with the publication of *The New Purchase; or, Seven and a Half Years in the Far West,* a memoir by Baynard Rush Hall, the first professor hired after the establishment of the State Seminary, the forerunner to Indiana University. Hall, who knew Whitcomb, lampooned a Monroe County politician with the Bunyanesque sobriquet, Insidias Catswell. Many readers recognized the "cold old bachelor" Whitcomb as the wily Catswell, who "never turned with the tide, but watching the ebb and flow, he always managed to turn a little before the tide."

In some respects, however, Whitcomb was an unlikely politician. Indeed, historian William Henry Smith noted, "He possessed but few of the arts of a politician, and was chosen to the high places he filled because of his commanding abilities." A passionate book collector who would leave his impressive, albeit eclectic, library to Asbury (now DePauw) University, the governor was frequently seen reading a book as he walked the streets of Indianapolis. This bibliographic absorption also provided convenient refuge for a weak memory for names—even, at times, the names of his friends.

Whitcomb, though, was not totally dispassionate. In particular, he was known for avuncular acts of kindness toward young people. One grateful recipient of the governor's consideration was Reuben A. Riley, a young lawyer who represented Hancock County in the 1845 and 1848 legislative sessions. Riley's admiration for the governor led him to name his second child—who would become Indiana poet laureate—James Whitcomb Riley.

As governor, Whitcomb also led efforts to establish benevolent institutions for the disabled, an initiative that had received little more than lip service from legislators absorbed by the financially disastrous public works projects. Advocates for the improved treatment of the mentally and physically handicapped had supported Whitcomb's election, and one of their leaders, Doctor John Evans, became the first private citizen to address a joint session of the general assembly. Whitcomb also worked personally with architect John Ekles on the design and construction of a new state prison at Jeffersonville that had been approved in the Bigger administration.

A school for the deaf was approved by the general assembly in 1843–44. An asylum for the mentally disabled, with Evans as director, was authorized two years later. A school for the blind would be established in the 1846–47 session. In each case, civic and grassroots advocates built public sentiment in favor of the institution. Whitcomb made timely choices, generating bipartisan support for each ongoing initiative, for which Democrats would get credit. Governor Thomas A.

Hendricks would later remark that Whitcomb "led legislators because it was safest for them to follow."

Resolution of the state's public debt dilemma began at Terre Haute in May 1845, when a representative of the bondholders, New York attorney Charles Butler, began promoting a financial settlement. When Butler met Whitcomb, he wrote to his wife, "He is one of the most cautious and timid men in the world; at the same time he is, I think, entirely honest and would be glad to have right done."

In his annual address in December, the governor made a strong appeal for a compromise, saying he anticipated receiving "liberal arrangements" for legislative consideration. A week later Whitcomb forwarded Butler's proposal to legislators, who adopted it with several amendments. Under the Butler Bill and revisions made a year later bondholders would receive ownership interest in the Wabash and Erie Canal in exchange for one half of the debt, with the balance refinanced by bonds carrying a reduced interest rate. The first Butler Bill was signed by Whitcomb on his sickbed on January 18, 1846, nine days after the Democrats nominated him for reelection.

Whitcomb's running mate in 1846 was Paris C. Dunning, the former junior partner at the Whitcomb and Howard law firm. The Whig candidate for governor was Joseph G. Marshall, the unsuccessful challenger to former Lieutenant Governor Jesse Bright for the U.S. Senate seat filled in December 1845. The Whig candidate for lieutenant governor, Godlove S. Orth, refused to canvass the state on behalf of the ticket and was replaced in May by former Putnam County legislator Alexander C. Stevenson. Results of the August 4 election were Whitcomb, 64,104 votes, to 60,138 for Marshall, with Liberty Party candidate Stephen C. Stevens polling 2,301 votes—an increase of more than 35 percent in the antislavery vote for governor. The election had not been closely contested until June, by which time many Indiana citizens were preoccupied with military matters. In May 1846 the Mexican War was declared, and President James K. Polk called on Indiana to provide three regiments of volunteers.

Indiana was completely unprepared for the military levy. The "cornstalk militia," whose members used cornstalks instead of rifles in their military drills and corn tassels in their hatbands in lieu of uniforms, was a subject of derision. Whitcomb arranged for lines of credit from each of the branches of the Indiana State Bank to outfit volunteers, and his nonmilitary adjutant general David Reynolds surpassed the quota, thanks largely to a nonpartisan outpouring of patriotism despite some Whig disdain for "Mr. Polk's little war." By war's end a year later, Indiana would provide a total of five regiments for the conflict, and the parsimonious governor recommended to the general assembly that his adjutant general receive a $100 salary increase.

Two months before the outbreak of hostilities with Mexico, on March 24, 1846, Indiana's fifty-year-old bachelor governor married Martha Ann Renick Hurst, a thirty-five-year-old widow. Whitcomb was married by his brother David, a Methodist circuit rider, in a ceremony at the bride's family home in Pickaway County, Ohio. A daughter was born to the couple on July 1, 1847. Sixteen days later Martha Whitcomb died, the first Indiana First Lady to die during her husband's term of office.

With reelection Whitcomb began to support efforts to establish free common schools in Indiana. The 1840 census showed that one in seven Hoosiers were illiterate, and the 1850 census would reflect an increase to one in five. A state tax to support public schools was especially controversial since many older, established communities had adequate schools financed locally, and some rural communities placed no premium on education. In his 1846 annual message Whitcomb urged the general assembly to revise the entire school system and place it under the charge of a state superintendent of schools. Caleb Mills, a longtime advocate of free schools, pressed a campaign for the next two years that led to enabling legislation in the 1848–49 legislative session and fundamental commitment to free schools in the Indiana Constitution of 1851.

Constitutional revision was a controversial topic on which Whitcomb remained neutral in the 1846 and 1847 legislative sessions. But when Democrats established majorities in both houses following the August 1848 elections, the governor made a detailed argument for a constitutional convention. In his annual message of December 6,

1848, the governor suggested a vote of the people in August 1849 and a schedule for a convention and ratification proposing that "the whole question would be disposed of before the Presidential election of 1852." The plan was adopted by the general assembly and supported by both major gubernatorial candidates in 1849.

Whitcomb's record of achievement was marred by a protracted dispute with the state senate over the nomination of Democrats to replace Whig judges on the supreme court. The conflict began in 1845 and continued for three years, and it went beyond party politics. Democratic factionalism appears to have been a factor, since Whitcomb's party enjoyed thin majorities in the upper house during all three years of the stalemate. Generally, though, Democratic intraparty conflict was kept from public view.

In December 1848 the Democratic caucus decided to replace the flamboyant Senator Edward A. Hannegan, whose term expired the following March. Whitcomb, who had been passed over for the senatorial vacancy filled by Jesse Bright, was elected U.S. Senator from Indiana on December 14, 1848, with seventy-five votes, while Hannegan received only fifteen.

During most of his Senate service Whitcomb was disabled, afflicted with "gravel," or kidney stones, and took little part in the debates, allowing his colleague Bright to dominate the Indiana delegation. He was being treated for his kidney disease when he died suddenly in New York City on October 4, 1852. He was buried with full Masonic honors in the Greenlawn Cemetery in Indianapolis. Much of his personal wealth had been donated to the American Bible Society, of which he was vice president.

Whitcomb's real estate holdings were distributed to family members, with his five-year-old daughter, Martha Renick Whitcomb, receiving Hazel Bluff, the estate five miles southwest of Clinton. Shortly after Martha married Kentuckian Claude Matthews in 1868, the couple moved to the Vermillion County farm. In 1892 Matthews was elected Indiana's twenty-third governor. First Lady Martha Matthews had her father's remains removed to Indianapolis's Crown Hill Cemetery and reinterred next to the grave of Governor Oliver P. Morton. In 1898, a year after Matthews vacated the governorship, a sculpture of his father-in-law by John Mahoney was dedicated at Indianapolis Circle Park, along with monuments to Indiana icons George Rogers Clark and William Henry Harrison.

Portrait by James Forbes (1869), Governors' Portraits Collection, Indiana Historical Bureau, State of Indiana.

FOR FURTHER READING

Carmony, Donald F. *Indiana, 1816–1850: The Pioneer Era*. Vol. 2, *The History of Indiana*. Indianapolis: Indiana Historical Bureau and Indiana Historical Society, 1998.

Carmony, Donald F., and Herman J. Viola. eds. "The New Purchase; or, Seven and a Half Years in the Far West." *Indiana Magazine of History* 62 (June 1966): 101–20.

Clark, Robert D. "Matthew Simpson, the Methodists, and the Defeat of Samuel Bigger, 1843." *Indiana Magazine of History* 50 (March 1954): 23–33.

Hall, Baynard Rush. *The New Purchase; or Seven and a Half Years in the Far West*. Princeton, NJ: Princeton University Press, 1916.

Marlow, William A. "Saga of Indiana: Gov. Whitcomb, Intellectual Giant." 1947. Indiana Clipping File. Indiana State Library, Indianapolis.

Smith, William Henry. *The History of the State of Indiana from the Earliest Explorations by the French to the Present Time*. 2 vols. Indianapolis: B. L. Blair Company, 1897.

Taylor, Robert M. Jr., et al. *Indiana: A New Historical Guide*. Indianapolis: Indiana Historical Society, 1989.

Van Bolt, Roger H. "The Hoosier Politician in the 1840s." *Indiana Magazine of History* 48 (March 1952): 23–36.

Walsh, Justin E. *Centennial History of the Indiana General Assembly, 1816–1978*. Indianapolis: Select Committee on the Centennial History of the Indiana General Assembly, 1987.

Whitcomb, James. *Facts for the People in Relation to a Protective Tariff: Embracing a Brief View of the Operation of Our Tariff Laws since the*

Organization of the Government, Including that of 1842. Indianapolis: G. A. and J. P. Chapman, 1843.

———. "Messages to the House and Senate 1844–48." *Documents of the General Assembly of Indiana.* Sessions 27–32. Indianapolis: J. P. Chapman, 1844–48.

Woodburn, James Albert. "Constitution Making in Early Indiana: An Historical Survey." *Indiana Magazine of History* 10 (September 1914): 237–55.

Woollen, William Wesley. *Biographical and Historical Sketches of Early Indiana.* Indianapolis: Hammond and Company, 1883.

Whitcomb's gubernatorial papers are in the Indiana State Archives, Indianapolis. His personal papers are in the William Henry Smith Memorial Library, Indiana Historical Society, Indianapolis.

Paris C. Dunning

December 26, 1848–December 5, 1849

THOMAS D. KOTULAK

PARIS C. DUNNING, NINTH GOVERNOR OF INDIANA, HAD A unique record of public service to the state. He was the only person in Indiana history to serve as governor, lieutenant governor, president pro tempore of the state senate, state senator, and state representative. A staunch Democrat and effective communicator throughout his career, he was repeatedly called upon to run for a wide range of leadership positions. Although his term as governor was relatively brief, it was noteworthy for resisting the expansion of slavery into free territories, championing greater popular sovereignty in state government, and expanding public education.

Born on March 15, 1806, in Guilford County, North Carolina, to James and Rachel North Dunning, Paris, the youngest of six sons, proved to be a promising youth. He was educated near his home at the Greensboro Academy in preparation for higher education at the state university in Chapel Hill. Following the death of his father, Paris joined his mother and an elder brother in moving to Bloomington, Indiana, in 1823. There he met and married Sarah Alexander in 1826. They had four children.

After coming to Indiana, Dunning taught school several terms before studying medicine in Louisville, Kentucky. Upon completion of his studies he spent a short time in practice at Rockville, Indiana, but was soon drawn to the study of law. Returning to Bloomington, he studied under Tilghman A. Howard and James Whitcomb. Given the latter's future as governor of Indiana and U.S. Senator, this career change proved

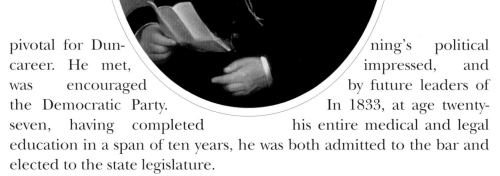

pivotal for Dun-ning's political career. He met, impressed, and was encouraged by future leaders of the Democratic Party. In 1833, at age twenty-seven, having completed his entire medical and legal education in a span of ten years, he was both admitted to the bar and elected to the state legislature.

Dunning was elected three times to represent Monroe County in the state house of representatives, serving from 1833 to 1836, and subsequently he was elected to represent Monroe County and part of Brown County in the state senate, where he served from 1836 to 1839.

After retiring from the state senate, Dunning returned to the private practice of law at Bloomington in 1840. He was called back to public duty in 1844, however, when he was selected by his party to be a presidential elector, casting his vote for James K. Polk and George M. Dallas. Two years later he was selected by Democrats to be their nominee for lieutenant governor, running successfully with former mentor Whitcomb, the party's gubernatorial candidate. When Whitcomb ran successfully for the U.S. Senate, Dunning succeeded him as governor in December 1848 and served out Whitcomb's term until December 1849.

This was a critical time for the nation and the state. On the national front, debate over slavery was becoming more strident and divisive. In

Indiana, moreover, there was mounting pressure for changes in the Constitution of 1816, which was seen by many as contributing to the state's domestic problems. Within this context, Dunning rose to the challenge of becoming governor. Although he served as the state's chief executive for only a year, he did not shirk from speaking out on these salient and often controversial public issues.

As governor, he clearly expressed his views on one of the most important national issues of the day, the extension of slavery into the newly acquired free territories. In his address to the Indiana General Assembly, Dunning suggested that legislators pass a joint resolution expressing the sentiments of the people on the issue of the extension of slavery. Aligning himself with the position of Union Democrats prior to and after the Civil War, Dunning said that "it is our imperative duty to assert our rights as members of the same great family, and manfully resist, by all legal and constitutional means, the further advancement of slavery into territory belonging to the General Government," adding that "bounds should be prescribed to the baleful influence of human slavery."

In addressing important issues specific to Indiana, Dunning advocated a progressive agenda, calling for a new constitutional convention after the people of the state had expressed their will: "It is most respectfully suggested that, in the discharge of this important duty, the members of the General Assembly should divest themselves of all party predilections, and make such an apportionment as will insure to the people of the State, irrespective of parties, a full and fair representation in that body." Dunning, for the most part, had his way. A historian's account of the composition of the constitutional convention stated that "they were generally representative citizens with much and varied political experience, and the rural and agrarian context of the pioneer economy is reflected by the variety of their occupations."

The resultant Indiana Constitution of 1851 also addressed Dunning's concern that "special legislation is a growing evil which has attracted much attention amongst the masses of the people, and to which much well founded opposition exists in the public mind." Once again, Dunning's position later prevailed. Article 4 of that document restricts the legislature in considering "local and special laws," thereby freeing lawmakers to consider more carefully laws of general application throughout the state.

Perhaps most important to Dunning's progressive vision for Indiana was his commitment to expanding free common schools. Calling it a matter of "greater importance," Dunning told the Indiana legislature: "I allude to the subject of Free Common Schools, in which the masses of the people are more immediately and vitally interested; it is upon them that our country mainly relies for her permanent peace and prosperity, and it is to their advancement and improvement in knowledge that our legislative action should be mainly directed." Dunning saw the expansion of public education in Indiana as vital to a flourishing democratic society. Having served as president of the board of trustees for Indiana College, which later became Indiana University, from 1838 to 1841, he early on demonstrated a commitment to the cause of public education. He thought that the future of the state was inextricably intertwined with an informed public, and having an informed public required universal access to at least an elementary education. The Indiana Constitution of 1851 adopted this position in Article 8.

Dunning was also progressive for his time regarding the educational opportunities for women: "The time will soon arrive when the fair daughters of Indiana will be enabled to acquire, within the borders of their own native State, an education which will place them in favorable comparison with those of the most highly favored portions of our country." This prediction was consistent with his other progressive positions stressing the importance of education for true popular sovereignty within the state.

Despite his short term of office, Dunning managed to refocus the agenda of political reform begun by his predecessor. His eloquence and popularity within the state assured a serious consideration of his views as Indiana embarked on the critical business of changing its constitution and engaging the national debate over the future of slavery.

After leaving the governor's office, Dunning returned to Bloomington to practice law. He again was called to politics in 1856, but declined the opportunity to run for Congress. Friends and other political supporters were not deterred from returning him to public service, and in 1860 he was nominated by the Democratic state convention to be a delegate to the national convention at Charleston, South Carolina, and later to the convention held in Baltimore. In both locations he supported the candidacy of Stephen A. Douglas over James Buchanan, and also served on the committee on platform and resolutions. When the Civil War broke out in 1861, Dunning declared himself, not surprisingly given the positions he had taken as governor, on the side of the Union. He subsequently worked tirelessly to raise Indiana's share of Union troops.

Also in 1861, he was once again elected to the state senate, this time without regard to party affiliation. In 1862 he was elected to a full term as state senator, having been endorsed by both the Democratic convention and the Union convention, and in January 1863 he was elected president of the senate. After Lieutenant Governor Conrad Baker assumed presidency of that legislative body at the next session of the legislature, Governor Oliver P. Morton went to Europe, and Baker thereafter assumed Morton's responsibilities as governor. At this point, Dunning was once again thrust into the leadership of the senate.

At the end of his term, Dunning was renominated to serve, but declined the honor. He also declined a repeated nomination for the U.S. House of Representatives, preferring as before to return to the practice of law in Bloomington. Having lost his first wife in 1863, Dunning married Ellen Lane Ashford in 1865. They had one son.

Though often involved in politics, Dunning remained committed to practicing criminal law. Indeed, as a local hometown newspaper put the matter, Dunning was "a lawyer of such marked ability as to have a reputation that was National, the success of a client being assured when P. C. Dunning was the counsel."

Dunning maintained an interest in public affairs, but mainly concentrated on his law practice and private life. Not surprisingly, given his interest and commitment to the law throughout his professional career, immediately prior to his death on May 9, 1884, at the age of seventy-eight, he had been listening to an argument in a case before a court in his adopted hometown of Bloomington. He was buried there at the Rose Hill Cemetery.

Portrait by James Forbes (1869), Governors' Portraits Collection, Indiana Historical Bureau, State of Indiana.

FOR FURTHER READING

A Biographical History of Eminent and Self-Made Men of the State of Indiana. Cincinnati: Western Biographical Publishing Company, 1880.

Bloomington Herald Tribune, June 3, 1968.

Bloomington Telephone, May 10, 1884.

Carmony, Donald F. *Indiana, 1816–1850: The Pioneer Era.* Vol. 2, *The History of Indiana.* Indianapolis: Indiana Historical Bureau and Indiana Historical Society, 1998.

London, Lena. "Homestead Exemption in the Indiana Constitution of 1851." *Indiana Magazine of History* 44 (September 1948): 267–80.

Myers, Burton D. *Trustees and Officers of Indiana University, 1826–1950.* Bloomington: Burton Dorr Myers papers, 1924–1951.

Portrait and Biographical Record of Boone and Clinton Counties. Chicago: A. W. Bowen and Company, 1895.

Post, Margaret Moore. *First Ladies of Indiana and the Governors, 1816–1984.* Indianapolis: Pierson Printing Company, 1984.

Thornbrough, Emma Lou. *Indiana in the Civil War Era: 1850–1880.* Vol. 3, *The History of Indiana.* Indianapolis: Indiana Historical Bureau and Indiana Historical Society, 1965.

Wright, Joseph, ed. *Official Report of the Governor's Messages.* Bloomington: Indiana University Library-State Documents, 1849.

Dunning's gubernatorial papers are in the Indiana State Archives, Indianapolis.

Joseph A. Wright

December 5, 1849–January 12, 1857

BRADFORD W. SAMPLE

IN 1850 GOVERNOR JOSEPH A. WRIGHT ORDERED AN INSCRIP-
tion placed on Indiana's contribution to the Washington Monument that read, "Indiana knows no North, no South, nothing but the
Union." A Free-Soil Democrat, unionist, and "thorough republican,"
Wright was more representative of the Hoosier State's population
than many who have held the post before or since. Wright urged the
state's citizens to embrace numerous reforms and innovations, while
also stressing political moderation. By the end of Wright's two terms
as governor, his beloved Union was headed toward Civil War, but the
reforms he pushed through the Indiana General Assembly or encouraged during his tenure set the foundation for institutions that continue to exist more than a century after his last day in office.

Born into a modest Washington, Pennsylvania, Quaker family on
April 17, 1810, Wright journeyed with his parents, John and Rachel
Seaman Wright, to Bloomington, Indiana, in 1819. Wright was the
couple's second son and shared family responsibilities with three
brothers and four sisters. His youngest brother, George G., became
a U.S. Senator from Iowa in the 1870s. John was a brick mason by
trade and helped to build Indiana University's first halls. He taught
these skills to his sons, which helped the future governor earn a living
from time to time when his law practice could not keep up with his
expenses.

Wright also used his masonry talents to pay his college tuition while
attending the Indiana State Seminary, later renamed Indiana University.

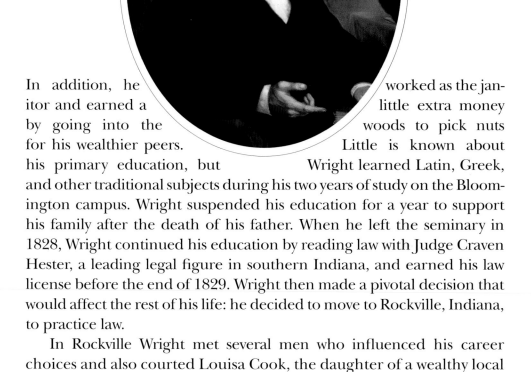

In addition, he worked as the janitor and earned a little extra money by going into the woods to pick nuts for his wealthier peers. Little is known about his primary education, but Wright learned Latin, Greek, and other traditional subjects during his two years of study on the Bloomington campus. Wright suspended his education for a year to support his family after the death of his father. When he left the seminary in 1828, Wright continued his education by reading law with Judge Craven Hester, a leading legal figure in southern Indiana, and earned his law license before the end of 1829. Wright then made a pivotal decision that would affect the rest of his life: he decided to move to Rockville, Indiana, to practice law.

In Rockville Wright met several men who influenced his career choices and also courted Louisa Cook, the daughter of a wealthy local farmer and the woman who influenced him to join the Methodist Church in 1837. The couple married on November 30, 1831, adopted a daughter in early 1832, and had their only son in October of the same year. Louisa Cook Wright was not particularly fond of politics, but was deeply devoted to her husband and ultimately approved of his decisions to run for elective office. She suffered from malaria during much of her adult life, but lived through her husband's first gubernatorial term, dying on May 21, 1852. Wright married Harriet Burbridge on August 15, 1854, and the couple had a daughter. Wright became a widower for the second time in October 1855. In 1863 he married Caroline Rockwill of New York City.

Wright's first two wives deeply influenced his positions on issues and encouraged his religious zeal by the depth of their own Christian piety, while the friends Wright made in Rockville steered him toward a long career in politics. William Perkins Bryant, state representative for Parke County and a fellow Rockville attorney with whom Wright shared an office, convinced the future governor to run for Bryant's seat after he decided to return to Kentucky. Wright ran successfully for the office, serving as the youngest member of the Indiana House of Representatives during the 1833–34 session. His support for a strong state bank cost him reelection, but he regained his seat in 1836. A year later the general assembly selected him for the post of prosecuting attorney of the First Judicial District. Not caring for the rigors required of a circuit-based court of the period, he succeeded in winning a state senate seat in 1839. At the conclusion of the 1840 general assembly, Wright returned to Rockville and entered into partnership with his mentor Tilghman A. Howard, a strict Methodist and a friend of President Andrew Jackson and Governor James Whitcomb.

After holding so many elective offices, Wright's positions on the issues were clear. He was somewhat independent of Democratic Party leadership, but was, by and large, a typical western Democrat. Wright spoke against the spread of slavery into new territories, but was not fond of abolitionism, believing that colonization would be the best option for both African Americans and Anglo Americans. He was an ardent expansionist and pro-Union, but equated the United States to a confederation. In local politics, Wright distrusted banks, raged against publicly supported internal improvements, and championed furthering public education, but believed that religious teaching should be a part of the curriculum. These values reflected the inclinations of most Hoosiers in the 1840s and 1850s and help to explain Wright's popularity. In contrast, Wright's chief nemesis, Democratic Party boss Jesse D. Bright, held slaves at his properties in Kentucky, stood against moral reform measures, and only believed in expansion and union when it appeared to aid the southern states or slavery.

A dynamic speaker, tall, and often described as hospitable and gentlemanly, Wright made a positive impression on voters. His ability to capture the confidence of people from all political parties remained a characteristic throughout his career. In 1843 he won a U.S. House of Representatives seat in a Whig-dominated district by three votes. In the next election he lost by 171 votes, but received 1,090 votes more than the 1844 Democratic presidential nominee. His success in 1843 and his close elections in 1845 and 1847 in the district that included Terre Haute brought him to the attention of Democrats around the state, who were looking to continue their dominance of state offices. After Wright backed Whitcomb's bid for the U.S. Senate, a position Whitcomb lost to Bright, Wright received Whitcomb's support for the Democratic gubernatorial nomination.

Campaigns in the 1840s and 1850s began at state conventions, where the party faithful determined the nominees. In 1849 Whitcomb maneuvered to win the presidency of the convention and chair the selection committee, and then made certain that Wright received the committee's unanimous endorsement. On the convention floor, Wright received two-thirds of the vote on the first ballot and easily secured the nomination. Many southern Indiana delegates were not happy with the choice, as Wright was suspected of having Free-Soil views. Segments of the party's platform could not have pleased them either, since it included two planks demanding slavery's exclusion from several new states or territories. Other planks included antibank and anti-internal improvement rhetoric common to Democratic Party campaigns since 1837.

During the 1849 campaign, Wright endeavored to speak throughout the state and planned one hundred speeches from April through August, but his health failed, and future Republican governor Oliver P. Morton spoke in his place after July 16. In his speeches, Wright reached out to all segments of society by recalling his own modest beginnings and demanding more opportunities for the average person. The Whigs recruited John Matson, and the Free-Soil Party placed James Cravens on the ballot against Wright. The campaign revolved around the issue of which party had the better record on keeping slavery out of the territories and which party was to blame for the state's debts. The Mexican War and the Wilmont Proviso generated heated sectional animosities in the mid- to late 1840s and increased the Free-Soil sentiment in the Hoosier State, so that by 1849 all three party platforms stood against slavery's introduction into new states. The state's Democratic leaning, Wright's proven antislavery proclivities before 1849, his gift of oratory, and his ability to reach out to all voters provided him with the widest margin of victory of any Indiana gubernatorial candidate to that point, receiving twice as many votes as the Democratic Party presidential nominee in 1848.

In his inaugural address, Wright continued the themes developed throughout his political career. Like many Hoosiers, he favored a revision of the 1816 state constitution that would include more elective offices and a commitment to public education. Being a good Jacksonian, he also wanted to more quickly pay off the state's debts and develop the internal improvements thought necessary for an improving economy through private enterprise. Reflecting on national events, he noted that Indiana was "one member of this great confederacy, and . . . it is our high mission to allay the excitement of one portion of this Union against the other."

Hoosiers in 1849 not only voted for governor, but also affirmed their preference for a new constitution. The 1851 constitution reflected the thoughts and concerns of the Democratic Party that dominated the convention and was widely hailed as a vast improvement over the old constitution. It charged the Indiana General Assembly to create the structure for a public school system, prohibited the state from investing in or owning a bank, prohibited the state from going into debt, expanded the number of elected offices, and added to the length of state office tenure. Reflecting the era, it also excluded African Americans from citizenship and prohibited them from settling in the state, urging African colonization instead. The issues Wright championed in his first term reflected the demands of the changing constitution, but he also branched out to include creating a more equitable property tax structure, providing adequate funding for and oversight of the state's benevolent and penal institutions, and strengthening Indiana's ability to compete economically.

For years Indiana's leaders had argued for a broad public school system to protect the citizens' ability to critically evaluate policy and encourage technological innovation, but these arguments went largely unheeded. The 1850 U.S. Census, which revealed Indiana as having the largest illiterate population of any northern state, embarrassed Indiana leaders and gave Wright, Caleb Mills (a Presbyterian minister who became known as the father of Indiana's public school system), and others the influence needed to force change. In 1852 the general assembly set the township as the administrative unit in charge of schools and provided for school funding through property taxes, for the first time in Indiana's history. To foster popular support for the education initiative and to adequately fund the system, leaders realized that higher and more equitable taxes would be needed.

Under Wright's guidance, district boards were established to review local decisions and state tax assessors began assessing property at its cash value, which included stocks and bonds for the first time on a consistent basis. This new assessment method yielded not only more revenue for the state, but also made taxation more equitable. With an increase in population during the 1850s, a rising economy, and a better system of taxation, Indiana was able to successfully launch its public education system and provide increased funding for the state's benevolent institutions, including the asylums for the blind and the insane.

Linked to his dedication to providing Indiana's citizens with better economic and social opportunities, Wright's thoughts and passions often led him to act outside of the realm of official state policy. Wright promoted what he called a "home" economic policy, consistently urging Indiana farmers and mechanics to buy goods from fellow Hoosiers whenever possible and to develop those industries or crops that Indiana denizens wanted but could not find at home. He urged the general assembly to conduct a geological and mineral survey because he wanted Hoosiers to create businesses based on its results to augment the state's agriculture base, so that Indiana's farming wealth would not be drained away to East Coast states, which dominated industry at the time. When Congress passed the controversial Compromise of 1850 and an air of bitter partisan and sectional rancor loomed over the country, Wright invited Kentucky's Whig governor, John J. Crittenden, to Indianapolis to show that both he and Wright "knew no North, no South, nothing but the common brotherhood of all working for the common good."

Although never a farmer, Wright favored agriculture and thought that it was the only true measure of wealth. During campaigns he endeavored to link himself to farmers, but his interest in farming was genuine rather than purely political. He wrote several well-received technical articles on cereals and grasses and spoke at agricultural society meetings in six states and Canada before the end of his second term. He encouraged experimentation in farming, such as crop rotation; the adoption of new crops in Indiana, such as flax; and soil conservation, sometimes well in advance of popular thinking. In 1851, at Wright's suggestion, the general assembly created a State Board of Agriculture and provided public funding for county organizations. Wright hoped that these agencies, and the fairs they would support, would provide a mechanism for the sharing of resources and information that would enable Hoosier farmers to be more efficient and more knowledgeable of advanced techniques.

By linking himself to the interests of the majority of Hoosiers, Wright increased his popularity over the course of his first term, but quarrels with Bright and Wright's reluctance to support some Democratic issues, such as Free or "Wildcat" banks, lessened the governor's influence with the leaders of the legislature's Democratic majority. Wright's veto of the Third State Bank Bill, the appointment of a few experienced Whigs to high offices and the courts over Democrats, and his general support of several reform measures and Free-Soil views cost him support within his own party, but endeared him to ordinary Hoosiers. Several personal letters reveal that Wright feared he would not be renominated in 1852 because of his position within the party, and his fears were not without merit. During the 1854 state Democratic Party convention, Bright gathered enough support to withhold a plank from the party's platform endorsing the governor's administration.

The Whigs halfheartedly placed Indianapolis businessman Nicholas McCarty against Wright in 1852. Both parties avoided the topics of temperance, the Compromise of 1850, and the Fugitive Slave Law, which were divisive issues to many in Indiana, concentrating instead on state finances and farming. The Democrats won in decisive fashion, but it was Wright who scored the biggest victory, polling almost 3 percent more than the Democratic presidential nominee and drawing support from both Free-Soil and Whig voters. Wright received 92,576 votes to McCarty's 73,641 and the 3,303 given to Cravens of the Free Soil Party.

Wright's second term, which lasted four years due to a change in the constitution, was much like his first. He continued to urge the general assembly to provide more funding for education, teacher training, and benevolent institutions. He remained a supporter of agricultural advances, speaking and writing on the growing of specific, nontraditional cereals and grasses in Indiana. He gained financial support from the legislature for the creation of a juvenile reformatory, first requested in 1851 and called for in the new constitution. Moreover, Wright not only asked for government support, but he also led by example, forming the first prison library with a personal donation of two hundred volumes. In addition, he succeeded in convincing the legislature of the need for the post of attorney general, which reduced the state's legal fees. Wright never received full support for his education measures or for his desire to establish an agricultural research station in Bloomington, and he failed to match the power of Bright within his own party. In his two terms as governor, however, Wright increased the social responsibility of the state, lowered the debt, lent his support for economic innovation, and, along the way, gained the trust of many Hoosiers from all political leanings.

In 1854 the Indiana Democratic Party split over the Kansas-Nebraska Act and state temperance legislation, and many of Wright's friends and closest supporters, forced from the party by the Bright majority, joined a mixture of groups that later became the Republican Party. In that year's election, Wright stumped for the Democrats, but remained silent on temperance, an issue that he supported due to his strong religious beliefs. For the first time in a generation, Democrats lost decisively.

Near the end of his second term, Wright began looking for a new political post. Some people from around the country wanted to make

Wright the next vice president, but the lack of unity within the Indiana Democracy probably made this impossible. Many state Democrats wanted him to be the next U.S. Senator, a position Wright desired. In a move to protect party unity at the 1856 state convention, however, Wright allowed Bright to continue as senator, with the agreement that in exchange for Wright's stepping aside, Bright would use his influence with president-elect James Buchanan to secure a cabinet position for the governor. Bright was again elected senator, but he made certain that Wright never received a cabinet position. Instead, Buchanan named Wright the U.S. Minister to Prussia.

For the next four years the former governor diligently served his nation, continually seeking redress for injuries inflicted upon German-born American citizens traveling to Prussia on business or visiting family. Some were harassed, not permitted to leave Prussia, pressed into military service, or defrauded, and Wright demanded that the Prussian government respect the rights of American citizens. When Buchanan left the White House in 1861, Wright returned to an America on the brink of rebellion.

In Indiana, Bright and his allies threw out of the party numerous Democrats with antislavery or Free-Soil views, including Wright. The former standard-bearer for the Democratic Party joined the Republican Party in 1861 and spoke on behalf of the Union cause and the Lincoln administration throughout the Civil War. Bright was later dismissed from the U.S. Senate, and Democrat-turned-Republican governor Oliver P. Morton appointed Wright to serve out the rest of Bright's term. In 1863 Lincoln sent Wright back to Germany as the Commissioner to the Hamburg Exposition and in 1865 appointed him Minister to Prussia. Ever true to his faith, Wright endeavored to establish Methodist churches in Europe. Indiana's tenth governor died in Berlin, Prussia, on May 11, 1867. His remains were interred in New York City at the request of his third wife.

An undergraduate residence hall opened in September 1949 on the campus of Indiana University in Bloomington was named in Wright's honor.

Portrait by Jacob Cox (before 1857), Governors' Portraits Collection, Indiana Historical Bureau, State of Indiana.

FOR FURTHER READING

Beeler, Dale. "The Election of 1852 in Indiana." Pts. 1 and 2. *Indiana Magazine of History* 11 (December 1915): 301–23 and 12 (March 1916): 34–51.

Brand, Carl F. "The History of the Know Nothing Party in Indiana." 3 pts. *Indiana Magazine of History* 18 (March 1922): 47–81; (June 1922): 177–206; (September 1922): 266–306.

Canup, Charles E. "Temperance Movements and Legislation in Indiana." *Indiana Magazine of History* 16 (March 1920): 3–37.

Carmony, Donald F. *Indiana, 1816–1850: The Pioneer Era*. Vol. 2, *The History of Indiana*. Indianapolis: Indiana Historical Bureau and Indiana Historical Society, 1998.

Crane, Philip. "Onus with Honor: A Political History of Joseph A. Wright, 1809–1857." MA thesis, Indiana University, 1961.

Holliday, P. C. "Hon. Joseph A. Wright." *Ladies Repository,* July 1859.

Jobson, Frederick J. *America, and American Methodism.* New York: Virtue, Emmins and Company, 1857.

Lincoln, Abraham, Papers. Library of Congress, Washington, D.C. American Memory Project, [2000 2002], http://memory.loc.gov/ammem/alhome.html.

McCord, Shirley S., comp. *Travel Accounts of Indiana, 1679–1961: A Collection of Observations by Wayfaring Foreigners, Itinerants, and Peripatetic Hoosiers.* Indianapolis: Indiana Historical Bureau, 1970.

Sobel, Robert, and John Raimo, eds. *Biographical Directory of the Governors of the United States, 1789–1978.* Vol. 1 (Alabama–Indiana). Westport, CT: Meckler Books, 1978.

Stoler, Mildred C. "Insurgent Democrats of Indiana and Illinois in 1854." *Indiana Magazine of History* 33 (March 1937): 1–31.

Thornbrough, Emma Lou. *Indiana in the Civil War Era, 1850–1880.* Vol. 3, *The History of Indiana.* Indianapolis: Indiana Historical Society, 1965.

Van Bolt, Roger H. "Indiana in Political Transition, 1851–1853." *Indiana Magazine of History* 49 (June 1953): 131–60.

———. "Fusion Out of Confusion, 1854." *Indiana Magazine of History* 49 (December 1953): 353–90.

Woodburn, James A. "Constitution Making in Early Indiana: An Historical Survey." *Indiana Magazine of History* 10 (September 1914): 237–55.

Wright's papers are in the Indiana State Library, Indianapolis.

Ashbel P. Willard

January 12, 1857–October 4, 1860

JAMES E. ST. CLAIR

THE ELECTION OF ASHBEL P. WILLARD IN 1856 GAVE INDIANA'S Democratic Party its fifth consecutive gubernatorial victory and a measure of satisfaction after it suffered a crushing setback in the off-year elections of 1854 at the hands of the upstart Fusion or People's Party. However, any jubilation by the party, which had been dominant in Indiana politics since the early 1840s, was short lived, as it now faced a formidable opposition party that demonstrated its staying power and prowess again in the late 1850s and throughout the next decade.

Slavery, the issue riving the nation North and South, likewise had fractured the Democratic Party and the state, also along a north-south axis. The defining breach in the Democracy, a term also in use then to identify the party, occurred at the state convention in 1854, was when support of the Kansas-Nebraska Act, which undid the Missouri Compromise of 1820 prohibiting slavery in a northern region of the western territories, became a litmus test of party loyalty. Anti-Nebraska Democrats, who tended to be from the northern part of the state, were further moved to rebellion over the party's stand against prohibition. In fact, the issue of temperance "contributed almost as much to the political revolt of 1854 as did the Nebraska question." A third element in the shifting political alignments was nativism, a reaction against the growing immigrant population in the state.

The odd coalition that formed in opposition to the Democratic establishment, which came to include Whigs, the anti-immigrant and anti-Catholic Know Nothings, and the antislavery Free-Soilers, later

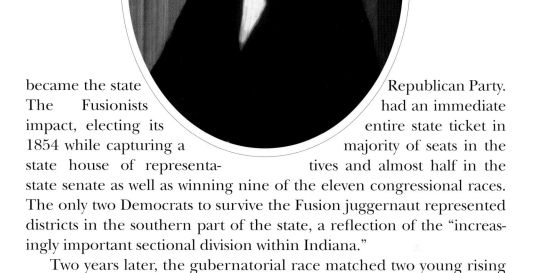

became the state Republican Party. The Fusionists had an immediate impact, electing its entire state ticket in 1854 while capturing a majority of seats in the state house of representatives and almost half in the state senate as well as winning nine of the eleven congressional races. The only two Democrats to survive the Fusion juggernaut represented districts in the southern part of the state, a reflection of the "increasingly important sectional division within Indiana."

Two years later, the gubernatorial race matched two young rising stars of Indiana politics, Willard and thirty-two-year-old Oliver P. Morton, a native of Wayne County in eastern Indiana and a Democrat until 1854. Willard's ascent since moving to New Albany in southern Indiana just eleven years earlier had been spectacular. In rapid succession, Willard, who was thirty-six by the time he was sworn in as Indiana's eleventh governor, had been elected to the city council in New Albany; to the state legislature, where at age thirty he became chairman of the House Ways and Means Committee; and then as lieutenant governor in 1852.

Willard was born on October 31, 1820, in Vernon, New York, to Erastus and Sarah Parsons Willard. His father was a farmer and later served as sheriff of Oneida County. Willard graduated from Hamilton College in Clinton, New York, in 1842 and then studied law with a judge in his home county of Oneida. Before finally settling in New

Albany in 1845 to practice law, Willard lived for a time in Michigan, Texas, and Kentucky, where he taught school in Carrollton and Louisville. His interest in politics led him to campaign for James K. Polk in 1844, and after making a speech in New Albany he so impressed city leaders that they asked him to move there. In 1847 Willard married Caroline C. Cook; they had three children, one of whom, Ashbel P. Willard Jr., died at the age of three of scarlet fever.

During the gubernatorial campaign of 1856, the two candidates made numerous joint appearances throughout the state, concentrating their debates mainly on the same divisive issues that had dominated political discourse in the state two years earlier. The issue of slavery, though, took center stage because of vicious fighting in "Bleeding Kansas" and the beating of Charles Sumner in the U.S. Senate chambers by South Carolina congressman Preston Brooks. Morton argued against the Kansas-Nebraska law and the possibility of slavery gaining a foothold in the western territories, though he would not interfere with slavery where it existed, and he also favored the immediate admission of Kansas to the Union as a free state. Willard, as did his party, endorsed the Kansas-Nebraska Act, saying that the question of slavery in the territories was a matter of popular sovereignty and states' rights. To him, the main issue was the preservation of the Union, and he urged his audience at one gathering to take "shelter under the Democratic roof till the present storm of faction should subside."

By all accounts, Willard's strength as a politician was his brilliant oratory. An Indiana newspaper reporter, in a decidedly unflattering remembrance of Willard, nonetheless recalled being dazzled as a young boy listening to him during an appearance in New Albany during the 1856 campaign. The reporter wrote: "His vocabulary was wonderful. Boy as I was, I felt the influence and beauty of the flow of words, and though understanding little of the matters discussed, I could not refrain from joining in the shouts and applause. It was a delight to listen to him." A sympathetic biographer of Morton's, however, said that while "Willard appealed to passion, imagination and prejudice, Morton [appealed] to the intellect and conscience."

During the campaign, Democrats, stung by their defeat two years earlier, did resort to overt appeals to racism, charging that the People's Party favored abolition; amalgamation, or mixing of the races; and giving blacks full social and political equality. For example, it was reported that in one Democratic neighborhood in Dubois County, several young ladies, all dressed in white, marched through the streets with a banner that read, "Fathers, save us from nigger husbands!"

The results of the governor's race, which Willard won by nearly six thousand votes, aptly demonstrated the polarized nature of the state at the time, with Democrats generally prevailing in southern counties and candidates on the People's ticket winning in northern counties. Willard carried the entire state Democratic ticket into office with him, while the house was again controlled by Democrats and the senate narrowly by the People's Party. The election also gave Democrats a six to five edge in the state's congressional delegation.

As an underscore to his Southern sympathies, Willard made a post-election trip to Jackson, Mississippi, where in an address to the state legislature he affirmed his support of slavery in the South, promising to protect the rights of whites to own slaves and to uphold the Fugitive Slave Law by sending any slaves who escaped to Indiana back to their owners. Later, at a reception at the governor's mansion, Willard, whose excessive drinking was so notorious that he took a public vow of abstinence if elected governor, was pitted against the state's attorney general in a drinking contest. Though the Mississippi official was considered the "best, heaviest and solidest" drinker in the southwest, he apparently was no match for the governor-elect, who emerged, according to an eyewitness account, "as cool and clear-headed and as steady on his pins at the close of the banquet as he was at the commencement."

Willard's tenure as governor, which did not extend to its four-year completion due to his death in October of 1860, seemed ill-fated almost from the start. Willard himself had unwittingly created the first conflict with the divided state legislature by his partisan actions in 1855 when he was lieutenant governor and presiding officer of the senate. At issue was the election by the legislature of a successor to John Pettit, a Democrat whose term as U.S. Senator was expiring. The People's

Party controlled the house and therefore would hold a majority in a joint vote of both assemblies. The senate, however, with Willard casting a tie-breaking vote, refused to go into joint session, leaving Indiana with only one Senator for two years. In 1857, when it was again time for the legislature to elect Senators, the political equation had been reversed. Democrats, in control of the state house of representatives, would hold a majority in a joint ballot, but the People's Party now controlled the senate and turned the tables by voting against a resolution for a joint session. Undeterred, Democrats proceeded to reelect Jesse D. Bright to another six-year term and to elect Graham N. Fitch for a four-year term. Despite protests by the opposition that the elections were invalid, both men eventually took their seats in the U.S. Senate, though more than a year later.

Besides the ill will this battle over senatorial elections generated, the partisan wrangling also caused the legislative session to end without approval of necessary revenue and appropriations measures. As a result, Indiana faced defaulting on the interest payment of its debt and closing of the so-called benevolent institutions in the state, which cared for the disabled. In addressing the first problem, Willard borrowed the necessary funds to pay the interest after the attorney general advised him that the state's obligation to bondholders was a perpetual one that needed no direct appropriation. Willard resisted recommendations to call a special session of the legislature to resolve the other issue and instead drafted a resolution of questionable legitimacy signed by him and the other state officeholders—all Democrats—directing the state treasurer to advance the funds necessary to reopen what were then called the Indiana Asylum for the Insane and the Institutions for Educating the Deaf and Dumb and Blind.

As the nation edged closer to civil war, though, state issues took a backseat in public attention to slavery, especially developments in Kansas, where proslavery forces rammed through the Lecompton Constitution in late 1857 that would have made slavery there inevitable. Widely branded a fraud and a travesty of popular sovereignty, the Lecompton question further split the Democratic Party in Indiana and strengthened the opposition, which in 1858 officially became the Republican Party. Most Democrats in Indiana as well as a majority of the Democratic press in the state supported the anti-Lecompton position of Stephen A. Douglas, who broke with President James Buchanan on the issue. Willard, however, endorsed Buchanan's support of Lecompton.

Republicans in the off-year elections of 1858 capitalized on the public's hostility toward Lecompton by campaigning almost exclusively on the issue, and as a result, they won majorities in both the state house and the state senate as well as winning eight congressional seats compared with three for the Democrats. Although the new general assembly was now controlled by the opposition party, Willard nevertheless called for a special session and asked legislators to rectify the inaction by the previous assembly by enacting revenue bills for the state and to make changes in the law for appraising taxable properties to reflect increases in their value. Both of these measures passed, though the governor's proposal to build a new state penitentiary in the northern part of the state to relieve crowding at the Jeffersonville facility was rejected. In this session, the legislature also passed a measure to revise the method of electing U.S. Senators, but Willard vetoed it as unworkable and unconstitutional, and members were unable to override the veto.

During the regular legislative session of 1859, Willard won approval of his plan for a new state penitentiary, which would eventually be built at Michigan City. The governor was not successful, however, in getting the legislature to repeal the Horse Thief Associations Law, an 1852 act that permitted private companies to form and function as law enforcement officials with the power to arrest and recover stolen property. Many people had been arrested and punished by these associations without the benefit of being tried before courts of justice, Willard noted in making his case for repeal. Other supporters for eliminating the law cited instances of "cruelties, murders and unrelenting inhumanities" that were committed by such associations.

Also during the 1859 session, a senate committee investigating the operations of the swamplands program in the state concluded it was rife with corruption and mismanagement on the part of both county and state officials. As a result of congressional action in 1850, more than a million acres of federal land in Indiana had been ceded to the state to be reclaimed for use in farming. The state administered sales of such land and used proceeds for drainage projects and levees. By the fall of 1857, the program was steeped in controversy over questionable land sales, failure by some reclamation contractors to perform the work the state had paid them to do, and the hiring of dishonest and inept county swampland commissioners, who were responsible for overseeing reclamation projects. It was in this regard that the senate committee castigated Willard for appointing as a commissioner a county treasurer who had embezzled $100,000 in funds due to the state for land sales.

Willard's troubles in 1859, though, extended beyond the state capital. In what had to be a great source of anguish and embarrassment for the proslavery governor, his brother-in-law, John E. Cook, was one of the raiders captured with the abolitionist John Brown at Harpers Ferry. However, despite advice from political friends to distance himself from the case, Willard went to the aid of his wife's brother, enlisting the services of noted criminal lawyer Daniel W. Voorhees to defend Cook and then traveling with him to Charles Town in what is now West Virginia for the trial. Willard's intervention on Cook's behalf, which included testifying at his trial and seeking a pardon from the governor after the conviction, actually increased rather than diminished his political standing back home. Still, his efforts and the spirited defense by Voorhees failed to save Cook's life; he was hanged in mid-December of 1859.

Although a young man, Willard had been plagued by serious respiratory problems for some time and, in fact, had been near death in 1858. In the fall of 1860, while making a speech at a state Democratic meeting in Columbus, he was stricken by hemorrhaging of the lungs. On the advice of his physicians, Willard, not yet forty years old, went to Saint Paul, Minnesota, in an attempt to restore his health. About a month into his stay, he suffered a relapse and died on October 4, 1860, thus becoming the first Indiana governor to die in office.

Portrait by George W. Morrison (1857), Governors' Portraits Collection, Indiana Historical Bureau, State of Indiana.

FOR FURTHER READING

Foulke, William D. *Life of Oliver P. Morton: Including His Important Speeches.* Indianapolis: The Bowen-Merrill Company, 1899.

Haffner, Gerald O. *The Hoosier Governor, Ashbel P. Willard, and His Times.* New Albany: Indiana University Southeast Bookstore, 1980.

Indiana Biography Series. Vol. 4. Microfilm. Indiana State Library.

Madison, James H. *The Indiana Way: A State History.* Bloomington: Indiana University Press; Indianapolis: Indiana Historical Society, 1990.

Thornbrough, Emma Lou. *Indiana in the Civil War Era, 1850–1880.* Vol. 3, *The History of Indiana.* Indianapolis: Indiana Historical Bureau and Indiana Historical Society, 1965.

Van Bolt, Roger H. "The Rise of the Republican Party in Indiana, 1855–1856." *Indiana Magazine of History* 51 (September 1955): 185–200.

Woollen, William Wesley. *Biographical and Historical Sketches of Early Indiana.* Indianapolis: Hammond and Company, 1883.

Willard's gubernatorial papers are in the Indiana State Archives, Indianapolis.

Abram A. Hammond

October 4, 1860–January 14, 1861

JAMES E. ST. CLAIR

IF EVER THERE WAS AN ACCIDENTAL GOVERNOR OF INDIANA, it was Abram A. Hammond, the state's twelfth chief executive. As lieutenant governor, he ascended to the office in the fall of 1860 following the death of Ashbel P. Willard, who had about three months remaining in his term. Hammond was not supposed to be Willard's running mate in 1856 in the first place, the nomination instead having gone to John C. Walker of La Porte County at the party's state convention.

However, according to most accounts, Walker later withdrew after it was discovered that he was too young to hold office, and party leaders picked Hammond. The real reason for the switch, other versions assert, is that the Democrats wanted to counter the successful coalition building of the surging People's Party by adding an old-line Whig like Hammond to the ticket. In any event, he defeated Conrad Baker for lieutenant governor by some five thousand votes.

Hammond, who was born in Brattleboro, Vermont, on March 21, 1814, to Nathaniel and Patty Ball Hammond, moved to Brookville, Indiana, with his parents when he was six years old. After completing a common school education, Hammond studied law with a local attorney, was admitted to the bar in 1835, and began practicing law in Greenfield in Hancock County, where he stayed for five years. In 1838 Hammond married Mary Ansden. They had one daughter. Beginning in 1840, Hammond began a fifteen-year odyssey that involved moving his practice to Columbus, Indianapolis, Cincinnati, back to Indianapolis, and then to San Francisco. During this period he served

briefly as pros- ecuting attorney in Columbus and judge of the Marion County Com- mon Pleas court. By 1855 Hammond was back in Indiana, setting up a law firm in Terre Haute.

On the great issue of the day, slavery, Hammond held the same views as his predecessor—that is, he supported the ownership of slaves as a constitutionally protected right to property, and he favored admitting Kansas to the Union under the Lecompton Constitution, which was tantamount to extending slavery westward. In his first and only message to the Indiana General Assembly in January 1861, Hammond made it clear that he valued preservation of the Union above all else, and he recommended that Indiana send representatives to a convention of border states to try to avert, in his words, "the horrors of disunion and civil war." At the subsequent so-called Peace Congress, all of Indiana's delegates voted against the most notable resolution offered there, the Crittenden Compromise, which offered major concessions to the South.

In his message to legislators, Hammond also proposed creating a subtreasury as an alternative to depositing state funds in banks and building a reformatory school for boys. The proposal for the former passed the legislature, while the latter did not, though a later general assembly did approve the establishment of what eventually became the Indiana Boys' School at Plainfield.

Hammond was not a candidate for governor in 1860, the party having nominated Thomas A. Hendricks in January of that year, well before Willard's death and Hammond's assumption of office. After his brief service as governor, Hammond continued to live and work in Indianapolis, though his health over time deteriorated. He suffered from rheumatism and asthma and walked with crutches. Believing that the warmer and drier climate out west might improve his condition, Hammond moved his family to Denver, Colorado. He died there on August 27, 1874. His body was returned to Indiana, and he is buried in Crown Hill Cemetery in Indianapolis.

Portrait by John Bayless Hill (1869), Governors' Portraits Collection, Indiana Historical Bureau, State of Indiana.

FOR FURTHER READING

Calhoun, Charles W. "'Incessant Noise and Tumult': Walter Q. Gresham and the Indiana Legislature during the Secession Crisis." *Indiana Magazine of History* 74 (September 1978): 223–51.

Post, Margaret Moore. *First Ladies of Indiana and the Governor, 1816–1984.* Indianapolis: Pierson Printing Company, 1984.

Woollen, William Wesley. *Biographical and Historical Sketches of Early Indiana.* Indianapolis: Hammond and Company, 1883.

Hammond's gubernatorial papers are in the Indiana State Archives, Indianapolis.

Henry S. Lane

January 14–16, 1861

JAMES E. ST. CLAIR

THE BRIEF TENURE OF INDIANA'S THIRTEENTH GOVERNOR, Henry S. Lane, was by design. Two strong candidates, Lane and Oliver P. Morton, were in contention for the Republican Party's nomination for governor in 1860. Lane, a stalwart in Indiana politics who had been instrumental in the founding of the state's party, and Morton, who had run a strong race for governor four years earlier, worked out a compromise to avoid a bruising battle over the nomination that might have jeopardized their party's chances in the fall election. Under the arrangement, Morton agreed to run as lieutenant governor but would become governor in the event that Republicans gained control of the Indiana General Assembly and in turn would then elect Lane to the U.S. Senate. The desired outcome having been achieved in the election, Lane resigned as governor just two days after being sworn in.

The statewide tickets in 1860 of the Republican and Democratic parties were stellar. Lane, besides his key role in the formation of Indiana's Republican Party, was a prominent figure in national Republican politics. He delivered the keynote address at the party's first national convention in Philadelphia in 1856 and was made convention chairman. Four years later, when the party met in Chicago, he helped engineer the nomination of Abraham Lincoln for president. Morton, best known as Indiana's legendary Civil War governor, later served for ten years in the U.S. Senate. On the Republican ticket in 1860 as candidate for reporter of the supreme court was a future

president, Ben-jamin Harrison. The Democratic candidates were Thomas A. Hen-dricks for gover-nor, David Turpie for lieutenant governor, and Michael C. Kerr for supreme court reporter. Hendricks, eventually elected governor on his third try, was vice president of the United States in Grover Cleveland's administration. Turpie, one of the state's most distinguished lawyers, was elected to two terms in the U.S. Senate. Kerr, who had served in the state legislature prior to his race for reporter, went on to become Speaker of the U.S. House of Representatives.

Lane's only message as governor to the state legislature came during a time of great public anxiety as Southern states, led by the actions of South Carolina, began seceding from the Union. He called secession a "dangerous heresy, fraught with all the terrible consequences of civil war and bloodshed, and leading directly to the utter ruin of all our institutions," adding, "This heresy has not yet poisoned the public sentiment of Indiana, and may God, in his kind providence, put afar off the evil day which shall witness its prevalence amongst us." Even at this late, dark hour, Lane, a native of Kentucky and ardent admirer of Henry Clay, "The Great Compromiser," seemed to hold out hope that war was not inevitable. He believed Southerners had been misled about the intentions of the newly elected Lincoln administration, claiming that it would not make war upon "the interests and institutions of the Southern people." Offering Indiana as an example of Northern amity, Lane said, "Whatever may be the condition of public sentiment in other sections of the Union, the people of our State would favor an amicable settlement of the existing difficulties between the different parts of the Republic."

A former Whig, Lane was elected to the Indiana House of Representatives in 1837 and served in Congress from 1840 to 1843. In the imbroglio over U.S. Senate elections in 1857 and 1858, Lane and William M. McCarty were elected when Republicans held the upper hand in the general assembly and Democrats Jesse D. Bright and Graham N. Fitch when their party dominated. When presented with both slates of candidates, the state senate, at the time firmly controlled by Democrats, elected to seat Bright and Fitch.

Lane was born on February 24, 1811, on a farm near Sharpsburg, Kentucky, in Bath County to James H. and Mary Higgins Lane. Educated by tutors in his home, he later studied law and was admitted to the bar at Mount Sterling, Kentucky, in 1832. In 1835 he and his first wife, Pamela Bledsoe, whom he married in 1833, moved to Crawfordsville, Indiana, where he opened a law practice. She died in 1842 from injuries suffered when the stagecoach she and Lane were in plunged over a cliff in Washington, D.C. In 1845 Lane married Joanna M. Elston, daughter of a prominent Indiana banker and businessman. When the United States declared war on Mexico in 1846, Lane organized a company of volunteers and was named major of the First Indiana Regiment and later promoted to lieutenant colonel. He served until 1848, though he and his men were never engaged in any battles.

In his one largely undistinguished Senate term, Lane, as expected, was fully supportive of Lincoln and the Union cause. At the end of his term in 1867, he returned to Crawfordsville, though he did not divorce himself completely from public service. He served on two commissions, one on Indian affairs and the other on improving the Mississippi River, as well as attending the Republican national conventions as a delegate in 1868 and 1872. He was also a delegate at the so-called Loyalist Convention of 1866 in Philadelphia that attempted to heal the breach between the Republican Party and President Andrew

Johnson over his Reconstruction policies. Lane died in Crawfordsville in 1881.

Portrait by Jacob Cox (1869), Governors' Portraits Collection, Indiana Historical Bureau, State of Indiana.

FOR FURTHER READING

"Governor Lane's Inaugural." *New Albany Daily Ledger,* January 15, 1861.

Montgomery County Historical Society. "Henry Smith Lane (1811–1881)." http://www.lane-mchs.org/lane.html.

Woodburn, James A. "Henry Smith Lane." *Indiana Magazine of History* 27 (December 1931): 279–87.

Woollen, William Wesley. *Biographical and Historical Sketches of Early Indiana.* Indianapolis: Hammond and Company, 1883.

Lane's papers are in the Lilly Library, Indiana University, Bloomington.

Oliver P. Morton

January 16, 1861–January 23, 1867

ED RUNDEN

TO ADMIRERS, OLIVER P. MORTON WAS A STRONG, DECISIVE, and effective leader, most notably during the Civil War, and one of the state's greatest governors. To detractors, he was a crafty opportunist who shifted positions according to the prevailing political winds and a power-hungry schemer who used questionable tactics to assemble and perpetuate his political machine. Whether knight or knave, though, Morton was the dominant figure of Indiana politics from his assumption of the governor's office in early 1861 to his death in late 1877.

Oliver Hazard Perry Throck Morton was born in the frontier settlement of Salisbury in Wayne County on August 4, 1823, to James Throck and Sarah Miller Morton. Morton's mother died when he was three years old, and he was raised by two staunchly religious aunts on a farm in southwestern Ohio. Their fervent beliefs may have contributed to Morton's later lack of interest in religion. As an adult he maintained no formal religious connection, unusual for that time.

The young Morton later returned to eastern Indiana, rejoining his family in Centerville, where they had moved after Salisbury failed to develop as a community. He left school at the age of fifteen to become an apothecary's clerk as the first step toward becoming a doctor. This job ended quickly following a dispute with the druggist. Morton next worked as a hatter's apprentice, but quit to enter Miami University in Oxford, Ohio, where he studied for two years. He left the university to study law in 1846 and within a short time was admitted to the Indiana bar at Centerville, where he practiced law

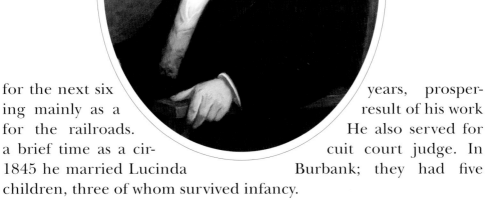

for the next six years, prospering mainly as a result of his work
for the railroads. He also served for
a brief time as a cir- cuit court judge. In
1845 he married Lucinda Burbank; they had five
children, three of whom survived infancy.

The state's fourteenth governor, he was the first to be born in Indiana. Morton began in politics as an antislavery Democrat but was expelled from the party at the Indiana state convention in 1854 for his opposition to the Kansas-Nebraska Act (which had made it possible for slavery to be extended into the western territories). He then joined with other anti-Nebraska Democrats in an amalgam of factions, including the temperance and nativism movements, to form the People's Party, the forerunner of Indiana's Republican Party.

In 1856 Morton ran for governor on the People's Party ticket, but lost to Democrat Ashbel P. Willard by about six thousand votes. Four years later Morton was the Republican candidate for lieutenant governor and became governor shortly after the election when the winning gubernatorial candidate, Henry S. Lane, was elected to the U.S. Senate by the Republican legislature as part of a prearranged deal.

Almost immediately Morton had to confront the fast-moving chain of events leading to the Civil War. His actions as chief executive and party boss during the tumultuous war years and the Reconstruction period illustrate how assessments of Morton have varied widely.

Morton was one of Abraham Lincoln's most capable and resourceful war governors, aggressively and successfully raising troops; supplying soldiers with uniforms, arms, and munitions; and ensuring treatment for the wounded. According to historian Emma Lou Thornbrough, "The role of the war governors was of crucial importance, and no governor played his role more valiantly or effectively than did Morton."

On the other hand, he was just as aggressive and successful in using the war as a way of amassing power, even if it sometimes meant using extraconstitutional means. Morton attempted to squelch dissent to his policies from Democrats and even members of his own party by branding as traitors those who questioned his actions. He used the existence of secret pro-Confederacy societies in the state to his political advantage, exaggerating their threat and insinuating they were part and parcel of the Democratic Party. One historian concluded, "Morton had zeal and ingenuity and administrative skill, but his emotions were unstable, and he was frequently filled with unwarranted terror." Even Lincoln was moved to remark, "Morton is a good fellow, but at times he is the skeeredest man I know of."

The plus side of Morton's Civil War ledger as governor is extensive. In late 1860 and early 1861, a period when many politicians vacillated, he was a strong voice of resolve, declaring the time for compromise and concession had passed and that it was essential to begin preparing for war. In a speech a few months prior to Fort Sumter, he said, "If it was worth a bloody struggle to establish this nation, it is worth one to preserve it." Visiting Lincoln in Washington, D.C., shortly before the outbreak of war, Morton assured the president of Indiana's support for the use of force to preserve the Union. When war did come and Lincoln issued his call for seventy-five thousand volunteers, Morton responded by offering to raise ten thousand in Indiana alone.

The state continued to be a reliable source of manpower throughout the war. In fact, Indiana ranked second in the percentage of men of military age to serve in the Union army during the war, contributing nearly two hundred thousand men to the cause. While most volunteered for service, some were paid bonuses ranging from $100 to $300 to enlist and a few thousand others were drafted. In addition, more than one hundred thousand served in the Indiana Legion, or state militia, which was formed to guard against internal threats and raids into the state, especially by Confederate troops crossing the Ohio River from Kentucky into southern Indiana.

Besides raising troops, Morton also took on the task of equipping them with arms, munitions, and uniforms. When the war started, Indiana had only a few thousand guns, most of which were outdated, and national arsenals were similarly ill-stocked. Consequently, Morton dispatched his own agents to scour this country and Europe to buy arms and equipment. In May 1861 a special session of the legislature appropriated $500,000 for this initiative and authorized the governor to borrow funds for additional purchases if needed. Acting on his own and without legislative authority, Morton established a state arsenal to manufacture ammunition. The facility employed as many as seven hundred workers and operated until April 1864.

Morton's concern for the welfare of Indiana troops continued after they left the state. He often visited training camps and battle-fields, sent aides to investigate the needs of soldiers in the field, frequently corresponded with officers of state regiments, and created a much-admired system of relief and medical care. Prominent in the effort to provide comfort and care to Hoosier soldiers was the Indiana Sanitary Commission, a vast voluntary organization that collected and distributed "foodstuffs, clothing, bedding, bandages, soap, whisky, wine, tobacco, writing papers, Bibles, and other books" to troops on the battlefield and in hospitals. According to one historian, "This state enterprise was close to the heart of Governor Morton, and he fostered it with meticulous care." The governor also established hospitals near battlefields to care for wounded soldiers who could not be returned to the state for treatment in Indiana hospitals. For all his efforts in behalf of the troops, Morton became known as the "soldiers' friend," an appellation he both "cherished and deserved."

Just as he worked hard to capture the hearts and minds of soldiers, Morton also endeavored to win over, or at least neutralize, political opposition. Here he revealed some of his rougher characteristics. At the outset of the war, he repeatedly called for an end to partisan politics and tried to unite Republicans and Democrats under the big tent of a Union organization. Some prominent Democrats responded to Morton's overture to join the Union movement, and he did appoint a number of Democrats to military positions. His most conspicuous show of unity was to name former Democratic governor Joseph A. Wright to the U.S. Senate in 1862 to replace Jesse D. Bright, who had been expelled for Confederate sympathies.

While Republicans praised the appointment as proof that Morton was sincere about the Union movement, many Democrats termed Wright a turncoat and "charged that Morton's nonpartisanship was in reality a device for weakening the Democratic party and building up the Republican." As the election year of 1862 gained steam, it became clear that the tenuous political unity formed following Fort Sumter was dissipating in the heat of the campaign.

Morton launched the first strike at the Republican-Union state convention that summer when he made the dramatic announcement that Indiana was infested by secret treasonable societies, and he obliquely implied that Democrats were involved. A few months later a federal grand jury, meeting in Indianapolis, issued a report on disloyal activities that seemed to buttress Morton's assertions, but the findings were suspect given that all the members of the jury were Republicans. A report on its findings included rumors published as facts, and it was printed and distributed as campaign material. The issue, however, failed to gain traction as dissatisfaction with the Lincoln and Morton administrations mounted. In particular, the concerns included military reversals that seemed to portent a much longer war than had been anticipated; additional calls for manpower including the imposition of a draft; an increase in tariffs; and limiting of personal liberties by the suspension of habeas corpus and the arrest of civilians by military authorities.

What sealed the Republicans' fate came in the waning days of the campaign when Lincoln issued his Emancipation Proclamation. The reaction was immediate and hostile among a majority of Hoosiers, who fervently supported the war to preserve the Union, but who were just as adamant that it not be turned into a crusade against slavery. Election results were decisive for Democrats, as the party's slate of state officers won by more than nine thousand votes, seven of the eleven congressional races went to Democrats, and the party controlled both houses of the state legislature by substantial margins. When the Indiana General Assembly convened in 1863, it did so in what has been described as "perhaps the harshest" political atmosphere in the state's history.

By his actions, Morton ensured there would be fireworks. He first planted stories in the Republican press that the Democrats had "plans for secession, armed uprisings, and sabotage" and, ignoring custom, he refused to appear in person to address a joint session of the legislature, releasing his message instead to the press and sending copies to each chamber. In return, Democrats devoted much of the session to attacking Morton and Lincoln, specifically denouncing emancipation, the loss of constitutional rights, and economic policies.

A meltdown between the two sides came when the Democrats drafted legislation to curtail Morton's patronage and his power over the state militia. To prevent action on the bill, Republican legislators bolted to break the quorum and fled to Madison, with Morton's approval, so they could cross the Ohio River into Kentucky if an attempt were made to force their return. The session ended without any significant legislation including appropriation bills being passed. With no spending measures enacted, Democrats expected Morton to call for a special session, but it never came, and the general assembly did not convene for almost two years.

Instead, Morton, through extralegal and extraconstitutional means, raised the necessary money to operate the state without legislative authorization, becoming a virtual dictator. He was able to accumulate more than a million dollars by borrowing from banks, using profits from the state arsenal, tapping into a War Department fund, and appealing to Republican county officials and private individuals for money. The governor kept funds in a safe in his office and created his own bureau of finance to disperse payments, bypassing the state treasurer and auditor, both of whom were Democrats. When Democrats raged against his actions, Morton resorted to his familiar tactic of branding his critics as treasonous rebel sympathizers and justifying his conduct "in terms of a patriotic desire to save the nation from its enemies." This constant drumbeat of accusation had the desired effect of blunting criticism and keeping public opinion on Morton's side.

Morton's scare tactics could not work indefinitely and the Union cause was buoyed when General John Hunt Morgan's Confederate cavalry raid into southern Indiana in July 1863 failed to result in a rising of pro-Confederate Hoosiers. The raid ended in failure, and Morgan was captured.

With his alarms of imminent internal insurrection fading and aware that Hoosiers were growing impatient for a resolution to the conflict, an anxious Morton wrote to Lincoln in early 1864 that political considerations "demand that the war shall be substantially ended within the present year." Morton also confronted a split in his party. Radical Republicans, led by the governor's perennial foe and outspoken abolitionist, George W. Julian, were dissatisfied with the moderate plan of reconstruction that had been outlined by Lincoln, while other Republicans were unhappy with the president's conduct of the war.

At the Republican-Union state convention in early 1864, however, Lincoln and Morton supporters acted before dissention could mobilize and sped through resolutions instructing delegates to the national convention to vote for Lincoln and proposing the nomination of Morton for governor by acclamation. The question of whether Morton was eligible to serve another term under the state constitution's limit of one four-year term within an eight-year period was brushed aside by the argument that he had been elected lieutenant governor, not governor, in 1860.

As they approached the election season, Indiana Democrats believed that their prospects were promising, given the prevailing gloom caused by dismal war news. The party selected Joseph E. McDonald, a lawyer and former attorney general, to oppose Morton. Neither he nor the party were a match for the wily Morton, whose quick moves crushed the opposition. The governor's masterstroke came by ostensibly demonstrating that the state Democratic Party had indeed harbored Confederate conspirators. This resulted from an episode, highly publicized and timed for maximum political effect, involving minor and fringe Democratic politicians, a secret society called the Sons of Liberty, and a plan to seize the state arsenal and release Confederate prisoners being held in Indianapolis. When Democratic leaders, including gubernatorial candidate McDonald, learned of the scheme, they said they were shocked that such a treasonable act was in the works and prevailed upon the plotters to call it off.

Morton, meanwhile, was fully informed of the plot by aides who had infiltrated the Sons of Liberty. Rather than acting beforehand to stop the conspirators, however, he waited until after the date set for the insurrection had passed to make his move. The leader of the group, Harrison H. Dodd, and his alleged accomplices were arrested, charged with treason, and tried before a military court, all developments that Morton used in his campaign.

The governor used other maneuvers to bolster his election chances, including pleading with Lincoln, in letters and visits to Washington, to arrange leaves for fifteen thousand Indiana troops so they could return home to vote, presumably for Morton, the "soldiers' friend." General William T. Sherman's counterargument that military considerations trumped political ones was more persuasive with the president, and few Hoosiers were furloughed. Morton had better luck in getting sick and wounded soldiers returned home in time to vote. He dispatched special agents to field hospitals to identify such troops and to arrange for their transportation back to Indiana. In all, some nine thousand were returned for the purpose of voting.

When Morton's campaign tactics were combined with Union gains on the battlefield, the race for governor turned into a rout. The incumbent beat his challenger by a margin of more than twenty thousand votes, and Republicans regained control of the general assembly while capturing eight of the eleven congressional seats. Even though the surrender at Appomattox came a few months after the election, Morton continued to find ways to exact political advantage from the war.

He still hammered Democrats as traitors, saying in a speech in 1866 that the "party may be described as a common sewer and loathsome receptacle, into which is emptied every element of treason North and South." Morton also persuaded the War Department to require that Indiana troops be discharged in Indianapolis instead of in Washington, as had been planned, so that he could stage and preside over elaborate homecoming celebrations for returning regiments. In addition, the governor actively promoted the growth of the Grand Army of the Republic in Indiana, a veterans organization that became in effect an adjunct of the Republican Party.

Morton served only two years of his second term, and for part of that time he was in Europe, where, on the advice of doctors, he had gone to rest and to seek a cure for the paralysis in the lower part of his body he suffered as the result of a stroke in the fall of 1865. Shortly after the 1867 legislature convened, Morton was elected to the U.S. Senate, an action even a few Republicans opposed, believing him to be ineligible to be elected while he was governor. Morton was reelected to the Senate in 1873 and served there until he died in 1877 in Indianapolis after suffering another stroke.

On the great issues following the war, Morton's performance followed a complicated trajectory as he abandoned centrist positions for far more liberal ones. Typical explanations given for this include sheer opportunism, a realization "the radicals were the real power in his party," and presidential aspirations. The shift was especially dramatic on the question of suffrage for African Americans. In his Richmond, Indiana, speech of September 29, 1865, while still governor, Morton argued African Americans were not ready to vote, saying it was inconceivable that people who had just been freed from slavery should be given "the full exercise of political power, not only to govern themselves and their neighbors, but to take part in the government of the United States."

Yet as senator four years later, in what his old adversary Julian called "a sudden and splendid somersault," Morton played a significant role in advancing through Congress the Fifteenth Amendment that guaranteed voting rights for African Americans. Morton also returned to Indianapolis to engineer the amendment's ratification by the state legislature. When Democrats resigned en masse to prevent consideration of the amendment, Morton devised a legal rationale for Republicans to act without a quorum present.

Similarly, Morton did an about-face on Reconstruction, switching from a position of support for President Andrew Johnson's cautious and generous approach to the restoration of Southern states to one of demanding harsh and uncompromising terms for readmission to the Union. He also zigzagged on the issue of currency contraction, which meant withdrawing greenbacks, so-called soft money, from circulation in favor of returning to specie, or gold and silver payment of debts. In 1868 he introduced a bill in the Senate for the resumption of specie payment; later he argued against rapid contraction of the currency, influenced most likely by hard economic times following the panic of 1873; and he returned to his original position in 1875 by voting for the Resumption of Specie Payment Act.

Morton was a serious contender for the Republican nomination for president in 1876 and was overwhelmingly endorsed by African American officeholders shortly before the party's national convention in Cincinnati. He placed second on the first round of balloting. He withdrew his name after the sixth ballot, and the majority of Indiana's delegates cast their votes for Ohio governor Rutherford B. Hayes, the party's eventual candidate. Morton did help decide who would become president as a member of the specially created and Republican-dominated Electoral Commission that was established to settle the disputed election between Hayes and Democrat Samuel J. Tilden, who had won a plurality of more than 250,000 votes. The fifteen-member commission, voting eight to seven along party lines to give Hayes every contested electoral vote, declared him the winner in the Electoral College tally by one vote, 185 to 184.

Portrait by Theodore Clement Steele (1916), Governors' Portraits Collection, Indiana Historical Bureau, State of Indiana.

FOR FURTHER READING

Foulke, William Dudley. *Life of Oliver P. Morton, Including His Important Speeches.* 2 vols. Indianapolis: Bowen-Merrill Company, 1899.

Hesseltine, William B. *Lincoln and the War Governors.* New York: Alfred A. Knopf, 1948.

Madison, James H. *The Indiana Way: A State History.* Bloomington: Indiana University Press; Indianapolis: Indiana Historical Society, 1986.

Morris, Roy Jr. *Fraud of the Century: Rutherford B. Hayes, Samuel Tilden, and the Stolen Election of 1876.* New York: Simon and Schuster, 2003.

Stampp, Kenneth M. *Indiana Politics during the Civil War.* Indianapolis: Indiana Historical Bureau, 1949. Reprint, with new preface by author, Bloomington: Indiana University Press, 1978.

Stoll, John B. *History of the Indiana Democracy, 1816–1916.* Indianapolis: Indiana Democratic Publishing Company, 1917.

Sylvester, Lorna Lutes. "Oliver P. Morton and Hoosier Politics during the Civil War." PhD diss., Indiana University, 1968.

Thornbrough, Emma Lou. *Indiana in the Civil War Era, 1850–1880.* Vol. 3, *The History of Indiana.* Indianapolis: Indiana Historical Bureau, 1965.

Walsh, Justin E. *The Centennial History of the Indiana General Assembly, 1816–1978.* Indianapolis: The Select Committee on the Centennial History of the Indiana General Assembly, 1987.

Morton's papers are in the Indiana State Library, Indianapolis.

Conrad Baker

January 23, 1867–January 13, 1873

RANDALL T. SHEPARD

CONRAD BAKER SPENT MUCH OF HIS POLITICAL CAREER standing just behind the larger-than-life figure of Oliver P. Morton, and the record of popular history has treated him as barely visible in Morton's shadow. Any fair look at Baker's contributions to the Civil War and to the era following it, however, leads inevitably to the conclusion that he not only made Morton's fame possible but also laid foundations for much of the state's progress through the balance of the nineteenth century and beyond.

In fields such as corrections, education, and the rights of women, Baker created a new state government readily recognizable more than a century later. By the time he left office, there was a House of Refuge for wayward boys at Plainfield, separate penal facilities for women and girls at Indianapolis, new universities at Terre Haute and West Lafayette, the state's first office building, and a home for veterans and their orphans at Knightstown. Though Baker's political light has faded, his name survives prominently in Baker & Daniels, the Indianapolis law firm he built with his gubernatorial successor, Thomas A. Hendricks.

Baker was born on a farm near Chambersburgh, Pennsylvania, on February 12, 1817, the son of Presbyterian farmers Conrad and Catherine Winterheimer Baker. He worked on the farm to the age of fifteen, then undertook collegiate study at what is now Gettysburg College. He left before graduating to read law in the office of Thaddeus Stevens, who was later famous as a leader of the "radical Republicans" who so tormented President Andrew Johnson in the years after the Civil War. Baker began

his own law prac-tice in 1839 at Gettysburg.

While studying in the Stevens office, Baker married Matilda Escon Sommers in 1838. The couple had two children before she died in 1855. Three years later, Baker married Charlotte Frances Chute, with whom he had four children, including a son they named Thaddeus.

The practice in Gettysburg lasted only until 1841, when the Bakers joined the general move westward in search of greater opportunity and settled in Evansville, Indiana. Besides building his law practice, Baker took an immediate interest in Evansville's civic and political affairs. He ran successfully in the election of 1845 as the Whig candidate to represent Vanderburgh County in the Indiana House of Representatives. This political service led to his election in 1852 as judge of the court of common pleas for Vanderburgh and Warrick counties, a post he held for about two years. Baker's local ascendancy paralleled that of his brother William, who launched a municipal career in the 1850s and became the only person to be elected mayor of Evansville four times.

"Judge" Baker was fresh off the bench when the new Republican Party put its first state ticket before the voters in 1856: Oliver P. Morton for governor and Conrad Baker for lieutenant governor. It was the same team that would prove so successful just eight years later, but 1856 proved to be a Democratic year. (Morton became governor in early 1861, moving up from lieutenant governor after Henry S. Lane resigned the office upon election to the U.S. Senate.)

When the Civil War broke out, Baker was still practicing law in Evansville. At a rally, called by Mayor William Baker for April 17, Conrad Baker proposed a resolution to the enormous crowd assembled that day at the county courthouse: "Our time, talents, fortunes, and lives are at the service of the government at this time of trial . . . without reference to the men or party by which it may be administered." There was a "wild demonstration of approval," and Baker administered a makeshift oath to those present.

The brothers set about the task of raising a regiment from the counties along the river. Conrad became a colonel in the First Cavalry and spent the early years of the war leading a regiment in the southwestern states. The correspondence and cable traffic between Baker and Morton was substantial. It suggested that Baker's special talent was not tactics but organization and a no-nonsense approach to the task at hand. When a soldier in the regiment complained directly to Morton about the food, Baker replied that he had made some changes and that as for the complainant, "I shall issue him double rations for a week . . . and insist on his eating them."

Baker eventually returned to Indianapolis to take up an appointment as assistant provost marshal. This assignment consisted chiefly of leading the recruiting drive for Indiana's enormous contribution of men to the Union armies, one of the very things for which the Morton administration became so famous. "I tender to you 50,000 men," Morton replied to Abraham Lincoln's first call for troops.

Morton had served nearly four years without a lieutenant governor when the Morton-Baker pair again went to the voters in 1864. Their victory margin of some twenty thousand votes was then considered a statewide landslide.

The Republican victory celebration of that year had hardly subsided when Morton suffered a paralytic stroke. The fact of his illness was apparent to all as he opened a special session of the legislature in November 1865 by delivering his address while seated, something that became rather common for him thereafter. Morton decided to travel to Paris to see a physician who had treated Charles Sumner, the abolitionist senator from Massachusetts, for a similar affliction, and informed the general assembly that Baker would administer the executive department during his absence. Morton left for Washington, visited with President Johnson, and then went to New York and on to Paris.

The five months of Baker's temporary leadership provided state government with a very different style of leadership. When Morton returned from Paris and the Republican majority elected him U.S. Senator in January 1867, a fight arose over the sentiments to be contained in commemorating resolutions of the legislature. Democrats were prepared to vote for resolutions that spoke well of Baker, but could not abide saying nice things about Morton.

Baker's service as acting governor featured the sort of groundbreaking plans that later characterized his own gubernatorial years. He launched a series of institutions that are still central to Indiana's life. Most dramatically, he laid the groundwork for two centers of higher education. Baker believed that an educated populace was crucial to the state's development. There needed to be more and better teachers, he believed, and accomplishing this goal required creation of a normal school.

There had been talk for nearly a decade about this need, but nothing ever came of it until Baker took office as acting governor. Baker was especially committed to ensuring that the school would focus on the students who were fixed on teaching careers, rather than on people who would use the normal school as a path to some other line of work. He let it be known that his decision on location would depend in part on what community was willing to make the best offer. The people of Terre Haute proved the most energetic suitors, and the result was that the institution now known as Indiana State University opened in 1870. He used the opening of the school to urge that Indiana's schools and universities be open for the advancement of women in education. Baker's views on the rights of women were strong ones for the time. In 1873 he transmitted a memorial of the American Woman Suffrage Association, saying, "I am willing to give my vote and influence in favor of conferring the right of suffrage on the women of Indiana."

Baker likewise saw opportunity for higher education in the act by which Congress transferred tens of thousands of acres to the states, which would in turn sell the public lands and use the proceeds to establish what became known as land-grant colleges. While Baker was acting governor, the general assembly voted to accept this gift for the benefit of agricultural and mechanical arts education. In his 1869 address to the legislature, Baker, by then elected to the office in his own right, declared support for the creation of an agricultural college, though he expressed doubt about whether the money then available was sufficient to the task. This declaration virtually crossed in the mail with the remarkable offer of John Purdue, who volunteered to donate $150,000 to the project so long as the college was located in Tippecanoe County and bore his name. Baker signed legislation setting this plan in motion in May 1869, and Purdue University opened soon after Baker left office.

Baker was also a leader in what today would be called corrections reform. Especially troubled by the conditions under which youth and women lived in the state's prisons, he allied himself with reformers such as the Quakers in pursuing more humane and effective institutions.

Baker was especially energized about creating a House of Refuge, something mandated by the 1851 constitution but never implemented. He urged action on this front while acting governor and raised the issue anew when he became governor. The legislature finally appropriated funds to launch the project, and Baker threw himself personally into details such as identifying and purchasing the necessary land. He eventually consummated the sale of land at Plainfield, and the institution known during much of its history as the Indiana Boys' School opened at the beginning of 1868 with inmates whose prison terms Baker commuted so that they could be transferred.

He was likewise dissatisfied with the conditions under which girls and women were incarcerated in the state prisons. On this, too, he allied himself with women's groups and other social reformers. The resulting political effort led to adoption of legislation creating a women's prison and a reformatory for girls located at a joint site in Indianapolis. As with the boys school, Baker pressed regularly for funds to complete this effort, and in the fall after Baker left office a new facility opened to receive inmates previously held at the Jeffersonville prison.

Baker was also the force behind the creation of an institution that would have tugged on the hearts of all citizens of the time: a place for disabled veterans of the Civil War and the many orphans the war produced. This was a project urged by Morton before leaving for Washington but never acted upon. Baker arranged for establishing the Soldiers' and Seamans' Home at Knightstown and guided its successful completion. After certain of its facilities were lost to fire in 1871, the Knightstown house became a place for orphans alone. The Indiana Soldiers' and Sailors' Children's Home continues to serve children in need some 130 years later.

The most contentious political issue during the Baker administration involved Indiana's ratification of the Civil War amendments to the U.S. Constitution. Indiana Democrats resisted all three of these. The Thirteenth Amendment, abolishing slavery, was ratified over their opposition while Baker was acting governor. Democrats also opposed the Fourteenth Amendment, designed to extend civil rights to blacks, when it was ratified in January 1867.

These debates were but a warm-up for the struggle over the Fifteenth Amendment, which assured blacks the right to vote. Baker submitted the proposed amendment to the legislature in March 1869. Democrats held a minority position in both houses and had no hope of winning in a vote on the merits. Their plan to block ratification was a dramatic one: the Democratic members of both houses resigned so that the quorum requirement of two-thirds could not be met. Baker immediately called special elections to replace those who had resigned. The voters in the affected districts promptly returned the same members to Indianapolis.

Baker placed the Fifteenth Amendment before the legislature again in May 1869. The Democratic position was unchanged. "We and the Democratic Party stand upon terms of bitter and undying

hostility. We ask no quarter and we give no quarter," said one prominent Democrat.

Democrat legislators once again resigned to prevent a quorum.
This time the Republican members met and voted to ratify the amendment anyway, taking the position that the constitutional requirement
for a two-thirds quorum meant two-thirds of those members holding
office. The Republicans ruling in Washington, of course, received
Indiana's ratification warmly, undeterred by claims of constitutional
irregularities. When Democrats later gained control of the Indiana
General Assembly, they voted to rescind Indiana's ratification, but it
was too late; the right of blacks to vote had become part of the U.S.
Constitution by then.

The Governors' Portraits Collection is yet another hallmark of Baker's legacy. In his 1869 legislative address, he observed that the state
had but a single such portrait and urged an appropriation so that the
state library might display such a collection. The legislature approved
up to $200 for each portrait, and Baker began by engaging an artist
who had painted a particularly effective image of his brother, William,
the mayor of Evansville. In the ensuing years, Baker personally corresponded with various other artists to begin building the collection
and wrote the families of former governors asking for photographs or
older portraits that could provide the basis for this collection.

Baker's career after leaving the governor's office took an ironic but
positive turn. He joined the law practice launched by his friend and
political opponent, Thomas Hendricks, whom Baker had defeated
during the 1868 election by a mere 961 votes, the closest contest in
history.

Hendricks had opened an office in Indianapolis in 1863 and associated himself with Attorney General Oscar B. Hord. They were joined
briefly by former Supreme Court justice Samuel E. Perkins. When
Hendricks was elected governor in 1872, he went to the statehouse
and Baker went to the law firm, which became Baker, Hord, and Hendricks. He stayed there until his death. Baker's son Albert and a lawyer named Edward Daniels left the firm to set up shop next door. All
the founders of Baker, Hord, and Hendricks died during the 1880s,

and the young Baker and Daniels assumed responsibility for the firm's business, which began operating under their name in 1888. It has long since become one of the nation's leading law firms, and it is still a place characterized by commitment to public affairs and to bipartisanship.

Portrait by James Forbes (late 1869 or early 1870), Governors' Portraits Collection, Indiana Historical Bureau, State of Indiana.

FOR FURTHER READING

Baker and Daniels Web site: http://www.bakerdaniels.com

Foulke, William D. *Life of Oliver P. Morton, Including His Important Speeches.* Indianapolis: Bowen-Merrill Company, 1899.

McCutchan, Kenneth P. *At the Bend in the River: The Story of Evansville.* Woodland Hills, CA: Windsor Publications, 1982.

Mueller, Arnold Ernst R. "Conrad Baker, Former Governor of Indiana." MA thesis, Butler University, 1944.

Baker's papers are in the Indiana State Archives, Indianapolis and the William Henry Smith Memorial Library, Indiana Historical Society, Indianapolis.

Thomas A. Hendricks

January 13, 1873–January 8, 1877

RALPH D. GRAY

WITH HIS ELECTION IN 1872, THOMAS A. HENDRICKS, THE nephew of Indiana's third governor, William Hendricks, became the first Democratic governor in a northern state after the Civil War. Previously, Hendricks served in Congress, both in the House of Representatives and the Senate, his senatorial career (1863–69) encompassing the final years of the Civil War and the first years of Reconstruction. Decidedly in the minority in these years (one of only twelve Democrats in the Senate), Hendricks had supported the Union during the war, but he steadfastly opposed most elements of "Radical Reconstruction" and also voted against the Civil War amendments to the Constitution—the thirteenth, fourteenth, and fifteenth. He also opposed removing President Andrew Johnson from office after he had been impeached by the House of Representatives.

Hendricks, who had previously run for governor in 1860 and in 1868, while still a senator, was successful on his third attempt. Unfortunately for him, however, his term in office, coinciding as it did with the postwar depression of 1873–78, was not to be an agreeable experience. The failure of Jay Cooke's banking house in New York in September 1873 plunged the nation into a serious and prolonged economic crisis, so the Hendricks years in office were marked by business failures, high unemployment, rapidly falling farm prices, and occasional strikes. Twice the governor authorized the state militia to quell labor disturbances among miners in Clay County and railroad workers in Logansport, the latter being upset by wage cuts and the use of black strikebreakers.

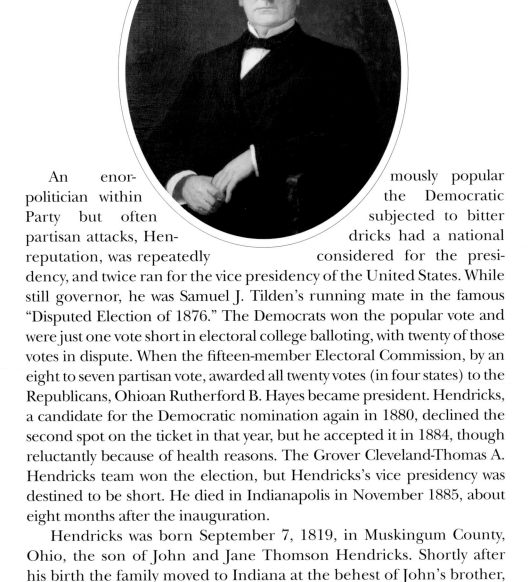

An enor-mously popular politician within the Democratic Party but often subjected to bitter partisan attacks, Hen-dricks had a national reputation, was repeatedly considered for the presi-dency, and twice ran for the vice presidency of the United States. While still governor, he was Samuel J. Tilden's running mate in the famous "Disputed Election of 1876." The Democrats won the popular vote and were just one vote short in electoral college balloting, with twenty of those votes in dispute. When the fifteen-member Electoral Commission, by an eight to seven partisan vote, awarded all twenty votes (in four states) to the Republicans, Ohioan Rutherford B. Hayes became president. Hendricks, a candidate for the Democratic nomination again in 1880, declined the second spot on the ticket in that year, but he accepted it in 1884, though reluctantly because of health reasons. The Grover Cleveland-Thomas A. Hendricks team won the election, but Hendricks's vice presidency was destined to be short. He died in Indianapolis in November 1885, about eight months after the inauguration.

Hendricks was born September 7, 1819, in Muskingum County, Ohio, the son of John and Jane Thomson Hendricks. Shortly after his birth the family moved to Indiana at the behest of John's brother, William, who was already a successful politician in the new state. The Hendricks family, after a brief two-year stay in Madison, settled in Shelby County in 1822, where the elder Hendricks was a successful and moderately prosperous farmer and businessman. The Hendricks home became a lively cultural center in the community. Young Thomas, fascinated by the conversation and discussions of the countless circuit-riding ministers, attorneys, and judges who visited the Hendricks home, acquired an early taste for both the law and politics.

He received his formal education at local schools and then attended Hanover College, graduating with the class of 1841, after which he undertook the study of law in Indiana and Pennsylvania. Admitted to the bar in 1843, he married Eliza C. Morgan of North Bend, Ohio, in 1845. Their only son, Morgan, died at the age of three in 1851.

A lifelong practitioner of the law, except for the times when his political offices precluded private practice, Hendricks's public service began in 1848 when he served a single term in the Indiana General Assembly. Subsequently a delegate to the state's constitutional convention in 1850–51, Hendricks was elected to the U.S. House of Representatives in 1851, but his support of Stephen A. Douglas, the principle of popular sovereignty, and the Kansas-Nebraska Act of 1854, which made slavery's expansion into those territories legally possible, led to his defeat in 1854. A new type of public service, however, immediately beckoned. At President Franklin Pierce's request, Hendricks became the commissioner of the General Land Office, serving four hectic years in a booming land-sales period for the country.

Hendricks returned to Shelby County in 1859 and then moved in 1860 to Indianapolis, where, besides running for governor that year, he established with Oscar B. Hord the law firm of Hendricks and Hord. The firm became Baker, Hord, and Hendricks in 1873, when outgoing governor Conrad Baker and Hendricks exchanged positions, the former to the law firm and the latter to the governor's office. Renamed Baker & Daniels in 1888, the company has long been one of the state's leading law firms.

Although Hendricks lost the gubernatorial race in 1860 to Henry S. Lane, with whom he held a series of joint meetings or debates similar to the Lincoln and Douglas debates in Illinois two years earlier, his sterling performance in the race led to his election by the Democratic-controlled state legislature to the U.S. Senate in 1863. There, as noted above, he insisted upon proper and constitutional procedures and opposed radical changes in the Constitution during a time of inflamed passion. Having "learned to hate one another as no people have ever hated," he asked, "are we now in the right spirit to change the fundamental law of the land?" He also repeated, in words often used against him later, his view that "this is a white man's Government, made by the white man, for the white man." Clearly, Hendricks was no friend of African Americans, but neither was he, as his political foes charged, a friend to slavery.

A change in control of the state legislature prevented Hendricks from having a second term in the Senate. Instead, after a narrow second defeat in the race for the governorship in 1868, Hendricks returned to his law practice while maintaining his political connections and activities. In 1872 he was again nominated for governor by the Democrats, and this time he narrowly edged out his Republican opponent, General Thomas M. Browne, a Civil War veteran, by a little more than a thousand votes, 189,424 to 188,276.

During his term in office, Hendricks not only had to deal with the problems of the economy but also with the volatile issue of temperance. When his first legislature in 1873 adopted the controversial Baxter bill, which provided for a strict form of local option, he signed it even though he personally favored a licensing system. He did so because the bill was constitutional and it represented the wishes of a majority in the legislature. In practice, however, the new law proved unworkable and was replaced by the next legislature in 1875 with the type of measure Hendricks preferred.

The two state prisons, particularly the older, dilapidated, disease-ridden one at Jeffersonville, created more concerns for the state. It was customary at that time to let nearby companies "hire" convicts to work for them, the pay to the state for this labor supposedly meeting the costs of their incarceration. But bad economic conditions, low pay, and venality, even criminality, on the part of the "South" prison officials required reforms. Conversely, the "North" state prison at Michigan City, more modern, efficient, and honestly administered, caused few problems, as did the new Female Institution for Women and Girls in Indianapolis, a combined prison for women and reform school for girls. Yet even at that facility sexual abuse charges were lodged against the superintendent that required a full investigation and eventual appointment of new leadership.

Amid the crises and problems, Hendricks did lay the groundwork for a new statehouse. The first one, used from 1835 on, was totally inadequate for the needs of the growing state and its increasingly active state legislature. The crumbling statehouse of the 1870s was too small to allow spectators a view of the legislature in session or to provide rooms for committee hearings and meetings. Instead, a variety of places around the city had to be rented for these purposes. Although Hendricks was no longer governor when the cornerstone for the handsome new statehouse, still in use today, was laid, he was the keynote speaker for that event in 1880.

As governor, Hendricks remained true to his principles of fiscal conservatism, morality, and strict adherence to the constitution. He did an acceptable job as chief executive, remained on good terms with members of both parties, and, in an age rife with graft and corruption, he was scrupulously honest and remained free of even any hint of scandal.

Not only did Hendricks's stature within the state and nation lead to his place on the Democratic Party's national tickets in 1876 and 1884, it also contributed to his place of honor among Indiana's political giants. His fame was such that, in 1890, when a towering statue of him was placed on the southeast corner of the statehouse lawn (facing, as it were, his adopted home of Shelbyville), the handsome bronze sculpture bore only a single word, HENDRICKS. In the 1990s, to avoid confusion between him and his uncle, the early Indiana governor for whom Hendricks County was named, two informative plaques were added to the base of the sculpture.

Hendricks's final years ended triumphantly as he was elected vice president of the United States in 1884. Not only did that continue the prominent role Indiana had played in presidential politics, as Hoosiers often joined with candidates from New York, providing both geographical and philosophical balance to the ticket, but Hendricks remained in politics with integrity, firm convictions, and the common touch. His death during a visit to Indianapolis in November 1885 was sincerely mourned by people throughout the state and nation.

Portrait by Theodore Clement Steele (1916), Governors' Portraits Collection, Indiana Historical Bureau, State of Indiana.

FOR FURTHER READING

Gray, Ralph D., ed. *Gentlemen from Indiana: National Party Candidates, 1836–1940.* Indianapolis: Indiana Historical Bureau, 1977.

Holcombe, John W., and Hubert M. Skinner. *Life and Public Services of Thomas A. Hendricks: With Selected Speeches and Writings.* Indianapolis: Carlon and Hollenbeck, 1886.

Memorial Addresses on the Life and Character of Thomas A. Hendricks . . . Delivered in the Senate and House of Representatives. Washington, D.C.: Government Printing Office, 1886.

Thornbrough, Emma Lou. *Indiana in the Civil War Era, 1850–1880.* Vol. 3, *The History of Indiana.* Indianapolis: Indiana Historical Bureau and Indiana Historical Society, 1965.

There are a few papers relating to Hendricks in the Indiana State Archives, Indianapolis.

James D. Williams

January 8, 1877–November 20, 1880

REBECCA S. SHOEMAKER

JAMES D. WILLIAMS, INDIANA'S SEVENTEENTH GOVERNOR, must have seemed to some during the term of his service, 1877–1880, as something of an anachronism. At a time when most men in public life were involved in business and the law, Williams was devoted to his life as a small farmer. At a time when the lifestyles of many public officials were examples of conspicuous consumption, Williams dressed modestly in garments made from the wool of his own sheep. At a time when many politicians were supporting the unwise monetary policies of the Gilded Age, Williams emphasized thrift and fiscal responsibility. Although he may have been out of step with the times in many ways, Williams enjoyed widespread support among Hoosier voters because he represented the traditional rural values that were reflected in most of their lives and backgrounds.

James Douglas Williams was born on January 30, 1808, in Pickaway County, Ohio, the son of George and Sarah Cavendar Williams. In 1818 the Williams family moved to Vincennes Township, Knox County, Indiana, the area in which James was to spend the remainder of his life. He attended school only through the fifth grade, then went to work on the family farm, taking over full responsibility for it and for caring for his mother and siblings after his father's death in 1828. As an adult he purchased and operated a farm of a few hundred acres in the community of Wheatland in Knox County, adding to his income through the operation of a gristmill. He specialized mainly in the production of grain crops, with a particular eye to

the study and implementation of improved meth- ods of production and the development of superior strains of grasses and grains.

Williams was known throughout his life for a habit of dress that reflected his farm roots. He adopted the habit of having his suits tailored from a denim or "jeans" fabric that his wife produced by spinning and weaving the wool from his own sheep, thus earning for himself the sobriquet of "Blue Jeans." The attire aroused little notice through much of his career, but after his election to Congress in 1874 comments by journalists and fellow congressmen soon made Williams's clothes an element of his political reputation, one which worked to his advantage when he campaigned on a platform emphasizing thrift and frugality. Williams culminated his sartorial career by taking the oath of office as governor in a silk-lined suit of jeans material, and he sat for his official portrait in the same attire.

Having been exposed to local political activities through the discussions of farmers who frequented his mill and the post office that he operated in his home, Williams began his political career at a relatively early age. He was appointed justice of the peace in 1839, serving in that position until he was elected to the state legislature in 1843. Thus began a career in politics that spanned the rest of his life. He served seven terms as a state representative between 1843 and 1869 and was a state senator from 1859 to 1865 and 1871 to 1872. He ran unsuccessfully for the U.S. Senate in 1872, being defeated by former governor Oliver P. Morton. He served one term, 1874–76, in the U.S. House of Representatives, resigning shortly before his term was over to accept the Democratic nomination for governor.

Williams's career in politics was paralleled by a long and active career in advancing agriculture in the state. Williams was more than just an ordinary farmer. He worked to improve the quality of the grain and grasses he produced and studied new techniques of production, focusing particularly on timothy, red clover, oats, and corn. He participated in local and regional farm organizations, joining his neighbors in forming the Knox County Agricultural Society in 1851 and serving as president of the District Agricultural and Mechanical Society of Southwestern Indiana, which was founded in 1858. When the Indiana State Fair was established in 1852, he quickly became one of its strongest supporters and participants, and he and his sons routinely won top awards for excellence in their production of such crops as timothy, oats, and clover. He served on the board of the Indiana State Board of Agriculture for more than two decades, including numerous terms as its vice president and president.

During his many years in the Indiana General Assembly, Williams focused on his two perennial concerns: the improvement of agriculture and keeping a careful eye on state expenditures. He believed farmers would have benefited from such proposals as a bill he drafted in 1857 to fund the completion of the Wabash and Erie Canal and one in 1871 to make railroad rates uniform throughout the state. His support for agriculture was perhaps culminated in 1865 by his guiding through the general assembly a bill designed to accept for Indiana the provisions of the federal Morrill Land Grant Act of 1862, which paved the way for the founding of Purdue University. In 1871 he added to this achievement by producing legislation concerning Purdue's governance. He also sponsored, in 1865, legislation in support of the growth of, and state support for, the Indiana State Board of Agriculture. Williams's attention to financial issues prompted him not only to monitor the expenditure of state funds, but also to become a supporter in the 1870s of the Greenback political movement. He heeded

Indiana voters' position that an inflationary money policy would ease their concerns about their continued financial straits, exacerbated by the panic of 1873.

It was undoubtedly a combination of his position on monetary issues and his long career as a prominent state Democrat that led to his nomination by the party for national office. Williams served the party well, not only in the legislature, but also as president of the Knox County Democratic Convention, as a member of the party's state central committee, and as a delegate to the national convention in 1872. In 1872 he was nominated for a seat in the U.S. Senate, running unsuccessfully against Morton. He was elected to the U.S. House of Representatives in 1874, carried to victory on a tide of economic dissatisfaction that enabled the party to sweep almost every state office that year.

As a member of Congress, Williams served as chair of the House Committee on Accounts, where he began immediately to cut what he considered unnecessary expenses, including not only many of the perquisites with which congressmen were normally furnished, but also the lemons and sugar for the traditional lemonade in the House cloakroom. Williams even had a difference of opinion on financial matters with President Ulysses S. Grant in the summer of 1876. Williams later commented in a speech that he was so angered by Grant's complaints that the Democratic appropriations bill was inadequate that he avoided future meetings with the president during his time in Washington.

Having been prevailed upon to run for governor of Indiana in 1876 because of his political experience and his position on the inflationary money policy, Williams resigned from Congress and returned to the state to campaign. His opponents in the campaign were Republican Benjamin Harrison and Greenback nominee Anson Wolcott.

The major issue of the campaign was the financial depression then facing the country and the inflationary money policy that many supported as a solution. The Republicans were also affected by continued publicity about the scandals of the Grant administration, then just ending. Responding to the sentiments of Hoosier voters, the three candidates took somewhat similar positions on the financial questions.

All three came out in favor of repeal of the federal Specie Resumption Act of 1875, which was designed to end the inflationary monetary policy that had been supported by the continued circulation of unredeemable greenback currency. The parties' platforms differed, however, on their proposed long-term solutions to the country's financial difficulties, with the Republicans favoring an overall conservative policy based on the gold standard and the Greenbacks willing to take the most radical steps to address the economic difficulties that bedeviled their blue-collar supporters. The Democrats took a moderate stand, calling for gradual movement toward a currency based on both gold and silver.

Williams's supporters made the most of his humble agricultural background and his emphasis on frugality, organizing "blue jeans" clubs and appearing at his rallies to sing songs touting his strengths. Williams's opponents took him on both on the stump and in the press, criticizing him particularly for his lack of wholehearted support for the state's commitment to the Union effort in the Civil War. The race was ultimately a very tight one, with Williams winning by a margin of 213,219 to 208,080. Wolcott, convinced that he could not win, withdrew six days before the election, and many of his supporters undoubtedly saw Williams as the most viable alternative.

Williams's governorship centered primarily on the state's financial difficulties, the effects of the panic of 1873 continuing to be seen in the increases in unemployment and in the number of bankruptcies. Since many of the causes were national in scope, there was not much the Williams administration could do to alleviate the distress. Williams suggested rather simplistically in his 1877 address to the general assembly that the solution was hard work and economy in government. Two years later he offered much the same antidote for continuing economic difficulties, urging the general assembly to cut spending by reducing the compensation of public officials and eliminating positions in the state's judiciary.

In spite of his tightfistedness, Williams was willing during his time in office to approve funding for a number of social initiatives, including increased funding for the state prison system; for the Indiana

Soldiers' and Sailors' Children's Home at Knightstown; for schools for the deaf, dumb, and blind; and for facilities for women at the state mental hospital. His sympathy for those who struggled financially was also evidenced, indirectly, in his veto of a bill calling for the licensing of physicians, surgeons, and midwives. He expressed concern that the new regulations would deprive older women and widows of the livelihood they earned by practicing medicine informally.

The most dramatic issue during Williams's term as governor was the impact on Indianapolis of the Great Railroad Strike of 1877. Rail workers walked off the job in protest when the Baltimore and Ohio Railroad announced that it was cutting the wages of its workers by 10 percent. Strikers in Indianapolis were determined to prevent any rail traffic through the city. Businessmen and other city residents called upon the governor to take military action to prevent loss of lives and property. When Williams refused to do so, probably because he did not want to damage Democratic support among blue-collar laborers, Judge Walter Q. Gresham and former Civil War general Benjamin Harrison organized a Committee of Public Safety to provide protection and a Committee of Mediation to hear the workers' grievances. Only after the workers had agreed to return to their jobs did Williams issue a proclamation calling for the resolution of the disputes by the courts.

The most enduring achievement of the Williams governorship was the initiative undertaken to erect a new statehouse. The bill for this purpose passed by the general assembly in 1877 bore the marks of Williams's abiding commitment to fiscal responsibility. The legislature appropriated $2 million for the project and stipulated that any cost overruns would be borne by the architect. Further, the architect was required to post a bond of $100,000 as evidence of his commitment to the project. Williams did not live to see completion of the edifice in 1887, but he would no doubt have been pleased to learn that $20,000 of the original appropriation was returned to the state treasury upon completion of the project.

Williams married Nancy Huffman, the daughter of a neighboring farmer, in 1831. They were married nearly fifty years, until her death on June 27, 1880. The couple had four children. Williams died in office on November 20, 1880, from a variety of physical ailments, including kidney and bladder diseases. His body lay in state in the Marion County Courthouse in Indianapolis, then in Vincennes. He was buried in the family plot in Walnut Grove Cemetery near his home on November 23, 1880.

Williams was not an innovative governor, and, indeed, was valued chiefly by his supporters for his steadfast adherence to the traditional values that formed the core of his personal and political existence throughout his adult life. His understanding of and commitment to the importance of agriculture as a key element in his own life and in those of much of the Hoosier population guided both his own career as a farmer and his dedication to the development of ways to promote and improve the state's agricultural economy. His focus on thrift and frugality was central to every aspect of his political career, from his days as a state legislator to his service in Congress and as governor. Williams's later political career was strongly influenced by his dedication both to the convictions of his constituency and to the principles that guided the Democratic Party at the time. While his proposed solutions to the financial crisis at the state level seemed somewhat simplistic, and his support of an inflationary money policy appeared unwise in the long term, his positions were in step with what the times and his supporters demanded. As governor, Williams did little to advance the state's economy or to move it forward in step with the rest of the country at the time. Though he represented the values that many Hoosiers saw as paramount, he also symbolized an era in Hoosier history that would soon be seen by many as out of step with the times.

Portrait by Henry M. Colcord (1878-79), Governors' Portraits Collection, Indiana Historical Bureau, State of Indiana.

FOR FURTHER READING

Burnett, Howard R. "The Last Pioneer Governor of Indiana." *Indiana Magazine of History* 22 (June 1926): 101–30.

Carmichael, O. B. "The Campaign of 1876 in Indiana." *Indiana Magazine of History* 9 (December 1913): 285–96.

Fort Wayne News-Sentinel. Undated clipping in the Indiana Biography Series, 4:183–84. Indiana Division. Indiana State Library, Indianapolis.

Indianapolis Sentinel, August 17, 1876.

Shoemaker, Rebecca S. "James D. Williams." *Traces of Indiana and Midwestern History* 8, no. 4 (Fall 1996): 27–30.

————. "James D. Williams: Indiana's Farmer Governor." In *Their Infinite Variety: Essays on Indiana Politicians*. Indianapolis: Indiana Historical Bureau, 1981.

Vincennes Western Sun, November 26, 1880.

Vincennes Western Sun and General Advertiser, July 31, 1847.

Williams, James D. Proclamation issued by Governor Williams during the railroad strike, on July 26, 1877. Broadside Collection. William Henry Smith Memorial Library. Indiana Historical Society, Indianapolis.

Williams's gubernatorial papers are in the Indiana State Archives, Indianapolis, and papers relating to Williams are in the Indiana State Library, Indianapolis.

Isaac P. Gray

November 20, 1880–January 10, 1881 and January 12, 1885–January 14, 1889

J. MICHAEL WALSH, DENNIS L. WALSH, AND JAMES E. ST. CLAIR

WHEN ISAAC P. GRAY BECAME GOVERNOR AFTER THE DEATH of James D. Williams on November 20, 1880, a newspaper account, in describing Indiana's new chief executive, said, "Under a pleasing exterior and suave manner he hides an indomitable will and aggressive character." Over the course of a political career that spanned more than a quarter of a century, Gray achieved great success through his determination and aggressiveness, but these traits also engendered a core of opponents who were able to thwart his more lofty ambitions for higher office, including the vice presidency of the United States.

Gray's iron will was never more in evidence than on May 13, 1869, when as the Republican president pro tempore of the Indiana Senate, he had the chamber doors locked as a vote on ratifying the Fifteenth Amendment to the Constitution was imminent to keep Democrats, who vehemently opposed the bill, from leaving and depriving the senate of a quorum. According to historian Jacob Piatt Dunn, one Democrat demanded: "Who dares lock senators in?" Gray shot back: "I do. The key is in my pocket. We have a right to break up unwarranted interference with the business of this assembly." As the roll call began, Democrats left their desks and crowded into the cloakroom, prompting Gray to order that they be recorded as present but not voting, ushering in a questionable parliamentary procedure that was cited as a precedent for counting quorum in later years in the U.S. House of Representatives. The tactic worked, the measure passed, and Indiana had the distinction of delivering the last ratification vote needed to make the amendment,

which extended   voting rights to
African   Ameri-   cans, part of the
Constitution. Gray's   actions, while successful for the moment,   came back to haunt him
years later, especially since he   eventually changed his party
affiliation from Republican to Democrat.

Isaac Pusey Gray, who served as Indiana's eighteenth governor for
a six-week period following Williams's death and then as its twentieth
for a full four-year term, was born on October 18, 1828, in Chester
County, Pennsylvania, to John and Hannah Worthington Gray, who
were Quaker innkeepers. When Gray was eight years old, the family
moved west, first to Urbana, Ohio, and then six years later to New
Madison, Ohio. While in New Madison, Gray began and ended his
brief formal education and became a clerk in a dry-goods store, later
becoming the store's owner. He married Eliza Jaqua on September
8, 1850. The couple had four sons, two of whom died in infancy. The
surviving sons became lawyers.

In 1855 Gray moved his family to Union City, Indiana, in Randolph County, where he opened a dry-goods store and quickly established himself as an energetic and well-regarded participant in civic
activities. His wife, who helped out in the store, encouraged him to
study law, which he did in his spare moments during store hours and
at night. Gray, who was admitted to the bar in 1861, said later that he
studied law not because he had a burning desire for the profession,

but that his real interest was in politics and he saw the practice of law as a critical credential for that career.

Gray hardly had time to establish his law practice before the outbreak of the Civil War. He was appointed a colonel and given command of the Fourth Indiana Cavalry, serving from the fall of 1862 to early 1863, when he resigned because of his dissatisfaction with not being given command of his entire regiment. Still, he was in command when two companies of the Fourth and two companies of the Fifth Indiana Cavalry fought against John Hunt Morgan and his soldiers at Munfordville on Christmas Day, 1862. In July of 1863 Gray was named colonel of the 106th Indiana Regiment, one of several dozen special "minuteman" units raised to repel Morgan's raids into Indiana. His unit disbanded after less than a week. Gray also organized the 147th Indiana Infantry Regiment and served as captain of the Randolph County branch of the Indiana Legion, the state militia during the war.

After the war Gray resumed his law practice as well as branching out into the grain business and banking, helping to establish Citizens Bank in Union City in 1865. For his first foray into elective politics, Gray, who had been a Whig in Ohio but became a Republican after moving to Indiana, dared to oppose the eminent Republican George W. Julian, a founder of the state GOP, for his seat in Congress in 1866. Gray lost the primary, but two years later he was elected to the state senate from Randolph County as a Republican and then was chosen by his colleagues as senate president.

Gray's heavy-handed tactics in ramming through ratification of the Fifteenth Amendment in 1869 won him praise in Republican circles throughout the state and nation, but his days in the party were numbered. In 1870 he declined the chance to serve as consul to St. Thomas, West Indies, after being appointed by President Ulysses S. Grant and confirmed by the U.S. Senate. Gray, repulsed by the scandals of the Grant administration, as were many Republican politicians, including Julian, joined the Liberal Republican movement. He was a delegate to the national convention of Liberal Republicans in Cincinnati, which nominated Horace Greeley for president in 1872. Following the defeat of Greeley, who was also the Democratic presidential nominee, the third-party movement he headed waned nationally, and Gray once again changed affiliations, this time to the Democratic Party.

It did not take long for the ambitious Gray to advance in his new party, but in doing so he also made enemies of a few powerful people who derailed his plans for even more exulted positions, mainly by using the Fifteenth Amendment imbroglio against him. In 1876 Gray was unanimously nominated for lieutenant governor on the ticket with gubernatorial nominee James D. Williams. Williams defeated the Republican candidate, Benjamin Harrison, by a little more than five thousand votes, and Gray won over his GOP challenger by a slightly larger margin. Although the currency question had become an important issue in Indiana in the 1870s, candidates for governor and lieutenant governor representing the Greenback Party, which advocated expanding the supply of paper money, received only about 3 percent of the vote.

In a strange set of circumstances, by the time Gray started his brief tenure as governor following the death of Williams in late 1880, he had already been defeated for his party's nomination for governor and had even lost his bid for reelection as lieutenant governor. At the Democratic state convention in June 1880, Gray was passed over as the party's nominee in favor of former congressman Franklin Landers of Indianapolis. Had it not been for his actions in "forcing ratification of the fifteenth amendment, he would undoubtedly have received the nomination." However, Gray was nominated by acclamation again for lieutenant governor. In the election for state officers, at the time held in October, the tandem of Landers and Gray lost to Republicans Albert G. Porter and Thomas Hanna.

Gray still had one more gambit to try before taking a brief hiatus from politics, and this one as well would come back to hound him in later years. With Republicans holding a decided edge in an 1881 joint vote of the Indiana General Assembly to select a U.S. Senator to replace Democrat Joseph E. McDonald, the election of the GOP candidate, Benjamin Harrison, was assured. Nevertheless, custom dictated that Democrats nominate McDonald as a courtesy. Gray, however, working behind the scenes, successfully lobbied Democrats to make him the nominee. It was something neither McDonald nor his allies ever forgot. Gray lost to Harrison by a vote of 81 to 62.

Once out of office, Gray resumed practicing law, but he was back on the political stage when state Democrats held their convention in the summer of 1884. A majority of the delegates favored Gray as the party's candidate for governor, though there were still rumblings about his Republican past and the ratification vote. The objections to his candidacy evaporated in the face of his evident support, and he was named the party's nominee by acclamation. In the general election, despite his failure to carry his home county, Gray defeated Republican William Calkins by nearly seven thousand votes. The Greenback and Prohibitionist candidates for governor drew very little support.

Gray had hardly settled in as governor before he set his sights on winning another office, specifically the U.S. Senate seat held by Harrison, whose term expired in March 1888. As with many best-laid plans, this one hit a snag when Lieutenant Governor Mahlon Dickerson Manson resigned in July 1886. This development presented the governor with precisely the dilemma his intraparty opponents had devised when they persuaded Manson to vacate his office and accept a low-level federal job. Gray, who could not resign as governor to run for the Senate with no reliable successor in the wings, turned to the attorney general for help and received an opinion that an election to fill the lieutenant governor's vacancy could be held in the off-year elections of 1886. That certainly suited Gray, who fully expected the Democratic candidate, John C. Nelson, to win. However, Nelson was upset by Republican Robert S. Robertson, who won by more than three thousand votes. In addition, as a result of the election, Republicans now controlled the Indiana House of Representatives by a 52 to 44 margin; four seats were held by members of the Greenback Labor Party. While Democrats remained in firm control of the senate with a 31 to 19 edge and had a margin of 75 to 71 in a joint vote, the four third-party votes presented a wild card.

With party alignments so close and partisan zeal at fever pitch, the 1887 general assembly was primed for a noisy and chaotic session, and not just because it was convened amid the sounds of construction as work continued on the new statehouse. The flash point was the election of Robertson as lieutenant governor. The house recognized his election, but senate Democrats, who were in the majority, deemed the midterm election unconstitutional and declared the lieutenant governor's office vacant. They appointed president pro tempore Alonzo Green Smith of Jennings County as acting lieutenant governor. Furious, Republicans even interrupted the opening prayer in the senate.

The uproar continued as Robertson took the oath as lieutenant governor on January 10 but was prevented from presiding over the senate by the January 13 ruling by the Marion County Circuit Court, an order he obeyed until it was lifted by the Indiana Supreme Court on February 23. Meanwhile, balloting for U.S. Senator began in the legislature on January 19. Gray, who by now had given up any thought of being a candidate, supported David Turpie, a former U.S. Senator, to oppose Harrison, who sought reelection. Turpie did not gain the necessary seventy-six-vote majority until the sixteenth ballot, but Republicans protested that the balloting was illegal because Smith was supposed to vote only in the case of a tie.

The situation at the statehouse escalated from contentious to riotous after the favorable state supreme court ruling for Robertson, who came to the senate on the morning of February 24 to assume its presidency as lieutenant governor. What ensued marked a "black day in the history of the General Assembly." Fistfights erupted. Robertson was manhandled by a doorkeeper, pushed toward the door, and ejected from the chambers. At one point, someone shouted, "Stop! I'm armed. I'll kill the man that touches me." With six hundred angry Republicans outside in the corridors ready to storm the doors to the senate and fifty armed doorkeepers inside, the threat of even more violence seemed likely. However, Robertson calmed the crowd, asking his followers to do "nothing of which you will be ashamed in your cooler moments."

Robertson was never installed as president of the senate, and lawmakers abandoned all legislating, the chambers refusing even to accept messages from one another. Still, the contretemps did have the positive effect of encouraging the national movement calling for a constitutional amendment for the direct election of U.S. senators, a proposition surprisingly supported nearly unanimously by the warring state senate.

Not surprisingly, the 1887 session had little to show in the way of accomplishments, though a few nonpartisan, noncontroversial measures were enacted, including those regulating the practice of dentistry and approving monuments honoring Schuyler Colfax, the former congressman and vice president of the United States, and former governor Thomas A. Hendricks, who was also a vice president as well as U.S. Senator and congressman. Three items from Gray's budget proposal to the legislature were also adopted: the initial appropriation to build the Soldiers and Sailors Monument in downtown Indianapolis, the building of "a school for the feeble-minded (children)" in Fort Wayne, and the rebuilding of the Soldiers' and Sailors' Children's Home in Knightstown, which had recently burned down.

During his term, Gray also focused attention on the rise of vigilante groups who used violence and even deadly force to impose their self-styled form of justice, and on the rampant problem of voter fraud and corruption in the state. The issue of ballot reform, brought to a head by the conspicuous abuses during the 1888 campaign, was addressed by Gray in his farewell message to legislators. Urging action on revision of election laws, Gray noted that "the public faith in the purity of elections has become shaken." At the behest of Gray, the attorney general investigated vigilantism in the state, in particular the activities of "white caps," a group akin to the Ku Klux Klan, which operated openly in several southern Indiana counties. The investigation resulted in legislation, passed by the general assembly in 1889, making it a crime when three or more people gathered for unlawful purposes while wearing white caps or masks.

After his term ended as governor, Gray again turned to his law practice, but did not abandon his efforts to seek higher office. Twice he came close to being nominated as vice president, only to have the prize go to someone else at the last moment, thus earning him the sobriquet of "Sisyphus of the Wabash." As Gray neared being nominated Grover Cleveland's vice presidential running mate in 1888 at the party's convention in Saint Louis, forces loyal to his nemesis, Joseph

McDonald, spread the word among southern delegates of Gray's work to ratify the Fifteenth Amendment. Southern votes swung to Allen G. Thurman, a former congressman and U.S. Senator from Ohio. A few days before Democrats met in Chicago in 1892 to select their presidential and vice presidential candidates, it was reported that Gray was a shoo-in for the second spot on the ticket headed by Cleveland. Again, however, the ratification story was told to southern delegates, and the nomination went to Adlai E. Stevenson of Illinois.

As a consolation, Cleveland in 1893 made Gray his first diplomatic appointment, as U.S. Minister to Mexico, where by all accounts he proved to be a respected and popular figure with the government. Gray died in Mexico City on February 14, 1895, of double pneumonia, having just returned to the country after a three-month leave in the United States. In a tribute to Gray, fellow Hoosier and Secretary of State Walter Q. Gresham said that he had discharged his duties "with singular diligence, fidelity, and very marked ability." President Porfirio Díaz of Mexico, who ordered flags to fly at half-staff in every government building throughout the country, praised him as "able a minister as the northern republic had ever sent to Mexico." The president also accompanied Gray's remains, along with a full division of the Mexican army and a civic procession, with the entire diplomatic corps of the republic in uniform, for the mile walk from the legation to the train station for the final trip to Indianapolis, where the body lay in state in the capitol before being transported to Union City for burial.

Positive assessments of Gray usually point to his strengths as a campaigner. Typical is this account: "He was a forcible speaker and especially strong in debate, being one of the most noted political canvassers Indiana ever had, and always in demand." A far darker view of Gray was presented in a newspaper report that discussed his behind-the-scenes efforts to position himself to run for president in 1892. The article said that he is a "small man of no attainments even in political knowledge" who is a "trickster . . . with no aim that he would not sacrifice friends and party to reach."

Portrait by Theodore Clement Steele (1888), Governors' Portraits Collection, Indiana Historical Bureau, State of Indiana.

FOR FURTHER READING

Cumback, Will. *Men of Progress, Indiana: A Selected List of Biographical Sketches and Portraits of the Leaders in Business, Professional and Official Life.* Indianapolis: Indianapolis Sentinel Company, 1899.

Dunn, Jacob P. *Indiana and Indianans: A History of Aboriginal and Territorial Indiana and the Century of Statehood.* 5 vols. Chicago: American Historical Society, 1919.

"Isaac P. Gray's Ambition." *New York Times*, July 18, 1890.

Lafollette, Robert. "The Adoption of the Australian Ballot in Indiana." *Indiana Magazine of History* 24 (June 1928): 105–20.

Phillips, Clifton J. *Indiana in Transition: The Emergence of an Industrial Commonwealth, 1880–1920.* Vol. 4, *The History of Indiana.* Indianapolis: Indiana Historical Bureau and Indiana Historical Society, 1968.

Reid, Richard J. *Fourth Indiana Cavalry Regiment: A History.* Olaton, KY: Richard J. Reid, 1994.

"Robertson Kicked Out." *New York Times*, February 25, 1887.

Stoll, John B. *History of the Indiana Democracy, 1816–1916.* Indianapolis: Indiana Democratic Publishing Company, 1917.

"Taking the Governor's Place." *New York Times*, November 21, 1880.

U.S. Congress. Senate. Pamphlet, January 13, 1896. 54th Cong., 1st sess., 1896.

Walsh, Justin E. *The Centennial History of the Indiana General Assembly, 1816–1978.* Indianapolis: Select Committee on the Centennial History of the Indiana General Assembly, 1987.

Gray's gubernatorial papers are in the Indiana State Archives, Indianapolis.

Albert G. Porter

January 10, 1881–January 12, 1885

JEFFERY A. DUVALL

VIEWED AS A "SAFE EXECUTIVE UNDER ORDINARY CONDI-tions," Albert G. Porter, only the second native son to become governor of Indiana, served his sole term in office with great competence and little fanfare. Having reluctantly accepted his party's nomination for the office in 1880, Porter declined to run for the U.S. Senate when the opportunity arose or to seek a second term as governor, preferring instead to return to private life.

The son of Thomas and Myra Tousey Porter, Albert was born on April 20, 1824, in Lawrenceburg, Indiana. His father, Thomas Porter, was a native of Pennsylvania who settled in Indiana after serving in the War of 1812. The senior Porter spent several years as the cashier of the Farmers' and Mechanics' Bank in Lawrenceburg and also served a term as recorder of Dearborn County. Following the death of his father-in-law, Thomas purchased his farm in Boone County, Kentucky, and took over the management of a ferry crossing that was attached to the property.

Working as a ferryman for his father, Porter earned enough money to begin attending Hanover College by age fifteen. After funds were depleted, his uncle, Omer Tousey, agreed to subsidize his education, stipulating only that he agree to attend a Methodist institution. Accordingly, Porter graduated from Greencastle's Indiana Asbury College (now DePauw University) in 1843. In 1844 Porter arrived in Indianapolis, where he quickly found employment in the office of the state auditor. That same year, he also briefly served as Governor James D. Whitcomb's unofficial

private secre- tary. Inspired by Whitcomb, Porter returned to Law- renceburg to study law in the office of Philip Spooner, father of Senator John C. Spooner of Wisconsin. Upon passing the bar in 1845, Porter returned to Indianapolis and entered private practice as a member of Hiram Brown's firm. On November 30, 1846, Porter married Brown's daughter Minerva. Porter and his first wife, who died in 1875, had five children. On January 5, 1881, he married his second wife, Cornelia Stone of Jamestown, New York. She died in 1886.

During his early years at the bar, Porter supplemented his income by writing digests of the state supreme court's opinions for the *Indianapolis Journal*. From 1851 to 1853 he served as the city attorney for Indianapolis. When an opening for the job of reporter of the supreme court occurred in 1853, Governor Joseph A. Wright appointed Porter to the post at the unanimous request of the justices. Running as a Democrat, Porter was elected to the same position by a large majority in 1854 and served for another two years. Increasingly uncomfortable with his party's stance on slavery, Porter joined a group of men that included his brother-in-law, Ignatius Brown, and helped to organize the Republican Party of Marion County in 1856. After completing his term as reporter of the supreme court, Porter was elected, as a Republican, to a seat on the Common Council of Indianapolis, where he served from 1857 to 1859.

In 1858 Porter was elected to Congress by a majority of one thousand votes in a district that the Democrats had carried by eight hundred votes in the preceding election. He was reelected to a second term in Congress in 1860. While a member of the House of Representatives, Porter served on the judiciary committee and became known both for eliminating the franking privilege and for his vigorous support of the prosecution of the Civil War. His most significant contribution to the war effort as a congressman was his report on the obligation of railroads that had received federal land grants and other subsidies to transport Union troops and munitions free of charge. Porter declined to run for a third term in Congress, mainly because of the small salary.

Returning to Indianapolis in 1863, he resumed his private practice and became head of one of the state's most successful and lucrative law firms. Between 1863 and 1877, Porter's partners included W. P. Fishback, Judge Cyrus C. Hines, his son George T. Porter, and future president Benjamin Harrison. Perhaps the most well-known case Porter's firm was involved in during these years was that of *Lambdin Milligan v. Alvin P. Hovey and Others*, which concerned the military's arrest of civilians in Indiana during the Civil War. In 1876 he was asked by the state Republican leadership to run for governor, but chose not to return to public service. In 1877 President Rutherford B. Hayes appointed Porter the first comptroller of the treasury. Serving from 1878 to 1880, he exercised judicial responsibility with great skill and settled numerous claims against the government, many of which dated back to the Civil War.

In 1880 Porter reluctantly accepted his party's nomination for governor. Republican leaders believed the gubernatorial election, the last one to be held in October, would predict the outcome of the national election in November. Viewing Porter as the strongest candidate for governor, the party placed his name in nomination while he was still in Washington and without consulting him. Amid concerns among at least some party workers that his penchant for formal dress—seen as an indication of his embrace of the eastern establishment—might prove to be a hindrance in the upcoming campaign, local Republicans were relieved when Porter arrived in Indianapolis in suitably casual attire, including a much remarked upon "cheap" straw hat, accepted the nomination, and launched what proved to be a vigorous and surprisingly enthusiastic campaign. After visiting all but five of the state's counties, and buoyed by an endorsement from the Knights of Labor thanks to his defense of striking railroad workers in 1877, Porter was elected to the state's highest office by a majority of seven thousand votes.

As governor, Porter advocated the allocation of $5,000 for a survey of the Kankakee swamp and other marshlands and upon the legislature's approval of the plan appointed John L. Campbell of Wabash College to conduct the survey. Porter then used Campbell's report to move forward on a long-standing plan to begin draining the surveyed land, eventually leading to the reclamation of 800,000 acres. In 1881 he also called upon the legislature to increase funding for the Department of Statistics and Geology, which led to the formation of two separate and well-funded new state agencies, the Department of Statistics and the Department of Geology and Natural History. Porter's administration also pushed the legislature to amend the state's mining regulations in order to protect the lives and health of miners, and its efforts also led to the creation of the State Board of Health, as well as the building of state hospitals for the insane at Evansville, Richmond, and Logansport.

In his inaugural address, Porter proposed the creation of a formal state Board of Visitors, the responsibilities of which would include inspecting all the benevolent institutions in Indiana. He suggested that the board consist of five members and maintained that two of the members should always be women. Also in 1881 Porter called on the general assembly to act on the question of women's suffrage, and he later recommended that "capable women physicians be appointed to have charge of the Woman's Departments of the hospitals for the insane." He also supported the appointment of professors of chemistry and agriculture, as well as expert mechanics, to the State Board of Agriculture. In 1883 both the Ohio and Wabash rivers overflowed, leading to the most devastating flood damage in Indiana history up to that date. In response, Porter pushed a $100,000 relief program through the legislature.

Perhaps the most difficult task Porter faced as governor arose in the wake of his party's proposal in 1881 that the state constitution be amended to grant the vote to women and to prohibit the manufacture and sale of intoxicating liquors in Indiana. In 1882 Democrats gained control of the general assembly, largely due to their opposition to the prohibition amendment. The following year, the state legislature quashed the proposed amendments and removed the governor's power to appoint officers and members of state boards and institutions. In similar fashion, the legislature created a metropolitan police board in Indianapolis and transferred management of the city's police department from the Republican-dominated city government. Porter argued that removing the governor's appointment powers and vesting them in the state legislature was inefficient and wasted legislators' time by locking them into "useless political controversies to the great detriment of the business which . . . members were elected to discharge." Having established his opposition to the legislature's actions, however, Porter chose not to engage it further on the issue and managed to maintain fairly cordial relations with what was essentially a hostile legislature during his final years in office.

Choosing not to run for a second term in 1885, Porter retired from politics and returned to private life in Indianapolis. In 1888, however, while serving as a delegate-at-large to the Republican National Convention in Chicago, he nominated his friend and former law partner, Benjamin Harrison, for president. Having actively participated in Harrison's campaign, he was rewarded by being appointed U.S. Minister to Italy, a post he held from 1889 to 1892. While in Italy, Porter played an important role in the negotiations between the United States and the Italian government following the deaths of Italian nationals in New Orleans during the Mafia Riots in 1891. He retired to Indianapolis in 1892 and spent his remaining years working on an unpublished history of Indiana. Porter died on May 3, 1897, and was buried in Crown Hill Cemetery.

Portrait by Theodore Clement Steele (1885), Governors' Portraits Collection, Indiana Historical Bureau, State of Indiana.

FOR FURTHER READING

Dunn, Jacob Piatt. *Indiana and Indianans: A History of Aboriginal and Territorial Indiana and the Century of Statehood.* 5 vols. Chicago: American Historical Society, 1919.

Phillips, Clifton J. *Indiana in Transition: The Emergence of an Industrial Commonwealth, 1880–1920.* Vol. 4, *The History of Indiana.* Indianapolis: Indiana Historical Bureau and Indiana Historical Society, 1968.

Reed, George Irving. *Encyclopedia of Biography of Indiana.* Chicago: Century Publishing and Engraving Company, 1895–[99].

Taylor, Charles W. *Biographical Sketches and Review of the Bench and Bar of Indiana, Containing Biographies and Sketches of Eminent Judges and Lawyers of Indiana, Together with a History of the Judiciary of the State and Review of the Bar from the Earliest Times to the Present, with Anecdotes, Reminiscences, Etc.* Indianapolis: Bench and Bar Publishing Company, 1895.

Walsh, Justin E. *The Centennial History of the Indiana General Assembly, 1816–1978.* Indianapolis: The Select Committee on the Centennial History of the Indiana General Assembly, 1987.

Porter's papers are in the William Henry Smith Memorial Library, Indiana Historical Society, Indianapolis and the Indiana State Library, Indianapolis.

Alvin P. Hovey

January 14, 1889–November 23, 1891

KATHY L. NICHOLS

EVEN IF ALVIN P. HOVEY HAD NOT BEEN ELECTED INDIANA'S twenty-first governor in 1888, he still would have earned a place in history for his past contributions to the state and nation as a lawyer, politician, judge, soldier, and diplomat. In fact, what Hovey did prior to becoming governor at age sixty-eight overshadowed his tenure as chief executive, which was cut short by his death on November 23, 1891.

That Hovey rose to any sort of prominence at all was remarkable, given his starting point in life. Born into poverty on September 6, 1821, in a log cabin near Mount Vernon in Posey County to Abiel and Frances Peterson Hovey, he was orphaned by the age of fifteen. Years later, Hovey recalled his "days of want and privation—bright days of sport and hope—and sad, sad, and gloomy hours, when the prospective future, would loom up before me." After receiving a common school education, Hovey set his sights on becoming a lawyer. Working by day as a bricklayer and by night studying law with local attorney John Pitcher, Hovey was resolved, as he put it, to "make myself fully master of the profession upon which I had just embarked."

After three years of preparatory reading, Hovey was admitted to the bar in 1843 at the age of twenty-two and then opened an office in Mount Vernon. In a few short years, his legal career and stature would be propelled by his work on a case that had attracted his interest when he studied in Pitcher's law office. The matter concerned the will of William Maclure, renowned geologist, educational reformer, and a partner of Robert Owen in his utopian experiment in New Harmony. Maclure, who

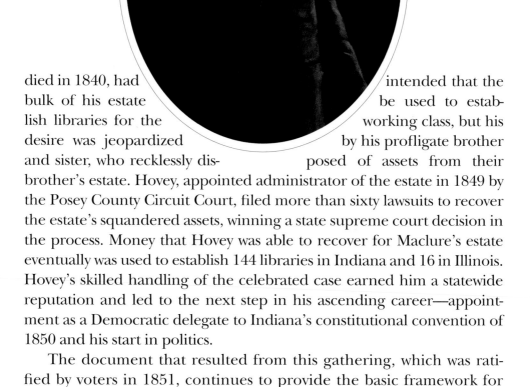

died in 1840, had intended that the bulk of his estate be used to establish libraries for the working class, but his desire was jeopardized by his profligate brother and sister, who recklessly disposed of assets from their brother's estate. Hovey, appointed administrator of the estate in 1849 by the Posey County Circuit Court, filed more than sixty lawsuits to recover the estate's squandered assets, winning a state supreme court decision in the process. Money that Hovey was able to recover for Maclure's estate eventually was used to establish 144 libraries in Indiana and 16 in Illinois. Hovey's skilled handling of the celebrated case earned him a statewide reputation and led to the next step in his ascending career—appointment as a Democratic delegate to Indiana's constitutional convention of 1850 and his start in politics.

The document that resulted from this gathering, which was ratified by voters in 1851, continues to provide the basic framework for Indiana government and its legal system. While reformist in some respects, the constitution was reactionary and racist in others. On the one hand, delegates, most of whom were Democrats and imbued with the spirit of Jacksonian democracy, approved making more offices elective rather than appointive, including judges; they prohibited the state from going into debt, a reaction to the failed internal improvements project; and they strengthened the state's commitment to public education. On the other hand, the convention not only refused to extend suffrage to women and African Americans, it barred African Americans from even settling in the state. It was Hovey, in fact, who proposed the clause to the suffrage provision that specifically excluded "negroes, mulattoes and Indians." He also opposed the homestead exemption, which was designed to give homeowners a measure of protection from creditors, on the grounds that it would legalize fraud and breed laziness.

Following the convention, it appeared that Hovey's political trajectory would continue climbing, but it was temporarily derailed when he was caught in the middle of a dispute between President James Buchanan and Stephen A. Douglas and by his service in the Union army during the Civil War. Fresh from his experience as a delegate, Hovey became circuit judge of Posey County, serving until being appointed by Governor Joseph A. Wright in mid-1854 to fill a vacancy on the state supreme court. At age thirty-two, Hovey became the youngest member of the high court up to that time and the first person who helped write the state's constitution to sit on the tribunal charged with interpreting the meaning of the document. Hovey's service on the court lasted less than a year; he was defeated in an election for a full term in the fall of 1854. Still, he managed to author "several opinions that seem to incorporate his convention experiences or, at least, to reflect his constitutional values." One case in particular, *Greencastle Township v. Black*, gave him the "opportunity to write from an enhanced perspective as a former convention delegate." Writing the majority opinion that struck down a statute allowing township taxes to pay for schools, Hovey said it violated the principle of uniformity in funding the common school system.

Following his defeat for the supreme court seat, Hovey was appointed U.S. Attorney for Indiana by President Franklin Pierce, but he was removed from office by Buchanan in 1858 for siding with Douglas in opposing admitting Kansas as a slave state. Hovey then ran for Congress from the First District as an anti-Lecompton Constitution Democrat, but was defeated by Democrat William E. Niblack, who was later elected to the state supreme court after a long congressional career.

At the onset of the Civil War, Hovey organized the First Regiment of the Indiana Legion and was commissioned a colonel. He later became a colonel of the Twenty-fourth Indiana Infantry, then was promoted to brigadier general because of his performance during the battle of Shiloh in Tennessee in 1862. He further distinguished himself as a division commander during the battle of Champion Hill in Mississippi in May 1863, winning praise for his efforts in this Union victory from General Ulysses S. Grant, who claimed that it was the key battle in the success of the Vicksburg campaign. Toward the end of 1863, Hovey suffered a personal loss when his wife, Mary Ann, whom he had married in 1844, died at age thirty-eight. The couple had five children, though only two survived into adulthood.

Although Hovey was briefly back at the front for the Atlanta campaign in 1864, he served out the remainder of the war as military commander for Indiana. He was commissioned brevet major general, an honorary promotion, and given responsibility for recruitment and quelling opposition to Abraham Lincoln and the Union cause by Southern sympathizers. In carrying out the former, Hovey raised ten thousand troops, selecting only young, unmarried men who became known as "Hovey's babies" because many were under the age of eighteen. For the latter, Hovey targeted members of two related secret organizations sympathetic to the Confederacy, the Sons of Liberty and the Knights of the Golden Circle. After the plot of a general uprising planned for Indianapolis in August 1864 was uncovered, Hovey ordered the arrests of dozens of alleged conspirators, including prominent northern Indiana lawyer Lambdin P. Milligan. The men were tried by a military court, and Milligan and two others were convicted of treason and sentenced to be hanged, though their executions were never carried out. Milligan, whose sentence was commuted to life in prison, appealed his conviction on the grounds that as a civilian he was not subject to military justice. In 1866 the U.S. Supreme Court agreed with Milligan in the landmark decision known as *Ex parte Milligan*, and he was freed from prison and returned to his law practice in Huntington County.

At war's end, Hovey resigned from the military, married for a second time, and accepted an appointment by President Andrew Johnson to head the U.S. diplomatic mission in Peru. Just prior to departure, his second wife, Rosa Alice, daughter of Caleb B. Smith, who had been in Lincoln's cabinet, became ill and died. Hovey served for five years in Peru, a time when the country was either at war with another country or was convulsed by internal revolutions. He returned to Mount Vernon in 1870 and resumed his law practice.

Hovey's political involvement, at least for elective office, appeared to have ended in 1872, when he declined the chance to run as the Republican candidate for governor, saying at the time that he was finished with politics. He changed his mind fourteen years later, however, when he accepted the party's unanimous nomination to run for Congress from the First District in the off-year election of 1886; he defeated his Democratic opponent, J. E. McCullough, by 18,258 votes to 16,901. Two years later he was unanimously nominated by the Republican Party for governor, joining a slate led by presidential candidate Benjamin Harrison, grandson of William Henry Harrison, Indiana's first territorial governor. Harrison, a distinguished Indianapolis lawyer, also had served one term in the U.S. Senate.

The election of 1888 in Indiana, even with favorite son Harrison at the top of the ticket, was highly competitive, and it was contentious, with Republicans and Democrats accusing the other of wholesale vote buying. In the governor's race, Hovey barely won, edging out Democrat Courtland C. Matson, a former four-term congressman, with 49 percent of the vote to 48.6 percent. Harrison won the state by 2,300 votes, and though he lost the total popular vote to incumbent President Grover Cleveland by more than 90,000 votes, he was elected president with 233 electoral votes to Cleveland's 168. Democrats in Indiana fared better in congressional and legislative races, winning ten of the thirteen House of Representatives seats and regaining control of both houses in the Indiana General Assembly.

Despite the division of power in state government, the legislature, which convened in 1889, "produced a very extensive record of reform legislation, some of it over Governor Hovey's veto but much of it bipartisan." One bipartisan measure adopted, which was spurred by the blatant buying of votes in the 1888 election, led to the creation of the secret ballot and made Indiana a leader in election reform. Under this new system, the state, not the political parties, as had been the practice, prepared ballots that were the same size and color and listed candidates in columns under their party affiliations, which allowed straight-ticket voting. Voters received the ballots on election day and marked them in secret. The new law also contained provisions for representation on local election boards and controlling access to and activities at polling places.

In an effort to suppress groups known as "white caps," who were self-appointed enforcers of moral and civic standards, Hovey and the general assembly reached an agreement on a law that provided for prison terms of two to ten years for those convicted of white capping, or vigilante activities. White Caps, secret organizations of white men generally found in southern Indiana, Harrison and Crawford counties in particular, took it upon themselves to mete out justice, usually lashes with hickory switches, to those they suspected of not living up to their responsibilities of being a good citizen. For example, a man might be punished for not taking proper care of his family by drinking too much or failing to cut enough wood for heating and cooking. Women could be disciplined for not keeping their houses clean. The governor and legislators also agreed on a bill creating a state board to determine which textbooks were used in public schools and mandating that the state pay for books.

Clashes between Republican Hovey and the Democratic-controlled general assembly, though, were inevitable, and the big fight erupted over patronage. The jousting followed a predictable pattern: the legislature passed laws giving it the power over appointments to governmental offices; the governor vetoed the bills on the grounds they were unconstitutional; the legislature then overrode the vetoes; and the issues eventually found their way to the Indiana Supreme Court. Although Republicans were dominant on the court when these cases were heard, decisions did not always favor Hovey. The court did, however, rule unconstitutional legislation that created local police, fire, and public works boards and gave the general assembly power to name members of these boards. The legislature did prevail in cases challenging its right to name trustees to the Indiana Hospital for the Insane and the state School for the Blind, the court ruling that it was constitutional for the general assembly to appoint governing officers of all benevolent institutions. Another tussle flared over the appointment of a state geologist who would head the newly created Department of Geology and Natural Resources. In its decision, the court, siding neither with the governor nor the legislature, ruled that the constitution required the office to be filled by a popular election.

While governor, Hovey was also involved in seeking national legislation that would provide pensions to Union veterans. It was an issue he championed when he was in Congress and one he continued to push while serving as president of the Service Pension Association of the United States, a lobbying group.

Portrait by Theodore Clement Steele (1889), Governors' Portraits Collection, Indiana Historical Bureau, State of Indiana.

FOR FURTHER READING

Dickson, Brent E., Thomas A. John, and Katherine A.Wyman. "Lawyers and Judges as Framers of Indiana's 1851 Constitution." *Indiana Law Review* 30 (1997): 397–408.

Elliott, Josephine Mirabella. "William Maclure: Patron Saint of Indiana Libraries." *Indiana Magazine of History* 94 (June 1998): 178–91.

Grayston, Florence L. "Lambdin P. Milligan—A Knight of the Golden Circle." *Indiana Magazine of History* 43 (December 1947): 379–91.

Hess, Earl J. "Alvin P. Hovey and Abraham Lincoln's 'Broken Promises': The Politics of Promotion." *Indiana Magazine of History* 80 (March 1984): 35–50.

Hovey, Alvin P. "Autobiography of Alvin P. Hovey's Early Life." With introduction and notes by Elfreida Lang. *Indiana Magazine of History* 48 (March 1952): 71–84.

Journal of the Convention of the People of the State of Indiana to Amend the Constitution. Indianapolis: Austin H. Brown, 1851.

London, Lena. "Homestead Exemption in the Indiana Constitution." *Indiana Magazine of History* 44 (September 1948): 267–80.

"The Milligan Case." *New York Times*, June 5, 1871.

Phillips, Clifton J. *Indiana in Transition: The Emergence of an Indus-*

trial Commonwealth, 1880–1920. Vol. 4, *The History of Indiana.* Indianapolis: Indiana Historical Bureau and Indiana Historical Society, 1968.

Post, Margaret Moore. *First Ladies of Indiana and the Governors, 1816–1984.* Indianapolis: Pierson Printing Company, 1984.

Hovey's papers are in the William Henry Smith Memorial Library, Indiana Historical Society, Indianapolis; the Indiana State Archives, Indianapolis; and the Lilly Library, Indiana University, Bloomington.

Ira J. Chase

November 23, 1891–January 9, 1893

ALAN K. WILD

THE POLITICAL ASCENSION OF IRA J. CHASE, WHO BECAME Indiana's twenty-second governor upon the death of Alvin P. Hovey in November 1891, was paved in large part by the recognition and prominence he had achieved throughout the state as a minister and official in the Grand Army of the Republic, or GAR, a formidable lobbying group of Union veterans. After a business failure, Chase, at the urging of friends, studied for the ministry in the Christian Church (Disciples of Christ). He came to Indiana in 1867 and began preaching at a church in Mishawaka, moving later to congregations in La Porte, Wabash, and Danville in Indiana and in Pittsburgh, Pennsylvania, and Peoria, Illinois. Chase, who served briefly in the Civil War, also became active in the Indiana branch of the GAR, winning election in 1887 to the top position of state commander and serving two terms as the organization's chaplain.

The early life of Ira Joy Chase, who was born on December 7, 1834, in Rockport, New York, to Benjamin and Lorinda Mix Chase, was something of a hardscrabble existence and one of frequent moves as the family struggled to make a living farming. Three months after he was born, the family moved to Medina, New York, and then when Ira was twelve, to Milan, Ohio. Young Chase attended Milan Seminary, where he was tutored for three years by a Presbyterian minister. The family then returned to Medina for a short period, and Ira continued his education. In 1855 the Chases moved again, settling on a small farm near Barrington, Illinois, about thirty miles northwest of Chicago. During

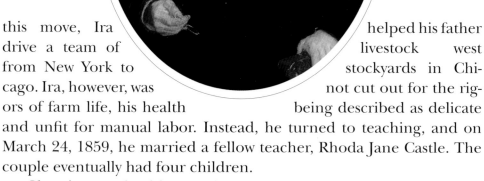

this move, Ira helped his father drive a team of livestock west from New York to stockyards in Chicago. Ira, however, was not cut out for the rigors of farm life, his health being described as delicate and unfit for manual labor. Instead, he turned to teaching, and on March 24, 1859, he married a fellow teacher, Rhoda Jane Castle. The couple eventually had four children.

Chase's poor health was also a factor in his abbreviated service during the Civil War. When the war broke out in 1861, he became the first man from Barrington to enlist in the Union army, helping to raise a company that became part of the Nineteenth Illinois Volunteer Infantry. Chase was made a sergeant, but because of his condition, saw limited action and was given the responsibility of drilling new recruits. As his health declined, he spent months in hospitals in Huntsville, Alabama, and Nashville, Tennessee, ultimately to be discharged from the army in late 1862.

Upon learning of her husband's illness, Rhoda left Illinois to be with him in Nashville, and when told that as a civilian she could not stay at the hospital to care for him, she enlisted as a nurse. Not long after the Chases returned to Illinois, Rhoda developed smallpox, which she likely contracted at the military hospital in Nashville. Chase spent five months nursing his wife back to health, but the disease left her blind and badly crippled for the rest of her life, another sixty years. Despite her handicaps, she participated actively in raising her children and in church and community activities.

Chase, meanwhile, had opened a hardware store in Barrington after his military discharge, but the business failed, in part because townspeople shunned the couple after Rhoda's bout with smallpox. Over the course of the next two decades, Chase established a reputation as a forceful preacher who had the "remarkable power to hold the interests of his audience," and as an effective voice for Union veterans through his work with the GAR. It was at this point that the state Republican Party came calling.

At their state convention in 1886, Republicans picked Chase, who at the time was on a religious mission to California, to oppose incumbent Fifth District Congressman Courtland C. Matson. Though he lost, Chase's strong showing in his first political outing put him in contention for the party's nomination for governor two years later. His candidacy was particularly favored by members of the temperance movement and churchgoers.

When it became apparent at the state Republican convention in the summer of 1888 that Hovey had the edge for the gubernatorial nomination, Chase moved to make the choice unanimous and accepted the lieutenant governor's position on the ticket, a gesture that won him the approbation of the delegates because it prevented a fractious fight. Four years later, when Chase, as the incumbent, filling out Hovey's term, sought the nomination to continue as governor, such good feelings toward him had all but dissipated. In fact, he was strongly opposed by the state party committee, including its chairman, and the *Indianapolis Journal*, the leading Republican newspaper in the state.

The anti-Chase effort was fueled by the feeling that the governor would jeopardize the party's chances in the fall election, in particular hurting the national ticket headed by President Benjamin Harrison, the illustrious Hoosier who was seeking reelection. Chase was viewed as poison at the ballot box for a variety of reasons. For one, his opponents noted, he insisted on preaching and making political speeches in the same city and on the same day, offending many, especially antitemperance voters. For another, he was considered anti-labor, a reputation burnished by his actions to kill a bill that would have made railroads liable for injuries caused to their workers through negligence by the companies.

In an effort to defeat Chase, state Republican leaders moved the site of the state convention to Fort Wayne from Indianapolis, where it had always been held up to then, and timed the meeting to coincide with the harvest. These actions were aimed at denying Chase support from his core constituency of farmers from the southern part of the state, whom party officials believed would not make the long trip to Fort Wayne, in the northeastern part of the state, and certainly not at harvest time. However, the plot failed and opposition to Chase evaporated "when special train after train unloaded regular delegates from the most distant parts of the State." Republican leaders, though, were right to be concerned about the party's prospects in the election that fall. In the governor's race, Chase lost to Democrat Claude Matthews by some seven thousand votes, about the same deficit in the state for Harrison, who was defeated by former president Grover Cleveland, the man he had beaten for the presidency four years earlier. Democrats also retained control of both houses of the Indiana legislature and won eleven of the state's thirteen congressional seats.

In his fourteen-month tenure as governor, Chase, who commuted daily by train from his home in Danville to the statehouse, was essentially a caretaker chief executive and left little in the way of accomplishments. He did attempt to use the office as a bully pulpit from time to time to advance legislation, but faced with a general assembly in the hands of the opposition party, he was largely unsuccessful. For example, legislators were unmoved by his plea to do something about the poor condition of Indiana roads. In a message to the general assembly, Chase said that Indiana roads were "wofully behind" those of other countries and states, adding that as a result, "For several months in each year the farmer is unable to do anything because of impassable roads. His teams are idle, and the profits of the months he has toiled are used up in doing nothing." Despite Chase's plea, poor road conditions persisted in the state into the twentieth century.

Chase also sought an additional $135,000 from the legislature for work related to Indiana's exhibit at the 1893 World's Columbian Exposition in Chicago. In his address to the general assembly, Chase said, "I cannot speak too strongly in behalf of this great work," adding that the Chicago World's Fair presented an opportunity for Indiana "to take her proper place in the front rank with the leading States of the Union." The legislature eventually appropriated $50,000, less than a third of what was requested, to complete work on the exhibit.

After leaving the governor's office, Chase returned to preaching full time. He died on May 11, 1895, at the age of sixty-one after being "taken suddenly ill" while conducting a religious meeting in Lubec, Maine. Chase's mark as a minister clearly outshone his brief political sojourn. Thirty-five years after his death, he was still being hailed by the Christian Church "as one of the outstanding evangelists and pastors for the past generation."

Portrait by Theodore Clement Steele (1892), Governors' Portraits Collection, Indiana Historical Bureau, State of Indiana.

FOR FURTHER READING

Barnhart, John D., and Donald F. Carmony. *Indiana: From Frontier to Industrial Commonwealth.* 2 vols. 1954. Reprint, Indianapolis: Indiana Historical Bureau, 1979.

Cassell, Frank A., and Marguerite E. Cassell. "Pride, Profits, and Politics: Indiana and the Columbian Exposition of 1893." *Indiana Magazine of History* 80 (June 1984): 93–121.

Cauble, Commodore Wesley. *Disciples of Christ in Indiana: Achievements of a Century.* Indianapolis: Meigs Publishing Company, 1930.

"Gov. Chase Renominated." *New York Times,* June 29, 1892.

Oval, Charles J. *Governors of Indiana: Illustrated.* Indianapolis: Oval and Koster, 1916.

Chase's gubernatorial papers are in the Indiana State Archives, Indianapolis.

Claude Matthews

January 9, 1893–January 11, 1897

DEBORAH A. HOWARD

CLAUDE MATTHEWS, A DEMOCRAT AND THE STATE'S TWENTY-third governor, came into office during a time of transition in Indiana. The state was experiencing turmoil in its transformation from an agrarian society to an industrial one, and, as a result, Matthews's time as governor would not be tranquil. Labor strikes, unrest among farmers, and a sustained economic depression all conspired to make his four years in office difficult. His troubles were compounded by the off-year elections of 1894 when Republicans, for the first time in twenty years, gained control of both houses of the Indiana General Assembly.

Matthews's calling in life had been farming, not politics. He was born on December 14, 1845, in Bethel, Kentucky, to farmers Thomas A. and Eliza Ann Fletcher Matthews. His mother died when he was four months old, and he lived with an aunt until he was thirteen. After his father remarried, he moved with the family to a farm near Maysville, Kentucky, showing an interest in raising livestock and studying agriculture as a young man. Matthews graduated from Centre College in Danville, Kentucky, in 1867, and then moved to a farm near Clinton, Indiana, in Vermillion County. A year later he married Martha R. Whitcomb, daughter of James D. Whitcomb, Indiana's eighth governor. They had three children who survived infancy.

At his farm, known as Hazel Bluff, Matthews raised grain and livestock and eventually became prominent for his expertise in improving the breeding of short-horn and Jersey cattle and trotting horses.

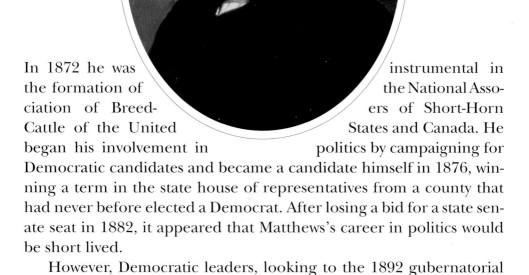

In 1872 he was instrumental in the formation of the National Association of Breed-ers of Short-Horn Cattle of the United States and Canada. He began his involvement in politics by campaigning for Democratic candidates and became a candidate himself in 1876, winning a term in the state house of representatives from a county that had never before elected a Democrat. After losing a bid for a state senate seat in 1882, it appeared that Matthews's career in politics would be short lived.

However, Democratic leaders, looking to the 1892 gubernatorial election, were casting about for a strong candidate to run for secretary of state in 1890, a race they saw as a critical preliminary to the governor's sweepstakes. In their searches, both major parties sought candidates who could blunt the rise of the People's or Populist Party in Indiana. The party had been gaining strength among disgruntled farmers and the working class with its platform of reform, which had as its signature issue increasing the money supply through unlimited coinage of silver.

The Republicans wisely picked Milton Trusler, a farmer in Fayette County and a top official of the state grange, an important farm organization. Countering, the Democrats, knowing they too needed a farmer of renown, recruited Matthews, who had the added credentials of being active in the Farmers' Mutual Benefit Association, one of the leading agricultural organizations in the state and a free-silver proponent. Matthews's candidacy was regularly and vigorously promoted by John B. Stoll, a leading Democrat and editor of the *South Bend Tribune*. The party's faith in Matthews was amply justified, as he delivered a resounding win, swamping the GOP challenger by nearly 20,000 votes, 233,881 to 214,302. The Populist candidate managed to poll only a little over 17,000 votes.

Two years later Matthews was named the party's gubernatorial candidate, opposing the incumbent Republican governor, Ira J. Chase. The People's Party, which had become the Populist Party by 1892, fielded a full slate of candidates for state offices headed by Leroy Templeton, a farmer, for governor. Matthews defeated Chase by a margin of seven thousand votes, and Templeton had a paltry twenty-two thousand votes, only about 4 percent of the total. Obviously, Populists in Indiana were never able to transfer widespread discontent among Hoosier farmers and laborers into success at the polls. The reasons, according to historian James Madison, had to do with voter loyalty to the two major parties and because the Populists "were too far from the center of Indiana's traditions."

Unhappily for Democrats and Matthews, the beginning of his new administration coincided with the panic of 1893, a severe nationwide depression that in Indiana inflicted massive unemployment, railroad bankruptcies, business failures, falling farm prices, and bank closings. Problems mounted the next year when the state was confronted by strikes in both the coal and rail industries. In the spring of 1894 miners in western Indiana, mainly in Clay, Daviess, Sullivan, and Parke counties, went on strike and forcibly halted trains hauling coal and either detached or derailed cars.

Matthews responded by sending nine companies of the state militia to the area to ensure safe passage for coal shipments. Just as the miners' strike was ending, railway workers at Pullman struck to protest low wages and adverse working conditions. When strikers seized the tracks at Hammond, Indiana, and stopped all traffic there, Matthews again called out the state militia to open the tracks. Because the general assembly was not in session and therefore could not appropriate money to pay the troopers, Matthews borrowed more than $41,000 on his personal credit to make the payments. He was later reimbursed by the legislature.

Besides quelling strikes, Matthews, described as having "correct and abstemious habits," also took actions against prizefighting and gambling on horse races in northern Indiana and against "white capping," a form of vigilantism, in southern Indiana. When the general assembly failed to pass his proposal to abolish prizefighting, he took possession of the arena in Lake County where fights had been held, and not long afterwards, "the building was torn down and regular prizefighting in Indiana ceased." Matthews had more success with the legislature when his proposed bill to close the Roby Racetrack in Lake County easily passed both houses. However, according to legend, a lobbyist for the racetrack paid the house clerk $500 to hide the bill to keep it from the governor. The ruse failed, and the bill was found and signed.

To suppress the "white caps," bands of vigilantes who terrorized people they suspected of immoral behavior, Matthews worked closely with local authorities in southern Indiana to rid their area of the lawless activity, offering in many cases "additional counsel to assist in the prosecution."

After the 1894 election, when Hoosier voters overwhelmingly went Republican to punish Democrats for the persistent depression, Matthews's battles were mainly with the GOP-controlled legislature. Two of the most contentious struggles, one provoking physical violence on the floor of the lower house, were over reapportionment and who had the power—the governor or the legislature—to make administrative appointments.

Once in power, Republicans moved swiftly in 1895 on the issue of redistricting, passing one bill that repealed the 1893 reapportionment bill passed by Democrats and another that redrew boundaries to favor their party. Though the legislature overrode Matthews's vetoes of both measures, the state supreme court later declared the 1895 act unconstitutional. Republicans also approved a bill that revoked a law passed under the previous Democratic-controlled general assembly that restored the governor's power to fill most administrative positions.

When Matthews had his secretary return the bill and his veto message to the lower house just a few minutes prior to adjournment, "Democrats and Republicans fought like beasts of the forest," with Democrats barging through locked chamber doors to get the governor's documents delivered in time and Republicans beating them back from reaching the Speaker. After the Speaker declared the house had adjourned before he received the bill, "fighting continued for another thirty minutes." Ultimately, the issue went to the state supreme court, which decided in favor of the legislature.

As Matthews neared the end of his term as governor in 1896, he became a candidate for the Democratic nomination for president of the United States. He was nominated at the party's convention in Chicago by Senator David Turpie of Indiana, and Hoosier delegates supported their favorite-son candidate until the fifth ballot, when the tide turned toward the fiery orator William Jennings Bryan, who had electrified the convention with his soaring "Cross of Gold" speech.

After leaving office, Matthews returned to Vermillion County, keeping active by working on his farm and making occasional public speeches. It was while delivering one such speech in Montgomery County that he suffered a stroke. He died three days later on August 28, 1898, at age fifty-two in Indianapolis. In its obituary, the *Indiana State Sentinel,* the state's leading Democratic newspaper, remembered Matthews as "an able, fearless and incorruptible executive, a wise party leader and counselor, a modest, unaffected and upright gentleman." He is buried in Clinton.

Portrait by Theodore Clement Steele (1893), Governors' Portraits Collection, Indiana Historical Bureau, State of Indiana.

FOR FURTHER READING

Bartholomew, H. S. K. "Governor Claude Matthews." *Indiana Magazine of History* 24 (December 1930): 271–78.

Carleton, William G. "The Money Question in Indiana Politics, 1865–1890." *Indiana Magazine of History* 42 (June 1946): 107–50.

———. "Why Was the Democratic Party in Indiana a Radical Party, 1865–1890?" *Indiana Magazine of History* 42 (September 1946): 207–28.

"Claude Matthews." *Indiana Sentinel*, August 29, 1898.

Dunn, Jacob P. *Indiana and Indianans: A History of Aboriginal and Territorial Indiana and the Century of Statehood.* 5 vols. Chicago: American Historical Society,   1919.

Madison, James H. *The Indiana Way: A State History.* Bloomington: Indiana University Press; Indianapolis: Indiana Historical Society, 1986.

Vermillion County, Indiana: History and Families. Newport, IN: Vermillion County Historical Society, 1988.

Walsh, Justin E. *The Centennial History of the Indiana General Assembly, 1816–1978.* Indianapolis: Select Committee on the Centennial History of the Indiana General Assembly, 1987.

Matthews's gubernatorial papers are in the Indiana State Archives, Indianapolis.

James A. Mount

January 11, 1897–January 14, 1901

CHARLES S. EWRY

WHEN JAMES A. MOUNT ENDED HIS FOUR-YEAR TERM AS Indiana governor on January 14, 1901, it was with great relief rather than reluctance. Eager to leave office and the state capital for his farm in Montgomery County, he called his final day as governor "the happiest day of my life . . . we are going back home to our beloved Shannondale farm, 'Willow Brook.'" Two days later, on the eve of departing for home, Mount, the state's twenty-fourth governor, died of a heart attack in his apartment at the Denison Hotel in Indianapolis. He was fifty-eight years old.

Mount, who had to be strong-armed into making his previous races for the state senate and Congress, actually had actively and aggressively sought the governor's office, confiding in friends his intentions to run two years before the state Republican convention in 1896. There, in competition with eleven other candidates, Mount was chosen the party's nominee on the seventh ballot. He then embarked on a grueling campaign around Indiana, making 130 speeches during a four-month period. Mount was accustomed to making speeches and traveling throughout the state, having visited every county as a lecturer at farmers' institutes, an extension program of Purdue University that provided instruction in various aspects of farming. In the election, Mount defeated his Democratic opponent, Benjamin F. Shively of South Bend, a former congressman and future U.S. Senator, by twenty-six thousand votes, at the time the largest plurality ever for a gubernatorial candidate in Indiana.

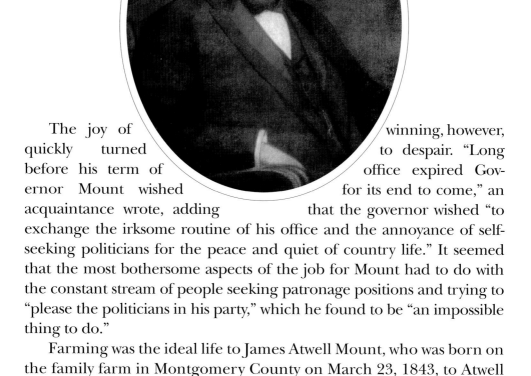

The joy of winning, however, quickly turned to despair. "Long before his term of office expired Governor Mount wished for its end to come," an acquaintance wrote, adding that the governor wished "to exchange the irksome routine of his office and the annoyance of self-seeking politicians for the peace and quiet of country life." It seemed that the most bothersome aspects of the job for Mount had to do with the constant stream of people seeking patronage positions and trying to "please the politicians in his party," which he found to be "an impossible thing to do."

Farming was the ideal life to James Atwell Mount, who was born on the family farm in Montgomery County on March 23, 1843, to Atwell and Lucinda Fullenwider Mount. One of twelve children, Mount's formal education was limited, attending school only during the harsh winter months when work on the farm stopped. His childhood days mostly were occupied by helping clear land in the dense forest around the family's crude log cabin and other routine farm work. At the outbreak of the Civil War, Mount, at age nineteen, enlisted in 1862 in the Seventy-second Indiana Infantry Regiment, which was part of the fabled Wilder's Lightning Brigade. In his three years of service in the Union army, Mount repeatedly showed courage in battle, most notably at the fierce and bloody battle of Chickamauga in September 1863, when he twice volunteered for the front line against a

Confederate infantry that outnumbered Wilder's forces by more than eight to one. As a skirmisher, or scout, in Sherman's drive through Georgia, he was credited with being the first soldier to cross the Chattahoochee River at Roswell on July 9, 1864.

After the war, Mount returned to Indiana and entered the Lebanon Presbyterian Academy in Boone County, one of eight such schools in the state offering students a classical education. He had to leave the academy after one year of study when his money ran out, but during his time there he became friends with a young woman, Kate Boyd, who shared his love of farm life. The couple was married upon her graduation from the academy in 1867, and they began their life together by renting a rundown three-room house on a farm in Montgomery County. After several years of hard work and careful management, they purchased the farm and all of its stock and equipment. The Mounts kept prospering and expanding, eventually owning five hundred acres of rich farmland and building an elegant $8,000 home for their family, which had come to include three children.

Mount's success as a farmer was due in large measure to his astute timing when selling livestock and crops, according to one of his contemporaries, who said, "He watched the trend of the markets very closely and always had something to sell when it would bring the best price." Both Mounts were generous in donating their time to share the secrets of their success with others, and were especially encouraging to young farmers who faced the same sorts of obstacles they did in the beginning. Kate, like her husband, was a frequent lecturer on the farmers' institutes circuit, sometimes giving several presentations a week. One author, commenting on Mount's lecturing at county institutes, said that "long before his name was considered in connection with high public office he had done much to mold and influence the destiny of the state as an agricultural center."

In 1888, over Mount's objections, the Republican Party nominated him for a state senate seat, a race he won in a normally Democratic district by six hundred votes. Two years later, again against his wishes, the party picked him as its congressional candidate in the Eighth District, but he was handily beaten as Democrats captured eleven of the state's thirteen congressional seats. Mount, who then finished out his two years in the state senate, was more receptive to party overtures to run for governor in the highly charged election year of 1896. Republican fortunes in Indiana and the nation were on the upswing as voters punished Democrats, the party in power, for the country's economic depression of the early 1890s. In the off-year elections of 1894, for example, Republicans captured both houses of the Indiana General Assembly for the first time since 1872, a dominance that continued into the early twentieth century. The party also won all of the thirteen congressional races.

In 1896 the political issue that overshadowed all others, both in Indiana and the nation, was the free and unlimited coinage of silver, heralded by Democratic presidential candidate William Jennings Bryan as the answer to the country's economic difficulties. With many in the agrarian reform movement in Indiana coalescing with Democrats around the free-silver issue, Republican leaders in the state, fearing a loss of support among farmers, saw Mount, the widely known and respected farmer, as the ideal standard-bearer. He proved to be just that, even topping the eighteen-thousand-vote plurality that GOP presidential candidate William McKinley received in the state by eight thousand votes.

Mount's unhappiness at being governor notwithstanding, his administration did help advance the state in several significant ways as Indiana continued its transformation from agriculture to industry. Perhaps the biggest achievement of his tenure was the enactment of the compulsory education law of 1897 that required children ages eight to fourteen to attend school. In step with the national reform and progressive movements of the time, the state also adopted laws to regulate businesses, control monopolies and trusts, improve worker health and safety, and ensure the quality of food and drugs. Additionally, a medical licensing board was established to screen applicants seeking to practice medicine, and the penal code was reformed to permit the possibility of parole to prisoners convicted of any felony except murder or treason.

An upturn in the business climate after the 1896 election made the economy less of a troubling matter for Mount and his administration, though there remained a number of other pressing problems that required attention. In the agricultural area, diseases were rampant among both crops and livestock. Commercial fruit production, which had been increasing in importance in the state, was threatened by disease and an infestation of pests. In response, Mount gained legislative approval for creating the position of state entomologist and for annual inspections of nurseries. Similarly, in an effort to prevent and control livestock disease, especially hog cholera, the general assembly approved Mount's proposal for a state veterinarian with powers to impose quarantines. Troubles for Mount also extended to the western Indiana coalfields and strikes by miners, mostly over wages. A two-member commission appointed by the governor to investigate the workers' complaints of inadequate pay sided with the miners. As a result of the commission's report, Mount "established a central relief committee to receive and distribute food and clothing to the needy strikers."

Another troublesome situation Mount faced involved getting blacks in Indiana an opportunity for military service in the Spanish-American War of 1898. When the War Department balked at activating two black infantry companies from Indiana unless they were commanded by white captains, Mount enlisted the aid of Indiana's Republican senator Charles W. Fairbanks to have the policy reversed. In a telegram to the senator, he said the "political situation" made it imperative "that Indiana [be] represented at the front by Colored men." Although small in number, black voters could make the difference in elections in the state because of the parity between the two main political parties. Mount and Fairbanks took their concerns to a receptive McKinley, who in turn had the War Department change its stand and allow the two units to be commanded by their black captains. The war ended before the black companies saw action, but the pressure by Mount and Fairbanks nevertheless "caused the War Department to modify its racial policy—a change which made it easier for other states to muster in Negro units with complete rosters of Negro officers."

During the last year of his administration Mount received national attention for refusing to grant an extradition request from Kentucky for the return of William S. Taylor, who fled to Indiana after being indicted for complicity in the murder of William Goebel. Taylor, a Republican, had defeated Goebel, a Democrat, in the bitter 1899 election for Kentucky governor. In the midst of an appeal by Democrats on the grounds of voter fraud, Goebel was shot as he was entering the statehouse and died a few days later. Taylor stayed in Indiana, where he became a successful insurance executive.

After her husband's death, Kate returned to Montgomery County and lived at the Willow Brook farm until her death in 1905. The Mounts are buried in Oak Hill Cemetery near Crawfordsville.

Portrait by James M. Dennis (ca. 1900?), Governors' Portraits Collection, Indiana Historical Bureau, State of Indiana.

FOR FURTHER READING

Bartholomew, H. S. K. "Governor James A. Mount." *Indiana Magazine of History* 33 (September 1937): 304–9.

Dunn, Jacob P. *Indiana and Indianans: A History of Aboriginal and Territorial Indiana and the Century of Statehood.* 5 vols. Chicago: American Historical Society, 1919.

Gatewood, Willard B. Jr. "Indiana Negroes and the Spanish American War." *Indiana Magazine of History* 69 (June 1973): 115–39.

Phillips, Clifton J. *Indiana in Transition: The Emergence of an Industrial Commonwealth, 1880–1920.* Vol. 4, *The History of Indiana.* Indianapolis: Indiana Historical Bureau and Indiana Historical Society, 1968.

Post, Margaret Moore. *First Ladies of Indiana and the Governors, 1816–1984.* Indianapolis: Pierson Printing Company, 1984.

Mount's gubernatorial papers are in the Indiana State Archives, Indianapolis.

Winfield T. Durbin

January 14, 1901–January 9, 1905

RAYMOND H. SCHEELE

WINFIELD DURBIN'S ELECTION VICTORY IN 1900 CONTINUED the Republican control of the governor's office during the Progressive Era. The abilities he developed as a businessman were the foundation of his political career. He often battled with members of his own party, always attempting to focus on policies establishing programs and reforms that would stimulate the economic and social growth of the state while balancing the progressive and the conservative wings of his party. At the same time, the major crisis he faced as governor was ultimately a moral crisis—lynching—and the manner in which he handled that threat in Indiana brought him national attention.

Winfield Durbin was the second Indiana governor to be born in Lawrenceburg, Indiana, following Albert G. Porter. Born on May 4, 1847, to William Sappington and Eliza Ann Sparks Durbin, he was the youngest of seven boys, one of whom was named Henry Clay Durbin, reflecting the family's interest in politics and public affairs. His parents moved to New Philadelphia, Indiana, while Winfield was still young. He attended public schools and worked in his father's tannery during the summers. He and his brothers enlisted in the Union army and joined the Sixteenth Indiana Volunteer Infantry Regiment, but Winfield could not serve immediately because of an arm injury. Later he helped form Company K of the 139th Indiana Volunteer Infantry and served from April 1864 to September 1864. He was the last Civil War veteran who would be elected governor of Indiana, and he always maintained his membership in the Grand Army of the Republic. After the

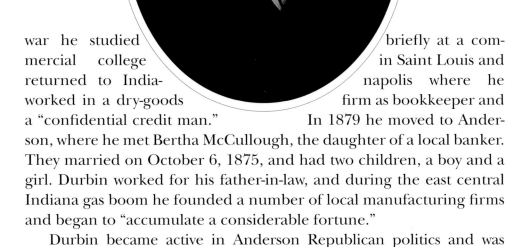

war he studied briefly at a commercial college in Saint Louis and returned to Indianapolis where he worked in a dry-goods firm as bookkeeper and a "confidential credit man." In 1879 he moved to Anderson, where he met Bertha McCullough, the daughter of a local banker. They married on October 6, 1875, and had two children, a boy and a girl. Durbin worked for his father-in-law, and during the east central Indiana gas boom he founded a number of local manufacturing firms and began to "accumulate a considerable fortune."

Durbin became active in Anderson Republican politics and was elected to the Republican State Central Committee in 1890. He served as a delegate to the GOP national conventions in 1892 and 1896. Governor James A. Mount brought Durbin onto his staff in 1897 and, when the Spanish-American War broke out, Mount appointed him colonel of the 161st Indiana Infantry Regiment, where he served from July 15, 1898 to April 30, 1899. The regiment served in Cuba for three months as an occupation force following the end of hostilities. It was reported after the war that Durbin based his leadership of the regiment on a simple premise: "I went on the theory that plain, common sense and business principles would apply to military life as well as to anything else," he said. This businesslike approach to life was well established in him by the time he received the Republican nomination for governor in April 1900. The Democrats sensed an impending loss and were "forced virtually to draft" their candidate for governor, John W. Kern. However, in November the competitiveness of two-party politics in Indiana continued to be demonstrated, and Durbin won with just 51.9 percent of the vote.

Durbin's inaugural address came on the heels of Mount's lengthy biennial message to the legislature, in which Mount addressed fifty-four specific issues, leaving Durbin to remark that he would "confine my remarks to generalities, rather than conventional recommendations." However, the new governor was very specific in stating his view of state government: he likened it to a private business, saying that "each taxpayer is a stockholder in State government," and proclaimed his gratification that "our institutions are upon a business plane, free from any bias of party management," using "the most approved business methods," and that "there is no logic or reason in a difference between the methods that prevail in successful private business not being applicable to those in public business." He made brief and passing references to agriculture, manufacturing, the gas boom, and veterans, but he did mention a problem that would become one of the hallmarks of his administration: lynching. Only two sentences were devoted directly to the issue: "Law and order must not be superseded by the slightest resort to, or the approval of, the injustice of vigilants [*sic*] with rope and masks. The hope of free institutions, the sanctity of the home, the safety of the citizen, the dignity of our manhood, rests on the respect for and the enforcement of law."

Lynching was a festering boil on the body politic, even in Indiana. While the exact numbers are unknown, at least sixty-one persons—forty-one whites and twenty African Americans—were lynched in Indiana between 1865 and 1903. Although more whites than African Americans were lynched, African Americans constituted only 2 percent of the state's total population and African American victims accounted for a third of those lynched. In 1886 an African American man was lynched on the Knox County Courthouse Square in Vincennes. In 1889 two white men were lynched at Corydon, and other lynchings occurred at Spencer and Shelbyville. In 1897 five white men accused of robbery were seized from the Ripley County Jail and hanged in the town square. Finally, in 1899, the state legislature passed an antilynching law that required a sheriff to petition the governor for military assistance if a lynching were threatened. The law allowed the governor to remove a sheriff from office who surrendered a prisoner to a mob. The very next year, however, three African American men accused of murder were lynched in Rockport, and a few weeks later an African American man was lynched from the Wabash River Bridge in Terre Haute. But no steps were taken to enforce the 1899 law. It was to fall on Durbin's shoulders to act.

In 1902 Durbin invoked the law and removed the Sullivan County sheriff after an African American prisoner was turned over to a lynch mob. His action ended lynchings in Indiana for nearly three decades (until two young African Americans, Abe Smith and Tom Shipp, were lynched by a mob in Marion in 1930), but it did not bring an end to racial tensions and violence. On July 4, 1903, a white Evansville policeman was slain and an African American man was arrested. A mob formed, and although the arrested man was moved out of Evansville, the mob continued to storm the jail. Upon request of the sheriff, Durbin called out Company E of the First Regiment of the Indiana National Guard. Durbin, in his final address to the Indiana General Assembly, described what happened:

> The Indiana National Guard, while defending the jail and other public property at Evansville against the attack of a mob ostensibly seeking to avenge the murder of a policeman . . . but actually engaged only in a senseless uprising against duly constituted authority, was fired upon after enduring for many hours the taunts and jeers of a large assailing party. The fire was returned by the soldiers of the Guard and by deputies stationed in the windows of the jail. The result was the killing of eleven persons, the wounding of many more, and the instant dispersal of the mob.

This incident bore in on Durbin. He not only confronted the mob through executive action, but he confronted the meaning of the mob to the democracy. He worried that his generation was losing the "inheritance" of free institutions and lapsing into "an era of commercialism." Such faltering in the defense of laws "prompts citizens of a Republic in the madness of animal fury to dash themselves insensately against the barriers erected by centuries of civilization between brute force and human rights." He compared the "sweep of the mob spirit" to "the rush of water through a sewer," and declared that if it became a contagion, the Republic will fall under the "sway of that dictator who proves himself to be the best leader of mobs."

Durbin's actions to crack down on lynching not only crystallized his views of liberty and order, but they also received national attention, and some observers thought his courageous stand merited a place on the Republican national ticket in 1904. The governor's mind was not totally consumed by the mobs, however. He continued to advocate several initiatives, many of which were consistent with the progressive agenda and often encountered opposition from conservative Republicans. In his biennial address to the Indiana General Assembly on January 8, 1903, he called for the creation of a juvenile court, which the legislature established after Durbin vetoed the first version because of constitutional reservations. He signed the second bill on March 10, 1903, and Indiana became the third state in the country to establish a juvenile court.

Durbin opposed a bill that permitted the consolidation of railroads and vetoed the measure, proclaiming that it put interests of big business against those of the people. He was concerned about election fraud and called for criminal penalties to be extended to those who sold their votes in addition to the law that penalized the purchasers of votes. When a special audit of Monroe County accounts revealed huge sums of public funds missing, Durbin showed his disgust of public corruption by threatening to remove the state university from Bloomington.

Durbin did not directly mention highways in his inaugural address, but he recognized the geographical advantage Indiana had in the Midwest and became a strong advocate of a state highway system to promote commerce. During his four years in office automobile traffic grew to the point that in his final address he called for "legislation regulating the speed and manner of handling" automobiles upon the "streets and highways of the state." It was also during Durbin's term that the Soldiers and Sailors Monument was completed in downtown Indianapolis. He proclaimed May 15, 1902, a public holiday in order to dedicate "one of the most majestic monuments in the world."

Durbin returned to Anderson and his business interests following his term as governor. When Governor Thomas R. Marshall proposed a new constitution for Indiana in 1911, Durbin returned to the public arena. Joining his successor, Governor J. Frank Hanly, the two Republicans railed against Marshall's proposal. Durbin opined that Marshall's new constitution "reminds me of the response that the girl gave to her first proposal. 'It's so sudden,' the girl said. The idea of a Governor trying to substitute for the organic law of a commonwealth a socialistic program conceived in a fortnight! It is positively absurd." In 1912 the state Republican Party—split down the middle by the formation of the Progressive Party led by Theodore Roosevelt—turned to Durbin as its nominee for governor. U.S. senator Albert J. Beveridge was the gubernatorial nominee of the Progressive Party, and Durbin finished a poor third in the race, with Democrat Samuel M. Ralston winning easily. Durbin returned again to Anderson, where he lived until his death at age eighty-one on December 18, 1928.

Portrait by Wayman Adams (ca. 1920?), Governors' Portraits Collection, Indiana Historical Bureau, State of Indiana.

FOR FURTHER READING

Biennial Message of Governor Winfield T. Durbin and Inaugural Address of Governor J. Frank Hanly. Indianapolis: Wm. Burford, 1905.

Durbin, Winfield T. Messages and Documents of Winfield T. Durbin, 1900–1902. Charles E. Wilson, comp. Indiana State Archives, Indianapolis.

"Durbin and Hanly Assail Marshall." *Indianapolis Star,* February 17, 1911.

Hoosier Heritage: Indiana Governors, 1800–1968. Hammond, IN: Sheffield Press, 1968.

Lambert, Louis E. "The Indiana State Board of Accounts." *Indiana Magazine of History* 55 (June 1959): 111–68.

Madison, James H. *A Lynching in the Heartland: Race and Memory in America.* New York: Palgrave, 2001.

Message of Governor Winfield T. Durbin. *Journal of the Indiana State Senate, Sixty-fourth Session of the General Assembly.* Indianapolis: William Burford, contractor for state printing, 1905.

Phillips, Clifton J. *Indiana in Transition: The Emergence of an Industrial Commonwealth, 1880–1920.* Vol. 4, *The History of Indiana.* Indianapolis: Indiana Historical Bureau and Indiana Historical Society, 1968.

Seeds, Russel M. *History of the Republican Party of Indiana.* Indianapolis: Indiana History Company, 1899.

Sullivan, Frank Jr. "Indiana as a Forerunner in the Juvenile Court Movement." *Indiana Law Review* 30, no. 1 (1997): 279–303.

Durbin's gubernatorial papers are in the Indiana State Archives, Indianapolis.

J. Frank Hanly

January 9, 1905–January 11, 1909

RAYMOND H. SCHEELE

A FULL CENTURY AFTER HIS TERM, JAMES FRANK HANLY continues to be one of Indiana's most controversial governors. He has been called an "enigmatic reformer"; "a cunning politician, a master of intrigue"; a "Don Quixote for prohibition"; and the hurler of "fiery anathemas" at Democrats. He advocated a decidedly progressive agenda, but in his forty-eight months as governor he was able to accomplish little that was to have long-lasting impact. During that time he perfected his thoughts on the moral calling of temperance, and it was that calling for which he is most prominently known.

The man who would confound and perplex his political party and most Hoosiers was born into poverty on April 4, 1863, in a log cabin near Saint Joseph, Illinois, about seven miles east of Champaign, Illinois. He was the youngest of seven children born to Elijah and Anna E. Calton Hanly. He began working as a farmhand and laborer at a young age to help pay household bills. His mother taught him to read, but she lost her eyesight when he was eleven, and he managed to obtain only about a year of formal schooling. On July 4, 1876, Hanly was inspired by the oratory in Champaign and started practicing public speaking. At sixteen "he started out alone to Warren county, Indiana, but his funds soon gave out and he had to walk most of the distance." He worked odd jobs, passed his teacher's licensing exam, and succeeded in saving enough money to enroll in a short summer course at Eastern Illinois Normal School. His dogged determination was evident early. It was the driving force in his political career.

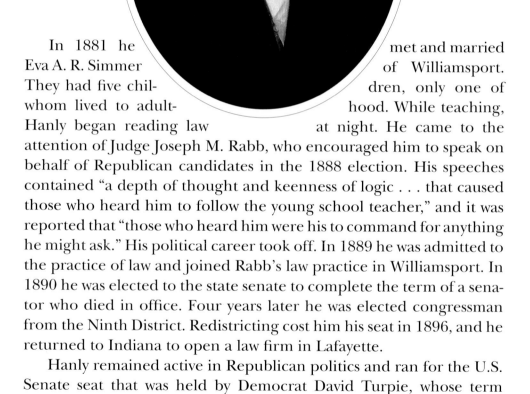

In 1881 he met and married Eva A. R. Simmer of Williamsport. They had five chil- dren, only one of whom lived to adult- hood. While teaching, Hanly began reading law at night. He came to the attention of Judge Joseph M. Rabb, who encouraged him to speak on behalf of Republican candidates in the 1888 election. His speeches contained "a depth of thought and keenness of logic . . . that caused those who heard him to follow the young school teacher," and it was reported that "those who heard him were his to command for anything he might ask." His political career took off. In 1889 he was admitted to the practice of law and joined Rabb's law practice in Williamsport. In 1890 he was elected to the state senate to complete the term of a sena- tor who died in office. Four years later he was elected congressman from the Ninth District. Redistricting cost him his seat in 1896, and he returned to Indiana to open a law firm in Lafayette.

Hanly remained active in Republican politics and ran for the U.S. Senate seat that was held by Democrat David Turpie, whose term expired in 1899. Hanly's major opponent was Albert J. Beveridge. The election was waged among the eighty-nine GOP members of the state legislature. Five candidates entered the race, and Hanly, with support from U.S. senator Charles W. Fairbanks, was the leading contender, garnering most of his support from legislators outside of Marion County. In a hotly contested election, after a dozen ballots, Beveridge was elected with forty-nine votes to Hanly's thirty-five. Beveridge's election opened a massive fissure in the Indiana Republican Party. Beveridge was competing with Fairbanks for control of the Indiana GOP at the same time issues such as temperance and women's suffrage, as well as the progressive movement, were shaking the two-party system in Indiana and the nation.

After Beveridge's victory, Hanly returned to his Lafayette law practice. He continued delivering speeches throughout the state, increasingly sprinkling his addresses with moral certitudes and phrases from Abraham Lincoln. His oratory resembled "old fashioned Methodist revivals" more than political assemblies. He was much in demand by lodges, veterans' groups, churches, and graduation audiences, and it was widely accepted that his travels were designed to build his political base for another run for high office, perhaps the U.S. Senate in 1904. The Republicans retained the governorship in the 1900 election and increased their majorities in both state legislative chambers. These victories, along with President William McKinley's assassination in September 1901, submerged the disputes in the Indiana Republican Party. The Democrats, meanwhile, continued to be split over issues raised by the "Great Commoner," William Jennings Bryan.

In August 1903 Hanly decided to seek the governor's chair in the next election and was easily nominated in the Republican state convention in April 1904. Later that summer the Republican National Convention nominated Fairbanks for vice president, vastly improving Republican fortunes in Indiana. But Hanly took nothing for granted. He spoke throughout the state, excoriating the Democratic Party, saying it was "without constructive ability" and "great only in its ability to destroy," and that Democrats were "for unholy and partisan purposes" to gain "a selfish end,—the obtaining of the 'flesh pots' of office." The national Democratic Party recognized Indiana's importance that summer when Thomas Taggart was elected national chairman. But Hoosier Democrats appeared to sense an impending defeat. They held two state conventions in 1904, one to select delegates to the national nominating convention and one to nominate their state ticket. Their efforts to separate the state ticket from the national nominees, however, were to no avail. "Never before in the history of Indiana was there experienced such a slump as occurred in the polls in November [for the Democrats]." Hanly defeated Democrat John W. Kern by more than sixty-four thousand votes, more than doubling the victory margin that Durbin enjoyed over Kern in 1900. All other state GOP nominees were elected, and the state senate seated thirty-six Republicans while the Indiana House swore in seventy-nine.

Hanly's 1905 inaugural address exceeded twelve thousand words and was replete with references to his religious beliefs and moral callings. He stated his "belief in the existence of a just God, in the teachings of the Christ, and in the immortality of my own soul" and justified his call for the construction of a new state hospital for the insane by proclaiming "the words of the great Teacher, for surely He must have thought of such unfortunate, stricken ones as these when He said, 'Inasmuch as ye have done it unto one of the least of these, my brethren, ye have done it unto Me.'" In a plea that would prove not to be salubrious for the Republican Party, he advocated a change in the liquor laws to allow the people to more easily stop the "traffic" because of its "unholiness."

Hanly's program was not overly ambitious, and his list of legislative accomplishments is viewed as "quite a limited one." One of his main achievements was the creation of the Indiana Railroad Commission, which was aimed at controlling abuses by the railroad and averting "the more radical sentiment of the country just now crystallizing in the demand for public ownership." Some progressive measures adopted during his administration included legislation to regulate trusts, railroads, and private banks and to outlaw "bucket shops" that illegally allowed what were basically wagers on security prices and commodity futures. During Hanly's term the legislature also established a legislative reference department in the Indiana State Library for the benefit of members of the legislature. Only one other state, Wisconsin, had provided for such an agency.

Not long into Hanly's governorship, major scandals erupted that heaped embarrassment upon his administration and that required his constant attention. Republican officeholders, including the state auditor, the secretary of state, and the state adjutant general, were found to have been misappropriating state funds for personal uses and, in the case of the auditor, to pay gambling debts that had been incurred on the property of the French Lick Springs Hotel, which was owned by Democrat Taggart. Hanly moved to limit the damage by insisting that the auditor resign. He appointed a three-person commission to investigate the amount of missing money and charged it with going back in time to investigate "officials whose terms have long expired," in order to maintain "that graft and peculation in Indiana has been bipartisan." He sought to shift the blame to Taggart, contending that Taggart's actions had received "exposure and condemnation" and this was "not the fault of the administration." Hanly pulled no punches: "[Taggart] alone is to blame. He knew when he established a Monte Carlo at French Lick that he was violating the law of the State." On July 3, 1906, Hanly sent state police officers to Orange County to raid the hotel casinos at French Lick and West Baden. They hauled away "nineteen slot machines, four roulette tables, two poker tables, two Klondike tables, one faro table, the famous French Lick Bookmakers' Club wheel, complete paraphernalia for making books on horse races, and many bushels of chips, cards, dice, and 'membership' cards." The state brought suit against Taggart and the owner of the West Baden resort seeking to revoke the charters of the companies and force the properties into receivership. The defendants were found not guilty.

The voters in the off-year election of 1906 did not punish the Republican ticket. For the seventh consecutive statewide election, the Republicans won the statewide offices and picked up one state senate seat. The Democrats took some solace in the state house of representatives, where they picked up twenty-five seats, but still were five seats short of a majority.

The final two years of Hanly's tenure focused more and more on the temperance issue. As one scholar concluded, "the governor's dedication to moral reform so outweighed every other possible consideration that critical issues were often neglected so that Hanly could conduct a crusade against vice."

On April 1, 1908, Hanly addressed the Republican state convention and insisted that the party include in its platform a "Local Option Law which shall permit the people of a county, should they so elect, by ballot at a special election, to exclude the saloons from the entire county." When the convention agreed to Hanly's local option plank, the governor was prepared to fight for its enactment. Three weeks before the general election, he called a special session of the state legislature and challenged it to pass the local option law. When the legislature agreed, the Republican nominee for governor, James E. Watson, contended that "it took my platform squarely out from under me." The 1908 gubernatorial campaign was as much a campaign against Hanly as it was a contest between Republican Watson and Democratic nominee Thomas R. Marshall. The Republicans had controlled the governor's office for twelve years, but Hanly "so completely demoralized, disorganized and disrupted the Republican party" that the Democrats won the next two gubernatorial races. During the 1908 campaign Marshall compared Hanly to a "dictator" who was "in violation of constitutional government" for calling the special session, and Watson ultimately blamed Hanly's actions for his defeat.

In the years following his governorship Hanly played a prominent role on behalf of the Anti-Saloon League, but he soon broke from it and other temperance groups to organize The Flying Squadron of America. Members of the Squadron scheduled speeches and rallies across the country to promote the total ban of liquor. Hanly served as chairman of the executive committee and was one of the most prominent and popular speakers on the circuit. Following his speeches in Boise, Idaho, in April, 1915, Idaho's major newspaper proclaimed that "it was to a species of old-time eloquence that we listened yesterday afternoon while Governor Hanly spoke."

The Flying Squadron professed that "Whenever a politician or an executive officer, or a political party prefers the liquor traffic above the public morals, such men must be set aside and such parties abandoned." And Hanly abandoned the Republican Party. In 1916 he accepted the nomination of the Progressive Party for governor of Indiana, but he quickly withdrew from that race to accept the Prohibition

Party's nomination for president of the United States. For the next four years he continued to campaign for Prohibition. He successfully argued a major case before the U.S. Supreme Court that advanced the cause of the Eighteenth Amendment. He died on August 1, 1920, from injuries sustained in an automobile accident in Ohio. He was fifty-seven years old.

Portrait by Wayman Adams (1913), Governors' Portraits Collection, Indiana Historical Bureau, State of Indiana.

FOR FURTHER READING

"Address of Gov. J. Frank Hanly." September 24, 1906, delivered at Tipton, Indiana. Indiana State Library, Indianapolis.

Braeman, John. "The Rise of Albert J. Beveridge to the United States Senate." *Indiana Magazine of History* 53 (December 1957): 357–82.

Boomhower, Ray E. *Jacob Piatt Dunn, Jr.: A Life in History and Politics, 1855–1924.* Indianapolis: Indiana Historical Society, 1997.

Fadely, James Philip. *Thomas Taggart: Public Servant, Political Boss, 1856–1929.* Indianapolis: Indiana Historical Society, 1997.

"The Flying Squadron of America, June 15, 1918." Indiana State Library, Indianapolis.

Garman, Harry O. "Biographical Sketch of J. Frank Hanly." Indiana State Library, 1940. (Garman was Hanly's son-in-law and notes that the sketch "was probably written by some person in the governors' office when Hanly was governor.")

Haggard, William S., ed. *J. Frank Hanly: Occasional Addresses.* Lafayette, IN, 1904.

Hanly, J. Frank. *Inaugural Address to the Sixty-Fourth General Assembly.* Indianapolis: Burford, contractor of state printing, 1905.

Indiana Governors, 1800–1968. Vol. 1, *Hoosier Heritage.* Hammond, IN: Sheffield Press, 1968.

Phillips, Clifton J. *Indiana in Transition, 1880–1920: The Emergence of an Industrial Commonwealth.* Vol. 4, *The History of Indiana.* Indianapolis: Indiana Historical Bureau and Indiana Historical Society, 1968.

Seeds, Russel M. *History of the Republican Party of Indiana.* Indianapolis: Indiana History Company, 1899.

Shipps, Jan. "J. Frank Hanly: Enigmatic Reformer." In *Gentlemen from Indiana: National Party Candidates, 1836–1940,* edited by Ralph D. Gray, 239–68. Indianapolis: Indiana Historical Bureau, 1977. Reprinted as "The Riddle of Governor Hanly." In *Indiana History: A Book of Readings,* edited by Ralph D. Gray, 214–20. Bloomington: Indiana University Press, 1994.

Stoll, John B. *History of the Indiana Democracy, 1816–1916.* Indianapolis: Indiana Democratic Club, 1917.

Temperance Legislation in Indiana: Governor Hanly's Speech on the Liquor Traffic, 1908. Pamphlet. Indiana State Library, Indianapolis.

The few items extant on Hanly are located in the Indiana State Library. Most are temperance related. Many of the papers from his gubernatorial years were destroyed.

Thomas R. Marshall

January 11, 1909–January 13, 1913

PETER T. HARSTAD

WHEN THOMAS R. MARSHALL WAS INAUGURATED AS INDI-
ana's twenty-seventh governor in 1909, industrialization, urbanization,
and immigration were reshaping the landscape of the state. Gary, a
company town destined to epitomize the best and the worst of industrial America, mushroomed on the shore of Lake Michigan and began
producing steel in 1909. Jobs in mills and factories attracted hired
men and unmarried women from the countryside, immigrants from
Europe, and African Americans from the lower South. Many newcomers to the industrial towns lacked skills to protect their own interests.
Some could not speak English. Issues of health, safety, and hygiene
plagued citizens in all parts of the state, particularly coal miners, quar-
rymen, meat packers, and railroad workers. Leaders of churches and
benevolent institutions lacked clout to temper dehumanizing decisions that came from boardrooms far removed from the workplace.
Indiana's labor laws were "some of the least progressive in the country." Prisons were full and there was social unrest. State and local
officials felt powerless to intervene even in the interests of exploited
children. As governor during these turbulent times, Marshall pushed
to find solutions to these vexing problems. He was considered, at least
by Indiana standards, to be a relatively progressive governor.

Thomas R. Marshall was born March 14, 1854, in North Manchester, Indiana. Previously, his parents, Daniel, a country doctor, and
Martha Patterson Marshall, had a daughter, but she did not survive
infancy. They had no more children, so Thomas was an only child.

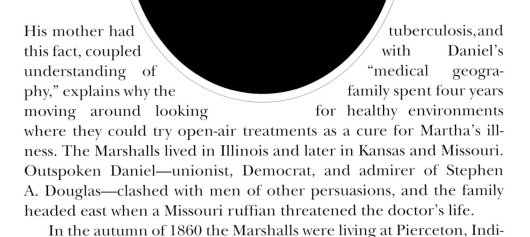

His mother had tuberculosis, and this fact, coupled with Daniel's understanding of "medical geogra-phy," explains why the family spent four years moving around looking for healthy environments where they could try open-air treatments as a cure for Martha's ill-ness. The Marshalls lived in Illinois and later in Kansas and Missouri. Outspoken Daniel—unionist, Democrat, and admirer of Stephen A. Douglas—clashed with men of other persuasions, and the family headed east when a Missouri ruffian threatened the doctor's life.

In the autumn of 1860 the Marshalls were living at Pierceton, Indi-ana, where Thomas enrolled in school. He spent six years in public school there, seventh and eighth grades in Warsaw, and the 1868–69 academic term in high school in Fort Wayne. Thomas received his sunny disposition and his Presbyterianism from his mother; from his father unswerving loyalty to the Democratic Party and sensitivity to human suffering. Each day of Thomas's youth began with a Presbyte-rian prayer "that began in Indiana and ended in China." Thereafter "we had a teaspoonful of quinine and then we had breakfast."

At age fifteen Thomas passed the Wabash College entrance exam and enrolled at the all-male, Presbyterian college at Crawfordsville. He showed no inclination to pursue his father's occupation nor to prepare for the Presbyterian ministry, as his mother had hoped. He studied classical Greek and Latin, modern French and German, mathematics, a cluster of critical-thinking courses, science, religion, military drill, and the U.S. Constitution.

Beyond the classroom Marshall joined Phi Gamma Delta fraternity, literary and debating societies, and the staff of the campus newspaper. He engaged in political activities and staunchly defended Democratic Party principles in debates. All of these activities had a strong influence on the undersized, brash young man. A defining moment came during the 1872–73 term when he defamed the character of a female lecturer and visitor to Crawfordsville in the columns of the student newspaper. She filed a $20,000 libel suit against Marshall and the *Geyser* staff, whereupon Marshall engaged the legal services of Benjamin Harrison. The future president extricated the students from their predicament, charged nothing, then exhorted the young men on ethics. "It was a great lesson to me," Marshall wrote, "and I have never again been sued for either slander or libel."

Elected to Phi Beta Kappa, Marshall graduated from Wabash College with honors in June 1873. As a result of the libel-suit episode in college, his father's political connections, and Saturday visits to courthouses, Marshall had met leading members of the Indiana bar, which fueled his interest in the law. He began studying law under the tutelage of his uncle, Woodson Marshall, but scuttled this plan to move to Columbia City with his parents. By the close of 1873 he was studying there in the office of Hooper and Olds. His preceptor, Walter Olds, opened an office in Fort Wayne and later became a judge of the Indiana Supreme Court. The Whitley County Circuit Court admitted Marshall to the bar on April 26, 1875, a month after he turned twenty-one.

The demand for legal services was booming in Whitley County and, by the late 1870s, Marshall and his partner, William F. McNagny, were involved with nearly half the cases before the local circuit court. McNagny attended to details of the law; Marshall worked the juries. Their influence spread throughout the Twelfth Congressional District of northeast Indiana. The affiliation between the two men lasted from 1876 until Marshall became governor.

In 1880 Marshall ran for the office of prosecutor in a two-county judicial district. He campaigned vigorously and carried Whitley County, but he lost the election because neighboring Kosciusko County was a Republican stronghold. He did not run for office again until 1908. Nevertheless, during those twenty-eight years people throughout Indiana came to know him because he spoke at rallies and conventions, supported candidates, and served on the Democratic State Central Committee beginning in 1896. Others came to know him through college, fraternity, legal, honorary society, church, and lodge affiliations. He developed a reputation as a quick-witted and engaging speaker.

Diverse elements came together to transform a gregarious county-seat lawyer into a successful gubernatorial candidate and then into a national political figure—some by force of character, others by organization and hard work, still others by what Marshall would term the will of God. His life appeared to be in order. He attended services regularly at First Presbyterian Church, taught Sunday school, served on the school board, organized the county fair, and contributed generously to charities. A Mason, he climbed the grades of the Scottish Rite to the thirty-third degree by 1898.

Beneath Marshall's genial exterior, however, lay a serious problem: he drank too much. Some mornings he could not function in court. He ultimately overcame his problem with the help of his wife, Lois I. Kimsey, whom he married in 1895, and often spoke at temperance meetings. Nevertheless, the issue of his drinking resurfaced in his campaign for governor in 1908, when temperance became a prominent campaign issue.

When approached about running for Congress in 1906, Marshall declined, then hinted that he might be interested in the office of governor. He would need backers and organizers as well as support from Thomas Taggart, leader of the Democratic Party in Indiana. These came in due course. A Republican friend from Wabash College convinced the journalist Louis Ludlow, Washington correspondent for the *Indianapolis Star*, to tout Marshall for governor, which he did in a column in the *Star* on September 3, 1907. Leading Twelfth District Democrats got on the Marshall bandwagon early and enthusiastically.

The liquor issue loomed large in 1908. The outgoing governor, J. Frank Hanly, a strong advocate of temperance, had pushed a reluctant legislature to adopt a countywide option law in a special session. This allowed counties to ban the sale of alcoholic beverages. It was not a popular measure. Taggart, a "wet," came to the state Democratic convention in March with his gubernatorial candidate, Samuel M. Ralston, in tow. A substantial anti-Taggart faction gathered around temperance candidate L. Ert Slack. In early balloting, Twelfth District delegates to a man remained loyal to Marshall. At a crucial point in the balloting, when it appeared that Ralston could not carry the day, Taggart swung the Ralston delegates to Marshall to head off Slack. On the fifth ballot Marshall received the nomination. He responded with a rousing call to party unity, including a reference to the apostle Paul, who had advocated medicinal use of wine. The convention selected Frank J. Hall of Rushville to run as lieutenant governor.

Marshall campaigned at his own expense against Republican nominee James E. Watson, whose party was badly divided between its progressive and conservative wings. In the campaign Marshall's opponents accused him of drunkenness, but leaders from across the political spectrum defended him. He poked fun at the miniscule distinctions that separated the two major parties on liquor issues. Watson supported the county option, while the Democratic platform called for local option, with city, ward, or township as the determining unit. Other planks called for direct election of U.S. senators, a new primary election law, and a litany of progressive measures similar to those in the Republican platform. Marshall's engaging personality helped him hold his party together and to cut into the margins of other parties. Marshall won by 14,809 votes out of 712,000 votes cast. His victory ushered in an eight-year period of Democratic dominance, aided by the fact that the progressives in the Republican Party split from the state party and joined forces with Theodore Roosevelt's Progressive Party. The Democrats won a majority of the seats in the state house of representatives, but failed to gain a majority in the state senate.

When Marshall assumed office, Indiana had no residence for its governor. The Marshalls leased a house in Indianapolis not far from the home of a scholarly Indianapolis Democrat, Jacob Piatt Dunn Jr., whom Marshall later called upon for one of his major initiatives, revising the state constitution.

Marshall's inaugural address on January 11, 1909, doubled as a sermon on progressivism. He declared that legislation "toward the making of men honest, or truthful, or industrious, or wise, is 'as idle as a painted ship upon a painted ocean.'" The legislature "cannot baptize the State. . . . What we need is not reform, but regeneration." He served notice on the trusts by asserting that the corporation is the creature of the state, and that "the creature cannot legally grow to be greater than its creator." The speech also fostered harmony, saying that in Indiana capitalists and laborers "are all brethren."

One of Marshall's objectives was to improve the procedures by which Indiana conducted its business and ran its institutions. This was evident in his approach to appointments. To keep from being overwhelmed by the office seekers who besieged him, Marshall tried to deal with them systematically. Distancing himself from the practices of Taggart, he attended to patronage by evenhandedly appointing to office Democrats from several factions of the party and reserving few patronage positions for himself.

He also engineered a plan that removed the process of selecting U.S. senators from smoke-filled caucus rooms and brought it closer to the people. At the time, U.S. senators were selected by the state legislature, but the true choice was made by the party caucus through a process that was often a raucous affair. Marshall got the state Democratic Party to agree to adopt a nominee before the general election in 1910 and to let the voters know in advance who the nominee was. They promised if they gained a majority in the state senate the announced nominee would be selected U.S. Senator. This reform presaged the passage of the Seventeenth Amendment to the U.S. Constitution, which established the direct election of senators, by three years.

Marshall also succeeded in getting the state legislature to create a State Board of Accounts, which gave his office power to hold state and local government employees accountable. It included a system of purchasing that in its first year, he claimed, saved over a half million dollars on school supplies alone.

Compassionate but not naïve, Marshall took personal interest in the state's penal system and saw to the pardoning of nearly three thousand prisoners, far more than his predecessors combined. In the same vein he throttled down a program of performing vasectomies on young males at the Jeffersonville reformatory.

In labor disputes Marshall used the state militia impartially to protect both the lives of workers and the interests of property owners, but he preferred arbitration. He was faced with a number of labor strikes that threatened violence, but Marshall tried to be evenhanded in these disputes. He thought his role was neither to break a union nor to help a union break an employer.

After the Democrats gained majorities in both houses of the Indiana General Assembly in the midterm election of 1910, Marshall turned to a progressive agenda of remedial and regulatory legislation. In keeping with his campaign promise regarding the sale of alcohol, the Democrats passed a township-option bill that only party diehards regarded as a reform measure. He pushed a progressive agenda related to child labor, correctional institutions, drugs, education, elections, hygiene, railroad safety, trusts, voter registration, and workman's compensation.

Passage of the mildly progressive legislation in the second half of his administration suggests that Marshall helped Hoosiers deal with some of the major problems spawned by the industrial age. Among his main achievements were the passage of a child labor law, an employer's liability law, a weekly wage law, and laws regulating railroads, telegraphs, and telephone companies. The legislature enacted a corrupt practices act and a voter registration law. Scholars who have analyzed the bills that Marshall signed into law during the second half of his administration characterize them as mild reform measures.

One of Marshall's chief reform initiatives was his failed effort to amend the state constitution. He had concluded that the difficult-to-amend constitution of 1851 was a deterrent to much needed change. He assigned to his friend and neighbor, Dunn, the task of drafting an entirely new constitution. People called it "The Tom Marshall Constitution," and it was presented to the legislature in 1911. Marshall's constitution had a curious blend of provisions, including such progressive measures as the initiative, referendum, and recall alongside restrictive voting eligibility requirements. It limited voting rights to male citizens of the United States above the age of twenty-one who had resided in the state for twelve months. The existing law permitted foreign-born males above the age of twenty-one to vote if they had declared their intention to become a U.S. citizen and had lived in the state for six months. Further, the proposed constitution established an English-literacy test for voter registration and imposed a poll tax for voting. The proposed constitution did not call for voting rights for women, despite the growing suffrage movement in the country. Marshall was adamantly against the idea of universal woman's suffrage, and when he was vice president he was caustically critical of the "everlasting clatter of the militant suffragettes." Marshall's proposed constitution also would have increased the size of the state house of representatives and state supreme court.

Rather than go to the trouble and expense of a constitutional convention as required by the state's constitution, Marshall presented his proposed constitution to the Indiana General Assembly, which approved not only the document but also the mechanism of letting the voters ratify the constitution. Frustrated Republicans charged that the proposed constitution would give the Democrats undue advantage at the polls and that the adoption procedure violated the governor's own separation of powers principles by usurping the power of the legislature. They convinced the Marion County Circuit Court to issue an injunction to keep the adoption issue off the ballot in the fall 1912 election. On appeal the Indiana Supreme Court sustained the decision of the lower court by one vote. Infuriated, Marshall argued that the judicial branch had overstepped its authority. There the issue stood at the close of Marshall's governorship in January 1913, pending review by the U.S. Supreme Court. Later that year the nation's highest tribunal denied the appeal. Thus Marshall failed in his attempt to accelerate change by replacing Indiana's 1851 constitution with a new one.

Some scholars have concluded that both "The Tom Marshall Constitution" and the means of adopting it were seriously flawed. There is merit in their arguments. However, the attention his proposed constitution gained him nationally may well have helped him in his quest for higher national office. His reputation had spread beyond Indiana, and he received speaking engagements from various parts of the country. He became a national political figure, and he went to the Democratic National Convention in 1912 with the goal of being nominated for president. Instead, he got the nomination for vice president, to run with the party's standard-bearer Woodrow Wilson. They defeated the Republican ticket in 1912 and again in 1916. Marshall became the first vice president since John C. Calhoun to be reelected.

Marshall was a popular figure in Washington. He was known for "his genial manner, his homely philosophy, his common good sense and his refusal to regard himself as different from other persons on account of the high office he held." He had a wry sense of humor and is perhaps best known for his famous line "what this country needs is a good five-cent cigar." There is no public record of his having made this statement; it is thought to have been overheard by a Senate secretary.

He is also remembered for the good judgment and character he displayed when Wilson was stricken with a cerebral stroke in the autumn of 1919. Many high-ranking officials urged Marshall to assume the office of president for the duration of Wilson's incapacity, but he refused to do so and said he would not consider such a suggestion unless it came from those closest to Wilson, with their insistence that such a move was essential to the public interest. Such a suggestion never came from Wilson's inner circle. They conspired to keep Marshall from visiting with the president and to keep the public in the dark as to the seriousness of Wilson's condition.

Marshall managed to serve as well as possible, despite the limits on his capacity as vice president. He presided over the Senate's debate and ultimate rejection of the League of Nations. He remained loyal to Wilson's vision for the League, although he later said that had he been president he would have been more flexible in dealing with the Senate. The impasse between Wilson and Marshall lasted until the end of their term of office in 1920.

After Marshall left public office he accepted speaking engagements, wrote his recollections, and served on the U.S. Coal Commission. He died of a heart attack on June 1, 1925, while on a visit to Washington, D.C. Upon learning of Marshall's death U.S. Secretary of State Frank B. Kellogg expressed a view widely held by others. He said Marshall "was a man of sterling ability and the highest character and won the respect of everyone whom he knew. . . . It was conceded on both sides of the Senate chamber that he was one of our best, fairest and ablest presiding officers."

At his request, Marshall was buried at Crown Hill Cemetery in Indianapolis by the grave of his foster son, Clarence Morrison, who had died at the age of ten. Morrison had been taken in by the Marshalls, who had no children of their own, and lived with them for four years before they moved to Washington. They had planned to adopt him, but he died before the legal steps were completed.

Portrait by Wayman Adams (1919), Governors' Portraits Collection, Indiana Historical Bureau, State of Indiana.

FOR FURTHER READING

Boomhower, Ray E. *Jacob Piatt Dunn, Jr.: A Life in History and Politics, 1855–1924.* Indianapolis: Indiana Historical Society, 1997. See especially chapter 5, "Dunn, Governor Thomas R. Marshall, and the Indiana Constitution."

Brown, John Eugene. "Woodrow Wilson's Vice President: Thomas R. Marshall and the Wilson Administration." PhD diss., Ball State University, 1970.

Harstad, Peter T. "Thomas Riley Marshall." In *The Vice Presidents: A Biographical Dictionary,* edited by L. Edward Purcell. New York: Facts on File, 2001.

Marshall, Thomas R. *Recollections of Thomas R. Marshall, Vice-President and Hoosier Philosopher: A Hoosier Salad.* Indianapolis: Bobbs-Merrill Company, 1925.

Thomas, Charles M. *Thomas Riley Marshall: Hoosier Statesman.* Oxford, OH: Mississippi Valley Press, 1939.

Seigel, Peggy. "Industrial 'Girls' in an Early Twentieth-Century Boom-town: Traditions and Change in Fort Wayne, Indiana, 1900–1920." *Indiana Magazine of History* 99 (September 2003): 231–53.

The Indiana State Archives, Indiana State Library, Indiana Historical Society, Indianapolis and the Whitley County Historical Society Museum (at Columbia City) all hold Thomas R. Marshall manuscripts and photographs.

Samuel M. Ralston

January 13, 1913–January 8, 1917

RAY E. BOOMHOWER

INDIANA'S CENTENNIAL GOVERNOR, SAMUEL M. RALSTON worked tirelessly to ensure the state commemorated its one hundredth anniversary of admission to the Union as the nineteenth state. Backed by the efforts of the newly created Indiana Historical Commission and the work of thousands of volunteers, the centennial observance saw the establishment of state parks, the beginnings of an improved road system, the creation of permanent memorials in numerous communities, the publication of historical volumes, and an overall awakening of interest in the history of the Hoosier State's heritage.

Ralston's role in the successful centennial celebration overshadowed his solid reform achievements as the state's twenty-eighth governor. Although the Lebanon Democrat, a close friend and ally of party boss Thomas Taggart, believed that the citizens of the state were "conservatively progressive," Ralston championed such measures as the creation of a public service commission to regulate utilities, a vocational education act, a child-labor law, an inheritance tax, a tenement housing act, a statewide primary system, a state farm for short-term offenders, and workmen's compensation. His administration also retired Indiana's debt.

A solid, affable man known from an early age as an outstanding orator, Ralston earned the affection of Hoosier voters, who elected him to the U.S. Senate over Republican challenger Albert J. Beveridge in 1922. Thanks to the efforts of Taggart, Ralston came close to capturing the presidential nomination at the Democratic National Con-

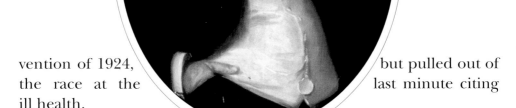

vention of 1924, but pulled out of the race at the last minute citing ill health.

Born on December 1, 1857, near New Cumberland, Tuscarawas County, Ohio, Ralston was the son of John and Sarah Scott Ralston. In 1865 the Ralston family moved to a four-hundred-acre farm near Spencer in Owen County, Indiana. While working on his father's farm, Samuel first became intrigued with pursuing a career in law after attending a trial before a justice of the peace. The financial panic that swept the country in 1873 caused the Ralstons to lose their farm and forced a move to Fontanet in Vigo County, where John leased land on which he mined coal. Working on farms during the summer, Samuel received his education during the winter, becoming a voracious reader.

Ralston also taught school to earn money for his further education. He attended the Northern Indiana Normal School in Valparaiso and also the Central Normal College in Danville, where he became involved in the Young Men's Democratic Club. In 1881 Ralston married Mary Josephine Backous of Connersville, but she died a year later. Ralston received his degree from Central Normal College in 1884 and began the study of law in the offices of J. C. Robinson and I. H. Fowler in Spencer. During his study, Ralston slept on a sofa in the law office in order to save money. He won admittance to the Owen County bar in January 1886. Looking to open his own practice, Ralston first considered Frankfort, but hearing about an opportunity for a young Democrat lawyer, he moved to Lebanon, the county seat of Boone County, where he formed a partnership with John A. Abbott.

In addition to his law practice, Ralston worked to support the Indiana Democratic Party, giving speeches on its behalf throughout the state and earning the respect and friendship of party leaders such as Taggart. However, Ralston's success with the party faithful did not translate into success for himself with voters, as in 1888 he lost a race to represent Clinton, Montgomery, and Boone counties as state senator. He subsequently lost two races for the secretary of state office in 1896 and 1898. Ralston had more success with his personal life, marrying Jennie Craven of Center Valley, whom he had met while a student, on December 30, 1889. The couple had three children: a daughter, Ruth, and two sons, Emmet and Julian.

With his continuing service to the party and his friendship with Taggart, Ralston seemed assured of gaining the top spot on the ticket—the gubernatorial nomination—when the Democrats gathered for their convention on March 25, 1908, at Tomlinson Hall in Indianapolis. At the convention, forces loyal to Taggart lined up in support of his candidate, Ralston. Meanwhile, those opposing Taggart's control over the party touted the candidacy of L. Ert Slack. With the convention deadlocked after four ballots, Ralston, pressed by his patron Taggart, announced his withdrawal from the race. With Ralston's withdrawal, voters quickly turned to a compromise candidate, Thomas R. Marshall, and he received his party's nomination on the subsequent ballot. Marshall would go on to defeat GOP candidate James E. Watson by more than fourteen thousand votes.

After his defeat, Ralston returned to his law practice in Lebanon, where he also served as president of the school board from 1908 to 1911. In 1912, following a successful term in office by Marshall, Ralston faced no opposition and received the Democratic nomination for governor at the party's convention on March 17 at Tomlinson Hall. Ralston was helped in the general election by a split in the Republican Party. The deep division between incumbent President William Howard Taft and Theodore Roosevelt had prompted

Roosevelt to bolt the party and establish the Progressive Party. A similar split occurred in Indiana, with the Progressives nominating Beveridge for governor while the Republicans turned to former governor Winfield T. Durbin. In the general election, Ralston received the largest plurality ever given a governor at that time and easily defeated Beveridge, who finished ahead of Durbin. Democrats also won control of both houses of the state legislature.

Taking office under a banner of "economy and reform," Ralston reminded the Indiana General Assembly that there existed among voters a growing wish for the "supremacy of the people over combinations of all kinds" and if the party in power failed to answer the demand it would "be repudiated by the people at their first opportunity." The legislature responded by establishing a public utilities commission to oversee telephone, gas, water, power, streetcar, and interurban companies. In addition, the legislature agreed with the governor's call for an overhaul of the state constitution, approving a series of amendments offered by Evan Stotsenburg, a Democratic state senator from New Albany. The amendments incorporated a number of changes sought during Marshall's term as governor. In addition, legislators passed along to voters a proposal for calling a constitutional convention. Hoosier voters overwhelmingly rejected such a convention during the 1914 election.

The most contentious issue facing Ralston's administration came in October 1913, when the Amalgamated Association of Street and Electric Railway Employees, foiled in its attempt to unionize approximately eight hundred workers at the Indianapolis Traction and Terminal Company, called upon motormen and conductors at the firm to strike to win union recognition along with higher wages and better working conditions. The company responded by firing striking workers and bringing in strikebreakers in order to keep its operation running. Responding to growing violence and the inability of the local authorities to maintain order, Ralston called out the Indiana National Guard. On the afternoon of November 6, thousands of workers gathered on the south lawn of the statehouse to protest the governor's action. Ralston left his office and spoke to the crowd, expressing sympathy for "the men and women who toil," but also called for an end to the violence and asked for the union's aid in preventing any more damage or injuries. He then successfully brought the firm and workers together to settle the strike.

Although Indiana voters in 1914 had rejected a call to celebrate the state's centennial by appropriating two million dollars for the construction of a memorial building to house the state library and other historical agencies, Ralston requested, and the legislature approved, a $25,000 appropriation and the creation of a nine-member Indiana Historical Commission charged with promoting a centennial celebration. The IHC sponsored historical pageants in communities throughout the state and, thanks to the efforts of conservationist Richard Lieber and others, developed Indiana's first state parks, McCormick's Creek and Turkey Run. The emphasis on the nineteenth state's past also sparked a general interest in Indiana history, with local historical societies formed or reactivated and the Indiana Historical Society seeing an influx of new members.

Leaving the governor's office with the state having a surplus of approximately four million dollars, Ralston returned to the practice of law, teaming with Indianapolis attorney Frederick Van Nuys. In 1922 he received the Democratic nomination for the U.S. Senate, going on to defeat a familiar opponent in Republican candidate Beveridge by approximately fifty thousand votes. As a senator, Ralston supported the paying of the bonus for World War I veterans and worked to reduce taxes. At the July 1924 Democratic National Convention in New York's Madison Square Garden, Ralston, with Taggart's backing, came tantalizingly close to capturing the presidential nomination that ultimately went to New York lawyer and West Virginia native John W. Davis. Due to ill health, Ralston withdrew his name from consideration for the nomination. Ralston died at his estate, Hoosier Home, located northwest of Indianapolis, on October 14, 1925. He was buried at the Lebanon Cemetery.

Portrait by Wayman Adams (1916), Governors' Portraits Collection, Indiana Historical Bureau, State of Indiana.

FOR FURTHER READING

Boomhower, Ray E. "Celebrating Statehood: Indiana's 1916 Centennial." *Traces of Indiana and Midwestern History* 3, no. 3 (Summer 1991): 28–39.

Dunn, Jacob P. *Indiana and Indianans: A History of Aboriginal and Territorial Indiana and the Century of Statehood.* 5 vols. Chicago: American Historical Society, 1919.

Hoy, Suellen M. "Samuel M. Ralston: Progressive Governor, 1913–1917." PhD diss., Indiana University, 1975.

———. "Governor Samuel M. Ralston and Indiana's Centennial." *Indiana Magazine of History* 71 (September 1975): 245–68.

Phillips, Clifton J. *Indiana in Transition: The Emergence of an Industrial Commonwealth, 1880–1920.* Vol. 4, *The History of Indiana.* Indianapolis: Indiana Historical Bureau and Indiana Historical Society, 1968.

Stoll, John B. *History of the Indiana Democracy, 1816–1916.* Indianapolis: Indiana Democratic Publishing Company, 1917.

Ralston's personal papers are located at the Lilly Library, Indiana University, Bloomington. His gubernatorial papers are in the Indiana State Archives, Indianapolis.

James P. Goodrich

January 8, 1917–January 10, 1921

DANE STARBUCK

"GIVE ME THE POWER, AND I'LL BE RESPONSIBLE FOR THE results," said James P. Goodrich during his run for the state's highest office in 1916. Known for his hard-hitting, decisive style, Goodrich would become best remembered as Indiana's "War Governor" due to the impact that World War I had on his term of office. He was one of the state's most accomplished chief executives. During his tenure, Goodrich established the State Highway Commission, the Department of Banking, and the Department of Conservation. Under the latter, many of Indiana's existing state parks were created. He assured the permanent status of the Indiana Historical Commission, and he reorganized the Public Service Commission. He signed the document ratifying Indiana's passage of the Nineteenth Amendment to the U.S. Constitution that extended the franchise to women and revamped Indiana's tax law, controlling public expenditures and saving state taxpayers more than $100 million.

James Putnam Goodrich was born on February 18, 1864, in Winchester, Indiana, two weeks before President Abraham Lincoln appointed a little-known general, Ulysses S. Grant, as commander in chief of the Union forces in the Civil War. The Goodrich family came to Indiana in 1832 when James's paternal great-grandmother, Rebecca Pearse Goodrich, a widow, left Virginia with eleven of her fourteen children. James's father, John Baldwin Goodrich, was an attorney who died prematurely of tuberculosis in 1872. James's mother, Elizabeth Edger Goodrich, was raised in Randolph County and was educated at Liber College in nearby Portland, Indiana.

Goodrich graduated from Winchester High School in 1881 in a class of nine stu- dents. Three note- worthy classmates were James E. Watson, a child- hood friend who would later become U.S. Senate Majority Leader from 1929 to 1932; John R. Commons, who became one of the most prominent U.S. economists of the twentieth century; and Cora Frist, whom Goodrich married in 1888.

After graduating from high school, Goodrich had planned on teaching school for one year and then matriculating at the U.S. Naval Academy in Annapolis, Maryland. He received a military appointment, but he had to decline because a severe hip injury, caused by a falling tree, prevented him from passing the academy's physical examination. Goodrich taught school for two years in Randolph County before matriculating at DePauw University in Greencastle, Indiana. At DePauw, Goodrich joined his childhood friend Watson, who began his college studies two years earlier, and became acquainted with Albert J. Beveridge, a brilliant student and orator, who would become a prominent U.S. Senator and gubernatorial candidate.

Goodrich quit college after two years for lack of funds and began to study law under John J. Cheney, a former circuit court judge, and Watson's father, Enos Watson. Goodrich went on to practice law with his uncle John Winchester "Ches" Macy and became involved with politics at the local level. Although he took an interest in a broad number of organizations, including the National Grange movement that advocated the interests of farmers, the Knights of Labor, and the Knights of Pythias, a philanthropic organization, his greatest interest was that of the Republican Party.

In 1897 Goodrich became chair of the Randolph County Republican Party and state Republican chairman in 1901. For the next ten years he traveled extensively throughout the state in support of local and statewide candidates. In particular, he had the difficult task of maintaining party unity at the same time he stroked the egos of such prominent and ambitious men as Charles W. Fairbanks, senator and vice president of the United States under Theodore Roosevelt, Beveridge, and Watson.

Goodrich stepped down in 1910 as state Republican chairman but remained on the executive committee of the national Republican Party. For the next few years he devoted himself to business and the practice of law. In December 1915 Goodrich returned to active politics when he announced his candidacy for governor. At the start of his campaign he gave a personal check for $40,000 to his campaign manager, John McCardla, and forbade him from receiving donations from any other individuals or organizations. Goodrich believed that by bankrolling his own campaign he could avoid obligations to political contributors.

His bid for the Republican nomination was fought out in Indiana's first statewide direct primary. He beat two opponents, Quincy A. Meyers and Warren T. McCray, by more than fifty thousand votes. In the general election he won the governor's office by defeating U.S. Representative John A. M. Adair from Portland by 47.8 percent to 46 percent. Goodrich received 337,831 votes; Adair had 325,060. Fellow Republicans Watson and Harry S. New both won U.S. Senate seats.

Goodrich's number-one goal of his four-year term was "efficiency and economy" in the administration of the state's duties. He immediately proceeded to prove it: his inaugural address lasted less than five minutes and he forwent the traditional inaugural ball in order to get down to business. He proposed abolishing many patronage positions, which he said only added to the bottom line, and overhauling the unjust tax system, making it more equitable between real property owners and owners of nontangible property.

Tax reform had been Goodrich's primary campaign issue. He thought that the tax system was grossly unfair to farmers because it taxed property but not the enormous intangible wealth that had been amassed in the state. Tax reform, however, would require an amendment to the state constitution. Indiana Supreme Court interpretations made it virtually impossible to amend the constitution through voter approval, so in 1917 Goodrich took the only route he thought was available to him—calling for a constitutional convention. He also asked the legislature to enact a statute calling for a constitutional convention and for the enactment of an excise tax on corporate property. On both efforts he was beaten by the power of those whose wealth was in intangible property. Their lobbyists succeeded in defeating the excise tax outright in the Indiana General Assembly and halting the constitutional convention through a lawsuit. In 1918 the Indiana Supreme Court ruled that the state legislature had no authority to call a constitutional convention, and that ended Goodrich's tax reform agenda. However, the tax reforms put forth by Goodrich did come to fruition some fifteen years later under the administration of Governor Paul V. McNutt. Some observers at that time credited Goodrich with planting the seeds for reforming Indiana's antiquated tax system.

Goodrich did succeed in getting a law passed in 1919 to make property tax assessment fairer by standardizing the methods used by local governments for assessing property. The law also enhanced the supervisory authority of the State Board of Tax Commissioners over local property tax assessment and borrowing through a new state tax commission. Ambiguity in the law led to a special session of the legislature in 1920, which restored some measure of local authority.

Goodrich's attempt to eliminate or consolidate governmental positions also met with strong opposition, especially from Democratic-leaning newspapers who referred to him as a "would-be Czar with a desire to centralize in the hands of the Governor complete control of the state's affairs." Goodrich's efforts to overhaul state government were stymied by more than just Democratic-leaning newspapermen. Two other events impeded his major restructuring plans. The first and most important was the United States's declaration of war against Germany on April 6, 1917, and the second was his contracting typhoid in August of that year after visiting a northern Indiana prison. For several weeks, the governor was bedridden at Methodist Hospital in Indianapolis, at times bordering on death.

Goodrich did not return to the statehouse from his illness until November. For the next several months he dealt with the state's coal shortage and the essential role it had in supporting the ongoing war effort. The previous May, Goodrich had established a State Council of Defense Committee to organize and direct the resources of the state for national use. Goodrich placed his good friend and state Republican Party chairman Will Hays in charge of the council. It proved to be one of the most successful statewide organizations of its kind in the country. By the war's conclusion, Indiana had supplied more than 130,000 troops, of which 3,354 soldiers and 15 nurses had been killed in battle or died of diseases. On the basis of percentage of population, this was more than from any other state in the nation. Equally important was the state's contribution in terms of production of food-stuffs and citizens' purchase of war bonds. Indiana was so successful in support of the troops that Newton D. Baker, secretary of war in the Woodrow Wilson administration, requested that other state councils go to Indiana and study the Hoosier council's methods.

The advent of the war caused Goodrich to change his mind about allowing the Indiana Historical Commission, created under his predecessor Samuel M. Ralston, to expire. He initially refused to sign the bill passed by the general assembly to make the historical commission permanent, but he came to realize that the organization could serve an important role by organizing a county-by-county history of Indiana's participation in the war. Reauthorized in 1919, with Goodrich's support, the Indiana Historical Commission became a permanent state agency. The name was later changed to the Indiana Historical Bureau.

Other aspects of Goodrich's dealings with wartime events were more problematic. The governor and state had to contend with blatant discrimination against citizens of German ancestry. American citizens of German blood were often ridiculed, discriminated against, and even lynched. In Indianapolis, most street names that were German or even German sounding were anglicized. By the winter of 1919, the state legislature, with the encouragement of the Indiana State Teachers Association, banned the teaching of German in all Indiana grade and high schools. Goodrich contested the legislation, but to no effect. He did issue a proclamation outlawing any conduct directed against any citizen because of his or her ancestry.

Against this backdrop Goodrich made one of his most controversial appointments, naming German-born Richard Lieber secretary of the Forestry Board. Lieber had three brothers who held the rank of colonel in the German army. Later Lieber would also hold the additional responsibilities of chairman of the Department of Conservation and director of the Indiana State Parks Committee. Lieber went on to become the father of Indiana's state parks system, establishing fourteen of Indiana's sixteen state parks by 1933.

In 1918, a year after his bout with typhoid, Goodrich suffered another personal misfortune. Driving back to his residence after attending a dinner party for a number of medical officers who were going abroad, he was struck by a streetcar and nearly killed. He suffered fractures of the hip, skull, ribs, and collarbone. Although the governor eventually recovered, he walked with the aid of a cane for the rest of his life.

In 1919 Goodrich signed two highly controversial amendments to the U.S. Constitution passed by the state legislature: the Eighteenth Amendment prohibiting the sale or consumption of alcohol and the Nineteenth Amendment extending the right to vote to women, a measure that Goodrich personally opposed. That same year Goodrich's name was floated as a favorite-son candidate for the 1920 national election. Although he certainly had the credentials to be a legitimate presidential candidate, by early 1920 Goodrich announced that he would not be a candidate for president. He later removed his name from consideration as vice president as well. He wrote to his friend New in April 1920, "I have no desire or ambition to do anything but finish my administration as best I can and then go back to my business. I am done with politics for ever and a day."

Goodrich's desire to forego public office can be at least partially attributed to his own disappointment in not accomplishing what he believed was attainable. For example, he was greatly frustrated by the failure of his own party, whose members dominated the legislature during his tenure, to support his reforms to eliminate more patronage positions and to revamp the state's antiquated tax code. He lamented in his unpublished biography that his fellow Republicans, who had supported these very same campaign promises before his election, "began to express grave doubts as to the wisdom and political expediency of so many new and unusual things."

Despite his failure to achieve tax reform and government reorganization, Goodrich was able to leave his impact on the state. One of his most notable accomplishments was the creation of the Indiana State Highway Commission, which laid out a system of state-maintained highways to reach every county seat and each town of five thousand or more residents. Clifton J. Phillips, writing about the state's transition from a primarily rural-agricultural society to a predominantly urban-industrial commonwealth, noted the significance of these developments: "It was a small beginning, but at long last a definite program of state responsibility for improved highways had been inaugurated in order to prepare Indiana to enter the dawning automobile age."

After stepping down as governor in 1921, Goodrich continued to make significant contributions to the state and nation for the next twenty years. At the behest of Herbert Hoover, then U.S. Secretary of Commerce and Director of the American Relief Administration, he traveled to the Soviet Union to investigate a terrible famine that existed in the Volga region of the recently formed country. This endeavor later took on a political mission as Goodrich met with Vladimir Lenin, Joseph Stalin, Leon Trotsky, and other senior Russian leaders to investigate the possibility of reestablishing diplomatic and commercial relations with the United States. Goodrich became a strong advocate of U.S. recognition for the Soviet Union. His wish was fulfilled in 1933 when President Franklin D. Roosevelt exchanged ambassadors with the Soviet Union, "practically the only occasion during his entire lifetime when he agreed with a Democrat."

Goodrich also served on the Great Lakes-St. Lawrence Tidewater Commission and the federal International St. Lawrence Waterways Commission. In 1929 President Hoover appointed Goodrich to the Commission on the Conservation and Administration of Public Domain. The commission was charged with evaluating how best to preserve and make use of millions of federal acres of land, primarily in the western states.

The former governor served in many other capacities. He was a member of the Wabash College board of trustees for thirty-six years, the last sixteen of which he served as chairman. He also served on the board of directors of the American-Russian Chamber of Commerce, the Theodore Roosevelt Memorial Trust, and the Presbyterian Theological Seminary in Chicago.

Some maintain Goodrich's greatest legacy to the state was in the business arena. His was truly a Horatio Alger story. From growing up in penury on a Randolph County farm immediately after the Civil War, he went on to become a major owner of a number of businesses with his brothers. In the process, his family formed a financial dynasty that lasted nearly one hundred years. Some of their business interests included holding controlling interest in a number of well-known Indiana corporations, including City Securities, the Indiana Telephone Company, the Ayrshire Colleries Corporation, Goodrich Brothers' Company (owning approximately forty grain and seed elevators), and numerous public utilities and banks. In the late 1930s James and his son, Pierre Frist Goodrich, his only surviving child, procured approximately a 20 percent interest in Central Newspapers, the newspaper chain established by Eugene C. Pulliam that owned, among others, the *Indianapolis Star*, the *Indianapolis News*, and Arizona's two largest newspapers, the *Arizona Republic* and the *Phoenix Gazette*. Pierre became a major figure in Indiana history himself. A corporate mogul, he exercised considerable influence in promoting intellectual causes and was one of the richest men in the state at the time of his death in 1973.

James Goodrich died on August 15, 1940, of a cerebral hemorrhage in his hometown of Winchester, where he is buried in the town's main cemetery.

Portrait by Wayman Adams (1920), Governors' Portraits Collection, Indiana Historical Bureau, State of Indiana.

FOR FURTHER READING

Goodrich, James P., Papers. Herbert Hoover Presidential Library, West Branch, Iowa.

Phillips, Clifton J. *Indiana in Transition: The Emergence of an Industrial Commonwealth, 1896–1920.* Vol. 4, *The History of Indiana.* Indianapolis: Indiana Historical Bureau and Indiana Historical Society, 1968.

Remy, Charles F. "Governor Goodrich and Indiana Tax Legislation." *Indiana Magazine of History* 43 (March 1947): 41–56.

Rhodes, Benjamin D. "Governor James P. Goodrich of Indiana and the 'Plain Facts' about Russia, 1921–1933." *Indiana Magazine of History* 85 (March 1989): 1–36.

———. *James P. Goodrich, Indiana's "Governor Strangelove": A Republican's Infatuation with Soviet Russia.* Selingsgrove, PA: Susquehanna University Press, 1996.

Starbuck, Dane. *The Goodriches: An American Family.* Indianapolis: Liberty Fund, 2001.

Goodrich's gubernatorial papers are in the Indiana State Archives, Indianapolis.

Warren T. McCray

January 10, 1921–April 30, 1924

TONY L. TRIMBLE

WARREN T. MCCRAY CAME TO THE GOVERNOR'S OFFICE WITH limited experience, having held only local office, and perceived by many as a political outsider. He promised government "grounded upon practical business principles." McCray advocated careful spending by government and a uniform budget system. Taxation should be subject to greater local control, and property tax assessment, McCray believed, should be based on true cash value.

McCray combined fiscal conservatism with the zeal of a progressive reformer. He supported significant expenditures to meet the "legitimate needs" of state institutions, including schools, mental health facilities, and prisons. Unfortunately, the reforms instituted during his administration were overshadowed by conflict with the Ku Klux Klan and the corruption that eventually forced McCray from office before completing his term.

A small farm near the future site of Brook, in newly formed Newton County, was the birthplace of Warren T. McCray. His parents, Greenberry and Martha Galey McCray, were childhood sweethearts who migrated north from Montgomery County after marrying in 1862. "Warnie," as he came to be known to friends, was born on February 4, 1865. McCray's birth followed that of an older sister, Fannie. A year later, his younger sister, Annie Eliza, was born, completing the family.

When Warren was five, his family left the farm and relocated to the town of Kentland. His father and uncle, Elmore McCray, formed a part-

nership in the livery and implement business. At the ripe old
age of nine, War- ren began his first
business venture. He planted vegetables on
an acre of ground owned by his father and went door-
to-door selling them. In his first year, he made enough money to buy
all of his clothes and open a small savings account. Thus encouraged,
Warren expanded his business to include caring for the cattle of townspeople who did not have sufficient room to graze them. Each morning,
Warren would ride around Kentland on his pony collecting the animals
and driving them to a pasture on the edge of town. In the evening, he
returned each animal safely home to its owner.

In April 1874 Elmore died suddenly at age thirty-nine. Greenberry
continued their business and formed a new partnership with John
Ade and E. Littell Urmston. Together, they purchased the Discount
and Deposit Bank of Kentland, and Greenberry became its president.
The bank became the centerpiece for future McCray family business
interests, and Warren found himself a member of one of the most
prominent families in Kentland.

McCray was educated in the Kentland public school system, graduating from high school in 1882. During his teenage years, the future
governor worked in his father's bank. He was always anxious to please
his father and this led him to make a choice that he "bitterly regretted" years later. He was given a choice. He could start a business

career with a full-time position in the bank, or he could go to college. McCray chose to go to work, but by age twenty-one he was growing restless. He wanted a business of his own. In late 1885 he formed a partnership with his friend Willis Kirkpatrick to purchase a local grocery business. In its fourth year, the business grossed $40,000. It was the first of a series of ventures that would make McCray a wealthy man. He invested in a variety of businesses—grain, mining, railroads, and, above all, land. Acquiring a good tract of land on which to farm and build a home was of paramount importance because then McCray could ask Ella Ade to marry him.

McCray and Ade had grown up together. It seemed only natural that their families, already joined in business, should be united in marriage as well. On June 15, 1892, McCray married the girl that he had "loved long before she knew anything about my interest in her." The newlyweds soon settled on their farm northwest of Kentland, which featured a large pond. McCray, perhaps tongue-in-cheek, called his home Orchard Lake. In the years ahead, Orchard Lake became a major destination for cattle dealers from all over the country.

Between 1893 and 1902 the McCrays had four children, two girls and two boys. Sadly, their first son died in infancy. As McCray's family expanded so did his business and with it his public visibility. McCray became interested in cattle breeding and chose to specialize in Herefords, hoping to establish a world-class herd. McCray's cattle auctions, held in his custom-built show barn at Orchard Lake, became legendary and his fortune and reputation grew.

McCray had shown little interest in politics beyond the local level. He served one term each on the Kentland school board and town board. He quickly gained a reputation for getting things done. After a series of devastating fires, which destroyed twenty-one buildings, including the local school, McCray oversaw reconstruction of the school and improvements to the town's water system so that such a calamity could not befall Kentland again. McCray said that he was elected to the town board because "the town had been dormant so long that it needed a new and aggressive administration." In short order, he fulfilled the voters' expectations. Plank railroad crossings were replaced with permanent gravel ones, Main Street was macadamized to eliminate the sea of mud that accompanied any sizable rain, and an electrical plant was installed to provide street lighting and electricity to homes at a fair rate. Ironically, the internal improvements that McCray oversaw also proved to be his undoing. He was defeated for reelection by disgruntled voters who did not like the increase in taxes needed to pay for modernizing the town. It was a lesson that McCray never forgot.

McCray's efforts as a local officeholder did not go unnoticed by leaders of the state Republican Party. In the summer of 1896 McCray was chosen as a delegate to the Tenth District Republican Caucus. He quickly learned two things: politics could be brutal, and he liked the limelight. In 1901 the McCrays traveled to Washington, D.C., for the inauguration of William McKinley. McCray returned home convinced that he had a future in politics. Just before the trip, McCray was notified that Governor Winfield T. Durbin had appointed him to the board of trustees of the Northern Hospital for the Insane in Logansport, a position he held for twelve years. The year 1912 brought still another appointment, this time to the State Board of Agriculture. Three years later, McCray was elected president of the board. Party regulars were beginning to mention McCray as a candidate for governor in 1916.

McCray's first run for governor ended in disappointment. Early in the race, McCray was the clear leader over James P. Goodrich of Winchester. But as the campaign progressed, Goodrich had too much political experience and too many connections for McCray to overcome. He easily defeated McCray in the primary. McCray came away from the experience unsure if he would ever run for office again.

Another year found the United States at war, and McCray, much too old for military service, wanted to contribute to the war effort. He chaired fund drives, served as a member and chairman of the Food Production and Conservation Committee, and accepted a commission as colonel of the Home Guards. Perhaps the most notable of McCray's wartime activities was Red Cross Day, a fund-raiser organized and hosted by McCray and his brother-in-law, George Ade, at Ade's Hazelden Country Club near Brook.

McCray's performance in the 1916 campaign created a positive impression on the Republican Party leadership. Approached to run again in 1920, McCray found himself in a struggle between his ego and his conscience. His first instinct was to stay at home and take care of his business and family, but his ego could not resist the lure of politics and high office. It appeared that Will Hays, the Republican National Chairman, would make a run, and McCray was unwilling to challenge him. In August 1919 Hays surprised many by announcing that he would not be a candidate. McCray found himself in a five-man race for the nomination opposed by James Fesler, Edward Toner, Edgar Bush, and Edward Jackson. McCray was attacked for his business practices and his "war record," but these attacks proved to be ineffective and McCray won the primary handily. The key to McCray's victory may have been the way that he reached out to the party's African Americans, gaining the strong support of their leader, George P. Stewart.

McCray's Democratic opponent was Doctor Carleton B. McCulloch, a prominent physician and war veteran. The fall election saw a record turnout, as high as 95 percent in some precincts. McCray was elected with nearly 55 percent of the vote, a landslide that saw Republicans elected at all levels of government.

McCray interpreted his victory as a mandate for change, and he was ready to oblige, but his inaugural address made it clear that the Progressive Era in Indiana was coming to an end. McCray called for less active government. He proclaimed to the Indiana General Assembly that the people wanted "a season of government economy and a period of legislative inaction and rest."

McCray became a strong advocate for education. During his administration the legislature passed a more stringent law governing compulsory school attendance and raised statewide standards for teacher licensing. He found funds to keep schools from closing and upgraded education programs in the prison system. He also oversaw construction of eighty-seven buildings, including several at the state fairgrounds, a new reformatory in Pendleton, and additions to the state hospitals.

Just as he had in Kentland, McCray took an interest in highway improvement. The highway system that the governor envisioned would be expensive to build and to maintain. Reluctantly, McCray authorized the introduction of a bill that would create Indiana's first gasoline tax. With the new revenue from the tax many roads were improved, and a much-needed bridge was built between Princeton and Vincennes at Hazelton. The most ambitious and controversial road project was the Lincoln Highway. At issue was the route the road would follow and whether there would be commercial development along the highway.

While McCray went about the state's business, two clouds were forming over his administration. The first cloud was wearing a white robe and preaching hatred. McCray clashed with the Ku Klux Klan when Secretary of State Edward Jackson granted the secret organization a charter. McCray publicly opposed allowing an organization whose officers refused to sign their names to be legally recognized by the state, and he took his case to the attorney general, who sided with Jackson. Unable to sway the governor, the Klan increasingly turned to Jackson as its representative in state government. During the remainder of McCray's term, the Klan challenged him at every turn. The feud reached its pinnacle when McCray vetoed a proposed "Klan Day," complete with nighttime cross burning, at the Indiana State Fair, and D. C. Stephenson attempted to bribe the governor through Jackson.

The second cloud was of McCray's own making. A wealthy man, worth a reported $3 million when he took office, McCray was facing bankruptcy. The value of his assets in land and cattle had been wiped out by the farm depression that hit the Midwest in 1921. Desperate to save his beloved Orchard Lake, he resorted to fraud to obtain loans. He received a loan for $155,000 from the State Agriculture Board, which he deposited in his personal bank account. Even more serious were his efforts to secure loans from various banks. After writing a large number of fraudulent promissory notes, some of which he forged with the names of other people, he attempted to sell these notes to banks that did business with the state as collateral for loans. Bank officials felt coerced into granting the loans because he had the power to withhold state funds from them. McCray faced charges in two different courts for his schemes of deception.

In March 1924 McCray was tried in the Marion County Criminal Court for embezzling $155,000 from the state, even though the debt had been repaid by a group of his friends. That trial ended in a hung jury on April 11, 1924, and ten days later he was brought to trial in the federal district court in Indianapolis for charges that he used the U.S. mail to sell and distribute his fraudulent promissory notes. During his trial he admitted what he did, but was adamant that he had no criminal intent. Nonetheless, he was convicted and sentenced to ten years in the federal penitentiary in Atlanta. After serving more than three years of his sentence, McCray was paroled. In 1930 President Herbert Hoover granted him a full pardon.

McCray returned to Kentland, where he was greeted warmly by his old friends and neighbors. Within five years he was financially solvent, and Orchard Lake was again a profitable farm. McCray died suddenly in his home on December 19, 1938. He is buried at Fairlawn Cemetery in Kentland, Indiana.

Portrait by Robert W. Grafton (1927), Governors' Portraits Collection, Indiana Historical Bureau, State of Indiana.

FOR FURTHER READING

"Autobiography of Warren T. McCray." Warren T. McCray Manuscript Collection. Indiana State Library, Indianapolis, Indiana.

Pardon File of Warren T. McCray. National Archives, Washington, D.C.

Stewart, George P., Papers. William Henry Smith Memorial Library. Indiana Historical Society, Indianapolis, Indiana

Feightner, Harold. Taped interview. Indiana State Library, Indianapolis, Indiana.

Niblack, John L. *The Life and Times of a Hoosier Judge.* N.p., 1973.

McCray's gubernatorial papers are in the Indiana State Archives, Indianapolis.

Emmett F. Branch

April 30, 1924–January 12, 1925

TONY L. TRIMBLE

ON THE MORNING OF APRIL 30, 1924, LIEUTENANT GOVER-
nor Emmett F. Branch rode the interurban from his home in Martinsville to Indianapolis, where he was to be sworn in as governor. It was
to be a ceremony with little fanfare in deference to Branch's predecessor, Warren T. McCray, who was forced to resign after being convicted of mail fraud. Promptly at 10:00 a.m., Branch appeared in the
governor's office. Facing Chief Justice Louis Ewbank, he exclaimed,
"Hello Judge. I've been looking for you. Come on, let's get this over."
The new governor was beginning his brief term amid a multitude of
questions resulting from McCray's sudden departure. To the press,
Branch would say only, "I have no statement to make until I make a
survey of affairs."

Branch had been a strong supporter of his predecessor's reform
program, and he wanted to build upon McCray's successes. First, however, he would have to reassure the citizens of Indiana that McCray's
legal problems had not compromised the government. The need to
investigate the administration of his friend was personally painful, and
it was reported that Branch sobbed as he took the oath of office.

Emmett Forrest Branch was born in Martinsville on May 16, 1874, to
Elliott F. and Alice Parks Branch. His father was a prominent leader in
the Republican Party, once serving as a member of the state committee
and later as Morgan County treasurer. One of four children, Emmett
was affectionately called "son" by many in the Martinsville community.
After high school, he attended Indiana University, where he played

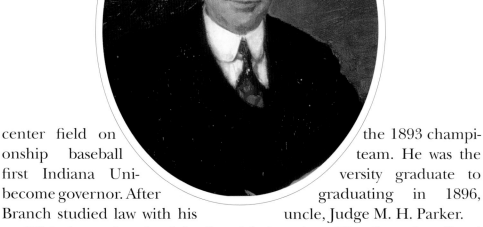

center field on the 1893 championship baseball team. He was the first Indiana University graduate to become governor. After graduating in 1896, Branch studied law with his uncle, Judge M. H. Parker.

With the outbreak of the Spanish-American War, Branch enlisted in the army, serving in Company K, 158th Regiment. He was discharged on November 4, 1898, with the rank of first lieutenant. From 1916 to 1917 Branch served on the Mexican border as a lieutenant colonel. World War I saw Branch assigned to the 151st Infantry as a colonel. He ended his military service in command of the 165th Depot Brigade at Camp Travis, Texas.

In between stints in the military, Branch passed the bar and established a successful law practice in Martinsville. In 1905 he married Katherine Bain, whose father was the editor of the *Martinsville Republican* and a former postmaster. Their marriage produced one son.

Branch began his political career in 1902. Following in the footsteps of his grandfather, Parminter M. Parks (Indiana Senate, 1841 and 1844), and great-grandfather, James Parks (Indiana House of Representatives, 1832), he ran for and was elected to the Indiana House of Representatives. Branch served three terms and was Speaker of the House in the regular 1907 and special 1908 sessions. During his term as Speaker, Branch outlawed the "omnibus" method of passing legislation. This unwritten rule allowed bills to be combined and then passed without discussion. With his election as lieutenant governor in 1920, Branch became president of the senate. During his tenure, the senate debated many controversial measures. Among them were bills to keep Memorial Day "sacred" by prohibiting races, games, and sports and to repeal the ban on teaching German in public schools. The latter provoked a series of angry exchanges that threatened to become violent. Order was restored only when Branch struck the podium so hard that he broke his gavel.

The immediate resignation of Governor McCray following his conviction in federal court left Branch with no time to prepare for the challenge ahead of him. "Everything was so sudden and surprising," Katherine Branch said, "that we scarcely knew what was happening. We were fond of the McCrays, and it was too bad it all had to happen." After shaking hands with hundreds of visitors, the new governor issued his first official statement in support of Child Health Day, which was being observed nationally on that day.

No one was more aware than Branch that his term would be brief and that he would be perceived as a "caretaker" until the next election in the fall. But Branch was not a man to settle for such a role. McCray's departure did not change the fundamental issues facing the state. Primary among them was the need for continued improvement of schools and highways, better health care for children, and completion of the expansion of the state prison system.

Branch sought increased expenditures for the improvement of railroad crossings on state and county highways, where the number of car-train crashes had become a serious problem. McCray had done much to improve funding for schools, but he had not completed plans for a facility to educate blind children. Branch began the process of selecting land and designing the Indiana School for the Blind. On October 7, 1924, the governor participated in the dedication of the new Riley Hospital for Children in Indianapolis, which continues to provide nationally recognized health services for Indiana's youngest citizens. In addition, Branch chose to involve the governor's office in a variety of patriotic causes, including voter registration campaigns, Flag Day displays, Red Cross promotions, National Defense Day, and Constitution Day.

Within a month after taking office, Branch found himself embroiled in a controversy over boxing contests. Indiana law allowed matches but not prizefights. A contest advertised as a boxing match was to be held in Michigan City on May 31, 1924. Protesters demanded that the fight be stopped because it was really a prizefight. Branch announced that he would not stop the fight but he would enforce the law to ensure that there was no prize involved. He sent Brigadier General L. R. Gigmilliat of Culver Military Academy to the contest as his observer and to enforce the law if necessary. Arrangements had quietly been made with General Harry Smith of the National Guard to provide whatever assistance might be needed. The boxing match proceeded without incident, and Branch established that the enforcement of Indiana law had not been compromised by McCray's illegal behavior.

On January 8, 1925, Branch delivered his only annual message to the legislature. He urged them to complete many of the reforms that had begun under McCray and continued during his short term. These included finishing the construction project at the reformatory in Pendleton to relieve overcrowding in the prison system and appropriation of funds to continue the improvement of public school facilities. He warned that Indiana's colleges would soon need more space to accommodate a growing number of students, as well.

Branch's term came to an end on January 12 with the inauguration of his successor, Edward Jackson. Branch returned to his home in Martinsville, where he spent the remainder of his life practicing law and managing his business interests. He was the president of the Branch Grain and Seed Company, a stockholder in the Martinsville Trust Company, and the owner of several farms in Morgan County. In 1929 Governor Harry G. Leslie appointed Branch to the State Armory Board. Branch died of a heart attack on February 23, 1932.

Portrait by Simon Paul Baus (1927), Governors' Portraits Collection, Indiana Historical Bureau, State of Indiana.

FOR FURTHER READING

"Branch Sworn In; Begins a Check of Affairs of State." *Indianapolis Star*, May 1, 1924.

Branigan, Roger D. Taped Interview. Manuscript Division, Indiana State Library, Indianapolis.

Post, Margaret Moore. *First Ladies of Indiana and the Governors, 1816–1984.* Indianapolis: Pierson Printing Company, 1984.

Walsh, Justin E. *The Centennial History of the Indiana General Assembly, 1816–1978.* Indianapolis: The Select Committee on the Centennial History of the Indiana General Assembly, 1987.

Branch's gubernatorial papers are in the Indiana State Archives, Indianapolis.

Edward L. Jackson

January 12, 1925–January 14, 1929

JASON S. LANTZER

THE 1920S WERE THE BEST OF TIMES AND THE WORST OF times for Hoosier Republicans. It was a time of prosperity in which the party was dominant at nearly every level across the state. Yet, Republicans had to grapple with the issues of Prohibition, the Ku Klux Klan, and corruption. The man the party picked to lead them, Edward Jackson, reflected all these tensions. His time as governor shows all that was right and wrong with Indiana politics and culture during this time.

Jackson was born on a farm in Howard County on December 27, 1873. His father, Presley, was a mill worker, and his mother was the former Mary Howell. The Jacksons were members of the Disciples of Christ denomination, an affiliation that the future governor retained for his entire life. As a boy Jackson delivered newspapers and worked for a time in a stave factory. On February 20, 1897, he married Rosa Wilkinson, with whom he had two daughters, Helen and Edith. After Rosa's death in October 1919, Jackson married Lydia Beaty Pierce on November 23, 1920. The couple adopted a son, whom they named Edward Jackson Jr.

Jackson opened a law office in Kennard at the age of twenty, though until it took off, he supplemented his income by working in a brickyard. A largely self-taught lawyer, he quickly became a sought-after attorney. By 1898 Jackson was working for the Henry County prosecutor, serving in that position in his own right from 1901 to 1906. He was elected judge of the Henry County Circuit Court in 1907, a position he held until 1914. In the process, he built up a solid political base.

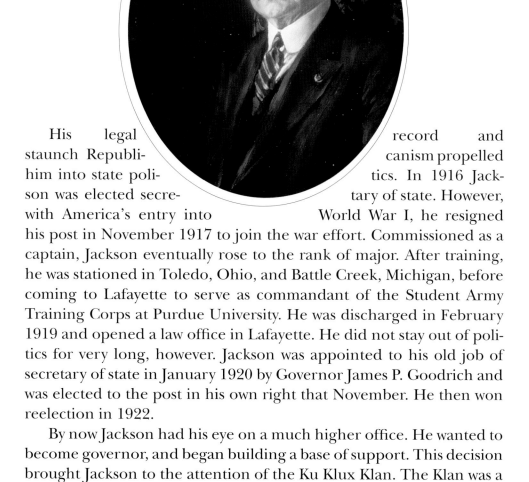

His legal record and staunch Republi- canism propelled him into state poli- tics. In 1916 Jack- son was elected secre- tary of state. However, with America's entry into World War I, he resigned his post in November 1917 to join the war effort. Commissioned as a captain, Jackson eventually rose to the rank of major. After training, he was stationed in Toledo, Ohio, and Battle Creek, Michigan, before coming to Lafayette to serve as commandant of the Student Army Training Corps at Purdue University. He was discharged in February 1919 and opened a law office in Lafayette. He did not stay out of politics for very long, however. Jackson was appointed to his old job of secretary of state in January 1920 by Governor James P. Goodrich and was elected to the post in his own right that November. He then won reelection in 1922.

By now Jackson had his eye on a much higher office. He wanted to become governor, and began building a base of support. This decision brought Jackson to the attention of the Ku Klux Klan. The Klan was a potent force in 1920s Indiana, and the hooded order could do much for Jackson's political future. The Klan, especially its Grand Dragon, D. C. Stephenson, saw Jackson as a candidate it could control. For his part, Jackson saw the Klan as an immensely popular, bipartisan group that had repackaged a message of morality, Americanism, Protestant- ism, and Prohibition lifted wholesale from the state's churches and patriotic organizations. It was seemingly a match made in political heaven. Instead, Jackson's decision to become friends with Stephenson brought him close to ruin and nearly into a prison cell.

With the Klan endorsement propelling him to victory in the 1924 Republican primary, Jackson hit the campaign trail hard. He promised to continue Republican prosperity, as well as guaranteeing full "civil and religious liberty for Jews, Catholics, and blacks," his way of publicly dodging the Klan's open support. Jackson defeated his Democratic opponent, Carleton B. McCulloch, by nearly one hundred thousand votes and carried ninety of the state's ninety-two counties. However, he did not lead all Republican candidates in the state, coming in well behind President Calvin Coolidge and some of the other statewide candidates. His victory had more to do with Republican strength in both the state and the nation than it did with the Klan's appeal.

Proof of this was soon apparent. Despite Republican dominance of the Indiana General Assembly and the assumed influence that it brought the Klan, the hooded order's legislative effort in 1925 was an abject failure, caused in large part by a rift between Stephenson and the national Klan organization. The Republicans did not need the Klan to get elected, but to exert any political influence in the state, the Klan needed to be attached to them. If anything, the Klan disturbed Republican elites and only had a perceived control over politics. Its bipartisanship brought in as many votes as its message of intolerance lost the candidates it supported.

While the Klan was omnipresent, the real issue for most Hoosiers was Prohibition. Indeed, the dry cause was very important to the course of Jackson's administration. At the behest of the Indiana Anti-Saloon League, the same 1925 legislature easily passed one of the strictest dry laws in the country, which Jackson eagerly signed. Known as the Wright Bone Dry Law, it increased penalties and inducements to prosecute violators, as well as closed some loopholes in Indiana's statues. The initially popular law was one the governor was soon to openly break.

One of the components of Indiana's dry code prevented the sale of medicinal whiskey in the state. However, when Lydia Jackson grew ill in 1925, the governor asked the attorney general to procure some.

Arthur Gilliom, who had previously obtained medicinal whiskey for his own sick children, did so as well for the state's first lady. When this incident became public knowledge, it produced a minor scandal. The public largely forgave Jackson, in part because he admitted to the charge while refusing to seek modification of the law. The state's dry forces claimed that Lydia had been rescued from death's door by prayer, not booze, and the matter was largely dropped.

High political theater occurred that fall, however, when Democrat U.S. senator and former governor Samuel M. Ralston died. Jackson quickly appointed Arthur Robinson to the seat, which caused some uproar. While Robinson was hardly an unknown within Republican circles, having been a state senator and judge in Marion County, he was not the most obvious choice for the post. Many Republicans, and a good number of Democrats, wanted Jackson to appoint Indiana's former senator, Albert J. Beveridge, to the vacant post. Robinson was characterized as a puppet for Jackson's own senatorial ambitions. There was also the specter of the Klan, as opponents claimed both Jackson and Robinson were beholden to the hooded order. But Jackson stood by his decision, and Robinson easily won reelection in 1928 and served into the New Deal.

Jackson became involved in a bitter state supreme court battle over the pardoning of the Indiana Anti-Saloon League's leader, the Reverend Edward S. Shumaker. In an internal 1926 report, Shumaker charged the attorney general and the state supreme court with lax enforcement of dry laws. Gilliom, who believed the League's voter guides and political clout made it too influential, and perhaps even part of a "super government" along with the Klan, brought contempt of court charges against Shumaker. After a protracted legal battle, the dry leader was about to serve his time at the state farm in 1927 when Jackson pardoned him. Gilliom, whose relationship with the governor was now strained, fought the pardon successfully in the Indiana Supreme Court, effectively limiting the power of granting clemency the state's chief executive has. Shumaker served his term in early 1929.

Jackson's problems with pardons were hardly over. When Stephenson found himself in legal trouble, the governor refused to grant him one. In 1925 the Klan leader was arrested following the death of Madge Oberholtzer, a young statehouse worker who accused Stephenson of forcing her onto a northbound train and raping and assaulting her. Following the assault, Oberholtzer took poison and went without medical attention for two days before Stephenson took her home. Before she died, about a month following the attack, Oberholtzer gave testimony that helped to convict Stephenson of second-degree murder, for which he received a life sentence. Stephenson's conviction for murder meant that there was no way Jackson could grant his friend a pardon. Angered, Stephenson began to leak information to the press about just how far he had taken the hooded order and its money in supporting Jackson in 1924. One of Stephenson's revelations nearly brought an end to Jackson's time as governor and tarnished his reputation forever.

While serving as secretary of state, Jackson approved the Klan's official charter over the objections of Governor Warren T. McCray. Jackson saw it as a prudent political step, to insure Klan support for his gubernatorial aspirations. In 1923, at the behest of the Klan, Jackson offered McCray a $10,000 bribe to fill the Marion County prosecutor's office with a man Jackson and the Klan supported. The governor refused. Soon after, charges emerged about fiscal improprieties that forced McCray to resign and led to his imprisonment in a federal penitentiary. Thanks to Stephenson's "black boxes" full of documents, Jackson's part in this story became clearer and led to formal criminal charges being brought against him. Despite the courtroom drama and calls from religious and civic groups that he do so, Jackson refused to resign. His wife stood by him and never believed the charges. The governor was saved from conviction and imprisonment only because the statute of limitations had expired. Though it generated plenty of headlines in an election year, the case did not hurt the Republican Party, which cruised to another victory in 1928, but it did end Jackson's political career.

All was not political intrigue and criminal accusations during Jackson's time in office. He was interested in better roads for the state, and he pushed for the creation of more state parks, adding eleven new ones during his four years in office. The George Rogers Clark

Memorial in Vincennes was also begun during Jackson's tenure. He stressed the importance of cutting the expenditures of state government in order to eliminate the debt, which was accomplished. Jackson was even able to cut taxes.

Nevertheless, his notoriety made him an outcast as a former governor. For a time, Jackson operated a law firm in Indianapolis, but in 1937 he retired from public life. He moved to a one-hundred-acre estate near Orleans in Orange County, where he raised cattle and started an apple orchard, and was active in local clubs. In 1948 Jackson suffered a massive stroke that left him largely bedridden for the rest of his life. He died at the age of eighty on November 18, 1954.

Portrait by Robert W. Grafton (1927), Governors' Portraits Collection, Indiana Historical Bureau, State of Indiana.

FOR FURTHER READING

Lantzer, Jason S. "Dark Beverage of Hell: The Transformation of Hamilton County's Dry Crusade, 1876–1936." http://www.connerprairie.org/historyonline/temperance.html.

Lutholtz, M. William. *Grand Dragon: D. C. Stephenson and the Ku Klux Klan in Indiana.* West Lafayette, IN: Purdue University Press, 1993.

Madison, James H. *Indiana through Tradition and Change: A History of the Hoosier State and Its People, 1920–1945.* Vol. 5, *The History of Indiana.* Indianapolis: Indiana Historical Society, 1982.

Jackson's gubernatorial papers are in the Indiana State Archives, Indianapolis.

Harry G. Leslie

January 14, 1929–January 9, 1933

ALFRED L. KNABLE JR.

WHEN HARRY G. LESLIE WAS SWORN IN AS INDIANA'S GOVernor in January 1929, he could not have foreseen the grave hazards that loomed. His term would coincide with the beginning of the unprecedented economic and social upheaval of the Great Depression. Unfortunately, Leslie did not have the luxury of hindsight. He did, however, possess ample experience in dealing with hardship. When trouble began with the stock market's tumble later that year it was not the first, or worst, unexpected crash of his life. He would call upon his long-honed personal skills and tested determination to help Hoosiers endure those first years of privation that would not end for more than a decade.

Leslie was born in Lafayette, Indiana, on August 6, 1878, to pioneer parents, Daniel and Mary Burkhart Leslie. His father was active in local politics and served for a time as Lafayette town marshal. While Leslie was still a small boy the family moved to the outskirts of West Lafayette. Growing up just northwest of Indiana's recently founded land-grant college, he and his siblings Frank and Amy were well within earshot of the trains rumbling to and from the city of his birth just across the Wabash.

From the family farm near Montmorenci, West Lafayette was only a brief journey. Leslie attended school there, and when economic circumstances forced him to strike out at an early age he found work as a grocery delivery boy. Courteous and memorable, the boy was well liked by everyone. Such comfortable familiarity paid off when he

was elected town clerk in 1898, less than one year after graduating from West Lafayette High School.

Leslie excelled in several sports in high school. After graduation he remained active in club teams and continued work at the grocery. His athletic ability helped him gain admission to Purdue in 1901. He starred in baseball and football and was captain of both squads his junior year. Such a dual honor in multiple varsity sports remains a feat unequaled at Purdue.

He also blossomed politically, being elected president of each of his five classes from 1901 to 1905. University life molded the young man, providing him with connections and skills he called upon throughout his life. He returned the favor. In later years he served as the university's first athletic director and remained active in alumni affairs. He even acquired a new name at Purdue. For reasons only a few friends from the university's foundry ever knew, he was donned "Skillet." The name stuck.

On the morning of October 31, 1903, Leslie boarded a wooden rail car reserved for members of the Purdue football team. The day promised much fanfare. The train was one of two "specials" carrying the team and its backers to Indianapolis to play their arch-rival Indiana University before ten thousand spectators in the new Washington Park stadium. The fact that the day marked the 101st anniversary of Purdue founder John Purdue's birth surely augured success.

The short trip had been festive. Just north of Indianapolis, Leslie moved from the second car where he had been joining in the singing of several fight songs back to the first car to collect his belongings. Others were beginning to stretch in the aisle, including fellow player Otis McCormick. Leslie greeted him with a smile. "Hello, Ott," he said, just as the whistle began to shriek and the emergency brakes locked to a squeal. The manager of the student newspaper yelled "Look out, boys!" but by then the wooden passenger car was already splintering around them. Engine 350 had turned around a bend and collided with seven northbound steel coal cars whose engineer never got the message to clear the main line for the "special." McCormick was thrown through a window, miraculously landing on his feet. All those seated around him were killed. Seventeen people died from their injuries. Leslie was among those taken to the morgue, where hours later undertakers detected a faint pulse. He lay near death for weeks. His slow recovery required several operations.

Throughout Indiana Leslie became a folk hero. Perhaps he had acquired the aura of providence bestowed upon those who survive such tragedy. Scarred and with a permanent limp, he returned to Purdue to complete his course work. He received his diploma in 1905, only one year behind schedule. He obtained his law degree from Indiana University in 1907 and opened a law office in Lafayette that same year. Leslie was coaching a local high school football team when a beautiful young woman named Martha Morgan caught his eye. He and Martha were married on August 16, 1910. Within a few years the Leslies had three sons—John (Jack), Richard, and Robert—each born about two years apart.

Leslie became active in local politics and in 1912 was elected treasurer of Tippecanoe County. His victory was notable as he was the sole Republican to win in that county's contests that year. From 1914 to 1924 he tried his hand at farming and also served as a bank president.

In 1923 he was elected joint representative from Tippecanoe and Warren counties to the 73rd Indiana General Assembly. His amiable, down-to-earth style made it easy for him to communicate effectively with constituents and make allies among colleagues. He was reelected to the house in 1925 and 1927, serving as Speaker during both sessions.

The contest for Speaker was set against a backdrop of efforts by the Ku Klux Klan to control the leadership and legislative agenda of the general assembly. The 1925 session has been labeled "the Ku Klux Klan session." While the Klan was still a significant force, its power was ebbing, in part because of a bitter split in the party between a faction of the Klan led by Walter Bossert and D. C. Stephenson, the longtime leader and most prominent klansman in the state. Bossert became Grand Dragon after Stephenson resigned that position in a break with the national Klan. In the 1925 session, the Bossert faction backed another candidate, while Stephenson and Governor Edward Jackson backed Leslie. Although Leslie did not seek Stephenson's support, he was most certainly aware of it. Leslie eked out a 42–39 victory in the Republican caucus contest and then was elected by the full house. It was considered "the most bitterly contested race of the era" for Speaker. Leslie fought the Klan influence in the house over several issues, including attempts to control committee assignments, education legislation, and its excessive lobbying tactics. He also confronted the Klan over other issues when he became governor.

During Leslie's term as Speaker, Stephenson was tried and convicted for the assault and second-degree murder of a young statehouse worker. He served twenty years in the Michigan City Prison. Leslie was one of the many governors who refused to grant clemency to Stephenson. Later when the question arose as to whether Stephenson could have been framed, Leslie replied: "Ninety percent of them [the prisoners in Michigan City] are serving time for things they did not do, because they should be where they are for the things they did do. Stephenson is one of the ninety percent."

As he did for most of his life, during the mid-1920s Leslie wore several hats simultaneously. He was appointed to the U.S. income tax department in 1924 as a division chief. From 1924 to 1928 he served as general alumni secretary for Purdue and manager of the *Purdue Alumnus.* Arguably, his greatest professional accomplishment during this time was his successful championing, as Speaker, of the fight for appropriations for the James Whitcomb Riley Hospital for Children in Indianapolis.

In early 1928 Leslie announced that he would be a candidate for governor in that year's Republican primary. The announcement was made with little fanfare and met with lukewarm enthusiasm. Among a field of ten hopeful candidates, Leslie ran fifth. With no aspirant receiving a majority, the contest would have to be decided at the state convention.

At the convention, preliminary polling failed to determine a clear victor. After six ballots, momentum seemed to be favoring Logansport native Fred Landis. Just as the last roll call was starting, a marching band rumbled onto the floor. Whether the band was sent in by Leslie supporters or premature Landis celebrants is as uncertain as the song they played. One thing is for sure. Whoever was responsible for the disruption bought the Leslie forces enough time to reorganize. Leslie won the nomination and in November defeated Democrat Frank Dailey by a margin of 51.3 percent to 48.1 percent to become the state's fifth consecutive Republican governor.

As governor, Leslie supported the effort begun as early as 1925 to repeal the direct primary and restore the state party convention for political nominations. Siding with Leslie on this issue were former governors Thomas R. Marshall and James P. Goodrich. In opposition was a combination of strange bedfellows, including the League of Women Voters, Jackson, Stephenson, and the Ku Klux Klan. Those who favored nomination by convention prevailed in 1929, Leslie's first year as governor, when the general assembly repealed the primary act of 1915.

Leslie and his family moved into the governor's mansion in early 1929 and enjoyed a honeymoon period that coincided with the tail end of the great bull stock market. The Leslies entertained many famous guests, including President Herbert Hoover and his wife, Charles Lindbergh and his wife, and Admiral Richard Byrd. They were skilled and gracious hosts, traits put to good use when Indiana hosted the national governors' conference later in Leslie's term. Leslie considered that event, held in French Lick and attended by

Governor Franklin D. Roosevelt of New York, a high point of his administration.

The "good times" came to an abrupt end with the stock market's crash in late 1929. The swift economic downturn brought with it labor unrest resulting in frequent strikes and soon thereafter wide-scale unemployment. Unprecedented drought assured that farmers were not spared from the difficulties. Leslie did little of significance to address the pressing economic needs stemming from the Great Depression, and although his approach was similar to other state and national leaders in the early stages of the Depression, his attitude was characterized as "unusually reactionary." For example, he established the Indiana Advisory Committee for Relief of the Unemployed, comprised mainly of businessmen. He warned the group about the problem with government relief, stating that "the greatest danger of a movement of this kind is pauperizing people." His address to the 1931 legislature made no mention of the issues relating to unemployment and relief. A year later he convened a special session of the legislature to consider only a proposal to reduce taxation. Although he did form the Reconstruction Finance Corporation, he did so reluctantly and requested aid only for a few cities. He expected local governments to take care of their own with little assistance from either the state or the national government. He even vetoed the first old-age pension act in 1931.

As the Depression began to take greater hold Leslie took action on several fronts. One of his most innovative policies was soon adopted on a large scale. His suggestion to a federal task force to employ down-on-their-luck farmers on road construction and repair projects was implemented nationally. In general, however, Leslie was more interested in helping individuals, rather than providing massive government assistance. He lobbied to maintain funding for Indiana's charitable institutions, and he took a personal interest in penal rehabilitation, making it a point to attend most meetings of the state's parole and pardon boards. Many individuals were successfully reintroduced into society because of Leslie's firm belief in second opportunities.

In August 1931, the day after Leslie's fifty-second birthday, Indiana received unwelcome national attention when two black men were lynched in a horrible spectacle in Marion. The men had been jailed for the assault of a white woman and the murder of her boyfriend. An angry mob of citizens dragged them from their jail cells, beat them, and then lynched them from a tree on the courthouse square. The perpetrators were never arrested or punished, although Leslie did issue a strong statement of condemnation.

During incredibly difficult times, Leslie remained accessible and genial. Mondays would find Leslie talking with statehouse reporters not only about current policy initiatives but also the weekend's football games. In the midst of such challenges it is remarkable that Leslie had time for other cares. He made the time, however, to take a personal interest in conservation efforts; particularly, he was instrumental in the formative stages of the state park system. His correspondences with Richard Lieber, the director of the state Department of Conservation, reveal a mutually fond working relationship.

Although most of the credit for the park system's successful development has been given to his predecessor, Jackson, Lieber seemed to believe Leslie equally deserving. In a letter written on his friend's last day as governor, Lieber stated, "What we have been able to do in the last four years is your monument for you made it possible." In a failure of prescience he ended the letter, "I may say with certainty that the best, the most productive and the most enjoyable years of your life lie before you."

After leaving office, Leslie helped organize the Standard Life Insurance Company of Indiana. He soon became the firm's president. He also stayed active in several fraternal organizations. He remained a sports fan, and although his name was mentioned for the job of baseball commissioner, the post never materialized.

He maintained many close friendships. One of the last to speak with Leslie was humorist and fellow Purdue graduate George Ade. Ade recalled Leslie was in a cheerful mood just hours before his unexpected death from heart disease in Miami, Florida, on December 10, 1937. He was fifty-nine.

The train that carried Leslie's body from Miami was met in Indianapolis by scores of people shocked by his unexpected death. He was buried in Lafayette, and Purdue has memorialized him in several ways. His legacy in Indiana exists in the presence of the world-renowned Riley Children's Hospital and in the state park system. At the time of Leslie's death, former Indiana Supreme Court justice Clarence R. Martin summarized the man: "He was always the same unpretentious, thoroughly homespun Hoosier. He was held in highest esteem by all of his associates."

Portrait by Robert W. Grafton (1929), Governors' Portraits Collection, Indiana Historical Bureau, State of Indiana.

FOR FURTHER READING

Feightner, Harold. Transcript of taped interviews. Manuscript Division. Indiana State Library, Indianapolis.

Lieber, Richard, Papers. Manuscript Division. Indiana State Library, Indianapolis.

Lutholtz, M. William. *Grand Dragon: D. C. Stephenson and the Ku Klux Klan in Indiana.* West Lafayette, IN: Purdue University Press, 1991.

Madison, James H. *Indiana through Tradition and Change: A History of the Hoosier State and Its People, 1920–1945.* Vol. 5, *The History of Indiana.* Indianapolis: Indiana Historical Society, 1982.

Post, Margaret Moore. *First Ladies of Indiana and the Governors, 1816–1984.* Indianapolis: Pierson Printing Company, 1984.

The Purdue Alumnus 25, no. 4 (January 1938).

Walsh, Justin A. *The Centennial History of the Indiana General Assembly, 1816–1978.* Indianapolis: The Select Committee on the Centennial History of the Indiana General Assembly, 1987.

Leslie's gubernatorial papers are in the Indiana State Archives, Indianapolis.

Paul V. McNutt

January 9, 1933–January 11, 1937

LINDA C. GUGIN

AS GOVERNOR, PAUL MCNUTT AMASSED UNPRECEDENTED amounts of power by centralizing authority in the office of governor, which in turn allowed him to achieve significant shifts in state government programs and policies, especially tax reform and socioeconomic legislation. The governor's office was supposed to be just a prelude to McNutt's pursuit of the presidency, but despite impressive achievements, these ambitions were never realized.

McNutt's election in 1932 occurred the same year that Franklin D. Roosevelt was first elected president, and his fate, for better and worse, was forever entwined with the president's. McNutt's successes in office were greatly enhanced by Roosevelt's popularity and his New Deal programs, but following his term as governor in 1937, McNutt's pursuit of the presidency was thwarted by Roosevelt and his close aides. The seeds for that downfall were sown in 1932, when McNutt, in a miscalculation of strategy, withheld the support of the Indiana delegation from Roosevelt's nomination at the Democratic National Convention until the very last minute. Neither Roosevelt nor his aides forgot that slight.

McNutt's formal entry into the arena of partisan politics at the state level occurred only two years prior to his election as governor, when he delivered the keynote address at the 1930 state Democratic convention. His rise to power is often described as "meteoric," but it seems that McNutt was destined for public office from an early age.

Law and politics were an integral part of his family background. McNutt was born in Franklin, Indiana, on July 19, 1891, the son

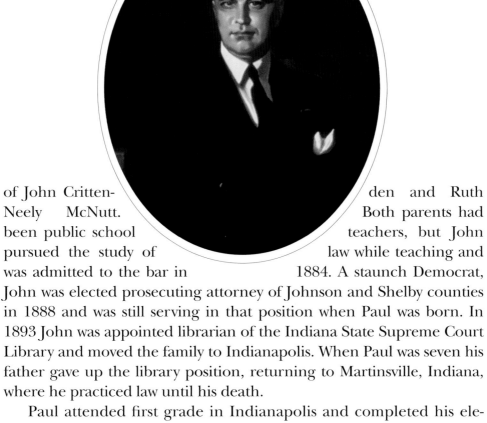

of John Critten-den and Ruth Neely McNutt. Both parents had been public school teachers, but John pursued the study of law while teaching and was admitted to the bar in 1884. A staunch Democrat, John was elected prosecuting attorney of Johnson and Shelby counties in 1888 and was still serving in that position when Paul was born. In 1893 John was appointed librarian of the Indiana State Supreme Court Library and moved the family to Indianapolis. When Paul was seven his father gave up the library position, returning to Martinsville, Indiana, where he practiced law until his death.

Paul attended first grade in Indianapolis and completed his elementary and secondary education in Martinsville. Despite the strong desire of his mother, a staunch Methodist, that he attend DePauw University in Greencastle, Paul chose Indiana University in Bloomington, where he established a distinguished academic record and honed his political skills through his active involvement in campus organizations. He was editor of the school newspaper, the *Indiana Daily Student*; president of the student union; president of Strut and Fret, a dramatic organization; and president of the senior class. His academic honors included membership in Phi Beta Kappa, Phi Delta Phi, and the Order of the Coif.

McNutt received his BA from Indiana University in 1913, graduating with high distinction. He attended Harvard Law School, mainly because his father wanted the prestige of a Harvard degree for his son. Even before he received his LLB from Harvard in 1916, McNutt had already been admitted to the bar in Morgan County, Indiana, in 1914 and had joined in his father's law practice. In 1917 he was appointed to the faculty of IU Law School but resigned within a year to enter the officers' training camp at Fort Benjamin Harrison. Although he was never sent overseas, he served in the military until the end of World War I, rising to the rank of major. He married Kathleen Timolat in 1918, and the couple had one daughter, Louise, born in 1921. McNutt resumed teaching at IU in 1919 and in 1925 was named dean of the IU Law School, a position once held by his great uncle Cyrus F. McNutt.

While serving as law school dean McNutt began laying the groundwork for his political career. He became actively involved with the American Legion, an organization with increasing political influence in the state. McNutt's rapid rise in the leadership hierarchy of the Legion helped to catapult him into the prominence essential for elective office. In 1926 McNutt was elected state commander of the Legion, and in 1928, despite long odds and after a skillful campaign, he was elected national commander. McNutt used both positions to establish his reputation as a polished speaker and dynamic leader. His talent and ability attracted another Legionnaire, Frank McHale, who became McNutt's closest political adviser and the chief architect of his political career.

In 1930 McNutt took the first major step toward the governorship when his supporters, led by McHale, succeeded in getting him chosen as temporary chair and keynote speaker at the state Democratic convention. The timing was propitious. The stock market crash the previous year had resulted in widespread economic hardship, which gave McNutt the opportunity to lambaste the Republicans for allowing the country to fall into economic chaos. McNutt gave a rousing speech that brought the conventioneers to their feet time and again and helped widen his recognition among the party regulars. He also introduced two themes that would become campaign issues in his bid for governor two years later—tax reform and economy in government.

Following his keynote address, McNutt campaigned actively for the Democratic slate of candidates. Although he received criticism from some quarters, especially Republicans, for engaging in partisan politics while serving as dean of the law school, he was not deterred. The Democrats won major victories in the 1930 elections, capturing all of the contested statewide offices and gaining a 75 to 25 majority in the state house of representatives. They also won ten of the thirteen seats in the U.S. House of Representatives. These results were a sharp reversal of the Republican domination of state politics in the previous decade, and many Democrats credited McNutt for the party's successes.

While McNutt benefited from the Democratic victories in 1930, he still had an uphill battle to get the party's nomination two years later. For the first time since 1916 party nominees for governor would be chosen by delegates to the state party convention. The Indiana General Assembly passed a bill in 1929 ending the Progressive Era experiment of nominating certain candidates, including gubernatorial candidates, in a statewide direct primary. McNutt was supported in his goal by a large contingent of veterans from the American Legion, who used the extensive Legion network throughout the state on his behalf. The power exerted by these "Young Turks" unsettled other factions of the party, particularly older members who saw them as a threat to their control over the party and its bounty of patronage. Controlling the "spoils of office" more than ideological differences had long been the primary motivating force for the state's political parties.

The anti-McNutt factions in the party were unable to stop what the *South Bend Times* called the "best organized political machine this state has ever seen," and McNutt easily won the Democratic nomination for governor in 1932. Before his campaign began in earnest, however, McNutt and his supporters turned their attention to the upcoming national convention, where the Democratic Party nominee for president would be chosen. Roosevelt, governor of New York, was the leading candidate. James A. McFarley, Roosevelt's campaign manager, sought a commitment from McNutt for the support of the Indiana delegation. McNutt resisted, and at one point Farley went so far as to ask him if he would accept the nomination for vice president. McNutt declined the offer, and despite numerous entreaties by the Roosevelt camp, he refused to budge. Roosevelt did get support from several Indiana delegates, but not enough to win the nomination on the first ballot. On the fourth ballot, when it was clear that Roosevelt had enough votes to secure the nomination, McNutt accepted the inevitable and threw his support to him. But it was too late to repair the damage he had done to his reputation with Roosevelt and Farley. They never forgot or forgave that "platinum blonde S.O.B." from Indiana.

McNutt's Republican opponent for governor was Raymond Springer, a circuit court judge who himself had been state commander of the American Legion. McNutt ran a masterful campaign. One innovation, the creation of McNutt-for-Governor clubs, was particularly effective. These organizations, established in every county of the state, served two important functions. One was to translate McNutt's public popularity into votes by attracting not only Democratic supporters but also Republicans and independents. The clubs also helped raise money, a major problem faced by the campaign. Members contributed $1 to $5. The state organization received 25 percent of the funds, and the county chapters kept the rest.

Boosted by his personal charisma and issues that struck a chord with the voters, the handsome and articulate McNutt far overshadowed his opponent. His general campaign theme was that the only way to overcome the economic ills of the Great Depression was to clean house by throwing out the Republicans from top to bottom. McNutt's main issues were tax reform, aimed at lowering the property tax and making the tax burden more equitable, and economy and efficiency in government. The party platform also included a promise for the establishment of a "just and equitable" old-age pension system, repeal of the law against prohibition, and reform of public utilities.

McNutt and his fellow Democrats won overwhelmingly. McNutt beat Springer by 192,330 votes, the largest majority ever received by an Indiana governor at the time. He became the first Democratic governor elected in twenty years. Democrats won all of the statewide offices and took all twelve of the congressional seats and the Senate seat. Most importantly the Democrats won control of both houses of the Indiana General Assembly by large margins—43 to 7 in the senate and 91 to 9 in the house. The era of Republican control in Indiana was clearly over, and a dynamic new governor was firmly in command, with enough support to pass just about any legislative proposals he submitted.

McNutt's election in 1932 produced a party realignment that lasted through the 1930s. Referring to the 1920s, historian James H. Madison observed, "seldom have the politics of two decades been so different." Whereas the 1920s had been the era of "caretaker" governors and limited government, the McNutt era expanded the power of the governor as well as the powers and responsibilities of state government.

The reforms promoted by McNutt fit into two categories. One set of reforms consisted of structural and procedural changes. Chief among these were the reorganization of the executive branch, establishment of the Hoosier Democratic Club, creation of a new system for licensing the importation and sale of alcoholic beverages in the state, and expansion of the state's regulation of public utilities.

Economy in government had been one of McNutt's key campaign issues, and his Executive Reorganization Act of 1933 was perhaps the most significant of his governmental reforms. The reorganization plan merged 168 separate agencies and commissions into eight departments: executive, state, audit and control, treasury, law, education, public works, and commerce and industry. With this reorganization McNutt also gained unprecedented powers to appoint and remove virtually any state employee, save those offices elected directly by the voters. The extreme centralization of power in the hands of the governor led critics to call the plan the "Mussolini bill" and the "ripper" bill.

Another institutional change was reform of public utilities, fulfilling a promise McNutt made during the gubernatorial campaign. The governor reduced the size of the Public Service Commission (PSC) from five to three members, appointed members less sympathetic to the utility companies, and created the position of Public Counselor to the PSC. This office was responsible for assuring that the public's interest was taken into account when the PSC debated rate hikes. The first public counselor to the commission was Sherman Minton, a Legionnaire and avid McNutt supporter, who is credited with saving rate payers over $3 million in rate reductions.

McNutt touted reorganization as a way to achieve greater efficiency in state government, and evidence suggests that savings did occur. The state moved from a deficit of more than $3.4 million to a surplus of $17 million during McNutt's tenure, and even neutral observers credit governmental reorganization, along with the establishment of the gross income tax, with helping to restore solvency to the state.

Besides promoting greater efficiency, the reorganization plan had other obvious benefits for McNutt. One was the national attention he received for it, a factor he anticipated would be helpful in his future bid for the presidency. The other obvious benefit was the extensive system of patronage it created. McNutt used this expanded patronage power to create the most powerful political machine the state had ever seen.

A central element of the McNutt machine was the Hoosier Democratic Club, popularly known as the Two Percent Club. State employees paid 2 percent of their wages or salaries to the party to fund political campaigns. While the administration claimed that these contributions were purely voluntary, it was widely assumed that failure to "contribute" would result in loss of a job. The Two Percent Club did produce substantial sums of money for the party, and it engendered party loyalty, but it also generated criticism and antagonism. After McNutt left the governor's office, the issue of the Two Percent Clubs came back to haunt him. In 1940, while he was actively pursuing the presidency, the Two Percent Club and several prominent state party leaders, including McNutt, were investigated for possible tax evasion. The issue was also raised in his confirmation hearings for Federal Security Administrator in 1939.

A third institutional change introduced by McNutt that also plugged into the patronage system was a measure that brought control over the importation, manufacture, and sale of alcoholic beverages.

In 1933 the Indiana General Assembly repealed the state's prohibition law shortly before ratification of the Twenty-first Amendment to the U.S. Constitution ended prohibition. The state legislature passed McNutt's Alcoholic Beverages Control Act that same year. The new regulations pertained to all alcoholic beverages, but the chief object of control was beer. Anyone wanting to import, manufacture, or sell beer required a license granted by the state, and they in turn had to pay fees and post bonds. Having a license amounted to a monopoly because the number of licenses was limited. Only the most deserving Democrats received licenses, and kickbacks and campaign contributions were a given. The list of licensees "read like a Who's Who of the McNutt faction of the Democratic Party." With the power amassed through the patronage appointments, the Two Percent Clubs, and alcoholic beverages licensing, the McNutt machine was able to control party nominations and government appointments for the rest of the decade.

McNutt also succeeded in achieving major substantive changes in government policies. Tax reform was at the top of the list. The goal of McNutt's tax reform was to reduce the high level of local taxes and to shift the tax burden away from property owners. He proposed a gross income tax bill that imposed a gross receipts tax on retailers and wholesalers and a gross tax on personal receipts. The highly controversial measure encountered stiff opposition from Republicans and retailers, but it passed the legislature the same day it was introduced with almost no debate, due to heavy-handed tactics used by McNutt that included suspending the rules. The tax law was effective in achieving McNutt's objectives of reducing reliance on property taxes and returning the state to fiscal solvency. It also had the effect of further centralizing power at the state level at the expense of local government.

Another important policy shift occurred in the area of relief legislation. While many of these policies were dictated by the need to participate in the various New Deal programs, the McNutt administration acted on its own to address the pressing economic dislocations resulting from the Depression. The development of liberal social-welfare programs starting in 1933 marked a significant shift in the direction of assistance to those in need. In keeping with the Hoosier values of self-reliance and limited government, the previous governor, Harry G. Leslie, had virtually ignored the growing problem of unemployment in the state. McNutt declared in his first inaugural address that "government may be a great instrument of human progress," and he identified providing food, clothing, and shelter for the destitute as the most pressing need in the state. One of the first pieces of legislation passed under his administration was an old-age pension program. Though limited in scope and stingy in benefits, it was an important shift in responsibility for poor relief from the local to the state level. It preceded the federal old-age assistance by two years. In 1935, when Congress passed the massive Social Security Act, the state responded quickly in passing welfare laws to conform to federal requirements for participating in national welfare programs and unemployment compensation.

The McNutt administration was also aggressive in pursuing assistance from the myriad of federal programs providing direct relief and work relief starting in 1933, including the Public Works Administration (PWA), the Federal Emergency Relief Administration (FERA), the Civil Works Administration (CWA), and the Works Progress Administration (WPA). The state readily established the necessary administrative structures needed to administer and coordinate these programs and was praised by the Roosevelt administration for its cooperation. McNutt's various relief policies produced perhaps his most enduring legacy—a more centralized, modernized, and professional welfare system. Granted, local governments still maintained substantial responsibility for administering poor relief, but their role was significantly reduced.

McNutt's liberal position on welfare programs was not matched in the area of labor relations. Indiana had the eleventh largest union membership in the country, and McNutt had courted labor in his campaign. His relationship with organized labor started off well when the general assembly passed several pieces of legislation favored by unions, including outlawing "yellow dog contracts," limiting antistrike injunctions, and strengthening safety standards for miners. However, his relationship with labor soured later when the governor declared martial law and used the Indiana National Guard to quell unrest in two strikes where violence occurred—in Sullivan in 1933 and the Terre Haute General Strike of 1935. He also maintained a permanent force of National Guard troops at Shakamak State Park to deter violence. Socialist leader Norman Thomas called McNutt a "Hoosier Hitler" for his aggressive intervention in labor disputes.

When McNutt's term of office ended in January 1937, his administration had greatly altered the landscape of Indiana politics. The powers he amassed were comparable in scope to the extraconstitutional powers assumed by Governor Oliver P. Morton during the Civil War. However, not all of his efforts had long-lasting effects. For one, the McNutt machine, despite its formidable power, was not able to overcome the internal factions of the party. While McNutt managed to dominate party nominations until the end of the decade, by 1938 things had begun to unravel. In order to maintain control, McNutt had to make a major and costly compromise by supporting the nomination of Frederick Van Nuys for reelection to the U.S. Senate, a decision that brought him into direct conflict with Roosevelt, who wanted Van Nuys out because he opposed his Supreme Court-packing plan. This was McNutt's first major break with the Roosevelt administration, but he distanced himself further from the president when New Deal programs lost their popularity. McNutt's motives in these matters can be attributed in part to his anticipated run for the presidency in 1940.

McNutt's highly touted reorganization act did not survive too long after his tenure. It was abolished in 1941 by a Republican legislature with the blessing of Governor Henry F. Schricker, a Democrat whose administration marked a return to a more passive chief executive. There were, however, more permanent and positive results of McNutt's administration. Chief among these were his reform of the welfare system, the establishment of the gross income tax, and returning the state to solvency.

In December 1936, on the eve of his departure from the governor's office, McNutt formally launched his bid for the presidency. One of his most ardent supporters, Minton (at the time a U.S. Senator), said, "as we bid you goodbye at the Statehouse, we bid you Godspeed toward the White House." McNutt was unaware that he had already reached the zenith of his political career.

In 1937 Roosevelt named McNutt to be High Commissioner to the Philippines, a position he held until 1939 when Roosevelt appointed him director of the new Federal Security Agency (FSA). At that time McNutt resumed his bid for the presidency, assuming that Roosevelt would not run for a third term. But the president waited until almost the eve of the convention to announce his intention to run again, dashing McNutt's hopes. He withdrew from the race, hoping that he might get the nod for vice president. McNutt's lack of support for Roosevelt in 1932 and again in the Van Nuys race in 1938, however, prevented him from serious consideration.

McNutt remained in the Roosevelt administration for several more years, holding various positions. During the war he chaired the War Manpower Commission while still serving as head of the FSA. In 1945 President Harry Truman appointed McNutt High Commissioner of the Philippines, where he helped bring about the transition to independence in 1946. McNutt remained in the Philippines as U.S. ambassador until 1947, when he retired from public service. He moved to New York and practiced law there and in Washington, D.C. for the next eight years. He returned to the Philippines one more time in 1955. Sailing with his wife on a world cruise to recuperate from illness and surgery, his health deteriorated rapidly as he neared the island. After landing at Manila he flew home to New York, where he died on March 24, 1955. He is buried in Arlington National Cemetery.

Portrait by Wayman Adams (1933), Governors' Portraits Collection, Indiana Historical Bureau, State of Indiana.

FOR FURTHER READING

Blake, I. George. *Paul V. McNutt: Portrait of a Hoosier Statesman.* Indianapolis: Central Publishing Company, 1966.

Jessup, Benjamin L. "The Career of Paul V. McNutt." PhD diss., Kent State University, 1995.

Madison, James H. *Indiana through Tradition and Change: A History of the Hoosier State and Its People, 1920–1945.* Vol. 5, *The History of Indiana.* Indianapolis: Indiana Historical Society, 1982.

Morgan, Iwan. "Factional Conflict in Indiana Politics during the Later New Deal Years, 1936–1940." *Indiana Magazine of History* 79 (March 1983): 29–60.

Neff, Robert R. "The Early Career and Governorship of Paul V. McNutt." PhD diss., Indiana University, 1963.

McNutt's papers can be found in the Wiliam Henry Smith Memorial Library, Indiana Historical Society, Indianapolis; the Indiana State Archives, Indianapolis; and the Lilly Library, Indiana University, Bloomington.

M. Clifford Townsend

January 11, 1937–January 13, 1941

JAMES L. MCDOWELL

THE GOVERNORSHIP OF M. CLIFFORD TOWNSEND PROVED a relative calm between storms in Indiana politics, connecting the proactive administration of Paul V. McNutt with one of the more acrimonious terms under Henry F. Schricker. Townsend did not achieve his goal of state government relaxing and consolidating its gains under the energetic leadership of his predecessor. But his tenure as the middle of three Democratic governors during a period of economic crisis and world conflict proved to be considerably more peaceful than the partisan rancor that characterized the term of his successor. The Townsend years, however, were not without conflict, in both the political and nonpolitical realms.

The son of David and Lydia Glancy Townsend, Maurice Clifford Townsend was born August 11, 1884, in rural Blackford County, Indiana. Raised on farms with his sister Myrtle, Townsend attended local public schools and completed high school in 1901. Over the next six years, he farmed, worked as a teamster in the state's oil fields, and taught in county schools while attending Marion Normal College, a school known for teacher education. After graduating from college in 1907, Townsend continued his teaching career until being selected superintendent of the Blackford County schools in 1909, a position he held for a decade. Thus established, he married Nora Adele Harris on Christmas Day 1910, and the couple had two daughters and a son.

Townsend left the Blackford County school position in 1919 and served a single term as a Democratic state representative in 1923, rep-

resenting Black- ford and Grant counties. From 1925 to 1929 he was Grant County superintendent of schools and also served on the executive committee of the Indiana State Teachers Association. Following an unsuccessful campaign for Congress in 1928, Townsend became educational director of the Indiana Farm Bureau the next year. His dual background in the fields of education and agriculture made Townsend an attractive running mate for Democratic gubernatorial candidate Paul V. McNutt in 1932. With McNutt forces in total control of the state convention, delegates nominated Townsend for lieutenant governor on the first ballot.

McNutt and Townsend won their separate races for the state's top two executive positions, each receiving more than 56 percent of the popular vote. The balloting also produced enormous Democratic margins in both state legislative chambers. In the subsequent legislative session, lawmakers increased the role of the lieutenant governor, assigning administrative duties to the office, including the position of commissioner of agriculture, in addition to the constitutional function of presiding over the state senate. Prior to that legislation, lieutenant governors had received only a token salary and worked only during legislative sessions. Townsend became Indiana's first full-time lieutenant governor.

Townsend's legislative duties proved little more than perfunctory in 1933. His main role in that session was maintaining legislative decorum in the upper chamber while forestalling any factional disputes over the administration's ambitious legislative program that included a revolutionary Executive Reorganization Act, a gross income tax to shift the state's revenue base from the property tax, and the sale of beer and wine under state supervision.

In 1935 Democrats continued legislative control, although with reduced margins. Townsend that year oversaw a somewhat more contentious senate, which defeated a proposal for a state personnel agency and a limited merit system that challenged the extensive patronage system that the administration had developed. Townsend was more involved in a special legislative session in 1936 that established agencies to comply with federal welfare legislation. Later that year, these agencies created a state personnel agency that was not only embraced by both McNutt and Townsend but also cited as a national guide for state personnel units.

Townsend's enhanced role as lieutenant governor gave him more visibility and political presence, but it was his staunch loyalty to the governor that won him McNutt's support for the Democratic gubernatorial nomination in 1936. Townsend was not unchallenged, however, in what would be one of the most acrimonious preconvention campaigns in state history. To illustrate the extent of the Democrats' divisiveness, while McNutt supported Townsend, Indiana's two U.S. senators each had his own candidate: Sherman Minton strongly supported Pleas Greenlee, the governor's former executive secretary and patronage chief, and Frederick Van Nuys, along with former state chairman R. Earl Peters, backed E. Kirk McKinney.

The bitter campaign extended even to the convention floor, where a fistfight among delegates supporting different candidates interrupted the gubernatorial balloting. In the end, however, McNutt's control of the state party machinery determined the outcome. Within twenty votes of winning on the first ballot, Townsend became the nominee when the other candidates accepted the inevitable and dropped out. The McNutt organization then engineered the single-ballot nomination of state senator Henry F. Schricker for lieutenant governor.

McNutt campaigned vigorously for the Townsend-Schricker ticket, and both U.S. senators and the defeated gubernatorial candidates also returned to the fold and publicly supported the slate. While stating he would be his own man as governor, Townsend in turn ran almost solely on the McNutt record and tied himself directly to President Franklin D. Roosevelt's first-term accomplishments. The approach was successful. Although he trailed Roosevelt by almost 70,000 votes, Townsend defeated Republican Raymond Springer by 180,000 votes.

In a postelection statement, the governor-elect suggested that national and state efforts had ended the Depression crisis so that Indiana would have little new to consider during his term. Townsend, holding that it was time that government "relaxed" after the hectic previous four years, told the Indiana General Assembly in 1937 that lawmakers should keep "new legislation to a minimum." The legislature, still safely in Democratic control, agreed with the governor's sentiment and produced little of major consequence in that session. Outside events, however, would make the governor's term—indeed, his first months in office—far more active than he intended or anticipated.

The initial incident was the devastating Ohio River flood of January 1937 that took place at the very outset of Townsend's administration. The surging waters that reached historic heights above flood stages from Lawrenceburg to Mount Vernon paralyzed communities along the state's southern border, resulted in martial law in Evansville, and necessitated the assignment of thousands of Works Progress Administration workers to flood cleanup. Townsend established a flood disaster relief program that aided thousands of displaced residents, but the total cost of restoration eliminated that portion of the state surplus allocated for a state office building.

On the heels of this natural disaster, a second set of episodes required the governor's involvement. A sit-down strike by United Auto Workers against General Motors at its Flint, Michigan, plant spread to other GM facilities, including one in Anderson, Indiana. Persistent, violent confrontations between union picketers and local strike opponents in January and February eventually forced Townsend to send in the Indiana National Guard, although only after Anderson's mayor requested assistance. In May 1937 steelworkers struck two plants in Lake County, but Townsend's mediation efforts helped forestall violence and enabled the plants to reopen in July. These events prompted the governor to propose the creation of the Indiana Division of Labor to provide for voluntary mediation of labor-management disputes.

Finally, a long-simmering political feud between Van Nuys and the McNutt-Townsend alliance came to a full boil in 1937–38. Although supported for the Senate nomination by McNutt in 1932, Van Nuys was never a part of the McNutt coalition. Considered "middle-of-the road" by national standards but a member of Indiana's "old guard" Democrats, Van Nuys opposed McNutt on various occasions after winning the Senate seat: in 1934 in a dispute over control of federal patronage in Indiana, in 1935 when he supported moving nomination of senatorial and gubernatorial candidates to the direct primary, and in 1936 when he attempted to reduce the governor's control over the state committee and opposed Townsend's nomination for governor.

The political pot boiled over in 1937 when Van Nuys opposed Roosevelt's plan to enlarge the Supreme Court. As a result, the president included Van Nuys among those he hoped to purge in the 1938 elections, and McNutt and Townsend supported the removal effort. Townsend in fact appeared at the White House to declare that Indiana Democrats would not renominate Van Nuys. Schricker appeared to be the choice to replace Van Nuys, even though he was also openly against the court-packing proposal.

Political realities eventually caused cooler heads to prevail. Dumping Van Nuys, if successful, likely would not only lead to a Republican capture of the Senate seat but, more importantly, damage McNutt's aspirations for the Democratic presidential nomination in 1940. An unsuccessful attempt to replace Van Nuys would be even more embarrassing to state Democrats and more harmful to McNutt's political future. McNutt convinced Townsend to drop his opposition, and the governor and other party leaders feigned harmony at the state convention that renominated Van Nuys.

In the November election, Van Nuys won reelection by just over five thousand votes, and the Democrats kept control of the state senate, but Republicans won the state house of representatives 51 to 49. Other than passage of some public health bills, the divided legislature in 1939 resulted in a stalemate. Lawmakers ignored Townsend's call for a new round of social legislation designed to counteract the economic downturn of the previous two years. Instead, they primarily engaged in partisan politics as the Republican house thwarted any administration proposals and the Democratic senate beat back efforts to repeal measures adopted during the McNutt governorship.

Despite the generally unproductive 1939 session, Townsend did achieve some notable accomplishments in his term. In addition to establishing the Indiana Division of Labor to authorize mediation of labor disputes, the Townsend administration also established pension programs for firemen in Fort Wayne, Indianapolis, and Terre Haute; began examinations for drivers' licenses; provided for free public school textbooks; and, not insignificantly, instituted the painting of school buses yellow as a safety measure.

Townsend did not involve himself in the Democrats' gubernatorial nomination process of 1940, neither endorsing nor overtly opposing Schricker's campaign. After leaving office, Townsend continued in public service as director or administrator of various federal agricultural programs from 1941 to 1943. He was the Democrats' unsuccessful candidate for U.S. Senator against Republican William E. Jenner in 1946. Following this defeat, Townsend lived in retirement on his farm in Blackford County until he suffered a heart attack in October 1954. He died on November 11 at the age of seventy and was buried in the Independent Order of Odd Fellows (IOOF) Cemetery in Hartford City.

Portrait by Cornelius Zwaan (1938), Governors' Portraits Collection, Indiana Historical Bureau, State of Indiana.

FOR FURTHER READING

Blake, I. George. *Paul V. McNutt: Portrait of a Hoosier Statesman.* Indianapolis: Central Publishing Company, 1966.

Burns, James MacGregor. *Roosevelt: The Lion and the Fox.* New York: Harcourt, Brace, 1956.

Madison, James H. *Indiana through Tradition and Change: A History of the Hoosier State and Its People, 1920–1945.* Vol. 5, *The History of Indiana.* Indianapolis: Indiana Historical Society, 1982.

Sikes, Pressley S. *Indiana State and Local Government.* Rev. ed. Bloomington: Principia Press, 1946.

Townsend's gubernatorial papers are in the Indiana State Archives, Indianapolis.

Henry F. Schricker

January 13, 1941–January 8, 1945 and January 10, 1949–January 12, 1953

JAMES L. MCDOWELL

HENRY F. SCHRICKER IS CELEBRATED AMONG INDIANA POLIT-
ical figures. He remains unique among those who have served as Indiana governor in that he alone was elected to two separate terms as the
state's chief executive. Under the original language of the Indiana
Constitution of 1851 (until amended in 1972), a governor was not
"eligible more than four years in any period of eight years." Schricker,
a Democrat, served from 1941 to 1945, returned to the private sector
for four years, and held the office again from 1949 to 1953.

His terms remain memorable for hostile encounters with opposition-controlled legislatures. In his first term, Schricker confronted
a Republican-dominated Indiana General Assembly that threatened
the administrative capacity of his office. His efforts ultimately led to
a landmark state supreme court ruling that the governor is the chief
executive. In his second term, Schricker successfully delayed implementation of a Republican legislative plan that jeopardized the state's
federal welfare funding until congressional action made the issue
moot.

Finally, his reputation remains that of an independent public servant whose trademark white hat symbolized his integrity. Schricker
was "independent" in that he was often at odds with others of his own
party and not always uncomfortable with positions taken by the opposition, and his personal integrity was unquestioned. His carefully cul-
tivated public image concealed a consummate politician who not only
carefully orchestrated his two gubernatorial nominations but also

enjoyed longer political success than did some more celebrated contemporaries.

Henry Frederick Schricker was born on August 30, 1883, in North Judson, Indiana, the second son and third child of Bavarian immigrants Christopher and Magdalena Meyer Schricker. He attended the Lutheran parochial school for five grades and received his eighth-grade diploma from the North Judson public school in 1897. While working in the family grocery and mercantile store over the next eight years, he obtained his only other formal education, a series of bookkeeping courses taken at a business college in South Bend. In 1905 Schricker read for the law under the tutelage of local attorneys while serving as deputy clerk of the Starke County Circuit Court. He was the unsuccessful Democratic candidate for county clerk in 1906, but was admitted to the Indiana bar the same year. Although Schricker practiced law for a short time, his career path took several different directions.

After serving as cashier of a small bank in Hamlet, Indiana, for about eighteen months, Schricker purchased the *Starke County Democrat*, a weekly newspaper published in Knox, the county seat, in 1908. Despite his lack of journalism training, Schricker ran the newspaper for eleven years, staunchly supporting Democratic candidates for offices from the courthouse to the statehouse and the White House. In 1914 Schricker married Maude L. Brown, the daughter of a prominent Knox physician. They had a daughter and two sons. Schricker returned to the banking business in 1919, selling the newspaper to become cashier of the Farmers Bank and Trust in Knox.

Schricker failed in his initial effort to be elected joint state senator from Starke and La Porte counties in 1924, but his rise to statewide prominence and some national notice began eight years later. The national Democratic tide of 1932 also engulfed Indiana, where the party carried all statewide offices and dominated both houses of the general assembly. Schricker was among a host of newcomers in the upper chamber as Democrats won twenty-five of twenty-seven senatorial races.

The legislative session of 1933 was dominated by the controversial Executive Reorganization Act pushed through by newly elected Governor Paul V. McNutt. Schricker opposed centralizing administrative control in the hands of one official but voted for the plan with "reluctance." He supported the unprecedented granting of power to the governor with an eye toward his own political future but also out of party loyalty. His allegiance to the party was one factor in Democratic senators electing him caucus chairman in 1935. On the basis of his record in the 1933 and 1935 sessions, which included laws that reformed the state's teacher tenure system, made his home county a separate judicial circuit, and reorganized the state police, voters in his district renominated Schricker for a second term in the 1936 Democratic primary. However, he did not make that race but instead became the compromise choice of the dominant McNutt faction for lieutenant governor.

The liberal M. Clifford Townsend and the more conservative Schricker comprised a formidable ticket. Aided considerably by President Franklin D. Roosevelt's overwhelming reelection margin, the tandem rode to victory, and Democrats retained control of both legislative chambers. Schricker's four years as lieutenant governor proved notable not for any governmental contributions but for his avoidance of political controversy—particularly the widening breach between the McNutt and Townsend factions that resulted from the attempted purge of Senator Frederick Van Nuys in 1938. As agricultural commissioner, a role assigned to the lieutenant governor, Schricker traveled frequently around Indiana, which enhanced his contacts with farmers as well as labor union members, local party officials, and average citizens across the state. In effect, Schricker conducted a four-year campaign for delegates to the 1940 Democratic state convention. At that conclave, neither McNutt nor Townsend supported Schricker, although they did not openly oppose him, and he won the nomination for governor on the second ballot.

In the 1940 campaign Republicans continued to oppose the McNutt reorganization plan, Democratic patronage policies and the Two Percent Club, and New Deal social legislation. For his part, Schricker largely ignored both the two previous Democratic administrations and the New Deal programs, running primarily on his personal popularity and his strength in rural areas. His strategy paid off, but barely. Schricker was elected governor by just 3,963 votes and was the only Democrat elected statewide. In addition to winning the state's electoral votes behind Indiana native Wendell Willkie, Republicans also elected a U.S. Senator and eight of the twelve members of the U.S. House of Representatives and, most importantly, gained control of both houses of the Indiana General Assembly—64 to 36 in the lower chamber and 31 to 19 in the senate. The Republican sweep presaged a turbulent initiation for the newly elected governor.

Republicans intended not only to repeal the 1933 executive reorganization act but also to enact legislation that reduced the governor to little more than a caretaker. Schricker attempted to head off their efforts by asserting in his inaugural address his opposition to the extensive control granted the governor eight years earlier, noting that he doubted the "wisdom of some of its provisions" and declaring that he supported a "return to the former standards of state government, maintained for many years prior to the Reorganization Act." However, he also noted that he opposed legislation already introduced that had "the unmistakable purpose of humiliating and embarrassing the present Chief Executive of our state." While he did not "crave dictatorial power," Schricker maintained that no governor could function effectively by reducing the powers of the office to "errand boy authority."

Despite Schricker's attempt at compromise, Republicans proceeded on what has been described as "one of the most thoroughly partisan ventures in Indiana history." The legislature repealed the 1933 statute, adopted the State Administration Act of 1941, and enacted additional laws that Democrats labeled "ripper bills." This legislative package eliminated many state agencies and revamped others, placing them in five newly established administrative departments, only one of which was directed solely by the governor. The new organization plan distributed the majority of state agencies into four departments. A commission of three elected state officials, the governor and two others, decided the appointments and policies of each department by majority vote. Under the prevailing political conditions, two Republican state officials could always outvote Schricker, effectively stripping him of his executive powers.

The governor vetoed all of these bills, but the Republican legislature overturned all but one. Following the legislature's adjournment, Schricker then obtained a temporary injunction in Marion County Circuit Court that barred other elected state officials from acting in accordance with the state reorganization legislation. Four Republican state officials, headed by Secretary of State James M. Tucker, appealed the lower court decision to the Indiana Supreme Court. After several months' deliberation, the state's highest court voided the Republican reorganization plan, essentially affirming that the governor is the "chief executive." In *Tucker v. State* the court ruled that the Indiana Constitution gave the governor the power to appoint and remove state administrative personnel and that legislative attempts to delegate this authority to other officials violated the separation of powers principle and was unconstitutional. The supreme court, which at that time consisted of four Democrats and one Republican, ruled strictly along party lines.

As the battle over executive branch reorganization dominated Schricker's first year, World War II overshadowed the remainder of his term. The governor and lawmakers tacitly agreed to put domestic policy modifications on hold for the duration. Republicans increased their majorities in both legislative chambers in the 1942 elections, but the partisan conflict was greatly reduced in the 1943 session. In his final two years, Schricker and the legislature worked together to maintain fiscal responsibility. When Schricker's term ended, Indiana had a general fund surplus of $57 million. But politics was not wholly absent. In 1944 Democrats nominated Schricker for U.S. Senator. Republicans swept all statewide races, however, with Schricker losing to incumbent Homer E. Capehart, although running some twenty-six thousand votes ahead of Roosevelt. Leaving the governor's office in January 1945, Schricker returned to the banking business as a vice president of the Fletcher Trust Company in Indianapolis.

Schricker retired from public life but not from politics. From his position at one of the state's leading financial institutions in the state capital, Schricker consulted frequently with Democratic lawmakers during the legislative sessions of 1945 and 1947. Toward the end of 1947, a group of Democrats, including recently elected mayors, initiated a "Draft Schricker for Governor" movement that the former chief executive did not discourage. Schricker, who "reluctantly consented" in May to formally enter the race, was nominated for governor by acclamation at the Democratic state convention in June. He led the Democratic state ticket to victory in November by defeating Hobart Creighton by more than 139,000 votes, although Republican Thomas Dewey narrowly carried Indiana's presidential vote. Schricker's victory made him the only person separately elected to two terms as governor under the original provisions of the 1851 constitution.

Another political struggle dominated Schricker's second term. This time, however, the battle was waged between the state and the national government over making welfare records public. Republicans had rebounded in the midterm elections, winning all the minor statewide offices and gaining control of both legislative chambers. In the 1951 session, Republicans passed legislation that made welfare rolls "public record and available for inspection," although this bill apparently conflicted with federal privacy requirements that states had to follow to qualify for public welfare grants. The legislature overrode Schricker's veto of the bill as soon as his message was delivered, and the national government acted almost as quickly to deny Indiana public welfare funds after the law became effective. This decision would have cost the state an estimated $18 million each year.

The governor then called a special session of the general assembly, but legislators could not resolve the looming financial crisis in the monthlong meeting. The legislature eventually passed a stopgap measure that delayed opening public welfare records for two years and provided for a new state-county funding formula in the event the national government again denied welfare funds to Indiana. This bill, which became law without Schricker's signature, became unnecessary when Congress finally rectified the situation. Senator William E. Jenner of Indiana was able to amend a major appropriations bill with a rider that provided no state could be deprived of federal funds for permitting public access to welfare disbursements.

The highlight of Schricker's remaining tenure was the 1952 presidential campaign. He served with Delaware governor Elbert Carvel as conominator of Illinois governor Adlai Stevenson for president at the Democratic National Convention in Chicago. The curious arrangement came about because Stevenson would not flatly reject a presidential bid but refused to stop either governor from placing his name before the convention. Delaware came before Indiana in the alphabetical roll call of the states, but Stevenson supporters did not want their candidate nominated by an easterner. They worked out a complicated arrangement by which Delaware yielded to Indiana, permitting Schricker, who had developed an excellent working and personal relationship with the Illinois governor, to deliver the first half of the nominating speech. When Schricker completed his part, the convention erupted into its first truly spontaneous demonstration, and Carvel finished the speech "to a tossing sea of Stevenson placards."

Schricker departed public office for the final time in January 1953. While he left a general fund surplus of $125 million, the state's frugal ways during his second term also left burgeoning problems with the state's educational facilities, highway infrastructure, and mental health system. In private life, he was one of the founders of the Wabash Fire and Casualty Insurance Company in Indianapolis. Schricker died on December 28, 1966, at the age of eighty-three. He is buried in Crown Hill Cemetery in Knox, where he had lived in retirement.

Portrait by Marie Goth (before 1943), Governors' Portraits Collection, Indiana Historical Bureau, State of Indiana.

FOR FURTHER READING

Fleming, Charles Francis. *The White Hat: Henry Frederick Schricker, a Political Biography.* Privately published, 1966.

Madison, James H. *Indiana through Tradition and Change: A History of the Hoosier State and Its People, 1920–1945.* Vol. 5, *The History of Indiana.* Indianapolis: Indiana Historical Society, 1982.

Martin, John Bartlow. *Adlai Stevenson of Illinois: The Life of Adlai E. Stevenson.* Garden City, NY: Doubleday, 1976.

Sikes, Pressley S. *Indiana State and Local Government.* Rev. ed. Bloomington, IN: Principia Press, 1946.

Tucker v. State. 218 Ind. 168 (1941).

Schricker's gubernatorial papers are in the Indiana State Archives, Indianapolis.

Ralph F. Gates

January 8, 1945–January 10, 1949

JASON S. LANTZER

RALPH GATES'S STORY IS THAT OF THE RESTORATION OF THE Republican Party in Indiana. He was noted as a "master politician," and in rebuilding the party in the age of the New Deal, he proved it, not just in the short term, but for the long term as well.

Gates was born in Columbia City, Whitley County, on February 24, 1893. His parents were Benton E. and Alice Fesler Gates. The devout Presbyterian family included three other boys, John, Scott, and Benton. Gates went to school in Columbia City, graduating from high school in 1911. He attended the University of Michigan, earning his bachelor's degree in 1915 and his law degree in 1917. He married Helene Edwards of South Whitley on October 30, 1919. Prior to their marriage, Helene attended the University of Chicago and was a teacher in Muncie. They bought a home, and he took a job in his father's law firm. Two children, Robert and Patricia, soon completed the family.

Gates served in the U.S. Navy during World War I. He enlisted as an ensign in the reserves and was attached to the Pay Corps in August 1917. He was promoted to the rank of lieutenant and began work for the War Risk Insurance Bureau, serving overseas from December 1917 until April 1919. Deployed to Ireland, Gates sold more than $1 million worth of war bonds to naval personnel. He was later assigned to France, where he was put in charge of building an airbase for the military. After the war, Gates turned down an offer to work with Herbert Hoover's Belgian relief effort so that he could go home.

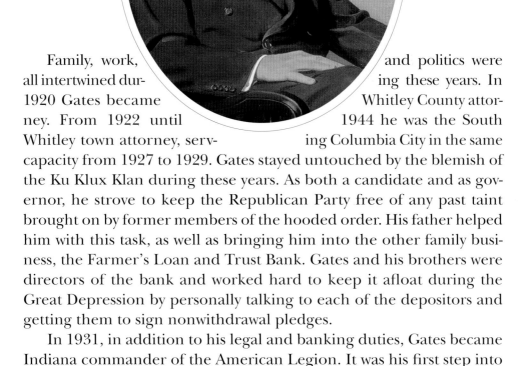

Family, work, and politics were all intertwined during these years. In 1920 Gates became Whitley County attorney. From 1922 until 1944 he was the South Whitley town attorney, serving Columbia City in the same capacity from 1927 to 1929. Gates stayed untouched by the blemish of the Ku Klux Klan during these years. As both a candidate and as governor, he strove to keep the Republican Party free of any past taint brought on by former members of the hooded order. His father helped him with this task, as well as bringing him into the other family business, the Farmer's Loan and Trust Bank. Gates and his brothers were directors of the bank and worked hard to keep it afloat during the Great Depression by personally talking to each of the depositors and getting them to sign nonwithdrawal pledges.

In 1931, in addition to his legal and banking duties, Gates became Indiana commander of the American Legion. It was his first step into politics outside of Whitley County and gave him innumerable contacts around the state that proved to be very important for his future. As governor, he would work to help bring the Legion's national headquarters to Indianapolis.

Gates grew up in Republican Party politics, his father having served as county chairman for a decade. That, much more than his paper route (he had been Thomas Marshall's paper boy), determined his choice of partisan loyalty. He served as the Whitley County chairman, as the Twelfth

Congressional District chairman, and as a delegate to the Republican National Convention in 1928, 1936, and 1940. In 1941 he became state chairman. Gates worked very hard during his tenure to get the Republican Party well organized in each of the state's counties. Those who opposed him found themselves outside of the party apparatus very quickly. He used this organization to seek the gubernatorial nomination.

At the 1944 state convention Gates was unanimously selected to carry the Republican banner in Indiana. Congressman Charles A. Halleck set the tone for the coming campaign in his keynote address blasting President Franklin D. Roosevelt, the New Deal, and Democratic domination of the state and nation since 1932, while also fully supporting the war effort. The convention brought Gates, Homer E. Capehart, and William E. Jenner together for the first time. The three Hoosier politicians were the future of Indiana politics. While they are rightly categorized as conservative, of the three, the war hero and short-term Senate nominee Jenner was by far the more rigid in his ideology. Capehart was a successful businessman whose Cornfield Conference in 1938 had helped to reinvigorate the state party. In an effort at promoting party unity at the 1944 convention, Gates opted not to openly support Capehart's opponent for the long-term Senate nomination. Following the convention, Gates was greeted with a large parade when he returned to Columbia City.

Gates was a strong believer in grassroots politics. His campaign style was to get to know people. He would go wherever there were voters, greeting them with his deep, friendly voice. Gates did not like to campaign alongside county chairmen, believing that they slowed him down and only let him talk to other Republicans. He was a firm believer in the idea that "a local problem can best be solved by local government." Gates charged that Hoosier Democrats had abandoned the leadership of the state to President Roosevelt and openly attacked the New Deal. During his campaign, Gates crisscrossed the state, spending much time in southern Indiana. But he rarely, if ever, spent the night outside of Columbia City and nearly always reported to work at his law office the next morning. By the end of the campaign he felt that he knew the state and its people very well. His instincts held true.

On Election Day, Gates defeated his Democratic opponent, Samuel D. Jackson, by a margin of 46,581 votes.

Gates was the first Republican governor in more than a decade. He vowed to Hoosier Republicans that he would not be another Paul V. McNutt, ruling as a virtual dictator over the state. Not that there was much fear of that. Even with patronage, the war-induced manpower shortage meant that there was no long line of seekers for poorly paid state jobs. In his inaugural address, Gates called on the three branches of state government to do their own jobs and do them well, but to not try and do the work of the other two. As governor, Gates offered no real change in government, but he did provide much-needed leadership to a state in transition from a wartime to a peacetime economy.

He was the right man for this task. Gates had no political debts, was attached to no party faction, and had the ability to reach politicians of both parties. Gates was a man of his word, and with few exceptions, knew how to pick good people for his administration. There was "tremendous energy" around the governor. He was a very hard worker and always seemed to be doing something, which had the tendency to wear out much younger aides.

Gates concentrated on the areas of industry, highway construction, and mental health while governor. He was determined to see Indiana make a successful transition to a peacetime economy. The governor realized that wartime spending would eventually end and that the state could not count on budget surpluses spurred by federal spending forever. He pushed and prodded the state legislature to increase funding for higher education for returning veterans. And he did his own part to help them, calling up the National Guard in December 1945 in order to bring returning Hoosier service men and women home to Indiana from jammed transportation centers all over the country. He became good friends with J. K. Lilly Jr. and received much help and advice on health care from Eli Lilly and Company. He also pushed for the construction of three mental-health facilities in the state.

Under Gates's guidance, the state passed a political convention reform law and raised the taxes on beer, liquor, and cigarettes. He also expanded the size of the state government to meet the demands of a changing postwar world. The departments of revenue, veterans affairs, and commerce all came into being during his time in office. He also created commissions on flood control and traffic safety. Gates pushed for the creation of Shades State Park and ordered the refurbishment of other parks in the system. He raised the minimum salaries for teachers, updated the Bureau of Motor Vehicles, and started a retirement fund for state employees.

Even though his party held better than a two-thirds majority in both houses of the legislature, Gates was not always successful. His plan for massive highway construction in the state largely came to naught because the Indiana General Assembly refused to allocate enough funds to receive matching federal dollars. This Hoosier mindset of not wanting big government help also plagued his attempts at getting money to local government. Still, he left office having increased the state's budget surplus by around $10 million.

Gates's greatest victory as governor was also one of his last in that role. During the 1948 Republican State Convention, he blocked Jenner from receiving the party's nomination for governor despite the senator having a two-hundred-delegate lead. Jenner was immensely popular in Indiana and had received more votes in 1944 than either Gates or Capehart. Never feeling completely at ease in Washington, D.C., the sharp-tongued Hoosier had his sights set on becoming governor, bending the state party apparatus around him in 1945 and 1946. The governor felt Jenner should stay in the Senate and got two of the other three candidates to rally around Speaker of the House Hobart Creighton of Warsaw to stop the Jenner bandwagon after the first round of votes. It was something few observers believed could be accomplished. Jenner never forgave him.

After leaving office, Gates retained his role as leader of the Indiana Republican Party, serving both the state and national parties in various roles. He surprised many by never seeking another political office, for he was rumored to be on the vice presidential short list in 1948 and was in Robert A. Taft's hotel room in 1952 when the Ohio Republican learned that the national convention was going to go with Dwight Eisenhower. Gates turned down a request that he run again

for governor in 1952, though he was by no means done with politics. Candidates such as Richard G. Lugar made the trip to Columbia
City to seek Gates's endorsement. He was still dispensing advice and
granting endorsements right up to his death, telling a reporter that
the Republicans made a mistake in picking Gerald Ford over Ronald
Reagan in 1976 and that Jimmy Carter was well intentioned but had
no grasp of politics.

After his one and only victory, Gates returned to his law practice in
Columbia City. He and Helene lived in the same house they had lived
in since they were married in 1919. They also enjoyed their cottage
on Crooked Lake, just outside of Columbia City. In retirement, Gates
indulged himself in reading about the Civil War and enjoyed spending time in his garden. He died on July 28, 1978. Gates requested a
simple service, telling his family that it would be all right with him if
they just played "Onward, Christian Soldiers" over and over again.

Portrait by Randolph LaSalle Coats (1946), Governors' Portraits Collection, Indiana Historical Bureau, State of Indiana.

FOR FURTHER READING

Madison, James H. *Indiana through Tradition and Change: A History of
the Hoosier State and Its People, 1920–1945.* Vol. 5, *The History of Indi-
ana.* Indianapolis: Indiana Historical Society, 1982.
Martin, John Barlow. *Indiana: An Interpretation.* Indianapolis: Indiana
University Press, 1992.
Pickett, William B. *Homer E. Capehart: A Senator's Life, 1897–1979.*
Indianapolis: Indiana Historical Society, 1990.

In addition to the sources cited above the following people contributed information for this essay: Patricia Gates McNagny, the Honorable James Heuer, Mary Trier.

Gates's gubernatorial papers can be found in the Indiana State Archives,
Indianapolis.

George N. Craig

January 12, 1953–January 14, 1957

HUGO C. SONGER

GEORGE N. CRAIG WAS THE PERFECT REPUBLICAN CANDI-
date for governor of Indiana in 1952 save one fact. He was a political
outsider confronted by a state organization tightly controlled by the
forces of U.S. senators Homer E. Capehart and William E. Jenner,
particularly the latter. Craig—trial lawyer, war hero, first World War II
veteran to be elected as national commander of the American Legion,
personal friend of Dwight Eisenhower, and a man who relished a good
fight—took on those forces and won, thereby incurring their eternal
wrath.

Every successful politician can name people who had a great effect
on his or her career for good or ill, and that was certainly true of
Craig. There were those without whose assistance at critical junctures
he would likely not have become governor and those who, though
close friends initially, almost brought him down, or at least tainted his
term of office.

Craig was born on August 9, 1909, in Brazil, Indiana, to Bernard
C. and Clo Branson Craig. After graduating from Brazil High School
in 1927, he attended the University of Arizona from 1927 to 1929. By
his own admission, he paid little attention to his studies and joined
a forbidden drinking fraternity, Kappa Beta Phi (the opposite of Phi
Beta Kappa). He returned home after only two years and decided to
become a lawyer like his father. When he sought admission to the Indiana University School of Law in Bloomington, he was apprehensive of
admission in view of his poor grades at the University of Arizona. He

had an inter-view with Paul V. McNutt, then dean of the law school, who would later play an impor-tant role in his career. Perhaps McNutt rec-ognized a kindred soul in Craig, and he admitted Craig to the law school. Taking his legal studies more seriously, Craig graduated in 1932. His future nemesis, Jenner, was a fellow classmate. Craig later said he and Jenner began arguing about issues while law students. In 1931, during his last year in law school, he married Kathryn Louisa Hilliger. After graduation, Craig returned to Clay County to practice law with his father.

The heart of the Great Depression was not a good time to begin the practice of law, but Craig honed his skills as a trial lawyer, trying every case he could, large or small, and developed forensic skills that would prepare him for a successful career in law and politics. Gravitating toward local politics, he was elected Clay County Republican Chairman in 1938, was named Brazil city attorney in 1939, and made an unsuccessful attempt at the state convention for the party's nomination for lieutenant governor in 1940. That experience no doubt influenced his attitude toward the nomination process because as governor he sought unsuccessfully to abolish the process of nominating state candidates at a state convention in favor of an open primary.

In February 1942 Craig received a commission as a first lieutenant and reported for duty to the Eightieth Infantry Division at Camp

Bedford Forrest at Tullahoma, Tennessee. He participated in the Normandy invasion on June 6, 1944, and saw action in France and Germany. Craig remained with the Eightieth Division throughout the war, serving as platoon, company, and battalion commander, and then at the regimental and division staff level. He met Eisenhower on several occasions when the general came down to division level, and his acquaintance with Eisenhower was to have an influence on Craig's subsequent career. For his combat duty Craig was awarded the Bronze Star with Oak Leaf Cluster and the Croix de Guerre. He was discharged in 1946 with the rank of lieutenant colonel.

After the war, eager to resume the practice of law, Craig returned to Brazil with his wife and two children, Margery and John. Almost immediately he became actively involved with the American Legion. He was elected commander of the Clay County Post, vice commander of the state, a national committeeman, and in 1949, national commander of the American Legion, having been nominated by McNutt.

Although he later denied having political ambitions following his election as national commander, Craig was aware that activity in the Legion was synonymous with holding high political office in Indiana. McNutt, governor from 1933 to 1937, had been national commander, and Ralph Gates, governor from 1945 to 1949, was a former state commander. Other prominent state politicians active in the Legion included Frank McKinney, who served as chairman of the Democratic National Committee; Frank McHale, McNutt's political adviser; John A. Watkins, Craig's Democratic opponent for governor in 1952; and several of the state's congressmen.

As national commander, Craig traveled all over the country, maintained his relationship with Eisenhower, and met many national and international luminaries. The cold war was in full sway, and Communism had no more virulent opponent than the American Legion. As commander, Craig made hundreds of speeches, many of them filled with cold war rhetoric. He once said, "You can't go slightly communistic any more than you can become slightly leprous or slightly dead." After fourteen months as commander, Craig returned to the practice of law in Indianapolis, where he had moved in December 1950.

Although Craig professed his intention to make the practice of law his permanent career, at the urging of his friends, many of them Legion associates, Craig secretly decided to seek the nomination for governor in 1951. He knew that as an outsider who was starting at the top he would be opposed by the top command of the Republican Party, especially Jenner and Capehart, as well as the GOP state chairman Cale Holder and virtually every district chairman.

To overcome this opposition, Craig developed a stealth campaign for the nomination. He defied the conventional practice of waiting until after the May primary in which convention delegates were chosen to seek support for his nomination. Having determined that three-fourths of the delegates to the nominating convention were reelected every time, Craig solicited the support of delegates from the two previous conventions prior to the primary. After the primary, he sought the support of the newly elected delegates. His strategy worked, although it took three ballots before he defeated the other six candidates. He attributed his victory to his Legion publicity, the support of newspapers throughout the state, and his progressive program.

At this time, the state Republican Party was wracked by internal strife that mirrored divisions in the national party. The major fissure in the party was over the Communist threat to America and who was best qualified to fight Communism at home and abroad. In 1952 the intraparty battle flared over the party's nomination for president. The party's right wing supported Ohio senator Robert A. Taft, while the more moderate wing supported Eisenhower. Jenner was nationally known for his staunch anti-Communist stand and was a strong supporter of Senator Joseph A. McCarthy of Wisconsin. Craig identified with the Eisenhower camp.

Craig's victory over the pro-Taft forces at the state convention was not without a price. He had incurred the enmity of those in control of the party such as Jenner and Capehart. Furthermore, Harold W. Handley, a member of the opposing faction, was nominated for lieutenant governor. His feud with these fellow Republicans plagued Craig throughout his term as governor and prevented him from achieving some of his major policy initiatives. He also was in a constant battle with them over the control of the state party organization.

Craig's campaign platform and his subsequent reform agenda was reminiscent of McNutt's ambitious agenda in 1933. However, McNutt enjoyed one advantage that Craig did not: full support of his legislative party. Craig's campaign platform was to upgrade state government in several categories, including workers' compensation and unemployment benefits; school construction and teachers' salaries; penal institutions; public health, and particularly mental health; and traffic safety. Running with the tremendously popular Eisenhower on the ticket, Craig overwhelmed his opponent John Watkins, lieutenant governor in Henry F. Schricker's administration, by 233,701 votes.

Following his inauguration in 1953, Craig submitted to the legislature a list of twenty-six proposals, all of them requiring enactment of new laws, and many of them costing money. Among his proposals was a plan, reminiscent of McNutt's reorganization plan, to set up a "little cabinet" that would have consolidated 141 state agencies under eleven department heads and centralized much power in the hands of the governor. Most of Craig's legislative agenda failed, including the reorganization plan.

The Jenner forces were arrayed against Craig and his ambitious agenda. Craig's lieutenant governor, Handley, was a Jenner man, as was John Van Ness, president pro tem of the state senate, one of the candidates he had defeated for the nomination at the convention. Crawford F. Parker, secretary of state, and Edwin Steers, attorney general, were political enemies as well. Craig also bears blame for the failure of his reorganization plan as well as some of his other legislative initiatives. He was faulted by legislative leaders, among them his own supporters, for not working closely enough with the party leaders before submitting his reorganization plan to the Indiana General Assembly. One senator observed that there were three parties in the general assembly, "two Republican parties (one anti-Craig and one pro-Craig) and the Democrats."

Craig was successful in creating a Department of Correction, enacting a Uniform Traffic Code, and increasing the state police by fifty patrolmen, which took it from thirty-second in national rankings to first. He established the first narcotics squad and expanded the police academy at Indiana University to year-round and included the training of state excise, conservation, and local law enforcement officials at the academy.

He established a new Mental Health Division and reformed mental-health programs in the state. Years after he left office, Craig said that the Muscatatuck State Hospital was the number-one accomplishment of his administration. He is credited with improving and expanding the state highway system and improving highway safety in the state. He fought with the legislature over one of his pet road projects—toll roads. He succeeded in getting the Indiana Toll Road in northern Indiana built, but the legislature dug in its heels on creating more toll roads, mainly because they did not want to enhance the governor's control over patronage positions.

Craig failed almost across the board with respect to his construction initiatives—a state office building, a facility for teenage offenders, and a request for fourteen million dollars for highway construction and for building a veterinary school at Purdue University. He was the first of several governors to experience the rejection of a proposed Indiana Port off Lake Michigan. In his final address to the legislature on January 11, 1957, he urged that body to abolish the death penalty, but this one last effort at reform was ignored by the legislature.

Budget issues were always a bone of contention between Craig and the legislature. One issue that carried over into the next gubernatorial campaign was the disappearing surplus. At the beginning of the 1955 legislative session, the state had a $21 million surplus, but by the end of Craig's administration it had disappeared. Two factors were mainly responsible. The Korean War bonuses, which the legislature passed over Craig's strong objections, cost $7.6 million. The former Legion commander said, "you can't put a bonus on patriotism any more than you can on motherhood." The remainder of the surplus was used to fund the construction of new classrooms. One-room schools were being phased out and school consolidation was proceeding apace, requiring much needed classroom space.

Craig's record of reform in Indiana gained him national prominence. Featured in a cover story in *Time* magazine in 1955, he was described as a "swift-footed, swashbuckling, lawyer-politician" and an "administrator by instinct." *Time* noted that he had been "praised by Eisenhower as one of the younger Republican officeholders who should be pushed up upward and forward in the Eisenhower G.O.P." In 1955 Eisenhower offered Craig the position of secretary of the army, but he refused the offer, saying he wanted "to finish what I started in Indiana." In later years, Craig said another reason for his rejection of the offer was his disdain for Charles Wilson, secretary of defense, whom he criticized for allowing the missile gap between the United States and the Soviet Union.

Late in 1956, as Craig was leaving office, a scandal broke that, unfortunately, was to overshadow his other accomplishments. Three persons, Virgil "Red" Smith, head of Craig's highway department; William Sayer, Craig's administration assistant; and Elmer "Doc" Sherwood, his close aide and former Legion friend, were convicted and imprisoned for bribery involving highway contracts. Craig was never implicated in the scandal, but on June 16, 1957, after leaving office, he testified before an Indianapolis grand jury. Emerging from the grand jury room, he took one more shot at those he regarded his greatest political enemies, the Indianapolis newspapers and Jenner. He charged that the writers critical of his administration during the highway scandal had "turned what should be a legitimate dignified inquiry into public affairs into a political vendetta aimed at me personally. The fanatical devotion and affection of these writers for Senator Jenner and their long hostility toward me is well known to most observers of Indiana politics."

Years later Craig was more philosophical about the scandal. He said, "The highway scandal bothered me for a number of years. But I've finally overcome the feeling that I should feel personally responsible for what happened—it was such a situation as could happen to any administration. Nobody can guarantee the honesty of employees any more than a bank president can prevent the cashier from stealing money and betting it on the horses." Asked for the basis of the differences between himself and Jenner, he responded: "Actually and fundamentally, philosophically, I don't think there was any. It was a clash of personalities—Jenner and I never agreed upon anything except the weather and we might have trouble with that."

Several years after the scandal broke, one political observer suggested that historians would come to "recognize the Craig years as a harbinger of an era of progressive change rather than one that began with high hopes and ended in scandal." Indeed, time has been kind to Craig's legacy. A 1981 column in the *Indianapolis Star* named him one of the ten best governors in the state's history, crediting him for his reorganization of state government, creating the Department of Correction, establishing the "most effective traffic safety program of any state in the nation," and laying the groundwork for programs that were created in the following two decades. Another observer said Craig was "one of the most important Indiana governors of the 20th century . . . [who was] one of the most progressive Republican administrators in Indiana."

In August 1957 Craig moved with his family to Annandale, Virginia, where he practiced corporate and international law. In March 1960, he became president of Audio-Dynamics Corporation, a firm specializing in leasing equipment to business and industry. Tiring of the Washington, D.C., scene, Craig moved to Los Angeles in 1965, where he again practiced law. Finally, in 1967 he returned to his hometown of Brazil, where he was the elder statesman, often taking calls from politicians and officeholders from Washington and Indianapolis who sought his advice. He continued the practice of law and served on the State Board of Law Examiners from 1976 to 1986. He died on December 17, 1992.

Portrait by Frances Norris Streit (1954), Governors' Portraits Collection, Indiana Historical Bureau, State of Indiana.

FOR FURTHER READING

Hanfield, F. Gerald Jr. "An Oral History Approach to the Administration of Governor George N. Craig: 1953–1957." *Proceedings of the Indiana Academy of Social Sciences* 14 (1979): 101–7. (Hanfield's work is based on the Oral History Project of the Indiana State Library. He lists numerous interviews that relate to the Craig years.)
"Warfare on the Wabash." *Time*, March 7, 1955, 23–26.

Craig's gubernatorial papers are in the Indiana State Archives, Indianapolis.

Harold W. Handley

January 14, 1957–January 9, 1961

JOSEPH L. WERT

HAROLD HANDLEY WAS ELECTED GOVERNOR AT THE HEIGHT of the Dwight Eisenhower era. While Indiana has traditionally been a conservative state, the politics of the state were even more conservative in the 1950s. This was particularly true of the Indiana Republican Party that, according to Indiana historian James Madison, touted the likes of Hoosier Wendell Willkie, Nelson Rockefeller, and Eisenhower as "too liberal." Handley could easily be tagged with a conservative label for his staunch anti-Communism and his strong opposition to various federal programs. He once described the expansion of the federal government as "part of the master plan of the radicals to disrupt American constitutional government." Despite his conservatism, Handley did support some moderate policies, such as increasing the state income and gasoline taxes.

Born on November 27, 1909, in La Porte, Indiana, Handley was one of three boys born to Harold Lowell and Lottie Margaret Brackbill Handley. In 1932 he graduated from Indiana University with a bachelor's degree in economics. While at IU, he befriended William E. Jenner, a fraternity brother who would later become a U.S. Senator from Indiana and whose seat Handley would try to fill upon Jenner's retirement. After graduation, Handley joined his father's furniture company in sales. Although Handley was seemingly a competent salesman, the company was forced to close in the late 1930s, along with thousands of other companies during the Great Depression. Afterwards, Handley had a brief stint in sales for a furniture company based in

North Carolina. It was during this period when Handley's inter-est in politics grew, and he formed the Young Republicans in La Porte. In 1936 he made an unsuccessful run for the state senate. He was elected four years later when Republicans scored major victories at the state level, gaining control of both houses of the state legislature, capturing eight of the twelve seats in the U.S. House of Representa-tives, and unseating incumbent U.S. senator Sherman Minton.

Handley served in only one session of the state senate. He resigned his seat in late 1941 in order to join the U.S. Army after the United States's entry into World War II. Despite his pleas to be sent overseas, he spent the war stateside, training infantry replacements for the Eighty-eighth Infantry Division. He was honorably discharged as a lieutenant colonel in 1946. During his time in the army, Handley met Barbara Jean Win-terble, a psychiatric nurse for the Red Cross stationed near Handley in the Mojave Desert. They were married on February 17, 1944. After his discharge, Handley and his wife moved back to La Porte, where he again worked in furniture sales and also as a salesman for a motion picture company. The Handleys had two children, Kenneth and Martha Jean.

In 1948 Handley resumed his political career with his election to another seat in the state senate. In 1952 the Indiana Republican Party nominated him to run for lieutenant governor. At this time, candidates for governor and lieutenant governor were chosen separately by the state party conventions. They did not run as a ticket, and Handley was not the choice of the Republican nominee for governor, George N. Craig. Aided by the Eisenhower landslide in 1952, both Craig and Handley were elected. Handley defeated his Democratic opponent, E. Spencer Dalton, by 230,420 votes. Handley's job as lieutenant governor was to preside over the Indiana Senate and serve as commissioner of agriculture and commissioner of commerce and industry, positions that would help him garner the support of both farm and labor groups in his run for the governorship in 1956. He is credited with bringing a number of new industries to Indiana.

When Handley sought the gubernatorial nomination, Craig actively fought to keep him from gaining it. He said that Handley was the only one of five candidates that was "unacceptable" to him. Several factors contributed to the estrangement between Craig and Handley. The most important factor was that they belonged to rival factions of the Republican Party. Craig belonged to the moderate wing that had favored Eisenhower over Robert A. Taft for the party's nomination for president in 1952. Handley belonged to the conservative wing that supported the nomination of Taft. The leader of this wing was Handley's ally Jenner, one of the most outspoken anti-Communist politicians of the day.

Differences between Craig and Handley emerged early in Craig's administration when Handley refused to support the governor's plan for reorganizing the state executive branch. Further, as lieutenant governor, Handley had been an outspoken critic of Craig as a result of a scandal in the highway department. Although Craig was never directly implicated in the scandal, three of his appointees were ultimately convicted for bribery and embezzlement in connection with contracts for highway supplies and equipment and the sale of land earmarked for the Indiana Toll Road right-of-way.

The 1956 gubernatorial campaign was dominated by three main issues. One was the corruption during Craig's term, another was the fiscal insolvency of the state, and the third was reform of mental institutions. Handley defeated his opponent, Democrat Ralph Tucker, by 227,475 votes. No doubt Handley was helped to victory by the overwhelming support for Eisenhower, who won the state by 398,903 votes.

Handley's style as governor was a laid-back, nonconfrontational approach. It seemed to work, because Handley was able to gain approval for most of his agenda. It helped that he was philosophically compatible with the Republican majority in both houses of the state legislature for his first two years in office, but he maintained good relations with the legislature even after 1958, when the Democrats gained control of the state house of representatives while the Republicans retained control in the state senate. In his centennial history of the Indiana General Assembly, Justin Walsh argues that Handley "enjoyed the least acrimonious relationship with the legislature during the era."

In his first year as governor, Handley was able to push through the legislature a 50 percent increase in the state's gasoline and income taxes, which earned him the name "High Tax Harold" from his political opponents. It also angered some of his conservative supporters in his own party, which was partly responsible for his defeat for the U.S. Senate seat in 1958. The tax increases, however, were deemed necessary because there was a burgeoning fiscal crisis in the state, as huge budget surpluses turned into record deficits during the Craig administration. Two things made these tax increases more palatable to conservatives and others. First, Handley was also able to push through legislation that made the automatic withholding of state income tax possible for the first time. This led to the discovery of thousands of tax cheats. Secondly, he was able to get most of the state property tax repealed.

There were other accomplishments in his administration. Early on there was the passage of the first right-to-work law for an industrial state. Handley was a supporter, but was not vocal about it, letting the bill become law without his signature so as not to anger his labor supporters, but that was not likely. Indiana was the first major industrial state to outlaw union shops. Handley's administration also began the construction of the interstate highway system in the state. He was able to get $1 billion in grants from the federal government, and by the end of his term more than one hundred miles of interstate highways were built throughout the state. Except for highway funds, Handley was a staunch opponent of federal aid for almost everything else, declaring that

"Hoosiers refuse to stand in line in front of the treasury in Washington with tin cups in their hands."

Handley oversaw the construction of the State Office Building in Indianapolis and the School of Veterinary Medicine at Purdue University. He also supported programs for the mentally disabled, building on the legacy left by Craig. In his first year in office Handley established a Retardation Study Committee, and in 1958 he funded a pilot program to train patients at Muscatatuck State Hospital for employment outside the institution. He continued his work on behalf of the mentally disabled after leaving office and in 1970 received the Drummer Boy Award of the Marion County Association for Retarded Children for his decade of service in advancing the care of the mentally disabled.

The most controversial aspect of Handley's term as governor was his run for the U.S. Senate seat being vacated by his longtime friend and mentor Jenner. By 1957 Jenner had decided he would not seek a third term in 1958 and apparently gave consideration to resigning early. The plan was for Handley to resign following Jenner's resignation so that Lieutenant Governor Crawford F. Parker could succeed him as governor. Then Parker would appoint Handley to the vacated Senate seat. The plan, which Handley's foe Craig said was a "shenanigan" that "would set the Republican Party back an entire generation," was never implemented.

With Jenner's help, Handley won the party nomination despite the lack of support from other top leaders of the party, including U.S. senator Homer E. Capehart and U.S. representative Charles A. Halleck, House majority leader. Handley's opponent for the seat was the Democratic mayor of Evansville, Vance Hartke, a rising star in the Democratic Party. He defeated Handley by a margin of more than 247,000 votes.

While Hartke's well-run campaign contributed to Handley's defeat, another major factor was obviously the large tax increases Handley had pushed through the legislature. Further, there was a downturn in the economy, both state and nationwide. In April 1958 the unemployment rate in Indiana was 10 percent, and although it had declined to 6.9 percent by mid-September this was still unacceptably high. Then there was also the highway scandal in the Craig administration, with which Handley was still unjustly associated. His tacit support of the right-to-work law hurt him among the state's union members. There was also the feeling of many, including those in his own party, that he should not have been running for another office so soon after taking the governor's office, especially when he had pledged to serve his full term. In fact, his candidacy brought about a court challenge concerning the legitimacy of his campaign. The case, which was argued before the Indiana Supreme Court, involved a provision of the Indiana Constitution that would have prohibited the governor from seeking another office while he was still in office. The court ultimately found that Handley was eligible to run, since the Senate seat is a federal office, and the Indiana Constitution could not prescribe qualifications for running for a federal office.

The day after losing the Senate race, Handley returned to the statehouse ready to continue his job as governor. He said, "We've got two more years of my administration." Banned by the constitution from serving consecutive terms, he left office in January 1961, retiring from politics. He lived in Indianapolis with his wife and operated a successful advertising and public relations firm. During this time he also served as cochair of the state Constitutional Revision Commission with former governor Matthew E. Welsh. The commission drafted several constitutional amendments.

Handley died of a heart attack at age sixty-two on August 30, 1972, while on a vacation trip to Rawlins, Wyoming.

Portrait by Donald Mattison (1959), Governors' Portraits Collection, Indiana Historical Bureau, State of Indiana.

FOR FURTHER READING

Madison, James H. *The Indiana Way: A State History.* Bloomington: Indiana University Press; Indianapolis: Indiana Historical Society, 1986.

Walsh, Justin. *The Centennial History of the Indiana General Assembly, 1816–1978.* Indianapolis: The Select Committee on the Centennial History of the Indiana General Assembly, 1987.

Handley's gubernatorial papers are in the Indiana State Archives, Indianapolis.

Matthew E. Welsh

January 9, 1961–January 11, 1965

JAMES PHILIP FADELY

THE ADMINISTRATION OF MATTHEW E. WELSH WAS SIGNIFI-
cant for the changes it brought in fiscal responsibility, governmental
efficiency, and social reform. Elected in 1960 at the beginning of a
decade of remarkable change in Indiana and the United States, Welsh
was arguably the most progressive governor since Paul V. McNutt.
Welsh's tenure in the statehouse was marked by a state budgetary crisis that required new sources of revenue, the streamlining of state
government, a reorganization of the state's educational system from
primary school through college, and responses to the fast-develop-
ing civil rights movement. At the center of these accelerating forces
of change in Indiana was the scholarly, dignified attorney from
Vincennes.

Matthew Empson Welsh was born on September 15, 1912, in Detroit,
Michigan. His parents, Matthew William and Inez Empson Welsh, both
natives of Jackson County, Indiana, had moved to Detroit, where his
father was secretary and legal counsel for an insurance company. His
father served as an industrial expediter for the federal government during World War I, and he sent the family back to Brownstown, Indiana,
where he became head of a small bank after the war. Later, a friend and
fellow banker offered him the position of head of an investment firm
in Vincennes, which led the family to Knox County in 1926. The senior
Welsh was active in Democratic politics, an interest he passed down to
his son. Welsh graduated from Lincoln High School in Vincennes in
1930 and went to the Wharton School at the University of Pennsylva-

nia, graduating in 1934. He then enrolled at the Indiana University School of Law in Bloomington, but after two years transferred to the University of Chicago Law School, where he completed his degree. Importantly, while in Bloomington, Welsh met Mary Virginia Homann of Washington, Indiana, whom he married in 1937, the year he received his law degree and passed the bar exam. The newlyweds settled into married life in Vincennes, where Welsh decided to practice law, and became parents of twins, Kathryn and Janet, in 1942.

In 1940 Welsh won a seat in the Indiana House of Representatives. Reelected in 1942, he resigned the following year to serve as an officer in the U.S. Navy during World War II. Like thousands of other servicemen, Welsh returned to civilian life in 1946. In 1950 President Harry Truman appointed him U.S. Attorney for the Southern District of Indiana, a post he held until resigning in 1952.

Welsh went back to his private law practice in Vincennes, but politics, clearly, was in his blood. In 1954, he ran successfully for the Indiana Senate. Only two years later, in 1956, Welsh narrowly lost the Democratic nomination for governor to Mayor Ralph Tucker of Terre Haute. The following year, and again in 1959, he was chosen as the Democratic floor leader in the state senate. Welsh's political star was rising and culminated in his election as governor in 1960 over Republican Crawford F. Parker. The gubernatorial election was very close, with Welsh defeating Parker narrowly by 1,072,717 to 1,049,540. While Welsh, the Democrat, was winning the Hoosier gubernatorial race, Democratic presidential nominee John F. Kennedy was losing Indiana to Richard M. Nixon by 222,762 votes. However, Kennedy eked out a victory nationwide in one of the closest presidential races in American history.

Welsh faced a daunting budget crisis upon taking the reins of power in January 1961. The state was in desperate financial shape. His predecessor, Governor Harold W. Handley, had proposed a budget for the 1961–63 biennium that was $18.2 million in excess of anticipated revenues. To his credit, Handley had attempted to deal with the budget situation in 1957 by winning a modest increase in the gross income tax in 1957. He paid the political price the following year when he lost his U.S. Senate bid after being branded "High Tax Harold." Both the property tax, the mainstay of local government, and the gross income tax were not effectively administered and could not produce sufficient revenue for the citizens' demand for public services.

To make matters more difficult, the 1960 election had given Welsh a Republican-controlled lower house and only a two-vote Democratic margin in the state senate. Despite the partisan challenges of this split, the 1961 legislature passed three Welsh initiatives designed to improve the efficiency of the tax structure. The first of these was the Property Assessment Act of 1961, which was the first recodification of the state's property tax law since 1919. The other two measures were designed to improve the administration of the state's revenue system. One created the Division of Tax Review in the State Board of Tax Commissioners, which supervised the administration of the property tax system, and the other established the Division of Audit in the Department of Revenue. These last two reforms were the first steps taken to create career staffs in areas of state government related to revenue. Employees in these areas now had to pass examinations for positions, and there was equal representation from each political party. To increase the productivity of the gross income tax, the state hired warrant investigators to help sheriffs in collecting unpaid taxes. Also, Indiana became the eleventh state to cross-check state and federal income tax returns.

However, revenue still fell short of expectations and even larger deficits loomed in the future.

The 1962 election produced a state legislature with both houses controlled by the Republicans. Welsh submitted a "balanced budget" that showed its destructive effect on education and also a "budget of needs" that detailed the need for additional funds. The difference between the two budgets was $447 million for the biennium. The legislature then mandated in December 1962 that the Commission on State Tax and Financing Policy study the state's fiscal situation. This commission recommended that the state adopt a 2 percent sales tax and increase the gross income tax by one-third. Despite this recommendation, the Indiana General Assembly was unable to pass a tax program or budget by the end of its session. Thus, Welsh called the legislature into special session on March 12, 1963, to resolve the issue. By the time the session ended on April 20, the legislature had passed the compromise "2-2-2 Plan." The tax plan called for a 2 percent retail sales tax with a $6 per capita credit against the state income tax; a 2 percent net income tax on individuals to replace the old gross income tax; and a 2 percent net corporate income tax as a minimum alternative to the gross income tax on corporations, at the rate of 2 percent or .5 percent depending on the source of income, the company to pay the greater of the two.

The legislature also passed Welsh's increase in the cigarette tax, which made possible the construction of two toll bridges across the Ohio River. These bridges, at Mauckport and Cannelton, spurred economic development in southern Indiana. Another major economic development achievement was Welsh's successful fight against powerful political interests in Illinois to secure a deepwater port on Lake Michigan in Indiana.

The effort to revamp the state's tax structure was the best example of Welsh's considerable political skill, combining leadership and compromise. He was joined in this effort by his Republican lieutenant governor, Richard O. Ristine, who cast the tie-breaking vote in the state senate to pass the sales tax. Welsh, as well as Ristine, paid a heavy political price for the new tax plan. His opponents now branded him

"Sales Tax Matt," and car plates appeared across the state proclaiming "Indiana—Land of Taxes."

Another key feature of the Welsh administration was the effort to streamline state government and to make it more effective and efficient. In addition to the previously mentioned professionalization of the State Board of Tax Commissioners and the creation of the Division of Tax Review and the Division of Audit in the Department of Revenue, Welsh succeeded in getting other reorganization measures adopted. In 1961 the general assembly passed his proposal to create a Department of Administration to achieve more efficiency and effectiveness in state government operations through reorganized purchasing, personnel, and administrative procedures.

The state highway department was also thoroughly reorganized during Welsh's tenure. The department had been run by a three-person, full-time commission appointed by the governor. This commission included two members of the governor's political party and one from the opposition. The patronage-driven commission had no clearly articulated division of responsibility among its members, resulting in considerable confusion, with members sometimes overruling one another. Welsh established the position of executive director, who had to be a civil engineer, and a four-person, bipartisan, part-time commission to set policy for the department. In a politically skillful gesture, Welsh retained Republican George Foster, an engineer who Handley had brought in earlier to study the problems in the department, as the first executive director.

The Department of Mental Health was created as well, consolidating the administrative responsibility for all eight state mental hospitals under the department instead of separate boards of trustees. The new department also had oversight for a range of other services, including two schools for the mentally retarded and a center for the treatment of alcoholics.

The Department of Correction underwent considerable change, with an emphasis on the rehabilitation of offenders. The state built a new reception and diagnostic center to screen all new inmates coming into the system. The Indiana Youth Center, a medium-security facility for young first-time offenders, was built and focused on rehabilitating its young inhabitants. Youth rehabilitation facilities were also established on state properties around the state. Reflecting his interest in cultural affairs as well as the impact of the Kennedy administration, Welsh issued an executive order in January 1964 creating Indiana's first arts commission, the Governor's Commission on the Arts. The spirit of change, focused on effectiveness and efficiency, permeated the administration of state government under Welsh.

Change was also the watchword of the state's educational system during Welsh's term as governor. He aggressively pursued the implementation of the 1959 School Corporation Reorganization Act, which eliminated ineffective and uneconomic primary and secondary school units. Under the act reorganization plans were to be developed locally by County School Reorganization Committees, then approved by the state commission, and finally, voted upon in a special referendum at the next primary or general election. Although this process was well under way when Welsh assumed office in January 1961, much of the implementation of the act took place during his tenure. The legislature passed amendments to the act in 1961, 1963, and 1965 to simplify, clarify, and make it more workable. By the time Welsh left office, the number of school units in the state had been reduced from 966 to 466.

Concerned about the relative lack of access to post-secondary education in Indiana, Welsh encouraged the general assembly to create the Post-High School Education Study Commission in 1961, chaired by Doctor John W. Hicks of Purdue University. The commission submitted its report to the legislature in 1963 with recommendations that the state accelerate secondary school consolidation; expand and fund regional campuses of Indiana and Purdue universities; establish a state-funded scholarship program for all Indiana colleges; and establish a new state school for vocational education. At the time nearly 30 percent of Hoosier high school students dropped out before graduation, and, of the remaining students, only 50 percent went on to a traditional college. In response to this report, the general assembly created the Indiana Vocational Technical College in 1963.

Welsh was an outspoken advocate for civil rights for African Americans. His leadership made Indiana one of the most progressive midwestern states with regard to civil rights in the early 1960s. Welsh provided leadership on this issue from the beginning of his term. In 1961 he persuaded the legislature to pass a civil rights law that made the Fair Employment Practices Commission, with five commissioners, an independent agency under the merit system. It doubled the commission's budget, broadened the coverage of the public accommodations law, and increased penalties for violators. Early that year, Welsh directed all agency heads throughout state government to end discrimination and to actively hire blacks at upper management levels. He issued an executive order on December 12, 1961, that required a nondiscrimination clause in all state contracts.

In 1963, the general assembly passed another law that gave the newly created Indiana Civil Rights Commission power to issue enforceable cease and desist orders when it discovered discrimination. Another Welsh executive order, on June 10, 1963, directed all departments of state government to prevent discrimination in places of public accommodation through their various licensing powers. Later that year, in August, he asked all state departments to appoint an equal opportunities officer to work with the civil rights commission to end discrimination in state government and throughout Indiana. Significantly, these initiatives in civil rights and equal opportunity for African Americans in Indiana preceded the federal Civil Rights Act of 1964. Of his accomplishments as governor, Welsh was most proud of the progress made in civil rights.

Welsh sealed his reputation as an advocate for civil rights when he stood in for President Lyndon B. Johnson against Alabama governor George C. Wallace in Indiana's Democratic presidential preference primary in 1964. Since Johnson chose not to enter any primaries, and neither Senator Birch Bayh nor Senator Vance Hartke would stand in for the president, Welsh decided to make the race. Johnson did not ask him to do so, but Welsh felt this was Indiana's problem. He feared that a Wallace victory in Indiana might have a negative impact on the state's political culture for a generation or longer. Welsh conducted a vigorous campaign across the Hoosier state in support of the president and his policies. He scored a resounding victory over Wallace, defeating him by a vote of 376,023 to 172,646. Wallace fared worse in the Indiana primary than he had a few weeks earlier in traditionally progressive Wisconsin.

A final highlight of the Welsh administration was a major change in the relationship between the state and the federal government. Ever since Franklin D. Roosevelt's New Deal increased the role of the federal government in national life, Indiana had exhibited an overt hostility toward Washington. The Hoosier position was embodied in House Concurrent Resolution Number 2, a symbolic but nonbinding resolution passed by the general assembly in 1947, which expressed Indiana's opposition to federal power as well as federal aid. This uncompromising attitude toward the federal government was overturned, quietly but surely, by Welsh. Now, with a new approach, Indiana no longer railed against federal aid but actively sought it.

Constitutionally prohibited from seeking a second term, Welsh returned to the practice of law in Indianapolis, which he continued until his death. He served as Democratic national committeeman from Indiana from 1964 to 1968. In 1965 President Johnson appointed him as the part-time chairman of the U.S. Section of the International Joint Commission for the United States and Canada, which protected water levels along the U.S.-Canadian border. He served in this role from 1966 to 1970. Welsh won the Democratic nomination for governor in 1972, but lost to Doctor Otis R. Bowen by a vote of 1,203,903 to 900,489 in the Nixon landslide over Senator George S. McGovern. The tax program passed nine years earlier in 1963 dogged him throughout this campaign, as Bowen charged that it had been a failure.

Welsh died in Indianapolis on May 28, 1995, at age eighty-two. His favorite saying, "It doesn't cost you anything to be a gentleman," summed up his life and career. He is buried at Memorial Park Cemetery in Vincennes.

Portrait by Edmund Brucker (1964), Governors' Portraits Collection, Indiana Historical Bureau, State of Indiana.

FOR FURTHER READING

Madison, James H. *The Indiana Way: A State History.* Bloomington: Indiana University Press; Indianapolis: Indiana Historical Society, 1986.

New, Jack. Interview with the author. February 28, 2004.

Walsh, Justin. *The Centennial History of the Indiana General Assembly, 1816–1978.* Indianapolis: Indiana Select Committee on the Centennial History of the Indiana General Assembly, 1987.

Welsh, Matthew E. *View from the State House: Recollections and Reflections, 1961–1965.* Indianapolis: Indiana Historical Bureau, 1981.

Welsh's papers are in the Indiana State Archives, Indianapolis and the Indiana State Library, Indianapolis.

Roger D. Branigin

January 11, 1965–January 13, 1969

RAY E. BOOMHOWER

KNOWN FOR HIS READY WIT AND LAUDED AS ONE OF THE
state's premier public speakers at events ranging from political conventions to 4-H club meetings, Roger Branigin, a Harvard-educated
attorney and Indiana's forty-second governor, received national attention in 1968 when he initially ran for the Democratic nomination for
president in the state's primary as a stand-in for incumbent Lyndon B.
Johnson. Upon Johnson's withdrawal from the race, Branigin continued as a favorite-son candidate against challengers Robert F. Kennedy
and Eugene McCarthy, both U.S. senators.

Branigin, whose administration presided over the state's sesquicentennial in 1966, shunned the usual trappings of the office, turning
down complimentary tickets to athletic events and the free use of corporate aircraft, and also kept a sharp eye on such state expenditures
as out-of-state travel by those in his administration. At his inauguration as governor, he noted: "It should never be necessary for anyone
to make gifts in order to do business with the state of Indiana. Conflict
of interest should be forbidden and absolute civic morality must be
the order of the day." Responding to criticism that he spent too much
time on such trivial matters, Branigin responded: "Perhaps we are saving peanuts, but we may save enough to open a peanut-vending business." The World War II veteran's common touch extended to often
handwriting, addressing, and posting his correspondence, dialing his
own telephone calls, and preferring train travel over flying. When one
day the heating system failed in his office, he remained as repairs were

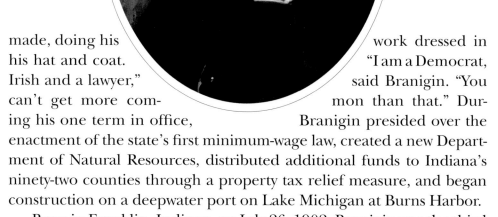

made, doing his work dressed in his hat and coat. "I am a Democrat, Irish and a lawyer," said Branigin. "You can't get more com- mon than that." Dur- ing his one term in office, Branigin presided over the enactment of the state's first minimum-wage law, created a new Depart- ment of Natural Resources, distributed additional funds to Indiana's ninety-two counties through a property tax relief measure, and began construction on a deepwater port on Lake Michigan at Burns Harbor.

Born in Franklin, Indiana, on July 26, 1902, Branigin was the third of four sons raised by Elba and Zula Branigin. All four sons followed in their father's footsteps by becoming lawyers, earning the elder Bra- nigin the moniker "Barrister of Branigins." A former schoolteacher, Franklin College graduate, and amateur historian, Elba Branigin maintained an extensive library that all of his sons used. Later in life Roger also amassed an impressive book collection, including many volumes on Indiana history that he later gave to the Franklin Col- lege library. Braingin received his education in the Franklin public schools and during his senior year in high school served as a cheer- leader when the school's basketball team, the "Wonder Five," won the first of its three straight state championships. After graduating from high school in 1919, Branigin attended Franklin College, where he majored in French, Spanish, and history and also pursued an interest in dramatics. Although an excellent student, Branigin did sometimes clash with school authorities, refusing to attend the school's compulsory chapel and being placed on probation after being caught smoking.

Upon his graduation from Franklin, Branigin attended Harvard Law School, receiving his law degree in 1926. For the next three years he worked in the prosecutor's office in Franklin. On November 2, 1929, Branigin married Josephine Mardis of Shelbyville; the couple had two sons, Roger Jr. and Robert. The next year Branigin began work as an attorney with the Federal Land Bank and Farm Credit Administration's Louisville office, which served a five-state area. Branigin, who became general counsel for the land bank, traveled extensively in his work giving speeches throughout Indiana and other states. "By the time I was 36," he later said, "I knew everybody in Indiana." In 1938 he left the land bank and joined a law firm in Lafayette. Later, he became a partner in the firm Stuart, Branigin, Ricks, and Shilling. Volunteering for service in World War II, Branigin worked in the contracts division of the Judge Advocate General's Office in Washington, D.C., later becoming chief of the legal division for the army's transportation corps.

A longtime Democrat and an admirer of former governor Paul V. McNutt, Branigin honed his political skills in a variety of nonelective positions, including serving as permanent chairman of the Democratic state convention in 1948, receiving an appointment by Indiana governor Henry F. Schricker as chairman of the state conservation commission, and serving as president of the Indiana Bar Association. In 1956 Branigin attempted to win the Democratic nomination for governor, but was defeated in his bid by eventual nominee Ralph Tucker.

Branigin had better luck in June 1964 when he captured the nomination on the first ballot at the Democratic convention held at the Indiana State Fairgrounds Coliseum. The 1964 gubernatorial campaign pitted Branigin against another Hoosier political veteran, Republican Richard O. Ristine. During his term as lieutenant governor under the administration of Democratic governor Matthew E. Welsh, Ristine had cast the tie-breaking vote in favor of the establishment of a sales tax in Indiana. This unpopular decision, coupled with the strong showing of incumbent president Johnson over GOP opponent Barry Goldwater, helped Branigin defeat Ristine by more than 260,000 votes—at that time the largest plurality in the state's history. Branigin had also received a front-page endorsement from the normally Republican *Indianapolis Star*, whose publisher, Eugene C. Pulliam, had been a friend of the Democratic candidate since his days as editor and publisher of the *Franklin Evening Star*. Democrats also captured both houses of the Indiana General Assembly for the first time since 1937.

Although he compared himself politically to Johnson as a "middle-of-the-roader with liberal leanings," Branigin had a conservative reputation among some Democrats, with one legislator calling him "the best Republican governor the Democrats ever had." As governor, Branigin wielded his veto power on such measures as legalizing abortion, outlawing the death penalty, and prohibiting the hiring of strikebreakers in labor disputes. A strong believer in the separation of powers between the administrative and legislative branches of government, Branigin nevertheless achieved significant success during his administration. Among the measures he championed were an increase in scholarships to students attending Hoosier institutions of higher learning, the passage of a mandatory vehicle inspection law, the repeal of the personal property tax on household goods, the expansion of the authority of the state's civil rights commission, and improvements to state correctional facilities, highways, parks, forests, and nature preserves. The governor failed, however, in an attempt to locate a federal atomic research center in Indiana.

Branigin received national attention in March 1968 when he agreed to run as a stand-in for Johnson in the Indiana Democratic presidential primary after the president had agreed to a number of proposals to aid the state, including funding for highways, reimbursement for funds spent on the Burns Harbor port, and aid on the establishment of a new park along the Ohio River. Just weeks after he had agreed to run in the primary on Johnson's behalf, the president, in a March 31 televised speech, shocked the nation by declaring he would not be a candidate for another term in office. "He left candidates shadow-boxing in the ring, hunting for an issue," Branigin said of Johnson's departure from the race. "He left pundits speechless. And he left me a favorite son."

Hoping to garner a stronger position for the state at the upcoming Democratic National Convention in Chicago, Branigin decided to remain in the race as a favorite-son candidate against McCarthy, who had run strongly against Johnson in the New Hampshire primary, and Kennedy, who had recently announced his candidacy. Although the national candidates received the bulk of the attention, Branigin, thanks to his popularity with Hoosier voters, appeared to have a chance at pulling off an upset. John Bartlow Martin, a Hoosier who served as a key Kennedy aide during the primary, initially believed that Kennedy's best chance would be to come in second in the race to Branigin.

Branigin embarked on a vigorous campaign throughout the state. A supporter of Johnson's policies in Vietnam, the governor focused mainly on securing a role for Indiana at the Democratic convention. He told a crowd in Franklin that "national issues are not at stake here. What is at stake here is who is going to represent the state of Indiana in Chicago." During the campaign, the Democratic governor received the wholehearted support of Pulliam's *Indianapolis Star*, which often attacked Kennedy. Referring to his time delivering copies of the *Star* as a young man, Branigin joked: "I used to carry Pulliam, and he has been carrying me ever since." Later in the race, the governor hinted to voters that if he won his home primary he might receive consideration as a vice presidential candidate with another Democrat, Vice President Hubert H. Humphrey. Branigin, however, lost the primary election to Kennedy (328,118 votes for Kennedy to Branigin's 238,700), but he did run ahead of McCarthy, who finished third.

After leaving the governor's office, Branigin returned to Lafayette and resumed his law practice. In addition to his term as governor, Branigin served as president of the Greater Lafayette Chamber of Commerce and the Harrison Trails Council of the Boys Scouts of America. He also served as a trustee of Franklin College, Purdue University, and the Indiana Historical Society. Talking to a reporter about his life, Branigin observed: "If I have one weakness, it's being myself. I never changed a damn bit, whether I was in the governor's office or not." He died in Lafayette on November 19, 1975, and was buried in Greenlawn Cemetery in Franklin.

Portrait by Helen Briggs Duckwall (1967), Governors' Portraits Collection, Indiana Historical Bureau, State of Indiana.

FOR FURTHER READING

Beasley, John. "Roger Branigin, Governor of Indiana: The View from Within." PhD diss., Ball State University, 1973.

Boomhower, Ray E. "A Voice for Those from Below: John Bartlow Martin, Reporter." *Traces of Indiana and Midwestern History* 9, no. 2 (Spring 1997): 4–13.

Farmer, James E. "The Individual Roger: Governor Branigin and the News Media." *Traces of Indiana and Midwestern History* 4, no. 2 (Spring 1992): 24–33.

Martin, John Bartlow. *It Seems Like Only Yesterday: Memoirs of Writing, Presidential Politics, and the Diplomatic Life.* New York: William Morrow, 1986.

Pulliam, Russell. *Publisher: Gene Pulliam, Last of the Newspaper Titans.* Ottawa, IL: Jameson Books, 1984.

Walsh, Justin E. *The Centennial History of the Indiana General Assembly, 1816–1978.* Indianapolis: The Select Committee on the Centennial History of the Indiana General Assembly, 1987.

Branigin's personal papers are located at Franklin College, Franklin, Indiana. His gubernatorial papers are in the Indiana State Archives, Indianapolis.

Edgar D. Whitcomb

January 13, 1969–January 9, 1973

RONALD J. ALLMAN II

THE TERM OF EDGAR D. WHITCOMB AS GOVERNOR REPRE-
sented a watershed in Indiana state politics. He was the last governor limited by law to a single term in eight years, making him a lame
duck as soon as he was elected. All governors who succeeded him had
the opportunity to serve two consecutive terms. Had this advantage
been available to Whitcomb he might have had a more distinguished
record as governor. However, he suffered other disadvantages. His
own Republican Party, which controlled both houses of the state legislature by substantial margins, was engaged in a "civil war," and Whitcomb ended up on the losing side. He was the leader of the old guard
of the party, the conservative wing based in rural areas of the state.
Pitted against him were the more moderate, urban-based party leaders, including Otis R. Bowen, Speaker of the Indiana House of Representatives and future governor. Further, Whitcomb never enjoyed
the full support of party members in either house of the legislature,
which prevented him from achieving some of his major legislative
objectives.

Although he is not considered one of Indiana's most effective governors, nonetheless Whitcomb left his mark on Indiana politics. His
more notable achievements include keeping the state solvent for four
consecutive years without a tax increase; a significant expansion of the
state's highway system, including 221 new miles of interstate highways;
improvement in highway safety through better construction of roads and
bridges; modernization of the state's system for enforcement and col-

lection of taxes; improvement of the state's mental health programs through the establishment of comprehensive community mental health centers; and the creation of the Higher Education Commission, which has governing authority over the system of state-supported colleges and universities.

Born November 6, 1917, in the small town of Hayden, in southeast Indiana, Whitcomb was one the four children of John and Louise Doud Whitcomb. He attended Indiana University in 1936 but dropped out due to financial concerns and later joined the army. As an aerial navigator of a B-17 bomber, Second Lieutenant Whitcomb was captured on May 7, 1942, the day after the fall of Corregidor, which left the Philippines in Japanese hands. Whitcomb escaped from a Japanese prison on May 22, 1942, by swimming eight miles in the shark-infested waters between Corregidor and the mainland of the Philippines. He was recaptured but escaped again, then served in the jungles with the Filipino underground. He was repatriated from China as a civilian under an assumed name in December 1943. His war experiences left him blind in his left eye, with a partial hearing loss and a bad back. Whitcomb later wrote a book, *Escape from Corregidor*, chronicling his war experiences.

After the war, Whitcomb returned to Indiana University to study law, received his bachelor of laws degree in 1950, and was admitted to the Indiana Bar in 1952. He became an attorney in Seymour and later practiced law in North Vernon and Indianapolis.

On May 20, 1951, Whitcomb married Patricia Dolfuss, a former model. The couple had five children: Tricia, Ann, Shelley, Alice, and John. They divorced in 1987 after thirty-six years of marriage.

Whitcomb was elected to the Indiana State Senate in 1951 and served until 1954. In 1954 Whitcomb unsuccessfully sought the Republican nomination for Congress, and ten years later lost a bid for the party nomination for U.S. Senate. In the mid-1950s Whitcomb served as assistant U.S. attorney for the Southern District of Indiana.

In 1966 Whitcomb was elected secretary of state, a position that was only a two-year term at that time. Although it was not an office with significant power, he used it to launch his bid for governor two years later. His chief opponent in that contest was the house Speaker, Bowen. Whitcomb's success in defeating Bowen was due largely to Marion County political boss L. Keith Bulen, an astute political strategist who was responsible for returning the Republican Party to dominance in state politics after a decade of Democratic control. At the state party convention, Bulen, leading a large contingent of Marion County delegates, joined forces with party leaders from other large counties to deliver the nomination for Whitcomb. Bulen's tactics created bitterness within the party and have been attributed with ending the practice of choosing gubernatorial candidates at state party conventions. In 1976 the state instituted the direct primary for selecting party nominees.

A staunch conservative, Whitcomb campaigned on principles of fiscal conservatism. He promised not to raise taxes and to make government more efficient. He defeated Democrat Robert Rock by 114,455 votes. His election was helped by the popularity of the Republican nominee for president, Richard M. Nixon, who outpolled the Democratic nominee Hubert H. Humphrey by 12 percent in Indiana. It was a banner year for Republicans. They gained substantial majorities in both houses of the state legislature and they won all major elections except the one for U.S. Senator, which was captured by incumbent Birch Bayh.

Although Whitcomb won the battle for the governor's office, he ultimately lost the war to control his party organization and the state legislature. Republicans controlled each of the two houses by more than a two-thirds majority, but "partly for ideological reasons and partly for his administrative style . . . Whitcomb found himself at odds with a majority of his own party in both Houses." Whitcomb represented the old guard within the party, whose base was in the more conservative rural areas of the state. Most of the members of the legislature had been elected after legislative reapportionment in 1965, which enhanced the representation of urban areas, bringing more moderate, urban-oriented legislators to power.

The two forces clashed over many issues, and the political editor of the *Indianapolis News*, Edward Ziegner, prophetically predicted that the 1969 session, the last biennial legislative session in the state's history, would see the "highest mortality rate in history" for legislative bills. Indeed the session proved to be "one of the least productive" in terms of proposed bills and resolutions passed.

One of the chief sources of disagreements was over taxes and state spending. In his state-of-the-state address, Whitcomb laid the blame for the state's fiscal plight on the "excessive spending and laxity in management" of the previous administration, and he promised to introduce greater efficiency in the operations of state government. To that end he created the Governor's Economy Program (GEP), comprised of sixty private-industry experts, to study state agencies and recommend strategies for making government operations more efficient and economical. Whitcomb credited the GEP with saving the state nearly $50 million over his four-year term of office.

Whitcomb ordered a 10 percent cut in the number of employees on the state payroll and revoked salary increases for some public officials. By closing tax loopholes and redesigning the revenue processing system, he increased revenues, collecting more in unpaid taxes than several of the previous administrations. Although the population of the state increased by only 1 percent during his administration, tax revenues increased by more than 8 percent without any new tax increases.

Despite allocating more money to most areas of the state budget compared with previous expenditures, the Whitcomb administration was the target of many protesters in his first term. The more vocal included schoolteachers, poverty protesters, black activists, and students at state universities protesting proposed fee increases.

Throughout Whitcomb's term, tax issues were the greatest source of conflict between the governor and Republican majorities in both houses. His chief protagonist on taxes was Bowen. They had significant differences over how to deal with the problem of property taxes levied by local governments, which was a great source of public discontent. Bowen promoted a plan to reduce reliance on property taxes by limiting their growth at the local level and replacing the lost revenues with an increase in the sales tax. Whitcomb opposed this plan because of his pledge not to raise taxes, by which he meant no increases in sales taxes or personal income taxes. Instead, he advocated local option taxes whereby local governments would have the option to levy sales taxes or individual income taxes on top of state levied taxes. Bowen's property tax plan was approved by the general assembly but vetoed by Whitcomb in 1971. However, when Bowen became governor in 1973, his property tax relief program was adopted and put into effect.

While Whitcomb was opposed to increasing sales or income taxes, he did ask the legislature to increase taxes on alcohol and cigarettes, extend the sales tax to services, and double the corporate income tax. None of his tax proposals passed.

Another hot-button issue that divided Whitcomb and the legislature was daylight saving time. This issue had simmered in the legislative process for several decades and divided along rural and urban lines, with the rural areas strongly opposed to daylight savings time. During Whitcomb's first year in office the general assembly passed a law that placed eighty counties on Eastern Standard Time year-round, meaning they could not observe daylight savings time. The remaining twelve counties in the central time zone were permitted to go on daylight saving time in the summer months. Whitcomb vetoed the legislation, drawing criticism that he had sold out to the television lobby, which preferred daylight saving time because it meshed better with the program schedules of the major networks and affected revenue generated by advertising. The legislature passed the bill again over Whitcomb's veto in 1971, and there the policy remained until the state adopted daylight saving time in 2005.

One of Whitcomb's major failures was his inability to assert control over the state party organization. The most visible evidence of this was his split with Bulen, who had become the kingmaker of the state Republican Party. Two short years after Bulen helped him achieve the governorship the two were engaged in a battle over control of party nominations. At the 1970 convention they disagreed on virtually all candidates for party nominations, and in almost every case the candidates backed by Bulen won. Whitcomb also lost the support of John Snyder, a onetime ally whom he had chosen as state party chair.

The split with Snyder precipitated Whitcomb's decision to end the state's Two Percent Club. Under this practice, established by Governor Paul V. McNutt in 1933, state employees were expected to "voluntarily" contribute 2 percent of their paycheck to the party in power. In 1971, after Snyder refused to use 2-percent funds to pay Whitcomb's bills for "political activities" such as trips, receptions, and photos, the governor announced that he was ending the 2-percent scheme for the five thousand state patronage employees under his control, depriving the state committee of a significant source of revenue. He declared at the time that he thought it was "inequitable to make payment of part of your salary to a Republican, or to any party, a condition of your employment for the State of Indiana." However, the program was resumed when a chair more friendly to Whitcomb replaced Snyder. When reinstituting the policy Whitcomb said that the collections would not be mandatory, nor would anyone be fired for refusing to give, but few refused to contribute.

Whitcomb achieved some noteworthy changes in the organization and administration of state government. He spent millions to computerize the Bureau of Motor Vehicles and criminal records. He created the Indiana Higher Education Commission by executive order in August 1971, establishing an independent body to oversee the educational needs of the state and to consider the interests of the higher education system in Indiana. The commission has final authority over any new campuses, colleges, or degree programs among the state-supported institutions of higher education. Whitcomb also established a statewide medical education system.

Whitcomb faced a constitutional crisis when the pocket veto was declared unconstitutional in Indiana. This crisis came about when the previous governor, Roger D. Branigin, did not sign thirty-three bills passed by the state legislature two days before the end of the legislative session, thus vetoing the bills. Among the vetoed bills were those that would give retroactive raises to past and present judges and change the inheritance tax distribution from 8 percent to Indiana counties to 90.8 percent. Branigin's pocket veto saved the state $10 million in taxes. Whitcomb asked the Indiana General Assembly to repeal the pocket-vetoed bills, which it did.

Another legal issue that left a black mark on the administration involved a court-ordered state payment of $12.7 million in disputed inheritance tax funds to Marion County. The administration refused the pay the funds. When the state auditor, Trudy Etherton, backed by the governor, continued to stall despite being threatened with a contempt-of-court citation, she was jailed for five minutes. The state paid the funds. Etherton was later appointed as commissioner of the Bureau of Motor Vehicles, where a scandal erupted over ten bureau "ghost employees" who were paid $40,000 for no work. Whitcomb redeemed his administration by firing the ghost workers and demanding restitution of funds.

When he left office, the assessment of Whitcomb's record by the media and other political observers was mixed, reflecting both pluses and minuses. However, the citizens of Indiana basically approved of his administration. He left office with a 50 percent approval rating. GOP State Party Chair James T. Neal observed, "He may not have been popular with a lot of politicians, but he was very popular with the man in the street. He said he wasn't going to raise taxes and he didn't."

After his time as governor, Whitcomb returned to his law practice and was director of the Mid America World Trade Association. In 1976 he ran against Richard G. Lugar for the Republican nomination for U.S. Senator, which Lugar won.

In 1985 Whitcomb closed his law office and worked with Christian Publishing Company until he retired. He traveled the country setting up a network of FM radio stations and took up sailing. In 1987 he sailed around the Mediterranean. This was a precursor for his solo sail across the Atlantic in 1990 at the age of seventy-two. Whitcomb left the Canary Islands on January 8, 1990, in a thirty-foot single-mast sailboat, the *Cilin II*, and set sail for Antigua. "It was just something I had to do," he said. He later attempted to circumnavigate the earth, but his journey ended on August 16, 1996, when he struck a coral reef in the Gulf of Suez and his sailboat sank.

In 1997 Whitcomb moved back into the house in which he grew up, in Hayden, Indiana. Then in 2000, at the age of eighty-three, he moved to a cabin on the Ohio River, in the thick of the Hoosier National Forest, with a battery as the only source of electricity. Spending his time canoeing, chopping firewood, fishing, reading, and writing, he said in 2004 that he no longer paid close attention to what happened in Indianapolis and that he liked the peace and solitude of his new home. "I'm in heaven," he said, "and don't even know it."

Portrait by Donald Mattison (1973), Governors' Portraits Collection, Indiana Historical Bureau, State of Indiana.

FOR FURTHER READING

Gray, Ralph D., ed. *The Hoosier State: Readings in Indiana History.* Vol. 2, *The Modern Era.* Grand Rapids, MI: William B. Eerdmans Publishing Company, 1980.

Ritchie, Alton J. *The Whitcomb Years.* Indianapolis, 1973.

Taylor, Robert M. Jr., Errol Wayne Stevens, Mary Ann Ponder, and Paul Brockman. *Indiana: A New Historical Guide.* Indianapolis: Indiana Historical Society, 1989.

Walsh, Justin E. *The Centennial History of the Indiana General Assembly, 1816–1978.* Indianapolis: The Select Committee on the Centennial History of the Indiana General Assembly, 1987.

Whitcomb, Edgar D. *Escape from Corregidor.* New York: Henry Regnery Company, 1958.

Whitcomb's papers are in the Lilly Library, Indiana University, Bloomington. His gubernatorial papers are in the Indiana State Archives, Indianapolis.

Otis R. Bowen

January 9, 1973–January 13, 1981

RAYMOND H. SCHEELE

OTIS R. BOWEN RAISED HIS RIGHT HAND AND TOOK THE oath of office as Indiana governor on January 9, 1973, while bombs were dropping on Vietnam and antiwar demonstrations were daily events. One month into his governorship the U.S. Senate established a Select Committee to investigate Watergate. Amid this national turmoil, Hoosier voters had chosen a methodical and matter-of-fact medical doctor to be their chief executive. Bowen had extraordinary experience, a keen political instinct, a firmness, a calmness, and a patience that was perfectly attuned to the moderate, conservative political culture of Indiana. As the first governor permitted to serve consecutive elected terms, he was to have a sweeping impact on politics and public policies. His methodical rise through the political ranks equipped him to emerge as the leader of the Indiana Republican Party and to fundamentally reshape the state's political and public policy structure.

Through all the events of the next eight years—happenings that would ruin dozens of political careers—Bowen's calm but firm leadership and straightforward policy initiatives resonated with Hoosiers. He maintained a popularity widely acknowledged as being among the highest of any governor in Indiana history.

Bowen considered himself to be a physician before all else. Born in Fulton County on February 26, 1918, he was the second oldest of five children of Vernie and Pearl Irene Wright Bowen. He was raised in the rural areas of north central and northwest Indiana, where his father was a teacher and coach. Like most young Hoosiers, Bowen played high

school basket-   ball, coached by
his father. Early   on he decided to
become a physician   and did not want to
be anything else, but the   cost of medical school
made him briefly consider   becoming a farmer or following his father into teaching. He had a resolute plan for his life's work,
and it did not include politics. Although politics was discussed in the
family and his uncle held the elective office of Fulton County Surveyor,
involvement in politics and public service "was not in my life's plan," said
Bowen.

Bowen graduated from Francesville High School in 1935. Unable
to afford private school tuition, he enrolled in Indiana University's
three-year premed program. His college years revolved around grades
and money. Bowen worked odd jobs to pay for room and board, but
his main efforts were put into his studies and he reported that he
"made A's and B's," receiving only one "C" in physics. Between his
sophomore and junior years, Bowen spent the summer in Crown
Point, Indiana, where his parents had moved. That summer he met a
young woman named Elizabeth (Beth) Anna Agnes Steinmann. They
were engaged five weeks after their first meeting, but they postponed
the wedding until February 25, 1939, so he could continue his education. Bowen's military commitment was fulfilled in the army ROTC
program, and he spent most of the summers of 1940 and 1941 in
training. On December 8, 1941, the medical school dean summoned

the students to a meeting where they heard President Franklin D. Roosevelt's radio address asking Congress to declare war on the Empire of Japan. Bowen recalled: "The hall became totally quiet as everyone lapsed into deep thought about what lay ahead. Ours was the first class to graduate in wartime. Graduation even was accelerated so we finished in May." He interned at a South Bend hospital and entered active duty on July 3, 1943. Dispatched to the Pacific theater, Bowen and his medical unit were assigned to the invasion force of Okinawa in April 1945. He returned to Indiana in January 1946, joining his wife and their young son in Bremen, Indiana, to start his civilian medical practice. During the next six years one daughter and two more sons were born. The youngest, Rob Bowen, was born on July 31, 1952. He was the one child to follow his father into public service.

Bowen became a Republican, following his mother's persuasion. His father was a Democrat, and when Bowen assented to local Republican leaders to run for Marshall County Coroner, his father teased him, calling him "politically unwise," but nonetheless enthusiastically supported all his son's candidacies. Bowen easily won the coroner's position in 1952, launching his political career.

Four years later Bowen ran for the local seat in the Indiana House of Representatives. In a hotly contested GOP primary, Bowen was first exposed to the factional infighting and personal assaults that permeated Indiana politics. He won the nomination by thirty votes and easily defeated his Democratic opponent in November.

With the Indiana General Assembly meeting only sixty-one days every two years, Bowen was able to balance his medical practice with his legislative and family responsibilities. His first session in 1957 was undistinguished, but Bowen enjoyed the give-and-take of policy making and spent his time learning the issues and procedures of the legislature. This session infected him with his "incurable disease": his love of public service and the challenges it holds for a person. However, his political career suffered a major setback in the 1958 reelection battle. It was a great year for Democrats. They gained control of the Indiana House of Representatives and elected a new Speaker, Birch Bayh. Bowen had lost his seat by four votes—the only electoral loss of his career. He won the seat back in 1960 and won the next five races by large margins.

The qualities that were imbued in Bowen—his attention to detail, his ability to diagnose symptoms and formulate treatments, his compassion for others, and his dogged determination to set goals and objectives and work to achieve them—were recognized quickly by other legislators, lobbyists, and public officials. In 1963 he had enough support to run for Speaker in the Republican caucus, but he challenged the sitting Speaker and was defeated. That session was one of the most contentious since the end of World War II, requiring a special session that lasted forty-two days. Governor Matthew E. Welsh had proposed the first sales tax for the state. Bowen voted for the tax after much "soul searching," reasoning that a tax increase was unavoidable and the sales tax was "less obnoxious."

Bowen survived the 1964 Democratic landslide, but the Republican losses were immense. The GOP house caucus was reduced to twenty-two members out of the one hundred seats. The previous Republican leaders were defeated, and Bowen won the post of minority leader.

The house Republicans rebounded in 1966, electing sixty-six members. Bowen was poised to become Speaker, but the GOP caucus vote was extremely close: he won by two votes. This was the "defining moment" of his political career. He now was in charge of the Indiana House of Representatives and would remain as Speaker until he was elected governor. Bowen acknowledged that if he had failed to become Speaker and serve six years in the position he "would not have been in the position to win election as governor."

In 1968 Bowen sought the GOP gubernatorial nomination but was defeated in the state convention by Secretary of State Edgar D. Whitcomb. L. Keith Bulen, the GOP boss of Marion County, engineered Whitcomb's nomination. Bulen constructed an alliance with other GOP leaders from urban areas and used every tactic to support his favorites. Bowen never forgot Bulen's opposition: "Bulen . . . heads my short list of people, in or out of politics, for whom I harbor ill feeling," said Bowen, pointing out that Bulen previously had attempted to defeat him as Speaker in the 1967 session.

With Bowen in the Speaker's chair and Whitcomb in the governor's office, the differences between the two Republicans were most pronounced on the issue of taxes. Indiana's tax structure had not been a major focus since the 1963 session, but Bowen carefully constructed a program that would substantially cut property taxes while replacing the revenue with a sales-tax increase. His package also called for limits on the growth of tax rates and levies for local governments and schools. Whitcomb was unalterably opposed to any tax increase, and Bowen's plan failed in the 1971 session. Bowen, however, had fashioned a centerpiece issue for his 1972 gubernatorial run, and he sensed a "howl" in the electorate for tax reform, promising that it would "become a roar."

The Whitcomb-Bulen forces were still arrayed against him, but Bowen easily won the nomination in the 1972 state convention, the last year Indiana was to nominate gubernatorial candidates in convention. Bowen's slogan was "He Hears You," and the voters spoke. He won a surprisingly easy victory over Democrat Welsh, carrying with him majorities in both legislative chambers.

In 1973 Bowen won another triumph, this time in the legislature. His tax restructuring plan passed narrowly, and the first policy achievement of Bowen's legacy was assured. His tax package would not be significantly altered for a generation. That summer dark clouds were gathering over the Republican Party. It was revealed before the U.S. Senate Select Committee that President Richard M. Nixon had taped his conversations in the White House, and the Watergate investigations led to his resignation in August 1974. Bowen was appalled by Watergate, calling it "public confidence unmet, public trust broken and public promise belied." The Democrats won a majority in the Indiana House in 1974, and Bowen was faced with divided party government. In 1976 Bowen easily won reelection over Democrat secretary of state Larry Conrad, and the Republicans recaptured control of the Indiana House but lost their senate majority. Finally, in 1978, the GOP, running on the slogan "The Bowen Team," won all statewide offices and majorities in both chambers. Bowen's control over the Indiana GOP was cemented and the Indiana Democrats were in disarray. Bowen was able to ensure that his lieutenant governor, Robert D. Orr, had an uncontested nomination for governor in 1980. Orr went on to serve two terms, enjoying GOP majorities in the state legislature.

Bowen considered his most popular accomplishment to be a vast upgrading of the state park and recreation system. His administration created five new parks, including the first urban park: White River State Park in downtown Indianapolis. In addition, two reservoirs were completed, Brookville and Patoka, and more than forty nature preserves were added to the system. Bowen prioritized these projects, insisting that each meet standards for flood control, water supplies, and recreation.

His administration accelerated the completion of Indiana's interstate highways by using state funds to complete the construction and having federal dollars reimburse the state. Bowen believed that the state had to have a complete modern highway system to retain its position as a transportation center. Late in his second term, he reorganized the State Highway Department, merging it with other transportation-related agencies into the Indiana Department of Transportation.

As a physician, Bowen was deeply concerned about the statewide emergency medical system (EMS). He convened a governor's conference on EMS in 1973 and moved quickly to implement the recommendations, including creating EMS response centers in existing hospitals, establishing training and equipment standards for EMS personnel, and adopting 911 as the statewide emergency telephone number.

Bowen's medical background also led him to insist on landmark legislation that limited medical malpractice claims to $500,000. He knew of other physicians who were forced to retire early after being sued. A patient's compensation fund was created by fees paid by doctors and hospitals, and state government became the insurer of last resort for doctors unable to obtain malpractice insurance. This reform was updated through the years, and the Indiana law served as a model for other states.

Personal tragedy struck the Bowen family just as the governor was concluding his second term. His wife Beth, suffering from bone cancer, died on New Year's Day 1981.

After turning over the governor's office to Orr, Bowen returned to the practice of medicine by teaching at the Indiana University Medical School in Indianapolis. In September 1981 he remarried. His new bride was Rose Crothers Hochstetler, a Marshall County native and former Bowen patient.

On November 5, 1985, President Ronald Reagan asked Bowen to serve as the sixteenth secretary of the U.S. Department of Health and Human Services. Bowen later characterized this cabinet position as one "with a lot of responsibility and little authority." His most notable achievement was the passage of the 1988 Medicare Catastrophic Health Care Act. Bowen had proposed the idea to Reagan, and it was well received in Congress. The plan covered the costs of catastrophic illness above a certain level for those on Medicare. Bowen proposed that it be paid for by a moderate flat tax on all Medicare recipients. The funding mechanism that was adopted, however, was a progressive tax, with wealthy seniors paying at a higher rate, up to $800 annually, than those who were less well off. The reaction among seniors was swift and furious, and within fifteen months of its passage, Congress repealed the act.

When Reagan's term ended, the Bowens returned to Bremen to enjoy retirement. Tragedy again struck when Rose was diagnosed with cancer. She died on January 21, 1992.

Later that year Bowen met Carol Lynn (Hahn) Flosenzier Mikesell at a political fund-raiser. Carol was a former patient. Their reacquaintance led to their marriage on February 5, 1993.

Portrait by Everett Raymond Kinstler (1978), Governors' Portraits Collection, Indiana Historical Bureau, State of Indiana.

FOR FURTHER READING

Bowen, Otis R. *Doc: Memories from a Life in Public Service.* Bloomington: Indiana University Press, 2001.

Scheele, Raymond H. *Larry Conrad of Indiana: A Biography.* Bloomington: Indiana University Press, 1997.

Watt, William J. *Bowen: The Years as Governor.* Indianapolis: Bierce Associates, 1981.

Bowen's papers are in the Bethel College library, Mishawaka, Indiana. His gubernatorial papers are in the Indiana State Archives, Indianapolis. Bowen speaks at the annual session of the Bowen Institute on Political Participation, Ball State University, Muncie, Indiana, and his remarks are recorded.

Robert D. Orr

January 13, 1981–January 9, 1989

RALPH D. GRAY

ROBERT D. ORR'S ELECTION AS GOVERNOR IN 1980 CUL-
minated more than thirty years of service to the Republican Party,
during which he worked his way up the ladder from precinct committeeman to county chairman and then state senator, followed by
eight years as lieutenant governor (1973–81) and finally eight more as
governor (1981–89). Orr's years in the state's highest office coincided
with Ronald Reagan's years as president and were marked, initially, by
attempts to recover from the recession of the early 1980s, high unemployment rates throughout the state, and a shortfall in state revenues
that threatened to produce a large state deficit, something prohibited by the state constitution. Orr successfully overcame these problems by increasing the state income and other taxes while pushing for
educational and economic development advances—areas in which he
had special interest and expertise. Indeed, his gubernatorial legacy
reflects major reforms in the public schools and significant improvement in the state's economic infrastructure.

Although a longtime resident of Evansville, Orr was actually born
on November 17, 1917, in Ann Arbor, Michigan, where his mother
had gone in order to continue being treated by the family physician
who had moved there. Orr was the son of industrialist Samuel Lowry
and Louise Dunkerson Orr, both of whose families had come to the
Ohio River community of Evansville in the early nineteenth century.

Robert, the youngest of three siblings, grew up in Evansville, attending the local schools and, to better his chances of being admitted to

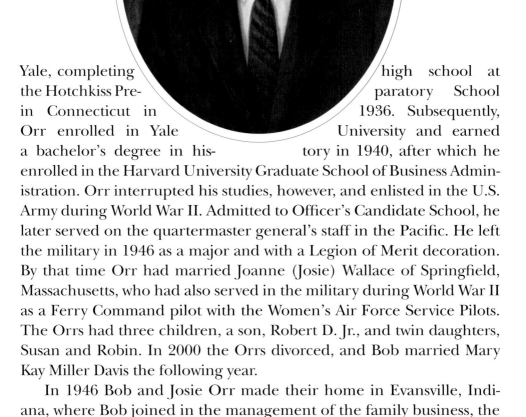

Yale, completing high school at the Hotchkiss Preparatory School in Connecticut in 1936. Subsequently, Orr enrolled in Yale University and earned a bachelor's degree in history in 1940, after which he enrolled in the Harvard University Graduate School of Business Administration. Orr interrupted his studies, however, and enlisted in the U.S. Army during World War II. Admitted to Officer's Candidate School, he later served on the quartermaster general's staff in the Pacific. He left the military in 1946 as a major and with a Legion of Merit decoration. By that time Orr had married Joanne (Josie) Wallace of Springfield, Massachusetts, who had also served in the military during World War II as a Ferry Command pilot with the Women's Air Force Service Pilots. The Orrs had three children, a son, Robert D. Jr., and twin daughters, Susan and Robin. In 2000 the Orrs divorced, and Bob married Mary Kay Miller Davis the following year.

In 1946 Bob and Josie Orr made their home in Evansville, Indiana, where Bob joined in the management of the family business, the Orr Iron Company, a more diversified company than implied by its name. Orr also became involved in a number of other businesses in Evansville, specializing in economic development as the community attempted to reconvert its substantial wartime industrial plants back to peacetime production. Orr assisted through buying local factories, refurbishing them, and finding new owners and industrial uses for the plants. He also served on the boards of numerous local companies including Erie Investments, Sterling Brewers, and Evansville Metal Products, as well as Dixson Inc. of Grand Junction, Colorado. He was highly active in local civic affairs, too, with leadership roles in the First Presbyterian Church of Evansville, the Rotary Club, the Evansville YMCA, Willard Library, and the Buffalo Trace Council of Boy Scouts of America. Orr was recognized in 1953 as the Jaycees Young Man of the Year and given its Distinguished Service Award. At the time he was an officer in thirteen service organizations and a director of twelve companies. Subsequently, Orr was a longtime member of the board of trustees of Hanover College.

In addition to his business and civic activities, Orr began to take part in Republican Party politics in 1950, serving first as a member and then as chairman of the Center Township Advisory Board in Vanderburgh County (1950–54). For eight years, he was a Republican precinct committeeman. During this time he also became treasurer of the Eighth District Republican Committee (1958–60). In 1965 Orr was elected chair of the Vanderburgh County Republican Central Committee, a position he held for six years. While in this position, Orr was elected to the Indiana State Senate in 1968, and he remained involved in state government for the next two decades.

In 1972 he was chosen by the Republican state party convention as the nominee for lieutenant governor. With the popular Otis R. Bowen, MD as the gubernatorial nominee, they were elected with a comfortable margin of 56.8 percent of the vote over former governor Matthew E. Welsh. Orr served as Bowen's loyal and hardworking lieutenant governor for the next eight years, the state constitution now permitting governors to serve a second successive term. The duties of the Indiana lieutenant governor include service as the state commissioner of agriculture and director of the Indiana Department of Commerce, giving that officer direct responsibility for promoting Indiana's economic development and the state's tourism programs. Orr's experience in Evansville served him well in this capacity, and he accomplished much, particularly in pressing forward the construction of Indiana's two Ohio River public ports, one at Mount Vernon, the other at Jeffersonville. He also cast five tie-breaking votes in the senate that kept Bowen's property tax relief program alive.

Tall and slender, his energetic physique capped by silver hair, Orr had a good speaking voice and he was quite popular both within the Republican Party and throughout the state. With the outgoing governor's approval, Orr easily won the Republican nomination to be Bowen's successor in 1980. The campaign slogan featured the Bowen connection—"Let's Keep a Good Thing Going"—and Orr, along with John M. Mutz as his running mate, defeated Democrat John Hillenbrand II by the largest margin in the history of the state at that time— 57.7 percent of the vote compared to 41.9 percent for Hillenbrand.

Despite this auspicious beginning, Orr's first year as governor was marked by difficulties. The state was in the midst of a recession, which had turned a budget surplus built up in the inflationary 1970s into a large deficit. To address these problems Orr proposed a series of tax relief and budget austerity measures to the Indiana General Assembly, while also advocating several economic development and government reorganization programs. His proposals led some legislators to label him a "do-nothing" governor. Orr's response was that "we should make do with what we have. If my unwillingness to recommend large tax increases is 'do nothing,' so be it." His approach irritated the state employees and schoolteachers, whose hopes for salary increases and better working conditions were dashed, and it did little to lighten the burden created by massive unemployment statewide. Nor were funds available to improve educational opportunities, particularly in math, science, and computer literacy, which were high on the governor's list of objectives.

In 1982, following the general election that continued Republican control of both houses of the legislature, Orr called the general assembly into special session in December to address the problem of a mounting state deficit, projected to be as high as $450 million in 1983, an election issue that the Republicans had downplayed but now needed to resolve. Accordingly, the state income tax was increased from 1.9 to 3 percent, and the state sales tax went up from 4 to 5 percent.

When the regular session of the legislature convened in January 1983, the taxation issue had already been taken care of, and other issues that Orr wanted to tackle could be addressed. Most troublesome was the matter of public utility reform. Utility rates, particularly on natural gas, had risen by 40 to 50 percent during the previous year. The legislature's response was a utility reform bill in 1983 that expanded the number of members on the state regulatory agency and limited the size and frequency of future rate increases. As Orr testified before the U.S. Senate Committee on Energy and Natural Resources in March 1983, however, the states had only limited ability to deal with such issues. Congress, he argued, was the responsible body for addressing these problems, and he urged it to act.

During these troubled times, Orr was forced to run for reelection. Easily renominated, he faced a strong challenge from W. Wayne Townsend, a state senator from Blackford County, in the general election of 1984. Only the second state governor constitutionally eligible to succeed himself since the Indiana Constitution of 1851 was amended in 1972, Orr continued the new two-term trend by narrowly defeating his Democratic opponent with 52 percent of the 2.1 million votes cast. This time, however, he ran at the bottom rather than at the top of the Republican ticket statewide.

During his second term Orr continued to make education and economic development his primary concerns. His "Prime Time" program reducing class size in the elementary grades and his "A+" program initiated to bring accountability to public education by measuring results and recording performance brought positive national attention to the state. Moreover, to provide even more financial support for these initiatives, the legislature again raised the state income tax from 3.0 to 3.4 percent. In another act of political courage, Orr reformed the state's license branch system, removing it from control by the political parties and making it a part of the Bureau of Motor Vehicles.

Orr also brought substantial foreign investment to the state, particularly through an arrangement concluded in 1981 that led to a new Subaru/Isuzu light truck and automobile plant in northern Indiana.

A controversial issue because of the size of the financial incentive package, Orr defended its feasibility and took pride in the financial benefits to the state that followed and the fact that his political opponents and critics have since followed suit in bringing other manufacturing plants to Indiana. The governor also continued his support of the Indiana Port Commission, which completed the construction of its three public ports on Lake Michigan and the Ohio River during the Orr years and bolstered Indiana's trade and connection with the world considerably. A forward-thinking administrator, Orr was convinced that a secure and prosperous future for the state required increased productivity at home and increased involvement in the global economy. This conviction was behind his creation of the Indiana Corporation for Science and Technology. Orr was deeply knowledgeable about the history of Indiana and did much to preserve and promote it. In his second term he launched "Hoosier Celebration '88," announced in his second inaugural address in January 1985, as a means to celebrate both Indiana's heritage and its promising future.

Orr, unlike his predecessor, did not have the satisfaction of seeing his lieutenant governor, Mutz, become his successor; instead, young Evan Bayh, son of former U.S. senator Birch Bayh, defeated Mutz in the next gubernatorial election. That change not only ended twenty years of Republican control in the Indiana statehouse and ushered in sixteen years of Democratic control, but it also marked the replacement of Indiana's oldest governor by the youngest. But Orr's career in public service was not over. In 1989 President George H. W. Bush appointed Orr to become the U.S. ambassador in Singapore, where he remained for three years and continued to bring increased economic development to his state and nation while also effectively serving his country. After retiring from public service in 1992, Orr continued to promote economic development as a consultant, working from an office in Indianapolis. He died on March 10, 2004, of heart arrhythmia following kidney surgery. He is buried in Crown Hill Cemetery in Indianapolis.

Portrait by Lucian Lupinski (1983), Governors' Portraits Collection, Indiana Historical Bureau, State of Indiana.

FOR FURTHER READING

Gray, Ralph D. *Public Ports for Indiana: A History of the Indiana Port Commission.* Indianapolis: Indiana Historical Bureau, 1998.

McKinney, Margaret. "The Orrs." *Evansville Courier and Press,* September 19, 1982.

Walsh, Justin E. *The Centennial History of the Indiana General Assembly, 1816–1978.* Indianapolis: The Select Committee on the Centennial History of the Indiana General Assembly, 1987.

Orr's gubernatorial papers are in the Indiana State Archives, Indianapolis.

Birch Evans Bayh III

January 9, 1989–January 13, 1997

CLIFFORD L. STATEN

AS A VERY POPULAR TWO-TERM DEMOCRATIC GOVERNOR IN a traditionally Republican state, the photogenic and media savvy Birch Evans Bayh established a solid reputation as a fiscal conservative and one of the "new" centrist, Clintonesque Democrats. He emphasized education and welfare reform, lower taxes, job creation, and efficient government. During this highly charged partisan era, Bayh, according to Ed Harris, the Democratic state representative from East Chicago/Gary, "would work both sides of the aisle." He was willing to work with Republican Party members in a pragmatic, compromising, and nonideological manner. "Evan" Bayh, as he is called, this practice continued in the U.S. Senate as a leader of the bipartisan centrist coalition. Those on the left of the political spectrum sometimes derisively refer to him as a "republicrat" while others characterize him as a midwestern "mainstream voice."

Bayh was born in Shirkieville, Indiana (near Terre Haute), on his family's farm on December 26, 1955, and it can be argued that he was destined for a political career. He grew up in one of the most prominent political families in the state. His father, Birch Bayh II, a hog farmer, served eight years in the state house of representatives, including two years as Speaker. Beginning in 1962 Bayh was elected to three terms in the U.S. Senate. Bayh grew up in Washington, D.C., in the spotlight of his nationally known father, who was responsible for drafting two amendments to the U.S. Constitution—the Twenty-fifth Amendment that provided for presidential disability and succession and the Twenty-sixth

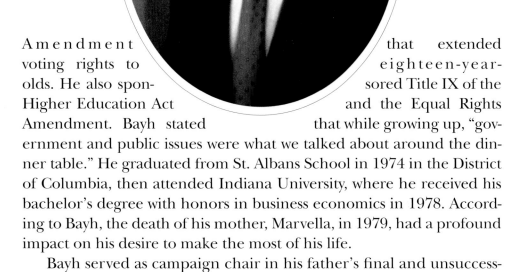

Amendment that extended voting rights to eighteen-year-olds. He also spon- sored Title IX of the Higher Education Act and the Equal Rights Amendment. Bayh stated that while growing up, "government and public issues were what we talked about around the dinner table." He graduated from St. Albans School in 1974 in the District of Columbia, then attended Indiana University, where he received his bachelor's degree with honors in business economics in 1978. According to Bayh, the death of his mother, Marvella, in 1979, had a profound impact on his desire to make the most of his life.

Bayh served as campaign chair in his father's final and unsuccessful 1980 Senate reelection campaign and received his law degree from the University of Virginia in 1981. He served as a law clerk for U.S. District Judge James Noland in 1982 and 1983. In 1983 he also worked for the Washington, D.C., law firm of Hogan and Harston, and the following year for his father's law firm in Indianapolis and the Wayne Townsend gubernatorial campaign. Bayh worked for the Indianapolis law firm of Bingham, Summers, Welsh and Spearman in 1985 and 1986. In 1985 he married Susan Breshears, and their twin sons, Birch Evans IV and Nicholas, were born in 1995.

In 1986 Bayh defeated Republican candidate Robert Bowen, son of former Governor Otis R. Bowen, in the election for secretary of state of Indiana. In the gubernatorial race of 1988 he and Frank O'Bannon

defeated the Republican Party ticket of John M. Mutz and Steve Goldsmith 53 to 47 percent. At the time Bayh not only was the youngest
governor in the United States but also the first Democrat elected as
governor of Indiana since 1964. In 1992 he and O'Bannon defeated
the Republican Party ticket of Linley E. Pearson and Robert Green by
a 62 percent to 37 percent margin, the largest margin of victory in the
any governor's race in the twentieth century.

When Bayh stepped into the governor's office, a centrist strategy
was not only a matter of choice for the young governor; it was a neces-
sity. The state senate was controlled by the Republicans, a fact of life
for Bayh throughout his tenure as governor, and the house of representatives was split fifty-fifty along party lines, resulting in an awkward
leadership structure of cospeakers and committee cochairs. In his first
term Bayh's relationship with the legislature was rocky, and many of
his proposals were met with hostility from Republicans. When his final
term as governor was nearing an end in 1996, Bayh said he regretted
not doing more after his first election to foster a better relationship
with the legislature and lamented that a more conciliatory strategy
might have headed off some of the animosity he experienced in his
first term.

In the first few months as governor Bayh set a conservative tone
by cutting government spending without laying off employees. He
started the Governor's Commission for a Drug Free Indiana, which
was designed to create and build partnerships at both the state and
local levels. In 1990 he created the Twenty-first Century Scholars Program to encourage low- and middle-income students in the seventh
and eighth grades to attend college. By signing a pledge to maintain a
2.0 grade point average, not use illegal drugs or alcohol or commit a
crime while in these grades, and to graduate from an accredited high
school and meet income qualifications, these students are provided
the resources to attend a university or college within Indiana.

Bayh frequently touted education as one of his top priorities,
and he pointed to increased spending for education as one of the
main accomplishments of his administration. However, the issue of
more equitable funding for public schools was the subject of a lawsuit

filed by school superintendents in several counties. The lawsuit was dropped when Bayh promised to intervene, but the backers of the lawsuit thought that Bayh did not live up to his promise. In 1992 Bayh became the president of the Education Commission of the States.

Economic development was another priority for Bayh. In 1992 he reached an agreement with United Airlines to build an $800 million airplane maintenance facility in Indianapolis. Three years later he convinced Toyota to build a truck plant in Princeton and Chrysler to build a new truck transmission plant in Kokomo.

Bayh won approval from labor unions when he issued an executive order in 1990 to extend collective bargaining rights for state employees, the International Union of Police Associations and the American Federation of State, County and Municipal Employees (AFSCME) workers, along with the Unity Team, an alliance between the American Federation of Teachers and the United Auto Workers. These collective bargaining rights were terminated for twenty-five thousand state employees in 2005 by Governor Mitch Daniels. Labor was disappointed when Bayh was complacent about changes in the prevailing-wage law pushed by Republicans. The new formula meant lower pay for construction workers on public projects.

Bayh accomplished significant reorganization of state government, especially in the area of social services. He had pledged in his campaign to rely heavily on a 1967 statute that gave the governor broad powers to reorganize state government, and he followed through on that pledge. In 1991 he restructured the area of social services by creating Step Ahead Councils in each county. These were designed to mobilize community leaders, agency representatives, and local service providers and to identify and address local needs in the area of childhood development. That same year Bayh initiated a massive overhaul of the state's bureaucracy for social services when he created the Indiana Family and Social Services Administration to better integrate the delivery of human services.

Welfare reform was one of the major accomplishments during Bayh's second term as governor. In December 1994, Bayh, with the support of the Republican-controlled general assembly, received permission from the federal government to implement a pilot project in welfare reform. The purpose was to "build a way for welfare recipients to work with business to build self-sufficiency and leave the public assistance rolls." In particular, it was designed to increase clients' employment, decrease reliance on welfare, make work more rewarding than public assistance, and to encourage responsible parenting. From December through May the state randomly assigned the entire welfare caseload into two groups for evaluation—one under Bayh's new Partnership for Personal Responsibility reform and the other under the old welfare system. With the project's focus on job replacement and job search, its initial success became a model of state welfare reform as Indiana experienced a significant drop in its welfare caseload through the year 2000 and an increase in clients' employment. Financially speaking, it was successful in that the savings in welfare payments actually were greater than the costs of the provision of extra employment and child-care services. Some critics of the reform suggest that even though many welfare recipients found jobs under the new program, on average they experienced little to no increase in income and simply became part of the working poor, with difficulty gaining access to adequate health-care insurance and child-care services. Others point out that much of its success was largely due to the fact that Indiana's public assistance levels had historically been among the lowest in the United States, and others argue that the success of the program simply mirrored the economic boom of the 1990s. Nonetheless, this was a clear illustration of Bayh's willingness and ability to work with members of the Republican Party in a significant policy reform effort. It also thrust Bayh and the state of Indiana into the forefront of the national welfare reform movement of the 1990s.

Medicaid, the state and federal health-care program for the poor and the elderly, proved to be one of the most intractable issues affecting the state budget. The program, which covered 600,000 residents, had become the fastest growing expense in the state budget. Bayh introduced a new managed-care scheme along with cuts in reimbursements to health-care providers. The changes were not popular but saved the state $500 million between 1993 and 1995. The problems stemming from the high cost of Medicaid caused Bayh to advocate his only tax increases. First he called for a new hospital tax to help balance the budget, and when this was rejected, he proposed a major increase in the cigarette tax, which was also rejected. Bayh's claim that the state went eight years without a tax increase during his administration can be attributed to legislative defeats rather than victories.

Bayh staunchly rejected a popular approach to solving fiscal problems—riverboat gambling—but the legislature overrode his veto in 1993. While he opposed raising funds from gambling, the revenues generated from the casinos helped to ease the state's budget problems and eventually contributed to the state's surplus.

Bayh continued to press for education reforms in the state by focusing on increased standards and assessment of student progress. In 1994 he served as chair of the National Education Goals Panel. That same year he helped to establish the CORE 40 curriculum for Indiana high schools. In 1995 he lobbied for passage of the Indiana Performance Assessment for Student Success (IPASS), a new statewide assessment test that never received funding. The next year the state raised the standards on its Indiana Statewide Testing for Educational Progress (ISTEP) exam by adding a writing sample.

In August 1996 Bayh delivered the keynote speech at the Democratic National Convention, an event that indicated he was viewed as a rising star in the national Democratic Party. However, his speech was pushed so late in the program to accommodate another speaker— Hillary Rodham Clinton—that it was viewed by a limited audience.

Bayh left office with a record of national leadership in welfare and education reform. In his eight years as governor there were no new tax increases, yet state funding for education increased each year. Indiana also experienced the largest budget surplus in its history at approximately $1.6 billion. Some of his detractors labeled Bayh a "caretaker governor" and pointed out that Bayh benefited from a strong national economy, the beginning of the Hoosier lottery, and new casino riverboat tax revenues during his terms as governor. Despite his critics, Bayh's record appealed to Hoosier citizens. He finished his second term with an approval rating of 80 percent, a level of support that bode well for his next political quest, U.S. Senator.

After finishing his second term as governor, Bayh took a lecturing position as the Harold A. "Red" Polling Chair of Business and Economics at Indiana University. In 1998 he defeated Republican Party candidate Paul Helmke to claim the U.S. Senate seat once held by his father. In this election he received 25 percent of the Republican vote. He was mentioned as a possible vice presidential candidate with Al Gore in 2000.

By 2005 Bayh was considered by many political pundits to be on the short list of likely candidates for the Democratic nomination for president, and there were signs he was starting his quest for the presidency. He assembled a team of advisers, began soliciting donors, and visited several of the battleground states. He raised his visibility in the Senate by taking a bolder stand against some of President George W. Bush's nominees for federal judgeships and U.N. ambassador as well as the president's conduct of the Iraq war. In June 2005 Bayh announced that he was stepping down as chair of the Democratic Leadership Council, a move speculated to leave him more time to explore a bid for the 2008 presidential nomination. Contemplating Bayh's possible candidacy for president, Brian Vargus, noted Indiana pollster, observed that: "The gubernatorial years for Evan Bayh will probably be regarded as a chapter in a much larger volume. . . . The chapter is going to be less significant than the chapters of the rest of his career, which I expect to be very distinguished."

Portrait by Michael Chelich (1993), Governors' Portraits Collection, Indiana Historical Bureau, State of Indiana.

FOR FURTHER READING

Bayh, Birch Evans. *From Father to Son: A Political Life in the Public Eye.* Indianapolis: Guild Press/Emmis Books, 2003.

Colander, Pat. "Legacy, Reality and the Future of Senator Bayh." *Lake Magazine* (Summer 2004).

Dieter, Mary. "Two-term Governor a Study in Caution." *Louisville Courier-Journal,* January 6, 1997.

U.S. Senator Evan Bayh Web site. http//www.senate.gov/~bayh/.

Bayh's gubernatorial papers are in the Indiana State Archives, Indianapolis.

Frank L. O'Bannon

January 13, 1997–September 13, 2003

CARY G. STEMLE

FRANK O'BANNON, INDIANA'S LAST GOVERNOR OF THE twentieth century and its first of the twenty-first century, was in many ways representative of a bygone era, especially in his calm, bipartisan approach to politics. Yet, he also presided during the period of rapid transformation fueled by technology, and far from avoiding the new wonders that confused many in his generation, he embraced them.

O'Bannon was just a little more than a year away from completing his second term as governor when he suffered a stroke while attending a conference in Chicago on international trade. His death five days later, on September 13, 2003, shocked the state and evoked eulogies that were effusive and sincere. He was hailed, even by those who opposed him politically, as a leader of substance who put public service above politics and self-aggrandizement and as someone known for fairness, decency, and integrity.

O'Bannon's entry into politics was practically foreordained. "I grew up in a political family," he once explained. "The idea was instilled in me that it's a way of serving, even with its weaknesses . . . it's basic and necessary." His grandfather, Lew M. O'Bannon, set the standard for the family, both as a public-spirited politician and newspaper publisher. A lawyer, Lew began his political career as county surveyor and county recorder and ran on an anti-Ku Klux Klan platform as the Democratic nominee for lieutenant governor in 1924. He was also chairman of the Democratic state convention in 1928, and he sought the party's

nomination for the U.S. Senate in 1932. In 1907 he purchased the *Corydon Democrat*, which became one of the state's most respected weekly newspapers and remains family owned and operated.

The political and publishing mantle then passed to Lew's son and Frank's father, Robert P. O'Bannon, who had a distinguished twenty-year career in the state senate, serving in such leadership positions as chairman of the State Budget Committee and chairman of the Senate Finance Committee. Upon his retirement from politics in 1969, Robert was rated by many as southern Indiana's most influential legislator since the Civil War days.

In 1970 it was Frank's turn. At age forty, he won the state senate seat that had been held by his father, and he insisted, in his characteristically scrupulous fashion, that it be done without trading on his father's name and reputation. "When I campaigned, I stressed my first name," he recalled. "My father never campaigned for me and I never asked him."

Frank Lewis O'Bannon was born on January 30, 1930, in Louisville, Kentucky, the third of five children of Robert and Rosella Faith Dropsey O'Bannon. They raised their family as Methodists and lived in a small house in Corydon, site of Indiana's first state capital and county seat of Harrison County. Frank was a good student and athlete and added to his growing renown when he saved his brother Bobby from drowning in Blue River as a teen. He was president of the class of 1948 at Corydon High School, became an Eagle Scout, and sang in a barbershop quartet.

O'Bannon earned a degree in government from Indiana University in 1952, then served two years in the air force as a first lieutenant. He returned to the state and earned a law degree at IU, then opened a private practice in Corydon in 1957. He worked for about a year at the family newspaper as a reporter and photographer while waiting for his law business to gain momentum. During this time he also married Judy Asmus, whom he had met at IU on a blind date. It was the perfect partnership. She shared his passion for public service, and over the years she became widely known and respected for her many civic and cultural activities, including work on early childhood development, historic preservation, the arts, and community involvement.

After being elected to the state legislature, O'Bannon quickly established himself as a rising star, doing it in his quiet and gentlemanly manner, demonstrating early on that he was to be a politician who preferred facts and figures to hell-raising speeches. It was also clear that he understood, as had his father before him, the importance of reaching across the aisle and working with the opposition. Simply put, he said, the "essence of the legislature is individuals getting along and getting things done." While still a freshman senator, O'Bannon moved into a leadership position as assistant minority floor leader, and when the Democrats gained control of the senate in 1977, he was named chairman of the finance committee. In handling the responsibility of helping decide how the state spent its money, O'Bannon exercised his power evenhandedly, refusing even to sponsor any general interest bills lest it be interpreted as a sign that he was trying to unduly exert his influence to get special projects passed for his district. The Democrats' majority position in the senate was short lived, and for the remainder of O'Bannon's time in the general assembly, from 1979 to 1988, he was minority floor leader.

O'Bannon liked to think of himself as a conservative Democrat, although his positions on issues defied precise pigeonholing. From the beginning of his service in the senate he was a strong advocate for tough environmental protection laws and championed the cause of opening up the legislative process to public scrutiny, stances of a more liberal bent. On the other hand, he had a conservative law-and-order side. When the U.S. Supreme Court ruled that all state statutes on death-penalty sentencing were unconstitutional, O'Bannon helped craft legislation to address the court's objections and restore capital punishment in Indiana. Also, as governor, he wanted to place a monument displaying the Ten Commandments on the statehouse lawn, an effort he abandoned when it was blocked by a court decision.

Speculation that the modest and earnest part-time legislator might be destined for bigger things surrounded O'Bannon almost from the beginning of his political career. He usually brushed such talk aside, saying that he preferred life in Corydon with his wife Judy and their three children, Polly, Jennifer, and Jonathan; his law practice; and his responsibilities with the newspaper publishing company. Still, he said, "You can't say absolutely no to the idea of running for a higher office because something might drop on you." For years Democratic Party leaders had urged O'Bannon to run for a statewide office, and the effort intensified as attention turned to the 1988 gubernatorial election. As early as 1985, O'Bannon was being touted by some as the party's best chance to win the governor's office for the first time since 1964. He finally acceded to the wishes of his supporters and announced his candidacy for governor, but so did the young and handsome Evan Bayh, the son of Indiana's former senator Birch Bayh.

Bayh, who had just run a surprisingly strong race in winning the office of secretary of state, immediately went to the front of the pack among Democratic hopefuls. He was the fresh face with wide name recognition and the advantage in fund-raising, and polls showed him beating O'Bannon in the primary by a substantial margin. After a meeting between the two candidates that Bayh requested, O'Bannon, ever the loyal party man, agreed to step aside and run on the Democratic ticket as lieutenant governor. In the fall, Bayh defeated the Republican candidate, John M. Mutz, who had been lieutenant governor, by a margin of 53 percent to 47 percent, a win made even more impressive considering that the Republican candidate for president, George H. W. Bush, beat his Democratic challenger, Michael Dukakis, in Indiana by 60 percent to 40 percent. Four years later, Bayh was overwhelmingly reelected, polling 62 percent of the vote compared with 37 percent for the Republican candidate, state Attorney General Linley E. Pearson.

In his eight years in the low-profile job of lieutenant governor, O'Bannon dutifully fulfilled his roles as president of the state senate and head of the departments of agriculture and commerce. During this period, he and his wife Judy bought and restored a house in a revitalized neighborhood near downtown Indianapolis and made it a welcoming place for children in the neighborhood. They also became active in a nearby church.

As Bayh neared the end of his two terms as governor, O'Bannon was the obvious choice to be his party's next gubernatorial candidate. He was unopposed for the nomination in 1996, and he chose Joseph E. Kernan, the popular mayor of South Bend, to run with him as lieutenant governor. The end of Bayh's reign also meant that O'Bannon would be leaving the senate, where he had spent a combined twenty-six years as a member and then as presiding officer. He was honored with a resolution signed by all fifty members and given the president's chair that he had used for eight years. Republicans joined their Democratic colleagues in saluting O'Bannon.

After being down in the polls by as much as eighteen percentage points at the start of the gubernatorial campaign in 1996, O'Bannon staged a remarkable comeback to defeat Republican Steve Goldsmith, then mayor of Indianapolis, by a margin of 51 percent to 47 percent. For its time, it was Indiana's most expensive race for governor, with the two candidates spending a combined $15 million, mostly for television advertising. One political writer, in assessing the race, believed Goldsmith erred in firing negative television spots at O'Bannon, suggesting they did not work "because it's almost impossible to find something negative about the man that would get voters stirred against him."

Four years later, Hoosier voters decided to keep O'Bannon in office, reelecting him and Kernan, by a margin of 57 percent to 42 percent for David McIntosh, who gave up his seat in Congress to make the race, and his running mate, state senator J. Murray Clark of Indianapolis. The win meant that O'Bannon, over the course of thirty years in politics, had never lost an election. Just as had been the case in 1996, attack ads did not work against the popular O'Bannon, and voters were not swayed by McIntosh's pledge to cut property taxes by 25 percent. And just like four years earlier, campaign spending by the two gubernatorial candidates reached record levels, close to $18 million, with a large share of the money raised going for television commercials.

In the nearly seven years he served as governor, O'Bannon put children and education among his highest priorities, a point he underscored by inviting to his inauguration in 1997 all fourth graders in Indiana, which is when students study Indiana history. More than twelve thousand were expected to attend, but near-zero temperatures on inauguration day kept many away from the ceremony, held outside the statehouse, the first such outdoor event since Governor Paul V. McNutt's in 1933. Four years later, the occasion moved indoors to the RCA Dome and again the invitation went out to a new group of Hoosier fourth graders; this time twenty-five thousand attended.

As O'Bannon assumed office in January 1997, advances in public education and support for children's programs as well as progress on a host of other pressing needs appeared well within reach due to the state's strong financial condition, and it was expected to remain healthy for some time to come. Unlike his two previous predecessors, Robert D. Orr and Bayh, who confronted recessions early in their terms, O'Bannon's administration had, at least in the beginning, almost an embarrassment of riches. The budget surplus, which resulted from soaring national and state economies and the thriftiness of the Bayh administration, was about $1.6 billion when O'Bannon took office, and there were projections that it could reach as high as $2.7 billion by mid-2001. That rosy forecast never materialized. Instead, shortly after O'Bannon's second term began, the nation entered a recession, exacerbated by the aftershocks of September 11, 2001, causing a downturn in the Indiana's economic health and shifting attention in the state capital from surpluses to deficits, from spending more to less, and from cutting taxes to raising them.

Back in the salad-and-surplus days of the late 1990s, however, it seemed that practically all things were possible. Naturally, O'Bannon's success in advancing his ideas on how best to use the windfall depended on forging agreements with legislators, and on that front, there was bound to be disharmony, especially since the governor faced a divided general assembly. During his time in office, Republicans dominated the senate, and the house was either split fifty-fifty between the parties or Democrats held a slight edge. Despite their differences, though, there was general agreement between the administration and the legislature that the state budget in the waning years of the twentieth century was strong enough to afford the rare opportunity of increased spending and tax cuts. When the state's cash surplus showed a balance of $2 billion at the end of the fiscal year 1998, O'Bannon said, "I'm confident that we will be able to do two things: No. 1, have tax cuts—property tax cuts. And No. 2, make some targeted investments in Indiana's future, particularly in education."

As O'Bannon entered the final year of his first term, he could point to progress in these two areas as well as in others. He noted, for example, in his state-of-the-state address in 2000 that "we have enacted $1.3 billion in tax cuts for Hoosier families and businesses since 1997," and he cited the start of a system of community colleges, which besides "their tremendous information-age potential . . . are also a great resource for lifelong learning." In his speech O'Bannon also hailed action on education reform, in particular the Education Roundtable he established with the Republican Superintendent of Public Instruction, Suellen Reed. The roundtable, which included teachers and members of the business community, developed curriculum standards for elementary and secondary schools and held the schools accountable for meeting them.

In addition, O'Bannon's first term led to increased funding for schools and universities as well as for highways and other public-works projects, five hundred more police officers, health insurance coverage for children from low-income families, and the creation of the office of Public Access Counselor, which fielded inquiries and complaints involving access to public records and open meetings. Through a bipartisan effort with legislators, O'Bannon was also able to use a portion of the state's share of the national tobacco settlement to fund a prescription drug program for seniors and an initiative on smoking prevention and education.

While O'Bannon relished the idea of bipartisanship, it was not always possible, of course, and breakdowns were inevitable. One such collapse occurred when the governor failed to win legislative approval for his number-one priority, the funding of full-day kindergarten. When his $111 million proposal went down to defeat in the 1999 session, the normally mild-mannered chief executive angrily blamed senate Republicans, claiming they had put politics ahead of children. Republicans, who had crafted a counter-plan of block grants that would have let districts spend the money on all-day kindergarten or other programs, in turn criticized the governor for refusing to compromise.

Another round of rancor was touched off when O'Bannon, using for the first time authority granted to governors by the legislature in 1981, suspended Indiana's 5 percent sales tax on gasoline when prices during the summer of 2000 shot up to $2 a gallon. The action, which saved motorists upwards of ten cents a gallon, was branded by some Republicans as a political move, coming as it did just a few months prior to the gubernatorial election. His opponent in that election, though, Congressman McIntosh, called it "the right thing to do," adding, "I applaud his decision to do this." Other events during O'Bannon's tenure that caused some political wrangling included the revelation that the person hired for a top position at the state's public employees retirement fund had a criminal record; a massive fish kill in a fifty-mile stretch of the White River from Anderson to Indianapolis; and problems of inadequate care at two state facilities for the developmentally disabled.

A break in partisan sniping came during O'Bannon's second term when the administration and legislators addressed mounting budget problems and court-mandated changes in the method of property-tax assessment with a sweeping deficit-reduction and tax-restructuring bill. The legislation, crafted during a special session of the general assembly in mid-2002, increased sales, cigarette, and gasoline taxes to generate the revenue necessary to fix the state's unbalanced budget and to cover the cost of tax relief for homeowners and businesses. Many business leaders praised the measure, believing its business-friendly mixture of tax reductions and incentives would improve the state's business climate and spur economic development. O'Bannon followed approval of this legislation with Energize Indiana, his long-range proposal, which was passed in a modified form by the general assembly, to fund and support high-tech initiatives that would diversify the state's economy and create additional employment opportunities for Hoosiers.

After passage of the legislation, O'Bannon set out on what was to be a twelve-city tour throughout the state to promote the plan. Just days after his death, one of the economic forums that had been scheduled went on as planned. O'Bannon's successor said the decision to hold the event was a conscious one. "He would have wanted it to go on," Kernan said.

Portrait by Michael Chelich (2001), Governors' Portraits Collection, Indiana Historical Bureau, State of Indiana.

FOR FURTHER READING

Ashley, Bob. "Gov. O'Bannon Must Watch Toes During Statehouse 'Delicate Dance.'" *South Bend Tribune,* November 10, 1996.

Colwell, Jack. "Democratic Trend Remarkable and Inevitable." *South Bend Tribune,* January 12, 1997.

"Frank O'Bannon Strives Hard to Be Loyal Opposition." *Louisville Times,* February 19, 1973.

Smith, Mike. "Indiana Gov. Frank O'Bannon Dies, Five Days after Suffering Stroke." The Associated Press, September 13, 2003, http://web.lexis-nexis.com/.

Stedman, Lesley. "The Governor's Race: O'Bannon's Theme: There's More to Do." *Louisville Courier-Journal,* October 29, 2000.

Weidenbener, Lesley Stedman. "He Felt a Private Duty to Offer Public Service." *Louisville Courier-Journal,* September 20, 2003.

O'Bannon's gubernatorial papers are in the Indiana State Archives, Indianapolis, and there are O'Bannon files in the Indiana Room, New Albany–Floyd County Public Library.

Joseph E. Kernan

September 13, 2003–January 10, 2005

JOHN E. FINDLING

THE SEVENTEEN-YEAR POLITICAL CAREER OF JOSEPH E. Kernan, who became the state's chief executive officer upon the death of Frank L. O'Bannon, was marked by his ability as a compromiser and consensus-builder, along with a keen interest in economic development issues. These qualities served him well as mayor of South Bend, lieutenant governor, and governor.

Kernan was born to Joseph E., an automobile parts salesman, and Marion Powers Kernan in Chicago on April 8, 1946. He was the oldest of nine children. The Kernan family moved to South Bend when Joe was in the fifth grade, and he graduated from St. Joseph High School in 1964. A Roman Catholic, Kernan earned a degree in government at the University of Notre Dame in 1968. The following year he enlisted in the navy and completed training as a flight officer. He was sent to Vietnam, where he was a reconnaissance attack navigator. His assignment took him on twenty-six missions over North Vietnam and Laos until his plane was shot down on May 7, 1972.

Kernan ejected from the plane and parachuted to the ground, where he was surrounded by North Vietnamese and made a prisoner of war. He spent ten months and twenty days in captivity, part of that time at the notorious "Hanoi Hilton," an urban prison camp where many captured American pilots were held. Released on March 27, 1973, he was later awarded the Combat Action Ribbon, two Purple Hearts, the Distinguished Flying Cross, and other commendations. He remained on active duty until December 1974.

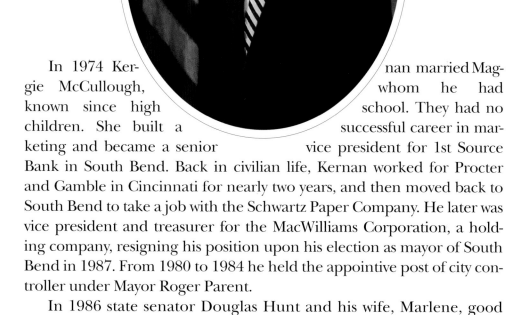

In 1974 Kernan married Maggie McCullough, whom he had known since high school. They had no children. She built a successful career in marketing and became a senior vice president for 1st Source Bank in South Bend. Back in civilian life, Kernan worked for Procter and Gamble in Cincinnati for nearly two years, and then moved back to South Bend to take a job with the Schwartz Paper Company. He later was vice president and treasurer for the MacWilliams Corporation, a holding company, resigning his position upon his election as mayor of South Bend in 1987. From 1980 to 1984 he held the appointive post of city controller under Mayor Roger Parent.

In 1986 state senator Douglas Hunt and his wife, Marlene, good friends of Kernan, urged him to run for mayor. He decided to try electoral politics and ran in the Democratic primary against Richard Jasinski, a well-known city commissioner. Jasinski, who considered himself the heavy favorite, ignored Kernan's request for a debate and focused his campaign on the controversial record of outgoing Mayor Parent, under criticism because of the construction of an expensive new baseball stadium. Kernan assembled a volunteer force of a thousand, campaigned quietly but effectively and exploited his popularity on the city's east side, and won the primary election by 473 votes out a total of more than 20,000. In the general election, Kernan faced a young, popular Republican, Carl Baxmeyer, a former aide to

U. S. Representative John Hiler. Both had similar ideas about city government, and the campaign revolved around their backgrounds and experience, as well as their links to unpopular politicians—Kernan to Parent and Baxmeyer to Hiler. On November 3, South Bend voters chose Kernan, giving him 53 percent of the vote in the closest mayoral race in thirty-two years.

In 1991 and 1995 Kernan was reelected with 76 and 82 percent of the vote respectively, as the Republican Party ran relatively weak candidates against the popular mayor. His easy reelections and candidacy for a top statewide position were clear testimony to the effective work Kernan did as mayor of South Bend. He made himself available to the people by instituting a monthly Mayor's Night In/Mayor's Night Out program, an idea borrowed from Mayor Jerry Abramson of Louisville, Kentucky.

Kernan emphasized economic development by focusing on the revitalization of the Studebaker Corridor, removing dilapidated buildings that had been vacant since the departure of the automobile company twenty-five years earlier, and he strongly supported Airport 2010, a plan to place light industry and other commercial activity on a 2,300-acre site near the Michiana Regional Airport. By his 1995 campaign, Kernan could claim that the city was in sound financial condition, that thirty-four more police officers patrolled the streets, and that the police department had been computerized. All of this was done without imposing a county option income tax, although Kernan spoke frequently of the benefits that extra revenue might provide.

When O'Bannon asked Kernan to join him in the 1996 governor's race, Kernan had served as mayor of South Bend longer than anyone else. He had been asked to run for the U.S. Senate against Representative Dan Coats in 1989 but had declined. In this instance, however, he was attracted by the idea of running with O'Bannon, with whom he had worked on economic development issues when O'Bannon was lieutenant governor. The O'Bannon-Kernan ticket was marked by compatibility between the two candidates, geographical diversity, and the factor of Kernan's urban expertise, important because the Republican candidate for governor was Steve Goldsmith, the mayor of Indianapolis.

Goldsmith had been a popular and highly visible mayor of Indianapolis, while O'Bannon, as lieutenant governor, had had few opportunities to claim the public spotlight. Political analysts predicted a close election, but the O'Bannon-Kernan team won with 51 percent of the vote to 47 percent for the Republican ticket. In the 2000 election O'Bannon and Kernan were reelected by a wider margin over U.S. Representative David McIntosh and his running mate, J. Murray Clark, winning 57 percent of the vote to just 41 percent for the Republicans.

As lieutenant governor from January 1997 until September 2003, Kernan was also head of the department of commerce and commissioner of agriculture. In these roles, he was instrumental in forming the bipartisan Agricultural Crisis Working Group to support farmers in economic distress, and he created an Insurance Industry Working Group to enhance Indiana's already strong insurance industry. In addition, as director of the commerce department, Kernan helped bring new industries into the state and helped others expand, although this process slowed after the beginning of an economic slump in late 2000. He also heightened Indiana's presence in the area of international trade through increased exports of the state's products. Finally, he chaired the 21st Century Research and Technology Fund that subsidized new initiatives in science and integrated technology.

Perhaps the area of greatest significance for Kernan was tax restructuring, an initiative he spearheaded after court rulings mandated changes in the existing property tax assessment system. A reassessment plan implemented in 2001 threatened to raise property taxes substantially, and thus, tax restructuring sought also to reduce these taxes while adopting other revenue measures to maintain the traditional manufacturing and agricultural sectors and increase the number of technology-related jobs. In June 2002 the legislature approved a tax-restructuring bill that lowered property taxes, raised the sales tax, and altered the business-tax structure designed to attract new industry. The measure "was regarded by folks on both sides of the partisan aisle as a smart, well-crafted package of reforms for Indiana."

Although it had become almost an Indiana political tradition that the lieutenant governor run for governor following the governor's second term, Kernan surprised Indiana Democrats when he announced in December 2002 that he would not run for governor in 2004. Although the O'Bannon-Kernan administration's popularity had declined in 2001 and 2002 because of the recession and the state's growing budget deficit, even Republicans believed that Kernan's decision was made for personal, family-related reasons rather than the prospect of losing the election.

But Kernan's world was turned upside down with the unexpected death of O'Bannon in September 2003. Kernan was credited for working effectively with leaders of the legislature and judicial branches to provide for a smooth transition of executive authority. As the new governor, Kernan selected Katherine (Kathy) Davis, a former state budget director and the Indianapolis city controller, as lieutenant governor, the first woman to hold that office. At the same time, Democrats were strongly urging Kernan to reconsider his decision not to run for governor in 2004. Finally, on November 7, 2003, Kernan announced that he would run for governor in his own right in 2004, with Davis as his running mate. Two announced Democratic candidates quickly withdrew from the race, leaving the nomination uncontested for Kernan. Republicans acknowledged Kernan's advantage as an incumbent but were quick to point out that Indiana's economic performance over the past three years would not be easy to defend.

Kernan said that he would not be just a caretaker governor while completing the sixteen months of O'Bannon's term, and he and Davis worked on several initiatives during those months. In the realm of education, he advanced the Community College of Indiana program begun under O'Bannon and attempted without success to persuade the legislature to approve a voluntary full-day kindergarten program. He also worked with Superintendent of Public Instruction Suellen Reed to increase high school graduation requirements for Indiana students.

By early 2004 there was still more to be done, and Kernan's state-of-the-state speech in January suggested the need for further property tax relief and other measures to create new jobs.

Kernan could take some credit for an economic rebound in the state during 2004. He worked with the legislature to make the business climate, including the corporate tax structure, more attractive to new businesses as well as to existing companies, bringing new jobs to the state. He created the Opportunity Indiana program, designed to award more state business to Indiana companies, and Indiana@Work, an innovative job-training program. Better economic conditions and fiscal responsibility at the state level decreased the budget deficit by half without a tax hike.

As more and more Indiana National Guard members were being called to active duty, Kernan worked with Adjutant General Martin Umbarger to ease the financial and social dislocation of foreign deployment on individuals and families. Kernan was also the first governor in forty-eight years to grant clemency in capital cases. His decision to do so in two cases contributed to the national debate over the justice and fairness of capital punishment, and Kernan called on the legislature to examine Indiana's capital-punishment system.

In the race for governor in 2004, Kernan was matched against Republican Mitchell E. Daniels, who was director of the Office of Management and Budget under President George W. Bush until he resigned in 2003 to run for governor. Daniels, in defeating Kernan by a surprisingly large margin of 53 percent to 45 percent, became the first Republican governor in Indiana in sixteen years. Republicans also won control of both houses of the legislature. Kernan returned to South Bend after leaving office and indicated in an interview in early 2005 that his career in elective politics was over, saying, "I just don't see myself running for office again." Reflecting on his brief tenure as governor, Kernan said, "What I am most proud of is the way we worked our way through the transition after Governor O'Bannon fell ill and passed away. There was no partisanship. There was cooperation . . . to make decisions during a difficult time."

Portrait by Mark Dillman (2005), Governors' Portraits Collection, Indiana Historical Bureau, State of Indiana.

FOR FURTHER READING

Fort Wayne Journal Gazette, January 2, 2005.

Indianapolis Star, November 6, 1996, December 10, 2002, October 10, 2003.

Louisville Courier-Journal, November 9, 2000.

South Bend Tribune, May 3, 6, November 1, 4, 1987, May 5, November 3, 8, 1991, November 5, 8, 1995, June 1, 1996, December 10, 2002, November 7, 2003, January 14, 2004.

Kernan's papers are in the Indiana State Archives, Indianapolis. Kernan's life and career are best studied through contemporary Indiana newspapers, especially the *South Bend Tribune* and the *Indianapolis Star.* In addition, biographical information may be found at http://www.statelib.lib .in.us/ and the Bulletin Broadfaxing Network, a digest of Indiana newspaper articles, available through http://web.lexis-nexis.com/.

Mitchell E. Daniels Jr.

January 10, 2005–current

JIM SHELLA

MITCHELL E. DANIELS JR. RAN FOR GOVERNOR PROMISING
to deliver change. In his first several months in office, he produced
sweeping changes ranging from the privatization of government services to the closing of license branches and the adoption of daylight
saving time. Along the way, Daniels, a Republican, earned a reputation
for being independent and strong willed, with a knack for generating
controversy that sometimes led to criticism even from more conservative members of his own party, as well as the Republican Speaker of
the Indiana House of Representatives.

Daniels's election itself constituted change. He restored Republican control of the Indiana statehouse for the first time in sixteen years
after saying repeatedly on the campaign trail that "every garden needs
weeding every sixteen years or so." He defeated conservative lobbyist
Eric Miller easily in the GOP primary and then won 53 percent of the
vote against Democrat Joseph E. Kernan. Kernan was the incumbent,
although he had served little more than a year after succeeding Frank
L. O'Bannon, who died in office. The last time an incumbent Indiana governor lost was in 1892 when Claude Matthews defeated Ira Joy
Chase, who had succeeded Alvin P. Hovey after Hovey died in office
in 1891.

The 2004 race was the most expensive political campaign in Indiana history, as the candidates spent a combined $23 million in a battle
that sometimes got personal. Democrats tried unsuccessfully to make an
issue out of the fact that, as a college student, Daniels spent a night in jail

in 1971 follow-
related arrest.
him to defend
corporate board that
IPALCO Enterprises, par- ent company of Indianapolis
ing a marijuana-
They also forced
his service on the
approved the sale of
Power and Light, a transaction that led to a drastic drop in stock prices, resulting in the loss of millions of dollars for shareholders and in retirement savings for some employees. Democrats also wanted voters to believe that Daniels, because of his service as an executive at Eli Lilly and Company, was responsible for high prescription drug prices. Through it all, Daniels stuck to his message, promising new jobs and change.

In winning, Daniels followed a unique campaign strategy that made use of a donated recreational vehicle that served as the candidate's mobile office as he toured the state full time. The vehicle, known as "RV-1," carried Daniels to multiple stops in all ninety-two counties, where he often appeared in a plaid shirt with the sleeves rolled up and sometimes a baseball cap. A half-hour "reality show" produced by the campaign and aired on television stations statewide chronicled his life on the road and served to reinforce the message that Daniels would represent the entire state. His campaign also made effective use of "My Man Mitch," a phrase coined by President George W. Bush that was used for ubiquitous green T-shirts, bumper stickers, and yard signs.

This effort to appear as a man of the people overshadowed a background that includes an Ivy League education and service to two presidents, as well as a career in business that made him a wealthy man. After selling all of his stock holdings to accept a job in the Bush administration, Daniels reported an income of over $27 million on his 2001 tax return.

Daniels, who is of Syrian ancestry, was born on April 7, 1949, in Monongahela, Pennsylvania, to Mitchell E. and Dorothy Wilkes Daniels. His father was a pharmaceutical salesman. The family also lived in Georgia and Tennessee before settling in Indiana when Daniels was in grade school. Daniels attended public schools before heading to Princeton University, where he earned a bachelor's degree in 1971. He then returned to Indianapolis to work in the office of Mayor Richard G. Lugar. It was there that he met Cheri Herman, who worked in the parks department. They were married in 1978, divorced in 1993, and remarried in 1997. They have four daughters: Meagan, Melissa, Meredith, and Margaret.

When Lugar won election to the U.S. Senate in 1976, he took Daniels along to Washington, D.C., to serve as his chief of staff. It was the first of a series of moves between Indianapolis and Washington for Daniels, who became the chief political adviser to President Ronald Reagan and the administration's liaison to state and local officials. While in Washington, Daniels earned a law degree from Georgetown University. He returned to Indiana in 1987 to serve as executive vice president and chief operating officer at the Hudson Institute, a conservative think tank, before joining Eli Lilly and Company, where he held positions as president of North American pharmaceutical operations and senior vice president of corporate strategy and policy. In 2001 he returned to Washington. This time Daniels served as director of the Office of Management and Budget under President Bush, who called him "the Blade" for his zeal to cut spending.

Because of that reputation and the nickname, some of Daniels's first moves as governor caught some conservatives by surprise. In his inaugural address, Daniels compared the job of revitalizing the Indiana economy to a barn raising. He said, "Those to whom life in Indiana has been the most kind must be willing to give back in accordance with their good fortune." Days later, in his first state-of-the-state address, it became clear that he was calling for a tax increase, a hike of 1 percent in the state income tax for those who earn more than $100,000 a year.

Even though Republicans controlled both houses in the general assembly, the plan never came to a vote. Instead, Daniels had to back down on his demands to balance the state budget in one year and to freeze school spending. In the meantime, the *Wall Street Journal* editorialized against the tax hike proposal, calling the governor "Mitch the Knife," and antitax lobbyists in Washington accused Daniels of being a traitor to their cause. Daniels eventually signed a two-year, $24 billion budget that contained a deficit in the first year and was balanced in the second.

One tax increase Daniels proposed, however, did pass. This one involved higher taxes on food and beverages in Indianapolis and surrounding counties to help finance a new professional football stadium for the Indianapolis Colts and higher hotel and rental-car taxes in Indianapolis to pay for the city's convention center expansion. Daniels took credit for saving a project launched by Indianapolis mayor Bart Peterson. Peterson's funding plan had failed, and because the Daniels plan also included state, rather than city, ownership of the new facilities, hard feelings between the Democratic mayor and the governor resulted.

There was probably no move by the new governor, however, that created more hard feelings than his plan to adopt daylight saving time. The controversial proposal forced the governor to use all of his powers of persuasion; it passed the general assembly by a single vote after failing twice. That started a new controversy over a possible change in time zones, with Daniels declining to recommend change. During the campaign, Daniels said he preferred a switch to the central time zone but was also open to the state being on eastern daylight time. In any event, he saw the time change as a necessary component to improving the state's economy.

As governor, Daniels continued using what worked for him as a candidate. A new recreational vehicle became his official mobile office, and he began holding town-hall meetings across the state on a regular basis. He stayed in people's homes while on the road, just as he did during the campaign, and work began on a new "reality show."

However, even the RV became a source of controversy as Democrats accused the governor of using it for political purposes in violation of state ethics rules on the use of state resources. He took the RV to a fund-raiser for state Representative Troy Woodruff in Vincennes. A report issued by the state's inspector general said the governor did nothing wrong in taking the RV to the event.

There were other controversies involving the first family's decision to live in their Geist Reservoir home rather than the official governor's residence on Meridian Street, and the governor's seeming intolerance for those who disagree with him. At mid-session in the general assembly he accused house Democrats of "car bombing" his agenda.

Yet, the hallmark of Daniels's service during his first year in office was change. He approved the closing of dozens of license branches over the objection of lawmakers, which prompted the house Speaker, Brian Bosma, to write him a letter warning of a "political buzz saw" and urging him to hold off. The governor's answer: "No." He split the Family and Social Services Administration into two agencies by creating the Department of Child Services. He revamped the Department of Commerce into a public/private partnership and created new rules for local school construction.

Daniels privatized prisons as well as food service in some prisons and mental hospitals, ended collective bargaining for state employees, and launched the first foreign trade mission to east Asia in eight years. He also created a program aimed at getting Hoosiers in better shape and another meant to deliver low-cost drugs to low-income seniors.

The rapid change produced a backlash among Hoosiers, too, and a relatively low approval rating. Survey USA, a national polling firm, pegged the governor's approval at just 42 percent in mid-May 2005, eleven points below his election percentage. That number increased to 47 percent in mid-July, but still left Daniels in the bottom half of governors nationwide in terms of approval ratings. The governor expressed no concern, and his staff repeatedly told reporters that they were not consulting polls.

Governor Mitch Daniels Press Photo.

FOR FURTHER READING

Lyman, Rick. "Focus on Indiana's Governor, a Tax-cutter Who Has Become a Tax-Raiser." *New York Times*, February 20, 2005.

Schneider, Mary Beth. "Daniels Welcomes Variety of Views, but Insiders Agree He's Calling the Shots." *Indianapolis Star*, April 19, 2005.

Weidenbener, Lesley Stedman. "Daniels Growing into Governor Role." *Louisville Courier-Journal*, May 9, 2005.

Index

Abbott, John A., 246
Abolition, 114, 127
Abortion, 349
Abramson, Jerry, 396
Adair, John A. M., 252
Adams, John, 18, 19, 28
Adams, John Quincy, 49, 61, 63, 66, 71
Ade, Ella. *See* McCray, Ella Ade
Ade, George, 263, 286
Ade, John, 261
African Americans, 149, 160, 163, 192,
    232, 264; colonization of, 65, 114,
    116; and citizenship of, 116; and
    civil rights for, 148, 157, 174–75,
    341–42; and military service, 214; and
    lynching, 218–19, 286
Agricultural Crisis Working Group, 397
Agriculture, 117, 118, 168, 172, 214,
    397
Airport 2010, p. 396
Alcohol tax, 356
Alcoholic Beverages Control Act, 295
Alexander, Sarah. *See* Dunning, Sarah
    Alexander
Allegheny County (PA), 29
Amalgamated Association of Street and
    Railway Employees, 247
American Bible Society, 102

American Federation of State, County
    and Municipal Employees, 379
American Federation of Teachers, 379
American Legion, 14, 290, 291, 317,
    322, 324, 325, 327, 328
American Relief Administration, 256
American Woman Suffrage Association,
    155
American-Russian Chamber of
    Commerce, 257
Anderson, 217, 221, 303, 391
Anderson, Deliah. *See* Boon, Deliah
    Anderson
Ann Arbor (MI), 368
Annandale (VA), 329
Annapolis (MD), 251
Ansden, Mary. *See* Hammond, Mary
    Ansden
Anti-Masonic Party, 25
Anti-Nebraska Democrats, 124
Anti-Saloon League, 229, 276, 277
Appomattox, 147
Arizona Republic, 257
Arlington National Cemetery, 298
Armstrong, John, 24
Army of the Northwest. *See* Northwest
    Army
Asbury College. *See* DePauw University

Asbury University. *See* DePauw University

Ashford, Ellen Lane. *See* Dunning, Ellen
  Lane Ashford

Asmus, Judy. *See* O'Bannon, Judy Asmus

Atlanta campaign, 193

Atomic research, 349

Audio-Dynamics Corporation, 329

Automobile plants, 373, 379

Ayrshire Colleries Corporation, 257

Backous, Mary Josephine. *See* Ralston,
  Mary Josephine Backous

Bain, Katherine. *See* Branch, Katherine
  Bain

Baker, Albert, 158, 159

Baker, Catherine Winterheimer, 152

Baker, Charlotte Frances Chute, 153

Baker, Conrad, 152

Baker, Conrad (governor), 110, 132,
  152–59, 162; (illus.), 153

Baker, Matilda Escon Sommers, 153

Baker, Newton D., 254

Baker, Thaddeus, 153

Baker, William, 153, 154, 158

Baker & Daniels, 152, 159, 162

Baker, Hord, and Hendricks, 158, 162

Ballot reform, 180

Baltimore (MD), 110

Baltimore and Ohio Railroad, 171

Baltimore Rail Road Company, 63

Bank of the United States, 45, 71

Banks and banking, 44, 45, 75, 76, 114,
  118, 133, 160, 176, 206, 317

Barbee, Clarissa. *See* Jennings, Clarissa
  Barbee

Barrington (IL), 198, 199, 200

Bath County (KY), 138

Baton Rouge (LA), 36

Battle Creek (MI), 275

Battle of Fallen Timbers, 19, 36

Battle of Monmouth, 34

Battle of Point Pleasant, 34

Battle of the Thames, 14, 23

Battle of Tippecanoe, 14, 23, 24, 30

Baxmeyer, Carl, 395, 396

Baxter bill, 163

Bayh, Birch, 342, 354, 362, 373, 376,
  387

Bayh, Birch Evans, III. *See* Bayh, Evan

Bayh, Birch Evans, IV, 377

Bayh, Evan, 5, 8, 11, 12, 13, 15, 373,
  376–83, 387, 389; (illus.), 377

Bayh, Marvella, 377

Bayh, Nicholas, 377

Bayh, Susan Breshears, 377

Ben-Hur, 81

Benton, Thomas Hart, 50

Berkeley (plantation), 18

Berlin (Germany), 120

Berryville (VA), 70

Bethel (KY), 204

Beveridge, Albert J., 221, 225, 244, 247,
  248, 251, 252, 277

Bigger, Ellen Williamson, 89

Bigger, John, 89

Bigger, Samuel, 85, 88–93, 97, 98;
  (illus.), 89

Bingham, Summers, Welsh and
  Spearman, 377

Blackford, Isaac, 62, 66, 67

Blackford County, 300, 301, 305, 372

Blake, Thomas H., 50

Bledsoe, Pamela. *See* Lane, Pamela
  Bledsoe

Bloomington, 95, 106, 107, 109, 110,
  111, 112, 119, 120, 289, 322, 337

Blue River, 386

Board of Internal Improvements, 74,
  78, 84

Board of Visitors, 187

Boise (ID), 229

Booker, Esther. *See* Ray, Esther Booker

Boon, Deliah Anderson, 50
Boon, Jesse, 48
Boon, Kessiah, 48
Boon, Ratliff, 48–50, 60; (illus.), 49
Boone County (IN), 212, 246
Boone County (KY), 70, 184
Bossert, Walter, 283
Botetourt County Committee of
   Correspondence, 34
Bowen, Carol Lynn (Hahn) Flosenzier
   Mikesell, 366
Bowen, Elizabeth (Beth) Anna Agnes
   Steinmann, 361, 362, 365
Bowen, Otis R., 1, 6, 7, 8, 10, 343, 352,
   354, 356, 360–67, 370, 371, 377;
   (illus.), 361
Bowen, Pearl Irene Wright, 360, 362
Bowen, Robert (Rob), 362, 377
Bowen, Rose Crothers Hochstetler,
   366
Bowen, Vernie, 360, 361, 362
Boxing, 271
Boy Scouts of America, 350, 370, 386
Boyd, Kate. *See* Mount, Kate Boyd
Braddock's Field (PA), 31
Branch, Alice Parks, 268
Branch, Elliott F., 268
Branch, Emmett, 10, 268–72; (illus.), 269
Branch, Katherine Bain, 269, 270
Branch Grain and Seed Company, 271
Branigin, Elba, 347
Branigin, Josephine Mardis, 348
Branigin, Robert, 348
Branigin, Roger D., 6, 346–51, 358;
   (illus.), 347
Branigin, Roger D., Jr., 348
Branigin, Zula, 347
Brattleboro (VT), 132
Brazil, 322, 323, 324, 329
Brazil High School, 322
Bremen, 362, 366

Breshears, Susan. *See* Bayh, Susan
   Breshears
Bridges, 339
Bright, Jesse D., 12, 95, 97, 100, 102,
   114, 118, 119, 120, 128, 138, 144
Brook, 260, 263
Brooks, Preston, 126
Brookville, 45, 60, 62, 70, 72, 80, 81, 90,
   132, 365
Brookville Hotel, 70
Brookville Repository, 66
Brown, Hiram, 185
Brown, Ignatius, 185
Brown, John, 130
Brown, Maude L. *See* Schricker, Maude
   L. Brown
Brown, Minerva. *See* Porter, Minerva
   Brown
Brown County, 107
Browne, Thomas M., 163
Brownstown, 336
Bryan, William Jennings, 208, 213, 226
Buchanan, James, 110, 120, 129, 192
Budget Advisory Committee, 4
Bulen, L. Keith, 354, 357, 363
Burbank, Lucinda. *See* Morton, Lucinda
   Burbank
Burbridge, Harriet. *See* Wright, Harriet
   Burbridge
Bureau of Motor Vehicles, 320, 357,
   358, 372
Burns Harbor, 347, 349
Burrous, Kermit, 6
Bush, Edgar, 264
Bush, George H. W., 373, 388
Bush, George W., 382, 399, 403, 404
Butler, Charles, 100
Byrd, Richard, 284

Calhoun, John C., 240
California, 200

Calkins, William, 178
Camp Bedford Forrest (TN), 323–24
Camp Travis (TX), 269
Campbell, John L., 187
Campbell County (KY), 70
Canada, 343
Canals, 46, 56, 62–63, 73, 82, 84, 88, 90,
    92, 96, 97, 100, 168
Canary Islands, 359
Canby, Israel T., 66
Cannelton, 339
Canonsburg (PA), 40, 53
Capehart, Homer E., 313, 318, 320, 322,
    325, 334
Capital punishment, 327, 349, 387, 399
Carr, John, 46, 67
Carter, Jimmy, 321
Carvel, Elbert, 314
Cass, Lewis, 46, 63, 66
Castle, Rhoda Jane. *See* Chase, Rhoda
    Jane Castle
Cemeteries, 50, 68, 85, 102, 111, 134,
    172, 188, 215, 241, 248, 266, 314, 351,
    373
Center Valley, 246
Centerville, 67, 68, 140
Central Newspapers, 257
Centre College (KY), 204
Chambersburgh (PA), 152
Champaign (IL), 224
Champion Hill, battle of, 193
Chapel Hill (NC), 106
Charles City County (VA), 18
Charles Town (WV), 130
Charleston (SC), 35, 110
Charlestown, 42, 46
Chase, Benjamin, 198
Chase, Ira J., 14, 198–202, 206; (illus.),
    199
Chase, Lorinda Mix, 198
Chase, Rhoda Jane Castle, 199, 200

Chattahoochee River (GA), 212
Cheney, John J., 251
Chester County (PA), 175
Chicago, 136, 188, 198, 199, 202, 208,
    350, 384, 394
Chicago World's Fair. *See* Columbian
    Exposition (1893)
Chickamauga, battle of, 211–12
China, 353
Christian Church, 198, 202
Christian Publishing Company, 358
Chrysler, 379
Chute, Charlotte Frances. *See* Baker,
    Charlotte Frances Chute
Cigarette tax, 339, 356, 381, 392
Cilin II (sailboat), 359
Cincinnati, 19, 23, 53, 62, 68, 71, 80, 94,
    149, 176
Citizens Bank, 176
City Securities, 257
Civil rights, 349; and African Americans,
    157, 341–42
Civil Rights Act of 1964, p. 342
Civil War, 8–9, 14, 110, 112, 140, 141–
    42, 144, 146, 152, 160, 170, 176, 186,
    192–93, 199, 211, 250, 297; Indiana
    troops raised for, 142–43, 154;
    veterans of, 148, 157, 198, 216
Civil Works Administration, 296
Claiborne, William C. C., 36
Clark, George Rogers, 103
Clark, J. Murray, 389, 397
Clark County, 30, 41, 42, 43
Clay, Henry, 24, 50, 61, 70, 72, 137
Clay County, 160, 206, 323, 324
Cleveland, Grover, 11, 137, 161, 180,
    181, 194, 201
Clinton (IN), 102, 204, 208
Clinton (NY), 125
Clinton, Hillary Rodham, 381
Clinton County, 246

Coal mines, 206, 214, 297
Coats, Dan, 396
Codification of laws, 52, 56, 65, 66
Colfax, Schuyler, 180
Colombia, 24
Colonization movement, 65
Columbia City, 234, 316, 317, 318, 321
Columbian Exposition (1893), 202
Columbus, 130, 132, 133
Commission on State Tax and
  Financing Policy, 339
Commission on the Conservation and
  Administration of Public Domain, 257
Committee of Mediation, 171
Committee of Public Safety, 171
Committee on Public Lands, 20
Commons, John R., 251
Communism, 324, 325, 330, 332
Community College of Indiana, 398
Compromise of 1850, pp. 117, 119
Connersville, 245
Conrad, Larry, 364
Constitutional Revision Committee, 335
Continental Army, 34–35
Cook, Caroline C. See Willard, Caroline
  C. Cook
Cook, John E., 130
Cook, Louisa. See Wright, Louisa Cook
Cooke, Jay, 160
Coolidge, Calvin, 276
CORE 40, p. 381
Cornfield Conference, 318
Cornstalk (chief), 34
Cornwallis, Charles, 35
Corporate income tax, 356
Corregidor, 353
Corydon, 22, 31, 37, 43, 45, 46, 52, 54,
  218, 385, 386, 387
Corydon Democrat, 385
Corydon High School, 386
County option income tax, 396

County School Reorganization
  Committee, 341
Covington, 82
Craig, Bernard C., 322, 323
Craig, Clo Branson, 322
Craig, George N., 5, 7, 10, 14, 322–29,
  332, 334; (illus.), 323
Craig, John, 324
Craig, Kathryn Louisa Hilliger, 323
Craig, Margery, 324
Craven, Jennie. See Ralston, Jennie
  Craven
Cravens, James, 115, 119
Crawford County, 195
Crawfordsville, 138, 139, 215, 233, 234
Creek (tribe), 35
Creighton, Hobart, 313, 320
Crittenden, John J., 118
Crittenden Compromise, 133
Crooked Lake, 321
Cross-cut Canal, 90
"Cross of Gold," 208
Crown Hill Cemetery (Indianapolis),
  85, 102, 134, 188, 241, 373
Crown Hill Cemetery (Knox), 314
Crown Point, 361
Cuba, 217
Culver Military Academy, 271
Cumberland Road, 56

Dailey, Frank, 284
Dallas, George M., 107
Dalton, E. Spencer, 332
Daniels, Cheri Herman, 404
Daniels, Dorothy Wilkes, 404
Daniels, Edward, 158, 159
Daniels, Margaret, 404
Daniels, Meagan, 404
Daniels, Melissa, 404
Daniels, Meredith, 404
Daniels, Mitchell E., 404

Daniels, Mitchell E., Jr., 5, 7, 16, 379, 399, 402–7; (illus.), 403

Danville, (IN) 198, 201, 245

Danville (KY), 48, 204

Daviess County, 206

Davis, A. J., 77

Davis, John W., 248

Davis, Katherine (Kathy), 16, 398

Davis, Mary Kay Miller. *See* Orr, Mary Kay Miller Davis

Daylight saving time, 356, 402, 405

Dearborn County, 42, 184

Death penalty. *See* Capital punishment

Deficits, 371, 398, 405

Delaware (state), 314

Delaware (tribe), 30

Deming, Elizur, 98

Democratic Leadership Council, 382

Democratic National Committee, 324

Democratic National Convention, 12, 240, 244, 248, 288, 314, 350, 381

Democratic Party, 3, 15, 24, 25, 48, 57, 61, 92, 94, 95, 97, 107, 108, 110, 112, 114, 115, 116, 118, 119, 120, 124, 125, 127, 128, 129, 132, 138, 141, 142, 144, 145, 146–47, 157, 158, 160, 161, 164, 169, 170, 172, 175, 177, 178, 181, 185, 188, 191, 201, 205, 206, 208, 213, 228, 233, 234, 235, 236, 237, 239, 244, 246, 247, 248, 277, 288, 290–91, 292, 293, 294, 295, 297, 302, 305, 310, 311, 312, 313, 314, 318, 324, 326, 333, 334, 348, 350, 354, 362, 363, 373, 376, 381, 382, 384, 387, 388, 390, 398, 402, 406

Democratic State Central Committee, 235

Democratic-Republican Party, 20

Denison Hotel, 210

Denver (CO), 134

Department of Administration, 340

Department of Agriculture, 5

Department of Banking, 250

Department of Child Services, 406

Department of Commerce, 370, 406

Department of Conservation, 250, 255, 286

Department of Correction, 326, 329, 340

Department of Geology and Natural History, 187

Department of Geology and Natural Resources, 196

Department of Mental Health, 340

Department of Natural Resources, 347

Department of Public Welfare, 3

Department of Revenue, 338, 340

Department of Statistics, 187

Department of Statistics and Geology, 187

Department of Transportation, 365

DePauw, John, 49

DePauw University, 15, 99, 184, 251, 289

Detroit (MI), 336

Dewey, Thomas, 313

Díaz, Porfirio, 181

Direct primary, 237, 252, 284

Disciples of Christ, 198, 274

Discount and Deposit Bank, 261

Discrimination, 255, 342

District Agricultural and Mechanical Society of Southwestern Indiana, 168

District of Louisiana, 21, 25

Division of Audit, 338, 340

Division of Tax Review, 338, 340

Division of Unemployment, 3

Dixson Inc., 370

Dodd, Harrison H., 147

Dolfuss, Patricia. *See* Whitcomb, Patricia Dolfuss

Douglas, Stephen A., 110, 129, 162, 192, 233

Draft, 142

Drummer Boy Award, 334
Dubois County, 127
Dukakis, Michael, 388
Dunlap's Creek (PA), 40
Dunmore, John, earl of, 34
Dunn, George H., 92
Dunn, Jacob Piatt, Jr., 174, 236, 238
Dunning, Ellen Lane Ashford, 110
Dunning, James, 106
Dunning, Paris C., 96, 100, 106–11; (illus.), 107
Dunning, Rachel North, 106
Dunning, Sarah Alexander, 106
Durbin, Bertha McCullough, 217
Durbin, Eliza Ann Sparks, 216
Durbin, Henry Clay, 216
Durbin, William Sappington, 216
Durbin, Winfield T., 15, 216–22, 227, 247, 263; (illus.), 217

East Chicago, 376
Eastern Illinois Normal School, 224
Economic booms, 217, 380
Economic development, 392, 396, 397, 399
Edgerton, Joseph K., 93
Education, 44, 64, 75–76, 83–84, 99, 101, 109, 114, 116, 117, 128, 152, 155–56, 171, 213, 264, 270, 271, 305, 314, 319, 327, 339, 341, 349, 353, 357, 368, 371, 372, 376, 378–79, 381, 389, 390, 391, 398
Education Commission of the States, 379
Education Roundtable, 390
Edwards, Helene. See Gates, Helene Edwards
Eggleston, Miles C., 81
1850 U.S. Census, 117
Eighteenth Amendment. See U.S. Constitution

Eighth District, 212, 370
Eightieth Infantry Division, 323, 324
Eighty-eighth Infantry Division, 331
Eisenhower Dwight, 320, 322, 324, 325, 326, 327–28, 330, 332
Ekles, John, 99
Electoral College, 24, 149
Electoral Commission, 149, 161
Eli Lilly and Company, 319, 403, 404
Elston, Joanna M. See Lane, Joanna M. Elston
Emancipation Proclamation, 144, 145
Enabling Act, 43
Energize Indiana, 392
Enlistments, 142
Equal Rights Amendment, 377
Equal Suffrage Society, 81
Erie Investments, 370
Escape from Corregidor, 353
Etherton, Trudy, 358
Evans, John, 99
Evansville, 92, 153, 187, 219, 303, 334, 368, 369, 370
Evansville Metal Products, 370
Ewbank, Louis, 268
Ex Parte Milligan, 193
Executive powers, 1, 3, 5–6, 7, 9, 12, 13, 46, 128, 143, 145–46, 188, 253–54, 288, 293, 294, 297, 308, 311–12, 379, 398
Executive Reorganization Act of 1933, pp. 5, 293, 297, 302, 310, 311
Extradition, 214–15

Facts for the People in Relation to a Protective Tariff, 97
Fair Employment Practices Commission, 341
Fairbanks, Charles W., 214, 225–26, 252
Fairfax County (VA), 33
Fairlawn Cemetery (Kentland), 266

Fall Creek Massacre, 65
Falls of the Ohio, 46, 56
Family and Social Services
    Administration, 5, 379, 406
Farm Credit Administration, 348
Farmer's Loan and Trust Bank, 317
Farmers' and Mechanics' Bank, 184
Farmers and Merchants Bank, 45
Farmers Bank and Trust, 310
Farmers' Mutual Benefit Association,
    205
Fayette County (IN), 205
Fayette County (PA), 40
Federal aid, 333, 343, 365
Federal Emergency Relief
    Administration, 296
Federal Land Bank, 348
Federal Security Agency, 298
Federalist Party, 20
Female Institute for Women and Girls,
    163–64
Fesler, James, 264
Fifteenth Amendment. See U.S.
    Constitution
Fifth District, 200
Fifth Indiana Cavalry, 176
Fifth Judicial District, 95
Financial crisis, 338, 339, 355
First Cavalry, 154
First District, 192, 194
First Indiana Regiment, 138
First Presbyterian Church (Columbia
    City), 235
First Presbyterian Church (Evansville),
    370
First Regiment, 192
1st Source Bank, 395
Fishback, W. P., 186
Fitch, Graham N., 128, 138
Fletcher, Calvin, 74
Fletcher Trust Company, 313

Flint (MI), 303
Floods, 303
Flying Squadron of America, 229
Fontanet (town), 245
Food Production and Conservation
    Committee, 263
Forbes, John, 28
Ford, Gerald, 321
Forestry Board, 255
Fort Benjamin Harrison, 290
Fort Duquesne, 29
Fort Harrison, 30
Fort Sumter, 142, 144
Fort Washington, 19
Fort Wayne, 92, 93, 180, 201, 233, 234,
    305
Foster, George, 340
Fourteenth Amendment. See U.S.
    Constitution
Fourth Indiana Cavalry, 176
Fowler, I. H., 245
France, 316
Francesville High School, 361
Frankfort, 246
Franklin, 288, 347, 348, 350, 351
Franklin College, 15, 347, 348, 350
Franklin County (NC), 48
Franklin Evening Star, 349
Frederick County (VA), 70
Fredericksburg (VA), 35
Free silver, 208, 213
Free-Soil Party, 115, 119, 124
Free-Soilers, 112, 115, 116, 118,
    120
French Lick, 228, 284
French Lick Bookmakers' Club, 228
French Lick Springs Hotel, 228
Frist, Cora. See Goodrich, Cora Frist
Fugitive Slave Law, 119, 127
Fulton County, 360, 361
Fusion Party. See People's Party

Gambling, 207, 228, 381

Gary, 232, 376

Gas boom, 217

Gasoline tax, 265, 330, 333, 392

Gates, Alice Fesler, 316

Gates, Benton, 316

Gates, Benton E., 316

Gates, Helene Edwards, 316, 321

Gates, Horatio, 34

Gates, John, 316

Gates, Patricia, 316

Gates, Ralph F., 5, 10, 14, 316–21, 324; (illus.), 317

Gates, Robert, 316

Gates, Scott, 316

General fund, 314, 319, 320, 327, 332, 333

General Land Office, 78, 162

General Motors, 303

George Rogers Clark Memorial, 278

Georgetown University, 404

Germany, 120

Gettysburg (PA), 153

Gettysburg College (PA), 152

Geyser (student newspaper), 234

Ghost employees, 358

Gibson, Elizabeth de Vinez, 28

Gibson, George, 28

Gibson, John, 15, 20, 23, 28–31, 32

Gibson County, 31

Gigmilliat, L. R., 271

Gilded Age, 166

Gilliam, Arthur, 277

Goebel, William, 215

Goldsmith, Steve, 378, 388, 396, 397

Goldwater, Barry, 349

Goodrich, Cora Frist, 251

Goodrich, Elizabeth Edger, 250

Goodrich, James P., 14, 250–58, 263, 275, 284; (illus.), 251

Goodrich, John Baldwin, 250

Goodrich, Pierre Frist, 257

Goodrich, Rebecca Pearse, 250

Goodrich Brothers' Company, 257

Gore, Al, 382

Government reorganization, 336, 340, 355, 357, 376, 379, 406

Governor's Commission for a Drug Free Indiana, 378

Governor's Commission on the Arts, 341

Governor's Economy Program, 355

Governors' Portraits Collection, 158

Grand Army of the Republic, 14, 148, 198, 200, 216

Grand Junction (CO), 370

Grange movement, 205, 252

Grant, Ulysses S., 169, 176, 193, 250

Grant County, 301

Gray, Eliza Jaqua, 175

Gray, Hannah Worthington, 175

Gray, Isaac P., 2, 13, 174–82; (illus.), 175

Gray, John, 175

Great Depression, 3, 7, 8, 9, 280, 285, 290, 292, 295, 303, 317, 323, 330

Great Lakes-St. Lawrence Tidewater Commission, 257

Great Railroad Strike of 1877, p. 171

Greater Lafayette Chamber of Commerce, 350

Greeley, Horace, 176

Green, Robert, 378

Greenback Labor Party, 178

Greenback Party, 177, 178

Greenbacks, 168–69

Greencastle, 67, 184, 251, 289

Greencastle Township v. Black, 192

Greenfield, 132

Greenlawn Cemetery (Franklin), 351

Greenlawn Cemetery (Indianapolis), 102

Greenlee, Pleas, 302

Greensboro Academy, 106
Greensburg, 52
Greenwood (estate), 35
Gregory, James, 89
Gresham, Walter Q., 171, 181
Gross income tax, 294, 295, 297, 302,
    338, 339
Guilford County (NC), 106
Guristersigo (chief), 35

Hall, Baynard Rush, 64, 98
Hall, Frank J., 236
Halleck, Charles A., 318, 334
Hamilton College (NY), 125
Hamilton County (OH), 62
Hamlet, 309
Hammond, Abram A., 2, 14, 132–34;
    (illus.), 133
Hammond, Mary Ansden, 132
Hammond, Patty Ball, 132
Hampden-Sidney College (VA), 18
Hancock County, 99, 132
Handley, Barbara Jean Winterble, 331
Handley, Harold Lowell, 330
Handley, Harold W., 10, 14, 325, 326,
    330–35, 338, 340; (illus.), 331
Handley, Kenneth, 331
Handley, Lottie Margaret Brackbill, 330
Handley, Martha Jean, 331
Hanly, Anna E. Calton, 224
Hanly, Elijah, 224
Hanly, Eva A. R. Simmer, 225
Hanly, J. Frank, 10, 221, 224–31; (illus.),
    225
Hanna, Thomas, 177
Hannegan, Edward A., 95, 102
"Hanoi Hilton," 394
Hanover College, 15, 57, 162, 184,
    370
Harmony Lodge of Free and Accepted
    Masons, 70

Harpers Ferry, 130
Harris, Ed, 376
Harris, Nora Adele. *See* Townsend, Nora
    Adele Harris
Harrisburg (PA), 24
Harrison, Anna Tuthill Symmes, 18, 23,
    25
Harrison, Benjamin, 18
Harrison, Benjamin (president), 13, 18,
    137, 169, 171, 177, 178, 186, 188, 194,
    200, 201, 234
Harrison, Christopher, 46, 48
Harrison, Elizabeth Bassett, 18
Harrison, John Scott, 18
Harrison, William Henry, 11, 14, 15,
    18–26, 28, 30, 32, 40, 41, 42, 43, 54,
    80, 81, 89, 90, 103, 194; (illus.), 19
Harrison County, 30, 42, 195, 385
Hartke, Vance, 334, 342
Harvard University, 289, 290, 348, 369
Hay, Ann Gilmore. *See* Jennings, Ann
    Gilmore Hay
Hayden, 353, 359
Hayes, Rutherford B., 149, 161, 186
Hays, Will, 254, 264
Hazel Bluff (estate), 96, 102, 204
Hazelden Country Club, 263
Hazelton, 265, 270, 319, 380–81, 391, 406
Health care: licensing, 171, 213;
    mental, 319, 327, 332, 340; medical,
    365, 366
Helmke, Paul, 382
Henderson (KY), 36
Hendricks, Abraham, 53
Hendricks, Ann Jamison, 53
Hendricks, Ann Parker, 53
Hendricks, Eliza C. Morgan, 162
Hendricks, Jane Thomson, 161
Hendricks, John, 52, 161
Hendricks, Morgan, 162
Hendricks, Thomas, 52

Hendricks, Thomas A., 11, 52, 97, 99, 134, 137, 152, 158, 160–65, 180; (illus.), 161

Hendricks, William, 11, 38, 41, 49, 52–58, 60, 78, 160, 161, 164; (illus.), 53

Hendricks and Hord, 162

Hendricks County, 72, 164

Henry County Circuit Court, 274

Herman, Cheri. *See* Daniels, Cheri Herman

Hester, Craven, 113

Hicks, John W., 341

Higher Education Act, 377

Higher Education Commission, 353

Hiler, John, 396

Hillenbrand, John, 371

Hilliger, Kathryn Louisa. *See* Craig, Kathryn Louisa Hilliger

Hines, Cyrus, 186

Hochstetler, Rose Crothers. *See* Bowen, Rose Crothers Hochstetler

Hogan and Harston, 377

Holder, Cale, 325

Holman, Jesse, 66

Homann, Mary Virginia. *See* Welsh, Mary Virginia Homann

Home Guards, 263

Hooper and Olds, 234

The Hoosier (Greencastle newspaper), 67

Hoosier Democratic Club. *See* Two Percent Club

Hoosier Home (estate), 248

Hoosier Lottery, 381

Hoosier National Forest, 359

Hoover, Herbert, 256, 257, 266, 284, 316

Hord, Oscar B., 158, 162

Horse Thief Associations Law, 129

Hotchkiss Preparatory School (CT), 369

House Concurrent Resolution Number 2, p. 343

House of Refuge, 152, 156

Hovey, Abiel, 190

Hovey, Alvin P., 2, 14, 186, 190–97, 198, 200, 402; (illus.), 191

Hovey, Frances Peterson, 190

Hovey, Mary Ann, 193

Hovey, Rose Alice Smith, 193

Howard, Tilghman A., 89, 90, 96, 97, 98, 100, 106, 114

Howard County, 274

Howell, Mary. *See* Jackson, Mary Howell

Hudson Institute, 404

Huffman, Nancy. *See* Williams, Nancy Huffman

Humphrey, Hubert H., 350, 354

Hunt, Douglas, 395

Hunt, Marlene, 395

Hunterdon County (NJ), 40

Huntington, Elisha Mills, 96

Huntsville (AL), 199

Hurst, Martha Ann Renick. *See* Whitcomb, Martha Ann Renick Hurst

Illinois Territory, 42

Illiteracy, 101, 117

Immigrants, 232, 239

Income tax, 333, 356, 368, 371

Indentured servitude, 21

Independent Order of Odd Fellows, 305

Indian Removal Act (1830), 83

Indiana Advisory Committee for Relief of the Unemployed, 285

Indiana Asylum for the Insane, 128

Indiana Bar Association, 348

Indiana Boys' School, 133, 156

Indiana Centennial, 244, 248

Indiana Chamber of Commerce, 5

Indiana Civil Rights Commission, 342

Indiana College. *See* Indiana University

Indiana Constitution: (1816), 1, 2, 9, 37, 43–44, 46, 56, 108, 116; and terms of governors, 1–2; (1851), 1, 2, 10, 85, 94, 101, 108, 109, 119, 191–92, 221, 308, 312, 313, 335, 370, 372; and terms of governors, 2; revision of, 237, 238–40, 247, 253

Indiana Constitutional Convention: (1816), 37, 43–44, 54; (1850–51), 85, 101–2, 108, 191–92

Indiana Daily Student, 289

Indiana Division of Labor, 304, 305

Indiana Farm Bureau, 5, 301

Indiana Federation of Labor, 5

Indiana General Assembly, 48, 70, 71, 72, 108, 112, 162, 168, 194–95, 213, 228, 238, 269–70, 276, 282, 331, 337, 338, 349, 352, 354, 362–63, 370, 385, 386–87, 399, 402; and power relationship with office of governor, 1, 2–4, 5, 6, 7–8, 9, 10–11, 12, 44, 64, 66, 67, 78, 102, 118, 127–28, 145, 188, 195–96, 201–2, 204, 207–8, 308, 333, 349, 356, 378, 391, 398; repeals indentured servitude laws, 21; and reapportionment, 49, 77, 207–8, 355; and roads and highways, 56, 320, 327; moves state capital, 56–57; governor addresses, 62, 109, 133, 264, 303; and construction of statehouse, 65, 77, 171; and internal improvements, 74, 82–83, 84, 90, 96, 98; and education, 75–76, 101, 116, 117, 119, 341; and taxes, 77, 91, 253, 339–40, 356, 364, 371–72, 390, 391–92, 397, 405; and state debt, 82–83, 91, 100; and removal of Native American tribes, 83; and revision of codes, 92; and institutions for the physically and mentally handicapped, 99, 126; and corruption and mismanagement issues, 129–30; and election of U.S. senators, 136, 163, 177, 178–80, 187, 201, 218, 237, 304–5; and appropriations for Civil War, 143, 145; ratification of the Fifteenth Amendment, 148–49, 157–58, 174–75, 176; and appropriation for Governors' Portraits Collection, 158; temperance and Prohibition, 163, 236, 295; and vigilantism, 180, 195; and women's suffrage, 187; and anti-lynching law, 218–19; and juvenile court, 220; and Indiana State Library, 227; and revisions to 1851 constitution, 239; and public utilities, 247, 372; and statehood centennial, 248; and teaching German in schools, 255, 270; and Ku Klux Klan, 283; and repeal of direct primary, 284, 291; and pro-union legislation, 295; and government reorganization, 297, 310, 311–12, 326, 340; and duties of the lieutenant governor, 301; and welfare rolls, 313–14, 379–80; centennial history of, 333; and creation of Indiana Vocational Technical College, 341; and civil rights, 342; and federal aid, 343; and daylight saving time, 356, 405; and repeal of vetoes, 358; and economic development, 392

Indiana Higher Education Commission, 357

Indiana Historical Bureau, 254

Indiana Historical Commission, 244, 248, 250, 254

Indiana Historical Society, 95, 248, 350

Indiana Hospital for the Insane, 195

Indiana Legion, 143, 176, 192

Indiana National Guard, 219, 247, 271, 297, 303, 319, 399

Indiana Performance Assessment for Student Success (IPASS), 381

Indiana Port Commission, 373

Indiana primary, 343, 346, 349, 350
Indiana Railroad Commission, 227
Indiana Sanitary Commission, 143
Indiana School for the Blind, 2, 195, 270
Indiana Seminary. *See* Indiana
    University
Indiana Sesquicentennial, 346
Indiana Soldiers' and Sailors'
    Children's Home, 157, 171, 180
Indiana State Bank, 101
Indiana State Board of Agriculture, 168
Indiana State Fair, 168, 265
Indiana State Fairgrounds Coliseum,
    348
Indiana State Library, 227
Indiana State Parks Committee, 255
Indiana State Police, 326
Indiana State Seminary. *See* Indiana
    University
Indiana State Sentinel, 208
Indiana State Teachers Association, 255,
    301
Indiana State University, 155
Indiana Statehouse, 164, 171, 179
Indiana Statewide Testing for
    Educational Progress (ISTEP), 381
Indiana Supreme Court, 2, 4, 8, 44, 66,
    102, 179, 185, 192, 195, 207, 234, 239,
    253, 277, 289, 308, 312, 335
Indiana Teachers' Seminary, 75
Indiana Telephone Company, 257
Indiana Territorial General Assembly,
    21, 37, 41, 43, 53, 54
Indiana Territory, 18, 25, 41, 42, 48, 70;
    governance of, 20–22; census of, 29,
    37
Indiana Toll Road, 327, 332
Indiana University, 15, 53, 57, 64, 75,
    92, 98, 112–13, 120, 220, 268, 269,
    281, 282, 289, 290, 322, 326, 330, 337,
    341, 353, 361, 366, 376, 382, 386

Indiana Vocational Technical College,
    341
Indiana Women's Christian
    Temperance Union, 81
Indiana Youth Center, 340
Indiana@Work, 399
Indianapolis, 52, 55, 56, 64, 65, 67, 71,
    72, 74, 76, 82, 85, 95, 99, 102, 132,
    134, 147, 148, 152, 157, 154, 162, 165,
    171, 172, 177, 181, 184, 185, 186, 188,
    193, 208, 210, 217, 246, 248, 254, 255,
    266, 268, 270, 279, 281, 282, 286, 289,
    305, 313, 317, 324, 328, 329, 334, 335,
    343, 354, 365, 366, 373, 377, 379, 388,
    389, 391, 397, 398, 404, 405
Indianapolis Circle Park, 103
Indianapolis Colts, 405
Indianapolis Common Council, 185
Indianapolis Journal, 185, 200
Indianapolis News, 257, 355
Indianapolis Power and Light, 403
Indianapolis Sentinel, 67
Indianapolis Star, 235, 257, 329, 349, 350
Indianapolis Traction and Terminal
    Company, 247
Inheritance tax, 358
Insurance Industry Working Group, 397
Internal improvements, 44, 45, 47,
    50, 52, 55, 56, 57, 61, 62–63, 70, 73,
    74–75, 76, 80, 82–83, 84, 88, 89–90,
    92, 96, 114
Internal Improvements Act. *See*
    Mammoth Internal Improvements
    Bill
Internal Improvements System. *See*
    Mammoth Internal Improvements
    System
International Joint Commission for the
    United States and Canada, 343
International Union of Police
    Associations, 379

IPALCO Enterprises, 403
Iraq war, 382
Ireland, 316
Iroquois League, 35
Italy, 188

Jackson (MS), 127
Jackson, Andrew, 24, 49, 50, 61, 71, 76, 96, 114
Jackson, Edith, 274
Jackson, Edward, 264, 265, 271, 274–79, 283, 284, 286; (illus.), 275
Jackson, Edward, Jr., 274
Jackson, Helen, 274
Jackson, Lydia Beaty Pierce, 274, 277
Jackson, Mary Howell, 274
Jackson, Presley, 274
Jackson, Rosa Wilkinson, 274
Jackson, Samuel D., 319
Jackson County, 336
Jacksonian Democratic Party, 61, 72
James Whitcomb Riley Hospital for Children, 270, 284, 287
Jamestown (NY), 185
Japan, 362
Jaqua, Eliza. *See* Gray, Eliza Jaqua
Jasinski, Richard, 395
Jaycees, 370
Jefferson, Thomas, 20, 21
Jefferson College (PA), 53
Jefferson County (IN), 54
Jefferson County (KY), 62
Jeffersonian Republican Party, 61, 72
Jeffersonville, 37, 41, 42, 65, 99, 129, 157, 163, 238, 371
Jeffersonville Land Office, 72
Jenner, William E., 305, 314, 318, 320, 322, 323, 325, 326, 328, 330, 332, 334
Jennings, Ann, 40
Jennings, Ann Gilmore Hay, 42
Jennings, Clarissa Barbee, 42, 46

Jennings, Ebenezer, 40
Jennings, Jacob, 40
Jennings, Jonathan, 1, 11, 22, 23, 32, 37, 38, 40–47, 48, 49, 54, 55; (illus.), 41
Jennings, Mary Kennedy, 40
Jennings County, 179
John, Enoch D., 70
Johnson, Andrew, 138, 149, 152, 155, 160, 193
Johnson, Lyndon B., 342, 343, 346, 349, 350
Johnson County, 289
Jones, Eleanor. *See* Wallace, Eleanor Jones
Jones, John Paul, 80
Judge Advocate General, 348
Julian, George W., 146, 176
Juvenile court, 220
Juvenile facilities, 119, 133, 152, 156, 164, 340–41

Kansas-Nebraska Act, 119, 124, 126, 141, 162
Kappa Beta Phi, 322
Kellogg, Frank B., 241
Kennard, 274
Kennedy, John F., 338, 341
Kennedy, Robert F., 346, 350
Kentland, 260, 261, 262, 265, 266
Kern, John W., 218, 227
Kernan, Joseph E., 394
Kernan, Joseph E. (governor), 2, 14, 16, 388, 392, 394–400, 402; (illus.), 395
Kernan, Maggie McCullough, 395
Kernan, Marion Powers, 394
Kerr, Michael, 137
Kickapoo, 37
Kimsey, Lois I. *See* Marshall, Lois I. Kimsey
Kirkpatrick, Willis, 262
Knights of Labor, 187, 252

Knights of Pythias, 252
Knights of the Golden Circle, 193
Knightstown, 152, 157, 171, 180
Know-Nothing Party, 124
Knox, 309, 310, 314
Knox County, 28, 166, 169, 336
Knox County Agricultural Society,
    168
Knox County Courthouse, 218
Knox County Democratic Convention,
    169
Kokomo, 379
Korean War, 327
Kosciusko County, 235
Ku Klux Klan, 180, 260, 265, 274, 275,
    276, 277, 278, 283, 284, 317, 384

La Porte, 198, 330, 331
La Porte County, 132, 310
Labor relations, 160, 204, 206, 238,
    247–48, 295–96, 303–4, 305, 333,
    334–35, 349, 379, 406
Lafayette, 73, 82, 92, 225, 226, 275, 280,
    348, 350, 351
Lafayette, marquis de, 65
Lake County, 207
Lake Erie, 56, 84
Lake Michigan, 63, 64, 232, 327, 339,
    347, 373
*Lambdin Milligan v. Alvin P. Hovey and
    Others*, 186
Lancaster (PA), 28
Land Act of 1800, pp. 20, 43
Landers, Franklin, 177
Landis, Fred, 284
Lane, Amos, 72
Lane, Henry S., 2, 11, 136–39, 141, 154,
    162; (illus.), 137
Lane, James H., 138
Lane, Joanna M. Elston, 138
Lane, Mary Higgins, 138

Lane, Pamela Bledsoe, 138
Laos, 394
Lawrenceburg, 90, 232, 327, 339, 347,
    373
League of Nations, 240
League of Women Voters, 284
Lebanon (IN), 244, 246
Lebanon (OH), 89
Lebanon Cemetery, 248
Lebanon Presbyterian Academy, 212
Lecompton Constitution, 128–29, 133,
    192
Lenin, Vladimir, 256
Leslie, Amy, 280
Leslie, Daniel, 280
Leslie, Frank, 280
Leslie, Harry G., 10, 271, 280–87, 296;
    (illus.), 281
Leslie, John (Jack), 282
Leslie, Martha Morgan, 282
Leslie, Mary Burkhart, 280
Leslie, Richard, 282
Leslie, Robert, 282
Lewis, Andrew, 34
Lexington (KY), 94, 95
Liber College, 250
Liberal Republicans, 176
Liberia, 65
Liberty, 89
*Liberty Hall Gazette and Cincinnati
    Mercury*, 80
Liberty Party, 98, 100
License branches, 402, 406
Licensing of alcoholic beverages, 295,
    302
Lieber, Richard, 248, 255, 286
Lilly, J. K., Jr., 319
Lincoln, Abraham, 9, 120, 136, 138,
    142, 144, 145, 146, 147, 154, 162, 193,
    194, 226, 250
Lincoln High School, 336

Lincoln Highway, 265
Lindbergh, Ann Morrow, 284
Lindbergh, Charles, 284
Local option law, 229, 236
Local option tax, 356
Logan (chief), 29, 30
Logansport, 160, 187, 263, 284
Lord Dunmore's War (1774), 29–30, 34
Los Angeles (CA), 329
Louisiana (MO), 50
Louisville (KY), 45, 106, 348, 350, 385, 396
Loyalist Convention, 138
Lubec (ME), 202
Ludlow, Louis, 235
Lugar, Richard G., 321, 358, 404
Lynching, 216, 218–20, 286

Maclure, William, 190–91
MacWilliams Corporation, 395
Macy, John Winchester "Ches," 251
Madison, 45, 53, 75, 82, 145, 161
Madison, James, 20, 31, 32, 46, 54, 206, 293, 330
Madison and Indianapolis Railroad, 90
Madison County, 65
Madison Daily Courier, 57
Madison Square Garden, 248
Madison Western Eagle, 53, 54
Mafia Riots, 188
Mahoney, John, 103
Mammoth Internal Improvements Bill, 74, 82, 88
Mammoth Internal Improvements System, 76, 80, 82, 84, 89, 90, 91, 96, 97–98
Manson, Mahlon Dickerson, 178
Mardis, Josephine. *See* Branigin, Josephine Mardis
Marion, 219, 286
Marion County, 85, 225, 277, 354, 358

Marion County Association for Retarded Children, 334
Marion County Circuit Court, 179, 239, 312
Marion County Courthouse, 172
Marion County Criminal Court, 266
Marion Normal College, 300
Marshall, Daniel, 232, 233
Marshall, Joseph G., 100
Marshall, Lois I. Kimsey, 235
Marshall, Martha Patterson, 232
Marshall, Thomas R., 10, 11, 221, 229, 232–42, 246, 247, 284, 317; (illus.), 233
Marshall, Woodson, 234
Marshall County, 362, 366
Martial law, 297, 303
Martin, Clarence R., 287
Martin, John Bartlow, 350
Martinsville, 268, 269, 271, 289
Martinsville Republican, 269
Martinsville Trust Company, 271
Masons, 235
Mathews, Martha. *See* Posey, Martha Mathews
Matson, Courtland C., 194, 200
Matson, John, 115
Matthews, Claude, 102, 103, 201, 204–9, 402; (illus.), 205
Matthews, Eliza Ann Fletcher, 204
Matthews, Martha Renick Whitcomb, 102, 204
Matthews, Thomas A., 204
Mauckport, 339
Maumee River, 56
Maysville (KY), 204
McCardla, John, 252
McCarthy, Eugene, 346, 350
McCarthy, Joseph A., 325
McCarty, Nicholas, 118, 119
McCarty, William M., 138

McCormick, Otis, 282
McCormick's Creek State Park, 248
McCray, Annie Eliza, 260
McCray, Ella Ade, 262
McCray, Elmore, 260
McCray, Fannie, 260
McCray, Greenberry, 260, 261
McCray, Martha Galey, 260
McCray, Warren T., 10, 252, 260–66, 268, 270, 271, 278; (illus.), 261
McCulloch, Carleton B., 264, 276
McCullough, Bertha. See Durbin, Bertha McCullough
McCullough, J. E., 194
McCullough, Maggie. See Kernan, Maggie McCullough
McDonald, Joseph E., 146, 147, 177, 178, 180
McFarley, James A., 291, 292
McGovern, George S., 343
McHale, Frank, 290, 324
McIntosh, David, 388, 389, 391, 397
McKinley, William, 213, 214, 226, 263
McKinney, E. Kirk, 302
McKinney, Frank, 324
McNagny, William F., 234
McNutt, Cyrus F., 290
McNutt, John Crittenden, 289
McNutt, Kathleen Timolat, 290, 298
McNutt, Louise, 290
McNutt, Paul V., 2–3, 5, 7, 8, 9, 11, 12, 14, 253, 288–99, 300, 301, 302, 304, 305, 310, 311, 319, 323, 324, 326, 336, 348, 357, 389; (illus.), 289
McNutt, Ruth Neely, 289
Medicaid, 380–81
Medical care. See Health care
Medical licensing. See Health care
Medicare Catastrophic Health Care Act (1988), 366
Medina (NY), 198

Memorial Park Cemetery (Vincennes), 343
Menominee (chief), 83
Mental Health Division, 327
Merrill, Samuel, 66
Methodist Hospital (Indianapolis), 254
Methodists, 92, 98
Mexican War, 94, 100, 101, 116, 138
Mexico City, 181
Meyers, Quincy A., 252
Miami (FL), 286
Miami (tribe), 46, 63, 64, 83
Miami County (OH), 80, 81
Miami University (Oxford, Ohio), 140
Michiana Regional Airport, 396
Michigan City, 129, 163, 271
Michigan City Prison, 283
Michigan Road, 63, 72
Mid America World Trade Association, 358
Midwives, 171
Mifflin County (PA), 80
Mikesell, Carol Lynn (Hahn) Flosenzier. See Bowen, Carol Lynn (Hahn) Flosenzier Mikesell
Milan (OH), 198
Milan Seminary (OH), 198
Militia, 100–101
Miller, Eric, 402
Milligan, Lambdin P., 186, 193
Mills, Caleb, 101, 117
Mingo (tribe), 15, 29–30
Minimum wage, 347
Mining, 187
Minton, Sherman, 294, 298, 302, 331
Mishawaka, 84, 198
Mississippi, 193
Missouri Compromise, 124
Mobs, 219, 220
Mojave Desert, 331
Monongahela (PA), 404

Monroe, James, 36

Monroe County, 96, 98, 107

Montgomery County, 208, 210, 211, 212, 215, 246, 260

Montmorenci (IN), 280

Moore, Harbin H., 66

Moravian Town (Canada), 23

Morgan, Daniel, 34

Morgan, Eliza C. *See* Hendricks, Eliza C. Morgan

Morgan, John Hunt, 146, 176

Morgan, Martha. *See* Leslie, Martha Morgan

Morgan County, 290

Morrill Land Grant Act of 1862, p. 168

Morrison, Clarence, 241

Morse, Samuel F. B., 85

Morton, James Throck, 140

Morton, Lucinda Burbank, 141

Morton, Oliver P., 2, 8, 9, 11, 14, 102, 110, 115, 120, 125, 126, 136, 140–50, 152, 153, 154–55, 157, 168, 297; (illus.), 141

Morton, Sarah Miller, 140

Mount, Atwell, 211

Mount, James A., 210–15, 217, 218; (illus.), 211

Mount, Kate Boyd, 212, 215

Mount, Lucinda Fullenwider, 211

Mount Sterling (KY), 138

Mount Vernon, 190, 194, 303, 370

Mount Vernon (plantation), 33, 34

Muscatatuck State Hospital, 327, 334

Muskingum County (OH), 161

Mutz, John M., 371, 373, 378, 387

N. Noble and Company, 71

Napoleonic Code, 65

Nashville (TN), 199

National Association of Breeders of Short-Horn Cattle of the United States and Canada, 205

National Education Goals Panel, 381

National Guard. *See* Indiana National Guard

National Republican Party, 82

National Republicans. *See* Jeffersonian Republican Party

National Road, 46

Native Americans, 15, 23, 29, 30, 33, 34, 35, 37, 43, 55, 56; treaties with, 18, 19, 20, 29, 46, 48, 63–64, 96; removal of, 61, 64–65, 73, 83

Neal, James T., 358

Nelson, John C., 178

New, Harry S., 252, 256

New Albany, 82, 125, 126, 247

New Cumberland (OH), 245

New Deal, 121, 277, 288, 295–96, 297, 311, 316, 318, 343

New Hampshire primary, 350

New Harmony, 190

New Madison (OH), 175

New Orleans, 71, 81, 188

The New Purchase; or, Seven and a Half Years in the Far West, 98

New Purchase Treaty, 46, 48, 49

New York (city), 298

Newton County, 260

Niblack, William E., 192

Nineteenth Amendment. *See* U.S. Constitution

Nineteenth Illinois Volunteer Infantry, 199

Ninth District, 225

Nixon, Richard M., 338, 343, 354, 364

Noble, Catherine Stull van Swearingen, 71

Noble, Elizabeth Claire Sedgwick, 70

Noble, James, 70, 71

Noble, Lazarus, 71

Noble, Noah, 1, 14, 67, 70–79, 80, 82; (illus.), 71

Noble, Thomas, 70
Noland, James, 377
Normandy (France), 324
North Bend (OH), 25, 162
North Carolina, 331
North Judson, 309
North Manchester, 232
North Vernon, 354
North Vietnam. *See* Vietnam
Northern Hospital for the Insane, 263
Northern Indiana Normal School, 245
Northwest Army, 23, 24, 31
Northwest Ordinance (1787), 21
Northwest Territory, 19, 20, 28

O'Bannon, Bobby, 385
O'Bannon, Frank L., 2, 8, 16, 377, 378,
    384–93, 394, 396, 397, 398, 399, 402;
    (illus.), 385
O'Bannon, Jennifer, 387
O'Bannon, Jonathan, 387
O'Bannon, Judy Asmus, 386, 387, 388
O'Bannon, Lew M., 384
O'Bannon, Polly, 387
O'Bannon, Robert P., 385
O'Bannon, Rosetta Faith Dropsey, 385
Oak Hill Cemetery (Crawfordsville),
    215
Oberholtzer, Madge, 278
Office of Management and Budget,
    399, 404
Officer's Candidate School, 369
Ohio River, 56, 63, 64, 90, 303, 339, 349,
    359, 370, 373
Ohio Territory, 35
Ohio University, 89
Okinawa, 362
Olds, Walter, 234
158th Regiment, 269
147th Indiana Infantry Regiment, 176
106th Indiana Regiment, 176

165th Depot Brigade, 269
161st Indiana Infantry Regiment, 217
139th Indiana Volunteer Infantry, 216
Oneida County (NY), 125
"Onward Christian Soldiers," 321
Open primary, 323
Opportunity Indiana, 399
Orange County, 279
Orchard Lake (farm), 262, 265, 266
Order of the Coif, 289
Orleans, 279
Orr, Joanne (Josie) Wallace, 269
Orr, Louise Dunkerson, 368
Orr, Mary Kay Miller Davis, 369
Orr, Robert D., 3, 365, 366, 368–74, 389;
    (illus.), 369
Orr, Robert D., Jr., 369
Orr, Robin, 369
Orr, Samuel Lowry, 368
Orr, Susan, 369
Orr Iron Company, 369
Orth, Godlove S., 100
Owen, David Dale, 83, 96
Owen, Robert, 190
Owen County, 245
Oxford (OH), 140

Panics and depressions, 3, 7, 8, 9, 45,
    55, 75, 83, 97, 160, 169, 170, 206,
    207, 265, 280, 285, 290, 292, 295,
    303, 317, 323, 330
Pardons, 266, 277, 278, 283
Parent, Roger, 395, 396
Paris (France), 155
Parke, Benjamin, 46
Parke County, 206
Parker, Ann. *See* Hendricks, Ann Parker
Parker, Crawford F., 326, 334, 337, 338
Parker, M. H., 269
Parks, 297, 320, 349, 365, 391
Parks, James, 269

Parks, Parminter M., 269

Partnership for Personal Responsibility, 380

Patoka, 365

Patronage, 3, 12, 73, 195, 211, 237, 252, 256, 291, 295, 302, 311, 319, 340, 357

Paul, John, 53

Peace Congress, 133

Pearson, Linley E., 378, 388

Penal code, 213

Penal rehabilitation, 285, 340–41

Pendleton, 65, 264, 271

Pensions, 305

People's Party, 124, 125, 127, 128, 132, 141, 205, 206

Peoria (IL), 198

Perkins, Samuel E., 158

Peru (South America), 193, 194

Peters, R. Earl, 302

Peterson, Bart, 405

Pettit, John, 127

Phi Beta Kappa, 234, 289, 322

Phi Delta Phi, 289

Phi Gamma Delta, 234

Philadelphia (PA), 36, 136, 138

Philippines, 298, 353

Phillips, Clifton J., 256

Phoenix Gazette, 257

Pickaway County (OH), 101, 166

Pierce, Franklin, 162, 192

Pierce, Lydia Beaty. *See* Jackson, Lydia Beaty Pierce

Pierceton, 233

Pike County (MO), 50

Pitcher, John, 190

Pittsburgh (PA), 29, 31, 198

Plainfield, 133, 152, 156

Political fund-raising, 292, 294

Political parties, 3, 7, 15, 16, 20, 24–25, 53–54, 61, 66, 67, 72, 82, 95, 98, 100, 102, 108, 115, 116, 118, 119, 120, 124–

25, 127, 128, 129, 132, 138, 141–42, 144, 147–48, 158, 161, 169–70, 175, 176–77, 178, 179, 185, 188, 194, 200–201, 205–6, 207, 212–13, 216, 217–18, 221, 225–26, 227, 228, 229, 233, 234, 235, 236, 245, 246–47, 248, 250, 274, 276, 277, 278, 288, 290–91, 292, 293, 294, 295, 302, 305, 308, 310, 311–12, 314, 316, 317–18, 319, 320, 322, 324, 325, 326, 330, 331, 332, 333, 334, 338, 348–49, 350, 352, 354–55, 356, 357, 360, 362–63, 364, 370, 371, 373, 376, 378, 379, 380, 381, 382, 384, 387, 388, 390, 391, 396, 398, 399, 402, 406

Polk, James K., 100, 101, 107, 126

Polke, William, 49

Poll tax, 239

Polling, Harold A. "Red," 382

Population, 60–61, 77, 355

Populist Party. *See* People's Party

Porter, Albert G., 177, 184–89, 216; (illus.), 185

Porter, Cornelia Stone, 185

Porter, George T., 186

Porter, Minerva Brown, 185

Porter, Myra Tousey, 184

Porter, Thomas, 184

Portland, 250, 252

Ports, 370, 373

Posey, John, 33

Posey, Martha Mathews, 34, 35

Posey, Mary Alexander Thornton, 35

Posey, Thomas, 14, 31, 32–39, 44, 54; (illus.), 33

Posey County, 190, 192

Posey County Circuit Court, 191

Post-High School Education Study Committee, 341

Potawatomi, 37, 63, 64, 83

Presbyterians, 92, 98

Princeton, 265, 379

Princeton University, 404

Prisons, 99, 116, 119, 129, 152, 156–57, 163, 170, 232, 238, 264, 270, 271, 283, 349, 406

Prizefighting, 207, 271

Procter, Henry, 23

Procter and Gamble, 395

Progressive Era, 216, 264, 291

Progressive Party, 221, 229, 236, 247

Progressivism, 232, 237, 238, 239, 244, 247, 260

Prohibition, 82, 188, 224, 230, 255, 274, 275, 276, 292, 295

Prohibition Party, 178, 229

Property Assessment Act of 1961, p. 338

Property tax, 253, 260, 292, 295, 302, 333, 338, 347, 349, 356, 364, 371, 389, 390, 391, 397, 398

Prophet, The, 23

Prussia. *See* Germany

Public records, 390

Public Service Commission, 250, 293–94

Public utilities. *See* Utility companies

Public Works Administration, 296

Pulliam, Eugene C., 257, 349, 350

Pullman strike, 206

Purdue, John, 156, 281

Purdue Alumnus, 283

Purdue University, 15, 156, 168, 275, 280, 281, 282, 283, 286, 287, 327, 334, 341, 350

Putnam County, 100

Quakers, 72, 112, 156, 175

Rabb, Joseph M., 225

Racism, 127

Radical Republicans, 146, 148, 152

Railroads, 63, 67–68, 73, 74, 82, 88, 90, 96, 160, 168, 171, 186, 201, 206, 220, 227, 281–82

Ralston, Emmet, 246

Ralston, Jennie Craven, 246

Ralston, John, 245

Ralston, Mary Josephine Backous, 245

Ralston, Ruth, 246

Ralston, Samuel M., 10, 221, 236, 244–49, 254, 277; (illus.), 245

Ralston, Sarah Scott, 245

Randolph County, 176, 250, 257

Rawlins (WY), 335

Ray, Esther Booker, 68

Ray, James B., 1, 14, 15, 44, 60–68, 95; (illus.), 61

Ray, Martin M., 67

Ray, Mary Riddle, 68

Ray, Phebe Ann Brown, 62

Ray, William, 62

RCA Dome, 389

Read, James G., 72

Reagan, Ronald, 25, 321, 366, 368

Recessions, 371, 389, 398

Reconstruction, 139, 141, 149, 160

Reconstruction Finance Corporation, 285

Red Cross, 263, 331

Reed, Suellen, 390, 398

Rehabilitation. *See* Penal rehabilitation

Republican National Convention, 188, 226, 318

Republican Party, 3, 15, 16, 119, 125, 129, 136, 138, 141, 144, 146, 148, 153, 175, 176, 178, 179, 185, 186, 188, 194, 200–201, 204, 207, 208, 210, 212, 213, 216, 217, 221, 225–26, 228, 229, 236, 246, 247, 250, 256, 263, 264, 274, 276, 277, 278, 284, 291, 292, 293, 295, 297, 305, 311, 312, 313, 316, 317–18, 319, 320, 321, 322, 325, 326, 330, 331, 332, 333, 334, 349, 352, 354–55, 356, 357, 360, 362, 363, 364, 370, 371, 373, 376,

378, 379, 380, 388, 390, 391, 396, 398, 399, 402

Republican State Central Committee, 217

Resumption of Specie Payment Act, 149

Retardation Study Committee, 334

Revenues, 338, 339, 355, 356, 364, 368, 371, 392; surplus, 381, 389, 390

Revised Code of 1831, p. 65

Revolutionary War, 14, 29, 32, 34–35, 89

Reynolds, David, 101

Richmond (IN), 187

Richmond (VA), 18

Riddle, John, 68

Riddle, Mary. *See* Ray, Mary Riddle

Riker, Dorothy, 45

Riley, James Whitcomb, 99

Riley, Reuben A., 99

Riley Hospital for Children. *See* James Whitcomb Riley Hospital for Children

Ripley County Jail, 218

Ristine, Richard O., 339, 348, 349

Riverboats, 381

Riverview Cemetery (MO), 50

Roads and highways, 43, 45, 56, 63, 64, 74, 82, 88, 96, 201, 220–21, 265, 270, 278, 314, 319, 320, 327, 328, 332, 333, 340, 349, 352, 365

Robertson, Robert S., 178, 179

Robinson, Arthur, 277

Robinson, J. C., 245

Roby Racetrack, 207

Rochester (VT), 94

Rock, Robert, 354

Rockefeller, Nelson, 330

Rockport (IN), 219

Rockport (NY), 198

Rockville, 106, 113, 114

Rockwill, Caroline. *See* Wright, Caroline Rockwill

Roosevelt, Franklin D., 12, 257, 285, 288, 291–92, 296, 297, 298, 303, 304, 310, 313, 318, 343, 362

Roosevelt, Theodore, 221, 236, 246, 252

Rose Hill Cemetery (Bloomington), 111

Roswell (GA), 212

Rotary Club, 370

Rover's Delight (plantation), 33

Rush, Benjamin, 18

Rush County, 89

Rushville, 89

"RV1," 403, 406

Saint Joseph (IL), 224

Saint Joseph High School, 344

Saint Louis (MO), 21, 180, 217

Saint Paul (MN), 130

Sales tax, 339, 348, 356, 363, 371, 391, 392, 397

Salisbury, 140

San Francisco (CA), 132

Sanders, Zerelda. *See* Wallace, Zerelda Sanders

Saratoga (NY), 34

Savannah (GA), 35

Sayer, William, 328

Scandals and corruption, 227–28, 265–66, 268, 277, 278, 328, 329, 332, 334, 358, 391

School Corporation Reorganization Act (1959), 341

School for the Blind. *See* Indiana School for the Blind

Schricker, Christopher, 309

Schricker, Henry F., 2, 5, 8, 297, 300, 302, 303, 304, 305, 308–15, 348; (illus.), 309

Schricker, Magdalena Meyer, 309

Schricker, Maude L. Brown, 309

Schwartz Paper Company, 395

Scott, Charles, 36

Scott, James, 66
Scottish Rite, 235
Second Bank of the United States, 76
Second District, 46, 67
Second State Bank, 76
Secret societies, 147, 193, 265
Service Pension Association of the United States, 196
Seventeenth Amendment. *See* U.S. Constitution
Seventh Regiment Indiana Militia, 70
Seventy-second Indiana Infantry Regiment, 211
Seymour, 354
Shades State Park, 320
Shakamak State Park, 297
Sharpsburg (KY), 138
Shawnee, 30, 34
Shawneetown (IL), 38
Shelby County, 161, 162, 289
Shelbyville, 52, 164, 218, 348
Sherman, William T., 147, 212
Sherwood, Elmer "Doc," 328
Shiloh, battle of, 193
Shipp, Tom, 219
Shirkieville, 376
Shively, Benjamin F., 210
Shumaker, Edward S., 277
Simmer, Eva A. R. *See* Hanly, Eva A. R. Simmer
Simonson, John, 41
Singapore, 373
Sixteenth Indiana Volunteer Infantry, 216
Skillman, Rebecca (Becky), 16
Slack, Ert L., 236, 246
Slaves and slavery, 21, 22, 29, 32, 37, 40, 42, 44, 45–46, 54, 55, 57, 65, 72, 73, 107–8, 109, 114, 115, 116, 120, 124, 126, 127, 128, 133, 141, 144, 152, 157, 162, 163, 185

Smallpox, 199, 200
Smith, Abe, 219
Smith, Alonzo Green, 179
Smith, Caleb B., 193
Smith, Harry, 271
Smith, Oliver H., 50, 57
Smith, Rose Alice. *See* Hovey, Rose Alice Smith
Smith, Virgil "Red," 328
Smith, William Henry, 99
Snyder, John, 357
Social Security Act, 296
Social services, 379
Soldiers' and Sailors' Children's Home. *See* Indiana Soldiers' and Sailors' Children's Home
Soldiers and Sailors Monument, 221
Soldiers' and Seamans' Home. *See* Indiana Soldiers' and Sailors' Children's Home
Sommers, Matilda Escon. *See* Baker, Matilda Escon Sommers
Sons of Liberty, 147, 193
South Bend, 84, 210, 309, 362, 388, 394, 395, 396, 399
South Bend Tribune, 206, 291
South Whitley, 316, 317
Southern District of Indiana, 354
Soviet Union, 256–57, 328
Spanish-American War, 214, 217, 269
Specie Resumption Act of 1875, p. 170
Spencer, 218, 245
Spencer County, 48
Spooner, John C., 185
Spooner, Philip, 185
Spring Grove Cemetery (Cincinnati), 68
Springer, Raymond, 292, 303
Springfield (MA), 369
St. Albans School, 377
St. Clair, Arthur, Jr., 20

St. Thomas (West Indies), 176
Stalin, Joseph, 256
Standard Life Insurance Company, 286
Stapp, Milton, 72
Starke County, 309, 310
Starke County Circuit Court, 309
Starke County Democrat, 309
State Administration Act of 1941, p. 312
State Armory Board, 271
State Bank of Indiana, 44–45, 82, 91
State Board of Accounts, 237
State Board of Agriculture, 118, 187, 263
State Board of Equalization, 91
State Board of Health, 187
State Board of Law Examiners, 329
State Board of Tax Commissioners, 253, 338, 340
State Budget Agency, 4
State Council of Defense Committee, 254
State Education Convention, 76
State Highway Commission, 250, 256
State Highway Department, 365
State income tax, 339
State Seminary. *See* Indiana University
Staunton (VA), 34
Steers, Edwin, 326
Steinmann, Elizabeth (Beth) Anna Agnes. *See* Bowen, Elizabeth (Beth) Anna Agnes Steinmann
Step Ahead Council, 379
Stephenson, D. C., 265, 275, 276, 277, 278, 283, 284
Sterling Brewers, 370
Steubenville (OH), 41
Stevens, Thaddeus, 152, 153
Stevenson, Adlai E., 181
Stevenson, Adlai E., II, 314
Stevenson, Alexander C., 100
Stewart, George P., 264

Stoll, John B., 206
Stone, Cornelia. *See* Porter, Cornelia Stone
Stony Point (NY), 35
Stotsenburg, Evan, 247
Stout, Elihu, 54
Stowe, Harriet Beecher, 73
Strikes, 171, 204, 206–7, 214, 297, 303–4
Strut and Fret, 289
Stuart, Branigin, Ricks, and Shilling, 348
Studebaker Corporation, 396
Student Army Training Corps, 275
Sullivan, 297
Sullivan County, 206, 219
Sumner, Charles, 126, 155
Survey USA, 406
Switzerland County, 54
Symmes, Anna Tuthill. *See* Harrison, Anna Tuthill Symmes
Symmes, John Cleves, 18, 23

Taft, Robert A., 320, 325, 332
Taft, William Howard, 246
Taggart, Thomas, 226, 228, 235, 236, 237, 244, 246, 248
Tallahoma (TN), 324
Tannehill, W. M., 67
Taxes, 55, 74, 82, 83, 91, 101, 116, 117, 239, 244, 248, 250, 260, 263, 265, 285, 292, 294, 302, 319, 330, 333, 334, 338–39, 343, 347, 348, 349, 352, 354, 355, 356, 358, 363, 364, 368, 371, 372, 376, 381, 389, 390, 391, 392, 396, 397, 398, 399, 405; reform of, 253, 256, 289, 290, 292, 295
Taylor, William S., 215
Taylor, Zachary, 30
Teachers' Seminary. *See* Wabash College
Tecumseh, 23, 30
Temperance, 163, 201, 224, 226, 227, 228, 229, 235

Templeton, Leroy, 206
Tennessee, 193
Tenth District, 263
Terre Haute, 73, 84, 92, 96, 100, 115, 133, 152, 155, 219, 297, 305, 337
Terre Haute General Strike of 1935, p. 297
Territory of Louisiana, 21
Test, Esther French. *See* Wallace, Esther French Test
Test, John, 81
Third State Bank Bill, 118
Thirteenth Amendment. *See* U.S. Constitution
Thornbrough, Emma Lou, 142
Thornbrough, Gayle, 88, 90
Thornton, Mary Alexander. *See* Posey, Mary Alexander Thornton
Three Percent Fund, 45, 73
Thurman, Allen G., 181
Tilden, Samuel J., 149, 161
Time magazine, 327
Time zones, 356, 405
Timolat, Kathleen. *See* McNutt, Kathleen Timolat
Tippecanoe County, 156, 282
Tipton, John, 63, 78, 83
Title IX, 377
Toledo (OH), 92, 275
Tomlinson Hall, 246
Toner, Edward, 264
Tousey, Omer, 184
Town, Ithiel, 77
Townsend, David, 300
Townsend, Lydia Glancy, 300
Townsend, M. Clifford, 300–306, 310, 311; (illus.), 301
Townsend, Myrtle, 300
Townsend, Nora Adele Harris, 300
Townsend, Wayne W., 372, 377
Toyota, 379

Trade, 397, 406
Trail of Death, 83
Transylvania University (Lexington, Kentucky), 94
Treaties, 18, 19, 20, 46, 48, 49, 96
Treaty of Greenville (1795), 19
Treaty of St. Marys, 46
Trotsky, Leon, 256
Truman, Harry, 298, 337
Trusler, Milton, 205
Tucker, James M., 312
Tucker, Ralph, 332, 337, 348
Tucker et al. v. State, 5
Tucker v. State, 312
Turkey Run State Park, 245
Turpie, David, 137, 208, 225
Tuscarawas County (OH), 245
Twelfth District, 234, 235, 236, 317
Twenty-fifth Amendment. *See* U.S. Constitution
Twenty-first Amendment. *See* U.S. Constitution
21st Century Research and Technology Fund, 397
Twenty-first Century Scholars Program, 378
Twenty-fourth Indiana Infantry, 193
Twenty-sixth Amendment. *See* U.S. Constitution
Two Percent Club, 3, 9, 293, 294, 295, 311, 357
Tyler, John, 24, 25, 96

Umbarger, Margaret, 399
Unemployment, 285, 296, 334, 368
Uniform Traffic Code, 326
Union City, 175, 176, 181
Union County, 89
Unions, 247, 248, 295, 303, 304, 311, 379
United Airlines, 379

United Auto Workers, 303, 379

Unity Team, 379

University of Arizona, 320

University of Chicago, 337

University of Michigan, 316

University of Notre Dame, 15, 394

University of Pennsylvania, 336

University of Virginia, 377

Urbana (OH), 175

Urmston, E. Littell, 261

U.S. Bank. *See* Bank of the United States

U.S. Constitution, 163, 377; Seventeenth
   Amendment, 11, 237; Fifteenth
   Amendment, 148, 157–58, 174–
   75, 176, 177, 181; Fourteenth
   Amendment, 157, 160; Thirteenth
   Amendment, 157, 160; Eighteenth
   Amendment, 230, 255; Nineteenth
   Amendment, 250, 255; Twenty-
   first Amendment, 295; Twenty-fifth
   Amendment, 376; Twenty-sixth
   Amendment, 376

U.S. Department of Health and Human
   Services, 366

U.S. General Land Office, 96

U.S. House of Representatives, 21, 24,
   46, 49, 54–55, 174; Ways and Means
   Committee, 85; Committee on
   Accounts, 169

U.S. Military Academy (West Point), 81

U.S. Naval Academy (Annapolis), 251

U.S. Senate, 24; Select Committee,
   360, 364; Committee on Energy and
   Natural Resources, 372

U.S. Supreme Court, 193, 230, 297, 304,
   387

Utility companies: regulation and
   reform of, 293–94, 372

Valley Forge (PA), 34

Valparaiso, 245

Van Buren, Martin, 24, 25

Van Ness, John, 326

Van Nuys, Frederick, 248, 297, 298, 302,
   304, 310

Van Swearingen, Catherine Stull.
   See Noble, Catherine Stull van
   Swearingen

Vanderburgh County, 48, 153, 370

Vargus, Brian, 382

Vehicle inspection law, 349

Vermillion County, 96, 102, 204, 208

Vernon (NY), 125

Veterans, 319, 320

Vetoes, 5, 6, 7, 22, 84, 194, 195, 208,
   312, 313, 349, 356, 358, 381

Vevay, 45

Vicksburg campaign, 193

Vietnam, 350, 360, 394

Vigilantism, 129, 180, 195, 207, 218, 286

Vigo County, 245

Vincennes, 20, 21, 22, 23, 28, 29, 30, 31,
   41, 42, 53, 54, 56, 82, 172, 218, 265,
   279, 336, 337, 343, 406

Vincennes Indiana Gazette, 54

Vincennes Township, 166

Vincennes University, 41

Vincennes Western Sun, 54

Voorhees, Daniel W., 130

Vote buying, 194–95, 220

Voting rights, 43, 239; women, 82,
   155–56, 187, 188, 192, 226, 250, 255;
   African Americans, 148, 157, 158,
   174–75, 192

Wabash, 198

Wabash and Erie Canal, 46, 50, 63, 67,
   73, 85, 90, 92, 97, 100, 168

Wabash College, 15, 76, 187, 233, 234,
   235, 257

Wabash Fire and Casualty Insurance
   Company, 314

Wabash Manual Labor College, 75
Wabash River, 56, 73, 90
Walker, John C., 132
Wall Street Journal, 405
Wallace, Andrew, 80
Wallace, David, 14, 72, 80–86, 88;
    (illus.), 81
Wallace, Eleanor Jones, 80
Wallace, Esther French Test, 81
Wallace, George C., 342, 343
Wallace, Joanne (Josie). *See* Orr, Joanne
    (Josie) Wallace
Wallace, Lew, 81
Wallace, Zerelda Sanders, 81–82
Walnut Grove Cemetery (Monroe City),
    172
Walsh, Justin, 333
War bonds, 254, 316
War Manpower Commission, 298
War of 1812, pp. 23, 24, 30, 36, 43, 55,
    80, 184
War Risk Insurance Bureau, 316
Warren County (IN), 224, 282
Warren County (KY), 48
Warren County (OH), 89
Warrick County, 48, 153
Warsaw, 233, 320
Washington (PA), 41, 112
Washington, D.C., 138, 142, 148, 155,
    157, 158, 169, 186, 240, 241, 263, 298,
    320, 329, 348, 376, 377, 404, 405
Washington, George, 33, 36
Washington Monument (Washington,
    D.C.), 112
Watergate, 360, 364
Watkins, John A., 324, 326
Watson, Enos, 251
Watson, James E., 229, 236, 246, 251,
    252
Wayne, Anthony, 19, 35, 36
Wayne County, 125, 140

Wea, 37
Webster, Daniel, 24
Welfare programs, 284, 296, 297, 302;
    reform of, 376, 379–80, 381
Welsh, Inez Empson, 336
Welsh, Janet, 337
Welsh, Kathryn, 337
Welsh, Mary Virginia Homann, 337
Welsh, Matthew E., 4, 7, 8, 10, 335, 336–
    44, 348, 363, 364; (illus.), 337
Welsh, Matthew William, 336
West Baden, 228
West Lafayette, 152, 280
West Lafayette High School, 281
Western expansion, 57, 61, 73
Westmoreland County (PA), 53
Wheatland, 166
Whig Party, 15, 16, 24, 25, 57, 72, 80, 82,
    84, 85, 88, 89, 90, 98, 100, 101, 118,
    119, 124, 132, 138, 153, 176
Whitcomb, Alice, 354
Whitcomb, Ann, 354
Whitcomb, David, 101
Whitcomb, Edgar D., 6, 7, 14, 352–59,
    363; (illus.), 353
Whitcomb, James, 1, 6, 11, 15, 92, 94–
    104, 106, 114; (illus.), 95
Whitcomb, John, 353, 354
Whitcomb, John W., 94
Whitcomb, Louise Doud, 353
Whitcomb, Lydia Parmenter, 94
Whitcomb, Martha Ann Renick Hurst,
    101
Whitcomb, Martha Renick. *See*
    Matthews, Martha Renick Whitcomb
Whitcomb, Patricia Dolfuss, 354
Whitcomb, Shelley, 354
Whitcomb, Tricia, 354
White, Hugh, 24
White Caps, 180, 195, 207
White River, 90, 391

White River State Park, 365
Whitewater Canal, 90
Whitewater River, 90
Whitley County, 234, 317
Whitley County Circuit Court, 234
Wick, William, 41
Wilder's Lightning Brigade, 211, 212
Wilkinson, James, 21, 36
Wilkinson, Rosa. *See* Jackson, Rosa
   Wilkinson
Willard, Ashbel P., 2, 124–31, 132, 141;
   (illus.), 125
Willard, Ashbel P., Jr., 125
Willard, Caroline C. Cook, 126, 130
Willard, Erastus, 125
Willard, Sarah Parsons, 125
Willard Library (Evansville), 370
Williams, George, 166
Williams, James D., 2, 13, 15, 166–73,
   174, 175, 177, 184–85, 204; (illus.),
   167
Williams, Nancy Huffman, 171
Williams, Sarah Cavendar, 166
Williamson, Ellen. *See* Bigger, Ellen
   Williamson
Williamsport, 225
Willkie, Wendell, 311, 330
Willow Brook (farm), 210, 215
Wilmot Proviso, 116
Wilson, Charles, 328
Wilson, Woodrow, 11, 240, 254
Winchester, 250, 258, 263
Winchester High School, 251
Windsor County (VT), 94
Winterble, Barbara Jean. *See* Handley,
   Barbara Jean Winterble

Wisconsin primary, 343
Wolcott, Anson, 169, 170
Woman's Christian Temperance Union,
   82
Women: and voting rights, 187, 188,
   192, 226, 239, 250, 255; and office of
   lieutenant governor, 16, 398
Women's Air Force Service Pilots, 369
"Wonder Five," 347
Woodruff, Troy, 406
Works Progress Administration, 296,
   303
World War I, 248, 250, 254, 255, 263,
   275, 290, 316, 336
World War II, 14, 298, 312, 319, 322,
   324, 331, 337, 348, 353, 362, 369
Wright, Caroline Rockwill, 114
Wright, George C., 112
Wright, Harriet Burbridge, 113
Wright, John, 112, 113
Wright, Joseph A., 2, 10, 11, 15, 95, 112–
   22, 144, 185, 192; (illus.), 113
Wright, Louisa Cook, 113
Wright, Rachel Seaman, 112
Wright Bone Dry Law, 276, 277
Wylie, Andrew, 53

Yale University, 369
YMCA, 370
Yorktown (VA), 35
Young Men's Democratic Club, 245
Young Republicans, 331
"Young Turks," 291

Ziegner, Edward, 355